Hermann Fischer's lively and original study of romantic verse narrative traces in comprehensive detail the origins and development of this poetic form in the late eighteenth and early nineteenth centuries. It brings together the longer epic verse tales of Scott, Byron and Southey and the more lyrical forms of narrative poetry in the romantic period, thus presenting familiar poems such as Shelley's *Alastor* and Keats' *The Eve of St Agnes* in the revealing but neglected context of the narrative genre and its history. Professor Fischer addresses the question of genre from a viewpoint that is both theoretical and historical, examining it in terms of form, structure and tone, and analysing its contemporary purpose and audience. Whilst looking at each of the major narrative poets in some detail, his study also proves illuminating in many areas of romantic literature, covering issues such as the role of the medieval revival and the decline of neo-classicism, the importance of popular sources such as the ballad and more literary influences such as the eighteenth-century heroic epic, and questions of changing taste and the reading public.

This edition, extensively revised and updated since the first publication of the work in German, makes Hermann Fischer's acclaimed study available for the first time in translation, rendering an important contribution to the field accessible to English-speaking students and scholars of romanticism.

European Studies in English Literature

Romantic Verse Narrative

European Studies in English Literature

SERIES EDITORS
Ulrich Broich, Professor of English, University of Munich
Herbert Grabes, Professor of English, University of Giessen
Dieter Mehl, Professor of English, University of Bonn

Roger Asselineau, Professor Emeritus of American Literature, University of Paris-Sorbonne
Paul-Gabriel Boucé, Professor of English, University of Sorbonne-Nouvelle
Robert Ellrodt, Professor of English, University of Sorbonne-Nouvelle
Sylvère Monod, Professor Emeritus of English, University of Sorbonne-Nouvelle

This series is devoted to publishing translations in English of the best works written in European languages on English literature. These may be first-rate books recently published in their original versions, or they may be classic studies which have influenced the course of scholarship in their world while never having been available in English before.

To begin with the series has concentrated on works translated from the German; but its range will expand to cover other languages.

TRANSLATIONS PUBLISHED
Walter Pater: The Aesthetic Moment by Wolfgang Iser
The Symbolist Tradition in English Literature: A Study of Pre-Raphaelitism and 'Fin de Siècle' by Lothar Hönnighausen
The Theory and Analysis of Drama by Manfred Pfister
Oscar Wilde: The Works of a Conformist Rebel by Norbert Kohl
The Fall of Women in Early English Narrative Verse by Götz Schmitz
The Rise of the English Street Ballad 1550–1650 by Natascha Würzbach
The Eighteenth-Century Mock Heroic Poem by Ulrich Broich

TITLES UNDER CONTRACT FOR TRANSLATION
Redeformen des englischen Mysterienspiels by Hans-Jürgen Diller
Shakespeare et la fête by François Laroque
L'Etre et l'avoir dans les romans de Charles Dickens by Anny Sadrin

ROMANTIC VERSE NARRATIVE

The History of a Genre

HERMANN FISCHER

Emeritus Professor of English at the University of Mannheim

Translated from the German by
SUE BOLLANS

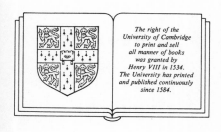

*The right of the
University of Cambridge
to print and sell
all manner of books
was granted by
Henry VIII in 1534.
The University has printed
and published continuously
since 1584.*

CAMBRIDGE UNIVERSITY PRESS

CAMBRIDGE
NEW YORK   PORT CHESTER
MELBOURNE   SYDNEY

Published by the Press Syndicate of the University of Cambridge
The Pitt Building, Trumpington Street, Cambridge CB2 1RP
40 West 20th Street, New York, NY 10011, USA
10 Stamford Road, Oakleigh, Melbourne 3166, Australia

First published 1991

Printed in Great Britain at the University Press, Cambridge

British Library cataloguing in publication data
Fischer, Hermann
  Romantic verse narrative: the history of a genre.
  (European studies in English literature).
  1. Narrative poetry in English, 1800–1837. Critical
  studies
  I. Title II. Series III. Romantische Verserzählung in
  England, *English*
  821.030907

Library of Congress cataloguing in publication data
Fischer, Hermann, 1922–
  [Romantische Verserzählung in England. English]
  Romantic verse narrative: the history of a genre/Hermann
  Fischer: translated from the German by Sue Bollans.
  p. cm. – (European studies in English literature)
  Translation of: Romantische Verserzählung in England.
  Includes bibliographical references.
  ISBN 0 521 30964 6
  1. English poetry – 19th century – History and criticism.
  2. Narrative poetry, English – History and criticism.
  3. Romanticism – Great Britain. I. Title. II. Series
PR589.N3F5713 1991
821'.0309145 – dc20 90-1579 CIP

ISBN 0 521 30964 6 hardback

WG

Contents

Preface

It is doubly problematic for an author to publish a new edition of a book of literary criticism twenty-five years after it was first written: he himself is no longer the person he was then, and literary studies are also no longer what they were a quarter of a century ago.

As far as the first part of the problem is concerned, I may perhaps say here without vanity that I have never felt obliged to dissociate myself in general from what my former self wrote about the English romantic tale in verse. While I readily admit that the book contained immaturity of judgement, gaps and the occasional misplaced emphasis, these were all of such a nature that with conscientious reworking and abbreviation it was possible to eradicate them without having to produce a completely new version, and even the thought that the English reading public of the 1990s would approach critically something that was presented to a German faculty in 1962 as a postdoctoral thesis did not force me to make drastic alterations. The second part of the problem is more difficult: is it possible in this period of structuralism, deconstruction and the introduction into literary studies of sociological questions, linguistic methodology, demystifying philosophy and semiotic, intertextual and ideologically critical approaches to literature to republish a genre study that 'naively' and eclectically amasses material to show what thoughts about genre in narrative poetry were current from 1798 to 1830? Has not the material collected then also since been rendered obsolete by more recent research?

Reading the relevant books from England and America,[1] however, went a long way towards allaying my fears on both counts. None of the studies on romantic poetry as a genre subscribes to the fashionable trends I have just mentioned, and none shows my approach and my results to be either erroneous or out-of-date and superfluous. This is because none of these monographs has been written with the same objective as my genre study.[2] My objective was to describe all the identifiable attributes of the genre, and support this with historical evidence in such a way as to reconstruct as far as it was possible the views of the times. It is for this reason that the study has been extensively documented with extracts from the leading periodicals.[3] Only when the 'romantic' tale in verse began to become something completely independent, when 'romantic poetry' in today's sense made it seem of questionable value or at any rate of only very secondary importance to identify works as particular types of poem, in other words with the work of Keats and Shelley, did I make cautious use of Northrop Frye's Theory of Modes and modern theories about the nature of romanticism – hopefully in a manner that will be found neither too speculative nor too epigonal. Since with traditional classification according to genre stylistic and, in the case of poetry, metric characteristics are also always involved, verse technique and style have been examined in a number of places in the book, which has often of necessity entailed brief text analyses.

The extensive documentation of contemporary reactions to the genre as reflected in the three leading periodicals, the *Edinburgh Review*, the *Quarterly Review* and *Blackwood's Magazine*, has been included out of the desire mentioned above to back up all statements made about the genre with examples from the literary views of the times, and also because the 'boom' in verse narrative between 1790 and 1830 represented a fashion trend: it is obvious that for this reason alone the way this was reflected in the media of the times should not be overlooked. Since, however, many of the critical assessments of the period can only be properly evaluated against the background of the critics' personal or political attitudes, the relevant information has often had to be inserted. In order to keep the genre history readable and not overload it with too many digressions, much of this subsidiary information has been assigned to the notes.

This book was accepted in 1961 by the Philosophy Faculty of the University of Munich as a postdoctoral thesis and was published in German in 1964 by the Max Niemeyer Verlag Tübingen. The study was inspired and promoted by the Munich Anglist Wolfgang Clemen, who died in March 1990. I should like to dedicate this new edition in English to his memory, in gratitude for the academic and methodological training which I received from him.

I would also like to thank Cambridge University Press for making this new edition possible, and the translator Sue Bollans, who applied her bilingual skills to this far from easy task with untiring enthusiasm and interest.

Abbreviations

CE	*Collected Edition of the Works of Robert Southey* (London, 1837| 8)
E Studien	*Englische Studien*
JEGP	*Journal of English and Germanic Philology*
MLN	*Modern Language Notes*
MLR	*Modern Language Review*
MP	*Modern Philology*
PMLA	*Publications of the Modern Language Association of America*
RES	*Review of English Studies*
BM	*Blackwood's Magazine*
ER	*Edinburgh Review*
QuR	*Quarterly Review*

Perhaps he will yet come who is to sing the greatest heroic poem, comprehending in spirit whatever was, what is, what shall be.

F. W. J. von Schelling, *The Ages of the World* (1811), quoted in M. H. Abrams, *Natural Supernaturalism* (New York, 1971), p. 256

It does not matter whether a poem be called an epic or a romance, an epistle or a dirge, an epitaph, an ode, an elegy, a sonnet, or otherwise, as long as it is full of the material of poetry.

Barry Cornwall, *Essays and Tales in Prose* (Boston, 1835), vol. II, p. 147

Introduction

This work is subtitled 'The History of a Genre'. It should be emphasized right from the start that it is not the intention of this author to develop an exclusive method of genre research. The problematic concept of genre excludes narrow schematization by its very nature: genres cannot be reduced to exact and absolutely valid definitions, since they are to a large extent subject to historical change. In the case of the specific genre that is to be studied here, moreover, the tendency in the romantic period for boundaries between genres to dissolve and even for the whole idea of genre to be regarded with hostility makes it practically impossible to apply a more precise method.

In the poetry of the romantic epoch, the genres might be compared with a network of subterranean water courses, and the researcher who is trying to follow the hidden lines of development with a water diviner who is obliged to obtain as many incomplete results as possible using all the methods at his disposal: observing the places where the underground streams come to the surface, i.e. where the poets are conscious of genre theory; divining for the development of taste; boring down into 'archetypal' ideas about genre; searching for the source, measuring and not least putting in additional colouring of his own to bring out the hidden changes of direction and mixtures.

It is not of course possible to talk about genres without definitive schematization. But such schematization cannot be justified as an end in itself, since it must always be imperfect and one-sided. It is only an unavoidable means to an end; and can only be defended if the end justifies the means. However, the end must not be to narrow down literary phenomena to fit them into a system for the system's sake, but rather to apply an adaptable system to the individual literary phenomena in order to be able to understand literature better from both a historical and an interpretative point of view. For this reason various approaches to the study of genre will be found existing side by side in this book. The focus is on the form, content, history or 'archetypal' aspects of the genre as the work of the individual poet seemed to require it.[1]

As just mentioned, this subject – the history of the romantic verse narrative genre – particularly necessitates abandoning a strictly dogmatic genre theory and keeping the method flexible, since the romantic period was one in which the boundaries between genres were dissolved and there was even hostility towards their very existence.

The literary form that is to be studied here is more convincing proof of this

1

than any theoretical considerations: it is harder to define as a genre than most other forms of poetry. For this branch of literature there is no binding terminology and there are no actual genre regulations. It is hardly possible to determine what length of poem, metre, level of style, stylistic attributes or themes are involved and there is not even a generally recognized name for the genre. While within the genre it did happen that successful works inspired imitation and initiated fashionable trends, resulting in the creation of 'schools' which emphasized and imitated a particular aspect, this was offset by the general tendency of the age towards originality and independent development of ideas from other sources, even to the extent of producing something so different that the original genre was only detectable as a remote influence.

The word romantic is thus also no guarantee of the kind of uniformity required of a historical genre such as the medieval court novel or the erotic epyllion of the Renaissance. The uniting factors that are implied by this description of a generation of poets are neutralized by the divisory aspects – the 'schools' and individual approaches – and the effect of these divisory aspects was so strong at the time that the collective name English Romantic Poets was not used for the poets of this epoch until after it was over.[2] Even today it can still be seen on closer inspection of precisely the forgotten narrative verse of the epoch, that the relative uniformity of other literary epochs – such as the Elizabethan period or the school of poetry from Dryden to Goldsmith – is missing in the period from 1798 to 1830. A time of radical change and liberation from centuries-old regulations and laws, it was a breeding ground for contrasting philosophies of life, political views and tastes.

The difference between great poets and minor poets, especially in the romantic period, is a particular example of such contrast: between poets who confronted the intellectual and artistic problems of the age and poets whose 'romanticism' consisted merely of imitating the superficial characteristics of the style change in order to be fashionable while intellectually remaining strongly bound to the thinking of the previous epoch. The many narrative poems of the romantic period cannot thus easily be accommodated within a uniform genre framework. The situation is so confusing and confused that, in W. M. Dixon's words: 'Distinguish and divide we may, but frankly it is not possible ... to propose a clue by means of which this labyrinth may be traversed. Type merges into type, classical forms into romantic to produce a confused panorama of scenes, characters, actions, where the distinctions that prevailed prevail no longer, where the old designations fail us.'[3]

Nevertheless, in the following study the attempt will be made not just to discuss the genre of the individual works one after the other and identify the models and influences that are blended into them, but also to bring out what the verse narratives of the English poets in the epoch from 1798 to 1830 do have in common in spite of all their differences, and to reveal a literary process in the midst of the variety that is characterized by a certain logic. Here the word genre is used less in the sense of a particular type of poetic form than in the sense of a tendency of the period in question, a common denominator that is there to be discovered in all these works. Thus, whenever the romantic tale in verse is referred to in this book as a genre, it is always with these qualifications in mind, as it were putting the word in quotation marks. Three further points should be made on this subject.

1. It will become clear in the course of this treatise that the length of a romantic tale in verse has hardly any influence on its qualification for the genre, which includes both poems of a few hundred lines and tales running to thousands of verses. It would be arbitrary to treat the latter as a separate genre.

2. Given the lack of definitive terminology for this whole field, it was not possible to avoid either describing the concepts involved in detail or inventing new expressions. The first solution encumbers the style, and the latter sometimes makes the text less easy to understand. The author has attempted to use whatever method seemed most appropriate for the particular subject in hand, while realizing that the pitfalls just mentioned could not always be avoided.

3. The aim of the study was not to give an overall picture of what during its history the romantic tale in verse consciously and unconsciously took over from other genres and what represented a new development. With an outline of this nature it would only have been possible to offer abtract hypotheses, which would not have been very convincing. The only way for the ideas of the book to appear to some degree substantiated was through the inclusion of as many provable details as possible, whereby the main interrelationships of the various aspects would automatically become clear.

The material to be evaluated was very extensive. The objective of the study could not be achieved by analysis of the works in question and the indications as to their genre alone. As well as dealing with the poems themselves, it was important to give ample space to the poets' own commentaries on their work and the opinions of the contemporary critics. In scarcely any other age have the literary problems and controversies been so richly documented as in the romantic period. For practical reasons it was not possible to include everything: of the many periodicals only the three most important are dealt with: *Edinburgh Review (ER)*, *Quarterly Review (QR)*, and *Blackwood's Magazine (BM)*. In addition to these three periodicals, reference is also frequently made to Hazlitt's *Lectures on the English Poets* (1818 – 19) and his *Spirit of the Age* (1825), which are valuable sources of information about contemporary views of English verse narratives.

The usefulness of what has been undertaken in this study will not be denied by anyone who has ever tried to find a chapter about the characteristics the romantic verse narratives have in common, or any separate discussion of this type of poetry as a genre in the current literary histories. This is not intended as a criticism. In all the 'compendia' and 'surveys' the authors have to decide on a compromise between the various dimensions of literary history – epochs, individual personalities, genres, trends, influences, schools, etc. – when organizing their material, and in the romantic period in particular classification by poet is more important than classification by genre. All that is being pointed out is that histories of literature do not investigate genre in the way that is being done here. However, even specialized histories of the epic or romance genres in European or English literature have not gone very far in this direction either. Many of these books end with an outline of the further development of narrative poetry in the later nineteenth century,[4] but since such works are always either based on classical normative definitions of the epic as well as of the metrical romance, or introduce a number of self-made definitions which blur rather than clarify the character of the genre to which the present study is devoted,[5] they are of no help to someone wanting to pin down the protean class of poetry that at the beginning of the nineteenth century was fashionable under such names as 'tale in verse', 'metrical tale', 'metrical romance', or just 'romantic poem'. To some extent today's unfavourable view of the decline of the epic genre in most narrative poems of that time has even resulted in these works being omitted from such studies. The connection of the most valuable examples of the romantic verse narrative genre – Keats' *Endymion*, *The Eve of St Agnes* and *Lamia*, Shelley's *Alastor* and *The Revolt of Islam* – with the fashionable 'metrical tales' of their period is thus lost sight of.

There have been very few scholars up to now who have been willing to embark on a study of this genre complex where both the themes and the form are so hard to define. The older standard works on the period from 1798 to 1830, for example, Saintsbury's *History of Nineteenth Century Literature* (1896) and his *Essays in English Literature 1780–1860* (1895), or Elton's *Survey of English Literature 1780–1830* (1924) do of course touch on this subject. H. A. Beers, in his *History of English Romanticism in the Nineteenth Century* (1901), shows a clearer view of genre in English romantic poetry than most earlier scholars when he maintains that Scott's verse narratives are the centre point of romantic development in England. In the *Geschichte der englischen Romantik* (History of English Romanticism) by Helene Richter (1916) there is, in Volume III 'Die Blüte der Romantik' (The Flowering of Romanticism), an entire chapter devoted to the descriptive poems and tales in verse from Pope to Southey, where with thorough knowledge of her subject the authoress sketches several important lines of development but then – as is the case with most histories of literature – pads this out with so much heterogeneous material that they are lost to view.

The most important older writings about the history and character of the type of poetry that is being examined here are two older works and three books written twenty to thirty years ago. A. C. Bradley's lecture on the 'Long Poem in the Age of Wordsworth' in *Oxford Lectures on Poetry* (1909) compresses into a very small space several important historical and critical problems. C. H. Herford's Introduction to his anthology of English verse narratives, *English Tales in Verse* (1924)[6] places the romantic tales in the wider context of verse narratives which do not claim to belong to the genre of the 'great epic poem' but go beyond the shorter ballad form and the story in verse of only a few lines. Both works, however, are so short that they are limited to an outline of their subject and only a few examples.

In *The Romantic Assertion* (1958) R. A. Foakes confirms some of this author's findings about the genre of long romantic poems. However, since his book is primarily about the relation between imagery and thought in romantic poetry and only occasionally in passing deals with the question of genre,[7] it does not render superfluous this attempt at a detailed genre history of the tale in verse from 1800 to 1830. Because of its particular slant, Foakes' book also focuses on different epochs: important romantic and Victorian poems are dealt with together and contrasted with the poetry of the seventeenth and twentieth centuries.

Karl Kroeber's *Romantic Narrative Art*, which was mentioned in the Preface, confirms my own work in many respects, in spite of the different objectives already described. It would be pointless to include in this monograph all the observations and quotes with which he supports his arguments and our two books may thus be considered as complementary studies each with a different emphasis. The same is true of Brian Wilkie's *Romantic Poets and Epic Tradition* (1965), that arrives at a similar conclusion in many matters to those of this book (particularly in the chapter entitled 'Epomania: Southey and Landor') and contains valuable additional material on some of the subjects I have dealt with. Wilkie of course concentrates exclusively on works which were consciously written by the romantic poets as epic poems, which I have only dealt with in passing – Wordsworth's *Prelude*, Shelley's *The Revolt of Islam*, Keats' *Hyperion* and Byron's *Don Juan* – so that the two books cannot really be said to overlap. Wilkie moreover admits in his Preface: 'this book is not a genre study as that term is often understood ... I am only secondarily interested in changing readers' ideas about what a certain literary form really is'.[8]

The general approach of Herford's Introduction draws attention to an important question: should not a history of the literary form known as the 'tale in verse' from Chaucer to the present time be written first, before a history of the romantic verse narrative genre is attempted? Herford's essay is too short to give more than an outline of such a history, and is thus not much more than a list of the best and most familiar achievements in this field of literature. A detailed history of the whole genre would without doubt be a desirable background to the specific study of romantic forms that is the object of this book. How much does the educated reader of our time know about generic continuities within the history of the shorter narrative poem in England, of that type of poem which does not claim to be an epic and for which 'tale in

verse' is the only possible collective term?[9] While we know individual names
and works that stand out from the general stream – Chaucer, the short
Renaissance epics composed by Marlowe, Chapman, Shakespeare, Drayton
and Southwell, and Dryden's *Fables*, etc., we seldom stop to consider that these
are not just isolated high points but are linked in a multitude of ways with
each other and with older – classical and medieval – traditions.

In special studies such as H. G. Wright's valuable book on *Boccaccio in
England from Chaucer to Tennyson* (1957) sections of this vast subject are dealt
with, and it is surprising to discover that in every period following their first
appearance the novellas of *The Decameron* were used as sources for tales in verse.
This is also the case with other works: with Ovid's *Metamorphoses* and other
classical tales, with certain material from the Middle Ages that was also
popular in the baroque and neo-classical epochs (such as the Arthurian cycle
of legends) and with biblical material. A monograph on verse narratives in
English literature would indeed be of great value. There is no such
monograph. In order not to leave this genre history of the romantic tale in
verse hanging in the air (it would be one of the later chapters of the missing
monograph) and in order instead to give it the solid foundation it needs, two
general chapters have been added preceding the study of the poetry itself. The
first provides the essential theoretical and terminological basis, the second
puts romantic narrative poetry in the context of English verse narrative and
deals with the situation at the end of the eighteenth century when romantic
narrative poetry began to be written.

But is all that is gained for a study of the history of the romantic tale in
verse as a distinctive genre a chapter on the history of a literary form that has
hardly ever been dealt with as a whole? It is hoped that the present study will
provide something more than this. Neither a mere historical survey nor a
classification of all these works according to an abstract genre system is felt
to be very valuable. The genre itself is being studied because the author
believes that by this means the surviving poetry of that time can be better
understood and defended against false judgements – provided of course the
concept of genre is not interpreted too narrowly or theoretically. With this
approach it is hoped to provide a deeper insight into the intentions of the
romantic poets, an insight that cannot be obtained by studying the outstanding
works out of context, as is the usual practice.

The ultimate purpose of this book is thus not to produce a system for
system's sake, nor a mere record of historic material, but to make living
poetry and artistic, intellectual and cultural phenomena that were important
right up until the beginning of this century more understandable. A revaluation of the mass of romantic verse narratives will nevertheless only
be possible in exceptional cases. Most of the poems are considered value-
less today, and this is not only attributable to changing fashions: their
absolute poetic value is often not very high. However, with respect to

quality assessment too a study of the genre history can also help to provide more objective standards.

The troublesome ambiguity of the word 'romantic' could not be avoided: it was already ambiguous in the early nineteenth century. It should be clear from the context which meaning is intended: whether the word still has something of the ironic nuance that it had in the eighteenth century; whether it implies the emotionalistic combination of feelings, sensation, adventure and surrender to love which made it appropriate to use 'romantic poetry' as a synonym for the verse narratives of Southey, Scott and Coleridge, etc.; whether it is to be understood purely as the term for the epoch from around 1795 to 1835; or whether it is being used in today's sense of the 'romantic school', in Friedrich Schlegel's sense, or to denote transcendentally idealistic poetry.[10] Where there is any danger of the meaning being misunderstood, clarifying explanations such as 'romantic in today's sense of the word' or 'romantic generation' have been added.

In closing, a few words about the limitation of the period to 1798 until around 1830. As already mentioned, this study also deals with the forerunners of the genre. They do not appear, however, before 1798, the year that is generally considered for other reasons too to mark the beginning of English romanticism. As far as developments after 1830 are concerned, a number of contemporary statements are included later in the book that clearly indicate a flagging interest in the genre at around this time.[11] Even though in England and America verse narrative of the romantic type continued to be produced for decades[12] – and even at the beginning of the twentieth century there were still new works that could be traced back to that fashionable genre[13] – the 1830s brought with them social changes, a new public, different tastes and new poets, who, if they went back to the verse narrative at all, either abandoned the form and content associated with the romantic tradition, or only developed those characteristics by means of which the great representatives of the younger romantic generation had already diluted the original type.

Finally, when the works were selected that are examined in greater detail to support the theses of this study, the aim was to provide as complete a picture as possible, but without unearthing every minor poet active in this area. Nothing would have been gained for example by including the numerous imitators of Scott – poets who even in their day were very much in the shadow of the man they copied and who only lasted a few years. The most gifted of these poets only differ from the head of the 'school' in that their work is less vivid than his, and to include them would add nothing new. As far as the unimportant poets who copied their models without talent are concerned however, it is as Scott said in the Introduction to *Rokeby* of 1830: '[they] at least lay hold of their peculiar features, so as to produce a strong burlesque', so that 'the effect of the manner is rendered cheap and common, and ... ridiculous to boot'. The criterion for the selection was provided by the reviews of the three journals already mentioned: those of the lesser poets whom the influential critics did not consider worthy of detailed discussion were not in general very important and had no decisive influence on the history of the romantic verse narrative.

Part I *THE GENRE AND ITS HISTORICAL CONTEXT*

1   Genre definitions

> The strong emotional repugnance felt by many critics toward any form of schematization in poetics is ... the result of a failure to distinguish criticism as a body of knowledge from the direct experience of literature, where every act is unique, and classification has no place. Whenever schematization appears in the following pages, no importance is attached to the schematic form itself, which may be only the result of my own lack of ingenuity. Much of it, I expect and in fact hope, may be mere scaffolding, to be knocked away when the building is in better shape.
>
> Northrop Frye, *Anatomy of Criticism*, 1957, p. 29

Literary kinds 'may be regarded as institutional imperatives which both coerce and are in turn coerced by the writer ...'. Genre should be conceived ... as a grouping of literary works based ... upon both outer form (specific metre or structure) and also upon inner form (attitudes, tone, purpose – more crudely, subject and audience). The ostensible basis may be the one or the other ... but the critical problem will then be to find the *other* dimensions, to complete the diagram.[1]

Towards a workable genre theory

These sentences from Wellek and Warren's *Theory of Literature* (1941) contain all that is needed in the way of a framework for any discussion of genre: the problematic conflict between the freely creative artist and tradition; the institutionalization of genre norms through description and repeated use of these norms; the varying scope of the notion of genre, which ranges from the universal categories lyric, epic and dramatic to traditional types of work – types by which as it were authors and readers may orientate themselves; and finally the breadth of each particular genre from the point of view of form and production as well as of conditions governing its reception by the public, a breadth which sometimes makes definition an extremely difficult business.

There have been occasional attempts, on account of the fact that all more precise regulations can be falsified, to deny the validity of genre classifications (in so far as they were not purely descriptions of the outer form such as Pindaric ode, or sonnet). However, this did not remove the genre problem, the need to speak of genres, to classify according to genre and study the history of genres. Everyone who approaches literature in this way is conscious of the shaky ground he is on;[2] and everyone sees himself obliged to be more precise about his own use of genre terminology even if only for pragmatic reasons and without making any claims that his use is the only valid one. This applies of course to the genre names that are used in this study, too, and particularly to the genres that form the background of the romantic verse narrative: the epic, the romance and the ballad.[3]

Some general remarks are necessary on this subject. Much of the confusion in genre research is probably due to the fact that the terms are used without sufficient understanding of the way in which every genre phenomenon is composed of many parameters or dimensions, which must all be taken into consideration. Hugo Kuhn, in his lecture on *Gattungsprobleme der mittelhoch-deutschen Literatur* (Genre Problems in Middle High German Literature)[4] provided a perfect example of how to avoid the problem. From his experience that neither general genre concepts – genres as the archetypes of poetic statement – nor historical genre names alone reveal the true relationships between the literary works that have appeared in the course of history, Kuhn, in complete agreement with the quote from Wellek and Warren with which this chapter began, says that there are three kinds of problems involved in establishing the character of a genre: *the problem of type*, which involves establishing the overall plan and model, the formative principle or idea on which every artistic production is consciously or unconsciously based; *the class problem*, where the sociological position of the piece of literature is explored, the area of society the work comes from and which it is addressed to, and the social traditions on which the writer feels obliged to base it; this also includes the social preferences and prejudices he has to take into account, no matter whether he affirms or rejects them; *the entelechy problem*, where the historical purpose of the genres is explored, or, to put it in more general terms, the literary intentions of a generation or social group. The important thing about this approach is that the historical element cannot be excluded from any of the three kinds of problem. The sole use of categories that are based on mere form is thus rejected.[5]

Can this approach be of assistance in reducing the complex genre history and terminology that is to be dealt with here to a few simple dimensions? It is very useful in the later sections of this study, where one historically clearly defined genre, the romantic tale in verse, is assessed. Here Kuhn's three kinds of problem are all in evidence, and are among the aspects that are studied.

However, a genre history is more than a description of the unique historic characteristic of the one genre. It consists rather of showing where the genre fits into the literary thinking – the 'mighty stream of tendency' – of a civilization by tracing the reasons for its development and the accompanying phenomena back as far as possible and thus revealing the intellectual background. The specific genre must be looked at in a wider context. Since, as has already been said, the romantic tale in verse has three different roots – epic, romance and ballad – we need a clear idea of what these three genres involve. We must know:

1. how these three genres were seen in the days of the romantic poets;
2. how the poets expanded these ideas themselves;
3. on which – generalized – ideas we want to base our assessment of their work.

An attempt will be made to clarify the first two points in the two sections on the 'initial situation' and the 'history of the romantic tale in verse'. The third point must, however, be dealt with now, in order to provide the assessment made in this book with a firm basis. The main difficulty with this third point is that on the one hand the problems cannot, as used to be the practice in normative genre studies, be narrowed down to concrete 'rules' which only apply to certain historical forms, and that on the other hand, through establishing the constitutive essence of all true epics, romances and ballads it is only too easy to arrive at formulas of too abstract a nature, which it was the intention to avoid.

The author proposes to deal with this difficulty in the following manner: If one were to assume that genre concepts were by nature comparable with the universals of medieval philosophy (which is not in fact so wide of the mark) then the problems could be solved in a similar way to that in which scholasticism solved the universals dispute. The genres would then exist for us *ante rem*, i.e., in their broadest sense they would correspond to certain modes of perceiving and experiencing the world that recur in all cultures, even though they would – in our special case – be considered mainly as social and cultural continuities within our civilization with which the genres are connected, as formal possibilities of expression, by a loose causal nexus. Here it is important to distinguish between the subconscious adoption of genre characteristics and their adoption by conscious choice. The genres would exist *in re*, i.e., these modes would repeatedly lead to similar or at least comparable genre characteristics which would constitute the essence of the genre. Finally the genres would exist *post rem*, i.e., one could only speak of them and define them by comparing the various realizations of each genre and summarizing in a kind of standardized formula the characteristics these have in common.

The old normative genre studies focused on the third point of view. Certain modern 'archetypal' genre studies tend to overemphasize the first aspect. And current histories of literature operate mainly with the second aspect. In this study it is a question of creating a synthesis of these viewpoints. The genres will be approached as something rooted in the general human understanding of the world throughout the ages, as something made tangible in consistent forms, and as a systematization of these tangibilities. This is both necessary and important because among other things, as everyone knows, genres in general and the three genres that form the basis of the romantic tale in verse in particular, appear in the course of history in two forms.

One is the 'natural' form, i.e., an early form governed by national, cultural and social conditions of the day, and the other consists of artificial forms, i.e., later uses of the once naturally created original type, which vary between close imitation and free versions; in these descendants, however, the form no longer necessarily reflects the 'world' of the epoch that is now making use of the genre, but rather goes back to the 'world' of the natural type (although a blend of the spirit of the age that imitates the earlier form is of course inevitable). It would be tedious in the extreme if this major distinction had to be included in all the theoretical discussions about the genre. In the definitions that are attempted the problem is to a large extent resolved: either these differences are shown to be of a secondary nature – where the themes and the urge to give expression to them in a particular way, viz. the expression and form of the original genre, are not essentially different from those prevailing in the period of its renewal – or they are so pronounced that the artificial forms cannot be said to belong to the original genre, since they have none of its main characteristics and bear only superficial resemblance to it.

The following chapter, in which the main characteristics of the epic, romance and ballad are accordingly described, may at first appear to be a digression. It will, however, be realized when the later sections are read that they have been written with the romantic tale in verse in mind. But the danger of the vicious circle is not to be feared. It can in any case hardly be avoided in discussions of genre: the decision about attributing a genre name to a work whose genre is doubtful always depends on the characteristics we ourselves have decided to assign to that genre. It was only by providing detailed definitions that it was possible to get away from the narrow approach of positivistic research into individual influences, imitations, adoption of subject matter and copies of style, and concentrate on the lines of development that are the heart of the matter.

Finally, as a further justification for this procedure, it is felt that this study of the character of the epic, romance and ballad genres as a product of European literary and cultural history does not represent late, retrospective theorizing about something that was remote from the romantic poets, something of which they were quite unconscious. The opinion of this author is rather that in this epoch, where the foundation was laid for so many elements of today's thinking, there was also a marked change in the approach to genres – in fact the change from the old normative evaluation of genres towards a more historically orientated evaluation which forms the basis of the following sections. The basic ideas that are presented in these sections with a precision derived from the historical perspective are reflected to a greater or lesser degree in the whole thinking of the romantics about genre, as expressed in both their works and their theoretical deliberations in prefaces, letters and reviews.

The romantic tale in verse developed in the area between what the ancient world and humanistic neo-classicists understood by 'a Great Poem' and the ideal the romantics were aiming at; i.e., in the area between the normative study of genre with its established 'workshop' principles and an absolute approach to genre which views it as a consequence of cultural history – and (it should be said right from the beginning) its history is the history of a significant failure; the exciting story of a literary epoch and a genre.

First genre definition: the epic

If we had a valid theory of poetry in which the rules of that art form were deduced from the unchanging laws of human sensibility which govern the original genres and fix their eternal boundaries, we should be fully aware of the essence of the epic genre. The critic's task would then consist only in the application of that already existing theory to each individual case. Until such a theory has been propounded however we have to content ourselves with coming to an agreement (however makeshift it may be) with our readers about the principles indispensable for the pronouncement of direct critical judgements on a given work of literature.

F. W. Schlegel, 'On Goethe's Hermann and Dorothea', in *Taschenbuch für 1798*, Berlin.

In order to show as clearly as possible what was intended by the theoretical statements in the preceding section, the first genre definition – that of the epic – will be based on the five elements that according to classic genre theory were integral parts of the epic, and the importance of each of these elements will be examined.[6]

Verse

The verse in the epic is closely connected with the nature of the genre – because of the quality of language required by the subject matter – but also with the presentation conditions of the authentic form: it had to meet the requirements of musical recitation, have lines that were easy to remember for the person reciting and also have the recurring rhymes and stereotyped attributes popular with less sophisticated listeners. If in later epochs the verse form was retained, it was not for the original reasons. In later periods poetic prose was quite as capable of reaching sublimity as verse, and the mode of presentation of former times no longer existed. However, verse had become an integral part of the genre, without which it no longer existed: in the absence of verse one in general no longer spoke of the epic, but either of history written in the form of a chronicle or of a novel. All attempts to extend the definition of the epic to apply to these two prose genres were unsuccessful.[7] No one would deny that there is a certain genetic relationship here, but the traditional type of epic in verse had such a lasting effect that it was considered to be the definitive form: the verse element, originally introduced for historical reasons, became an inherent part of the epic concept.

Heroic subject matter

This dates from the ages when a very high value was placed on heroism in battle. Later on the kind of person considered as a model for society changed, world orders underwent transformation and military heroism became less important than other virtues. However, a significance beyond the mere interest in the individual destinies of the characters – be it religious, ethical, national or political – is an inseparable part of the epic, in the same way as the verse. Without it the epic becomes a romance or a verse novel, no matter how many 'private' deeds of a military nature it might contain. The heroic subject matter is thus only apparently a way of introducing a historically limited aspect into the timeless concept of the epic that we are looking for. If heroism is interpreted in its broadest sense, i.e., as the hero's standing the test of trials he engaged in in the interest of something over and above his individual concerns, then it may be said to be an essential characteristic of the epic genre, one of its inherent components throughout the ages.[8]

Mythology and supernatural agency

This element takes the ideas already suggested in connection with the heroic subject matter a little further. The epic was originally poetry about man and the gods. Is the mythological or religious aspect thus also an integral part of the epic concept? Renaissance and neo-classical scholars in the seventeenth and eighteenth centuries often interpreted the genre definition of the epic in this way. However, is an epic that has no mythological apparatus, no gods and no God, unthinkable? Would such a work have to be consigned to another genre – just as the epic without verse is a chronicle or novel and without an all-embracing interest a verse novel?

In his epic *Pharsalia* Lucan managed without gods, and was praised for it by Voltaire, who himself also left out the mythological apparatus, or rather replaced it with allegories in his *Henriade*. In England a similar reaction by more enlightened thinkers against the mythological apparatus first manifested itself as early as 1650, in Thomas Hobbes' 'Answer' to Davenant's Preface to his *Gondibert*. Dryden and Hurd on the other hand insisted that the divine and the supernatural belonged to the epic. It is for us to decide who we think was right.

When the heroic subject matter was discussed above, it was already clear that the contents of epic poetry are largely dependent on the contemporary cultural situation: if a particular age is not primarily military in its orientation, the epic heroes will not be heroes in battle, but in some other sphere.

The dependence of the contents of epic poetry on the cultural situation is an established fact. Wolfgang Kayser summarized the problems implicit in this as follows: 'The epic as such appears to signify ... the story of the whole world.'[9] What he means by the whole world is rather unclear. He seems to be thinking of the world view of a self-contained national group or historical epoch. In his interpretation all epics 'open up' or interpret the worlds of this nature in which their stories are set. Here it should be said that there is a difference between the explicit description of the life, opinions, norms and phenomena of a particular period or people contained – in Kayser's opinion – in the epic, and the interpretation of the world suggested, according to Martin Heidegger, by means of signs and symbols in every true literary work. In order to avoid confusion, the more modest expression 'all-embracing interest' has been selected in this text; it is, however, used in the same sense as Kayser's 'opening up of the world'. If we now also apply the theory of the dependence of epic subject matter on the contemporary historical situation to the question of mythology in the epic,[10] we must concede that an age that is uninterested in religion and metaphysics will be perfectly capable of creating epics with no Mount Olympus, no gods and no intervention of supernatural powers in human fates. Atheistic societies could thus produce atheistic epics. This idea seems quite plausible, but should be looked at more closely.

The history of literature has shown that the true epic is less likely to flourish the less the people of a particular age are bound by general 'beliefs'. What is here being called an 'all-embracing interest' – and Kayser refers to as the 'whole world' – is then narrowed down to an interest in a particular class within this world, or an interest in private fates and individual problems. The transition from the heroic *chanson de geste* to the courtly romance is an example of such a narrowing of interest to focus on a certain class: while for example the *Chanson de Roland* still embraces the whole world of occidental Christendom – even the simple soldier is worthy of inclusion – Chrestien de Troyes focuses instead on the problems, morals and conduct of the social class from which the knights and the members of court were drawn. (This is not the place to draw exaggerated conclusions about the cultural situation in the twelfth and thirteenth centuries, and these examples have been mentioned only in order to indicate a general direction, without passing any judgement.)

The transition from general to private interests is characteristic of the inner difference between the epic and the novel. The way for this is paved by the romance, one of the preliminary stages of the novel.[11] On the subject of the 'world content' of the epic, E. M. W. Tillyard quotes Lascelles Abercrombie, in whose opinion the epic should express the 'accepted unconscious metaphysic' of its age, and adds that, depending on the nature of this 'unconscious collective metaphysic', the epic is quite a suitable vehicle for this important task in a given epoch: 'not every accepted unconscious metaphysic can prompt an epic. If for instance it is predominantly elegiac or nostalgic, it cannot serve ... Only when people have faith in their own age can they include the maximum of life in their vision.'[12]

Two points should be made here. 1. The correctness of Tillyard's assertion is undermined by the fact that in the course of history the original classic form of the epic became the common form, and was thus also used as the genre model even when the above condition was no longer met. Ages that were no longer 'epic' still based their long narrative poems on the classical model. The completely 'unepic' eighteenth century that abounded in literary imitations of classical culture and adopted classical genre models, resulted, in England for example, in a considerable number of works that are epics as far as the form is concerned; and it was a long time before the romantic generation stopped presenting themes and problems that were no longer of general relevance, clothed in a traditional genre form long since robbed of its true spirit. It is thus always important to make a distinction between the true epic and the epic style, between the epic where the genre form is a natural product of the poem's message and that where it is merely an exercise in imitation.[13]

2. The term 'accepted unconscious metaphysic' should not be too closely equated with 'religiously based collected consciousness'. The alternative is to say that every 'all-embracing interest', even if it is national or political, somehow becomes a sort of religion. Today's situation in Iran or in some communist countries would be a relevant example of this.[14] 'Accepted unconscious metaphysic', 'all-embracing interest' and 'interpretation of the whole world' are thus all attempts – each with a slightly different emphasis – at the same thing: an expression for something timeless but nevertheless taking place in the course of history, something that is part of the essence of the epic and that it would be too restricting to describe as mythology; furthermore they are attempts to remove all the historical limitations that result from defining the contents and nevertheless keeping the historical aspect as an integrating formal component of the genre.

'High argument' presented in a 'style sublime'

A further requirement that is often made of the epic is that this form of literature should have an exemplary subject and a tone to match. Is this an essential element of the genre, or is it a consequence of the relativity of the historical aspect?

This exemplary aspect of the epic has its historical origins in the derivation of the genre from the songs praising the deeds of a ruler, either living or dead, and in many cases revered as a god. Even later on, when the epic expanded to become a long narrative poem about gods and quite human heroes, the exemplary nature of the subjects and the appropriately elevated tone were retained and hence became inseparably bound up with the genre. It is totally inappropriate to say this is belied by the mock heroic – from the

Batrachomyomachis to *Hudibras* and *The Rape of the Lock*. The mock heroic was always a separate genre which focused solely on the ridiculous and had quite different objectives from the 'metaphysical' epic, in the sense in which the word metaphysical is being used in this text. This genre never set out to establish its approach as the only valid one and to deny the sublime aspects of life. Its similarity to the serious epic was limited to the parodying of its external features.

In what category, however, should we place such a basically serious work as Byron's *Don Juan*? 'More a mixture of wormwood and verdigris than satire' was how Shelley, who greatly admired the poem, described it in a letter to Peacock dated 8 October 1818. Byron commented himself about his poem: 'if you must have an epic, there's Don Juan for you. I call that an epic; it is an epic as much in the spirit of our day as the Iliad was in that of Homer. Love, religion, and politics form the argument, and are as much the cause of quarrels now as they were then.'[15] This would at first glance appear to have been meant ironically, like so many of Byron's statements. However, there is no denying the fact that he really considered *Don Juan* to be an epic, of a kind that was appropriate to the times, and many people would nowadays support the view that it is the first and perhaps the only epic that is representative of the modern spirit. The comic, ridiculous and ignoble aspects are not, as in the mock heroic, a deliberately selected side of life without any intention on the part of the poet of denying its sublimer sides, but are rather a way of looking at the whole world which is based on more complicated motives. Here the poet deals with all the phenomena of the world and sees it as neither primarily noble nor primarily comic, sees it without illusions, sceptically, naturally and with a cynicism that is only a front for an extremely sensitive nature. In order to defend himself against the oppressive foolishness and sadness, the banality, violence and senselessness of the world he has exposed, the poet distances himself from reality by means of a kind of comic stylization, a defence consisting partly of a particular kind of satirical tone, and partly of the consciously 'prosaic' verse language and the parodical epic form.[16] Such a work could claim to express the accepted unconscious metaphysic of the disillusioned, prosaic modern world, and when Byron compared *Don Juan* with Homer's *Iliad* as an 'epic ... in the spirit of our day' this is certainly one of the ideas he had in mind.

But is *Don Juan* really an epic? From what has already been said about the genre, this would not appear to be the case. The scepticism of the work is evidence of what Tillyard calls an 'elegiac or nostalgic' ... 'unconscious metaphysic'. Even if this approach were considered representative of the whole romantic period, or in other words 'accepted', it could still never form the basis of an epic poem. An age that is 'elegiac or nostalgic' does not believe in itself, and according to Tillyard such belief is the prerequisite for the creation of epics.

It cannot, however, be maintained that Byron's perspectives are representative of his age. The romantic poets did, it is true, often find the gradual disappearance of all myths and metaphysics in the new age hard to accept. Some romantic critics (similarly to Hegel in connection with sublime poetry) did also speak out against the modern world because of its 'prosaicness' and its view of reality as something based on mere factual experience as well as because of the absence of myths and miracles.[17] The preference of the romantic age for material from distant or past worlds is indeed an indication of its dissatisfaction with the present. Nevertheless many romantic poets still believed in the possibility of creating new myths, or at least in the power of genius to give empty old myths new, subjective interpretations. R. A. Foakes even took the 'Romantic Assertion' of a positive world vision as the starting point for his book of the same name on romantic and Victorian imagery. The romantic poets did not therefore have to give up all ideas of writing the true epic poem (as defined here in a wider sense) right from the start. This is the key to much that will later be said about romantic verse narrative.

Byron's *Don Juan* is thus according to all that has emerged here not a true epic: it is a reflection of the contemporary world through one individual character, who cannot automatically be described as representative of his whole generation (whether he may be called a prophet of the spirit of the twentieth century is quite a different question). *Don Juan* is a verse novel, much of it autobiographical, where satirical language and verse and the epic form are used for the sake of effect and expressive force but it is not a poem with an 'all-embracing interest' offering an interpretation of the 'accepted unconscious metaphysic' of the age of Goethe, Wordsworth, Coleridge, Chateaubriand and Hegel, to name only a few contemporaries. There is in fact nothing about this poem to justify classifying it as a representative epic of the romantic period, even if we fully share Goethe's admiration for it.

There is, of course, *The Prelude*. *The Prelude* is undoubtedly the most interesting, and may be the most successful, attempt to combine the traditional epic genre with the romantic concept of poetry, comparable, at least in its historical importance, with Milton's achievement in the epic genre. It in no way detracts from Wordsworth's greatness to say that *The Prelude* owes its 'organic' wholeness to its biographical and thematic plan and to the fact that it contains the 'archetype' of the quest journey rather than to the invention of a genuinely epic, i.e., narrative, structure. Wordsworth himself certainly thought of both *The Prelude* and the 'great poem' *The Recluse* which never materialized as epics.[18] Wilkie and, to some extent, Kroeber here and elsewhere reach different conclusions owing to their neglect not only of traditional but above all of contemporary views of genre. Wilkie does not propose to write a 'genre study in the usual sense', and Kroeber pays 'scant attention to any problems of influence'.[19] Both critics organize their books not as typologies of romantic verse narrative but 'topically', and in so doing rule out many considerations without which genre studies are hardly valid. Calling *The Prelude* a 'personal epic', as Wilkie does, may be defensible 'topically', but in the light of both the epic tradition and the various modern definitions of the epic on which the present study bases its argument it is in itself a contradiction. This also holds for the planned *Recluse* – unless we are prepared to concede that the 'accepted unconscious metaphysic' of the romantic age is idealistic individualism (which is patently contradicted by what was said above of Byron's *Don Juan*); and even then its predominantly 'elegiac or nostalgic' world view could not, according to Tillyard, produce an epic. Or, to use Northrop Frye's terminology, 'the theme of the boundary of consciousness, the sense of the poetic mind as passing from one world to another, or simultaneously aware of both'[20] is the 'typical episodic theme' of romance.

We cannot, of course, know whether Wordsworth's contemporaries would have felt *The Prelude* was an epic, as the poem was not published before 1850, and even then the fact that it was presented as 'the preparatory poem ... to ... a Philosophical Poem containing views of Man, Nature, and Society' in the Advertisement ruled out the possibility of its being considered as a heroic poem or epic. Coleridge, the addressee and one of the very few readers of the original version in 1805, certainly allowed it the loftiness and greatness it claimed, but in his poem *To William Wordsworth: Composed on the Night after his Recitation of a Poem on the Growth of an Individual Mind* the phrases he uses in describing and extolling it surely do not place it within the epic tradition: he calls it 'that Lay/More than historic, that prophetic Lay' (ll. 2 – 3); he finds its theme 'hard as high' (l. 11); and he stresses above all its prophetic and philosophical character: 'An Orphic song indeed/A song divine of high and passionate thoughts' (ll. 45 – 6), 'a linked lay of Truth' (l. 58). If we consider that Scott's verse narratives were thought of by his contemporaries as epics and as 'Homeric' in character it is easy to see that the non-epic features of *The Prelude* – its subjective, biographical, often lyrical and generally philosophic manner and the generic traits of the verse epistle (addressed to Coleridge), the confession (in Rousseau's line) and the reflective poem (as in Thomson, Cowper, Akenside, etc.) that is also contained – excluded it from being thought of as an epic poem.

The epic hero

The points to be made here are almost self-evident. In the earliest epics the heroes are high-ranking personalities – kings, dukes and aristocratic commanders of armies; and these are often even shown to be descended from gods or goddesses. Classical decorum, according to which only the high-ranking in society can have noble and tragic fates, is just as applicable to the epic as it is to all other types of poetry. It is the reflection in literature of the social values of classical culture.

Later on this aspect is retained, partly as the legacy of the classical period, and partly as the reflection of the social structure in the poets' own countries; however, with the spread of Christianity the main focus shifts in the direction of nobility of character (which is of course usually paired with nobility of origin). This is certainly one of the reasons why Virgil had much more influence on European literature than Homer, and why this influence continued even into the eighteenth century. Tasso, for example, says that an epic hero must be morally perfect, equipped with the virtues required by the court, and must be a great war hero.[21] This is obviously limited to a particular historical period, and is too narrow an interpretation. If we once again want to eliminate everything that is historically limited from our approach without totally excluding the historical connection, then the hero of an epic would, for example, have to be a model character in the world 'opened up' in the work. If this is a republic, he will not have to be a monarch, nor even a nobleman. If it is barbaric, the manners of the court will not be required. If it is not primarily warlike, he will not have to prove that he is an exemplary or rather 'representative' character (since moral perfection is not automatically obligatory for a hero – we only have to think of Homer's Achilles) mainly by deeds on the battlefield. If it is unheroic or individualistic ... but here we must stop. For now we come up against the same limitations that were encountered when the question of the exemplary subject and matching tone was discussed: an age where there are no longer any representative characters held up as examples for people to copy, or whose representative characters are not suitable for ennoblement in this type of poetry, cannot produce an epic. A Machiavellist, however immoral, could perhaps still be an epic hero, as could a priest who triumphed over all resistance through the sheer force of his personality and without the assistance of weapons. A Biedermeier epic, on the other hand, or an epic set in an individualistic, capitalist society, would be unthinkable. In such contexts novels in verse, idylls and tales in verse are all possible. However, any attempts at a serious interpretation of the current world view in a lofty, heroic style would be artistically unsatisfying, flawed and possibly even ridiculous.[22] Equally unsuccessful would be any attempt to interpret the *Zeitgeist* of past heroic ages, or in other words draw on historical material. One 'world' can only produce genuine poetic interpretations of similar or related worlds.

There is one further question to be discussed in this connection: which world is it that the epic is interpreting? If, as Kayser says, the epic represents the 'opening up of a world', it must be made clear from the outset that most epics are in fact dealing with two 'worlds'. One is that which has furnished the material for the story, but the other is the world in which the poet is living. Between the two there often lie hundreds of years.[23] What is being 'interpreted' is then much less the world from which the story is taken than the world of the storyteller. The 'Homeric world', for example, is less about the world of the late Mycenaean Ionic period (around 1400 to 1150 BC) with its chthonic religions[24] and different cults varying from region to region, that formed the background to the Trojan War, than about the archaic world (eighth century and later) with its anthropomorphic gods and genealogical interests.[25] Here both world views blend together to produce a single martial *Weltanschauung*: in spite of the considerable differences between the 'accepted unconscious metaphysic' of the two epochs, no distinction is made between them. On the other hand, even in a poem dating as far back as *Beowulf* the tension between the original Germanic story of the hero and warrior and the Augustinian Christian interpretation it is given in the poem[26] is sometimes so noticeable that the unity of the work is almost jeopardized. In the worldly baroque epic of the seventeenth century the 'historic' and heroic world of the plot is usually only a stylistic 'cover' for the contemporary period that is the real subject of the poem: far from being a picture of true heroism it deals with the complicated code of honour and gallantry of the court in Versailles and London.[27] But as we have already seen, limitation of the subject to a particular class runs counter to the spirit of the genuine epic. Later on we shall see that even the poets of the early nineteenth century with their taste for historicism were unable for a number of reasons to produce true epics.

On the basis of the five points discussed above, it is now possible to summarize what has been learned about the epic.

First we saw that the verse, in spite of its historical origins, is an inseparable part of the genre. The same was also found to be true of the heroic subject matter, although in place of the expression 'heroic' the more comprehensive term 'all-embracing interest' was used. The idea that the epic should contain mythology was expanded even further and Abercrombie's term 'accepted unconscious metaphysic' was applied. Here, however, the word 'metaphysic' was given a much broader meaning: it was equated with the 'world' that, according to Kayser, is interpreted in the epic. It was also found that all epics deal with exemplary subjects in a matching tone. On the subject of the epic hero, it was shown that this is closely connected with the previous questions (heroic subject matter, exemplary subject) and that such a hero must be a model character in the world being interpreted in the epic. If the world in question has no such representative characters, or if they are in no way heroic, no true epic can be produced.

After this preliminary investigation of the most important aspects of the epic genre, a definition of the concept itself will now be attempted, not however the traditional normative type of definition but rather a flexible system that outlines the essence of the true epic. A definition that summarizes the epic in a single sentence would also be out of place, since with so many factors to be taken into consideration it would always be obscure as well as syntactically unwieldy. What will instead be offered is a kind of description which will contain the relevant characteristics of every 'dimension' of the genre. This method will, it is hoped, greatly facilitate the brief definition of the integrating elements of the genre concept and provide a practical means of comparing the different genres.

Initial situation. A poet narrates to a like-minded reading or listening public.

Nature of presentation and external form. The epic is sung, recited or written, and has a self-contained plot in the form of a long poem with the appropriate rhythms and metres. The form is highly conventional.

Intended public. A national public or one where everyone shares similar views of the world and which is united by a single all-embracing interest.

Content. An all-embracing interest and, in the widest sense of the word, heroic theme to which the public in question can relate, in the guise of a story.

Poetic intention. The interpretation or illumination of the world, focusing on what the intended public consider to be its true and essential aspects.

Tone and style. Of a level appropriate to the truth and significance of the statement being made. Little dynamic shading in the narrative through changes of tone, and on the other hand many stereotyped elements.

Reality content. Subject matter that is close to reality, i.e., reflecting the main cultural and ritual characteristics of an experienced or 'believed' reality,[28] however stylized the form of the poem may be.

We will encounter the epic again in the following section on the romance genre: the precise distinction between these two genre types is something that we will have to bear in mind later, when the history of romantic narrative literature in verse is discussed.

Second genre definition: the romance

The woes of Troy, towers smothering o'er their blaze,
Stiff-holden shields, far-piercing spears, keen blades,
Struggling, and blood, and shrieks – all dimly fades
Into some backward corner of the brain:
Yet in our very souls, we feel amain
The close of Troilus and Cressid sweet ...
John Keats, *Endymion* II, 8ff.

Here it is particularly difficult to separate the 'absolute' genre concept from its historical context. As is well known, the word romance had a succession of different meanings in the course of its history, which only shows how vague it is as the name of a genre. Originally all it referred to was the Romance vernacular language, but subsequently it came to mean a story in this language, then the narrower concept of the court novel in verse, followed by the bourgeois minstrel form of this court novel and the prose version of it, and finally any fictional story in prose or verse – thus on the one hand novels from the *Morte d'Arthur* to *Arcadia*, *Don Quixote* and *Tom Jones*, and on the other metric narrative poetry from the *Chanson de Roland* to the minstrel romances, the Spanish *romanceros*, *Orlando Furioso* and Scott's tales in verse. All these meanings have been incorporated in the word as it is used today, and it has also acquired pre-romantic and romantic associations, so that romance – according to the context – can stand for all the things that have just been listed and in addition for 'the world of romance', i.e., everything that resembles the stories told in romances. In order therefore to establish what is meant here by romance, arbitrary limits must be set.

The most important arbitrary limit is the verse form. Since the original presentation conditions for the romance were similar to those for the epic, the verse form has more or less the same historical origins in both genres. Even if it has not been automatically implied by the word romance as a genre name for a long time – since the word is also used to refer to the prose novel – for the purposes of this study the verse form must nevertheless be retained as a characteristic of the genre; and whenever the name romance is used for the genre, what is implied is therefore always 'metrical romance'.

The starting point for the definition of the romance, in addition to the historical background, will of necessity be the genre that has just been analysed, the epic. It is also the genre to which the romance is most closely related, and with which it has the external form of the longer tale in verse and certain themes in common. The essential difference between the two seems clear enough, but it is nevertheless hard to define precisely. 'Romantic' features – adventures, miracles and the characters' 'private' concerns – are to be found in the epics, in the *Odyssey* and in *Beowulf*, just as epic, heroic aspects are to be found in the romances. Many Italian epics and the works of Spenser are even distinct mixtures of the two genres. W. M. Dixon, who is from the outset sceptical about all attempts to differentiate between genres, thus has this to say about separating the epic and the romance: 'It may please us to distinguish, to untwine and unlay the composing strands, but no one can indicate the moment at which poetry ceases to be heroic because it is too romantic.'[29] He then nevertheless embarks on a list of differences. The epic, he points out, has its roots in its country of origin, whereas the romance concentrates on far-away, foreign and exotic settings; the main emphasis in the epic is on the illumination of historical truths and causalities and on the real historical characters, or at least characters who are believed to have existed, whereas the romances were written to entertain, and not only go far beyond experienced or 'believed' reality but also blur the distinctive personalities of the characters with 'sentimental subtleties' of a general nature and emphasis on the plot. Furthermore, although both genres feature military engagements, in the epic, battle is a 'way of life', whereas in the romance it is more of an adventure, a social obligation or a class tradition, which is often pushed into the background by other themes, in particular court life and love. While the epic is by nature a homogeneous whole, the romance is a mixture of influences as a result of its Germanic, Celtic, classical and oriental roots. It proved thus impossible to blend the wealth of material into great poems as the author of the *Odyssey* was able to do, and the lengthy cycles of the Arthurian romances and the mammoth verse novels with classical themes never attained the rank of the great epic. Even the very best achievements of the genre – Dixon names the *Chanson de Roland*, Ariosto, Tasso and Spenser – are merely 'peaks of a submerged continent', fragments of a genre that has largely sunk into oblivion. In an attempt to reconcile all these different aspects, Dixon concludes: 'Any narrative poetry if it be sufficiently impressive is epic.' ... 'Impressiveness' – breadth of vision, sublimity and grandeur, significance and profound truth – this is what in his opinion distinguishes the epic from the romance and puts it on a higher plane.[30] Much of what this critic wrote in 1912 seems curiously dated and arbitrary, but it is not hard to see that all that is basically meant by impressiveness is the 'all-embracing themes', the 'interpretation of the world' and the 'accepted unconscious metaphysic' which were discussed in the section on the epic.

C. H. Herford also describes the differences between the epic and the romance in a similar way.[31] While the romance, like the heroic song and the classical epic, is a long story with one or several heroes at the centre of it, the main emphasis is on the novella aspect and the exciting external event: the sense of the 'tragic cry', however – which in Herford's opinion is the greatest achievement of a serious narrative poem – is completely lacking. In all Middle English romances subject matter that is often not very different from the best in world literature is wasted; profound description of character is totally lacking, and where tragedy is involved, its impact is lost through details of feeling or an external solution devoid of tragic understanding. The Germanic sense of conflict gives way to a conception of the hero in which a conflict situation is not possible since all resistance melts before him, and the mysticism of the Celts becomes merely a source of superficial events and curiosities. Herford blames the medieval idea of tragœdia as the simple decline of fortune for the disappearance of tragedy in the Germanic and modern sense.

Dixon's classical bias is replaced by a 'Germanic' bias in Herford's text. His understanding of 'impressiveness' is not quite the same as that of Dixon, but their approaches are nevertheless similar and roughly in accordance with the view that is presented in this study. Tragedy – as we understand the word today – has after all always involved the conflict of great individuals with a 'world' and its laws, demands and unavoidable obligations. Herford's 'tragic cry' thus also implies the existence of an 'all-embracing interest' or 'world'. Both Dixon's and Herford's definitions of the genre are biased in favour of the epic. This is easily explained by the reference both authors make to medieval English poetry, where there are scarcely any outstanding examples of the romance genre of the calibre of the great Middle High German and French verse romances. Should the general point that is being made here thus be included in our present definition of the romance (to do so would mean classing the great, profoundly intellectual Middle High German or French verse novels as epics in order to uphold the theory that there is less 'impressiveness' in the romance than in the epic); or should it rather be left out altogether?

As unsatisfactory as this may be, for the purposes of this study of English romances, there is no alternative but to take the former course. It is particularly important to keep in mind the conditions in England and the view the pre-romantic and romantic poets had of the nature of the medieval romance genre (in particular Scott, who was a connoisseur of Middle English romance literature). The romance in their eyes was always bound up with the primitivistic idea of the untaught minstrel, the natural genius who with unsophisticated feeling and inborn imagination told stories about the real world and his own fantasy worlds. It occurred to hardly any of these poets that the medieval romance could be a symbolic structure full of deep meaning, reflecting a complete theological and political concept of the world.

The fact that the greatest English romantic poets then went on to invest the romance with the same kind of meaningful symbolic structure that we now perceive in the great medieval romances is irrelevant: they proceeded, full of a sense of complete originality, with their brand new, up-to-date themes, without, as has already been mentioned, any idea of the deeper meaning embodied in the most important medieval models for the genre. If one wanted to identify the common characteristics of the genre in the two periods, complicated modern theories would have to be applied. While it will not be possible to avoid these theories later on, to bring them in now would spoil all attempts to construct the simple genre theory framework that it essential at this stage.

It may thus be said, bearing in mind that once again arbitrary limits are being set, that the romance – not so much in the sense of the medieval genre as of the romance as a general concept – differs most noticeably from the epic in its more moderate pretensions, the less comprehensive scope of its problems and its less elevated tone. All the other respects in which they differ can be summed up by saying that since the romance is not trying to be a great 'world poem' it does not have to be long.

The unity which holds the romance together is not a 'world', i.e., a society which comprehends itself as a community united by a common history, it is not the life of a hero important in and for this 'world' owing to his historical mission and commitments, but rather an imaginative plot centred on one or more heroes from a particular sector of society. It is united not so much by a compelling course of events as by a framework provided by the story, the mythological or legendary element and the preliterary or literary tradition, into which the poet works a sequence of any number of adventures. While they are usually rounded off with the return home or the marriage of the protagonist or a reconciliation, they must not be concluded so definitively that new beginnings and adventures are excluded.[32]

Just as the time in these poems is not actually a historical one in spite of the frequent historical references, but is rather an age of knights and fairy tales,[33] the setting of the romance is also unreal. The adventures either take place in faraway, exotic fantasy lands or the real places named, even the poet's own home country, are transformed into magic lands. Equally magical and unreal – or portrayed in an unusual light – are the deeds and events described in the romances, even if they do reflect the customs and sociological order of a certain historical epoch and sometimes come closer to reality with their description of the psychological aspects and of the life of the lower classes than the elevated epic. Even when a historical personality is made the hero of a romance, the emphasis is not on his historical mission, of which only the legendary aspects remain, but on his individual problems (in particular those relating to love and adventure) and the colourful and fabulous events in which he becomes involved. For this reason the subject matter and themes of the romances are much less confined to national settings than those of the true epics. Thus for example Charlemagne can blend with Carl Martel or Louis VII of France, as is the case with certain *chansons de geste*.

The relationship to reality is thus the opposite to that of the epic: the epic, with its reference to real historical events (even though these are padded out with mythology or legendary material) and closeness to reality in its portrayal of the simple details of outward life (which however is lost in the literary epic), is realistic as far as the subject matter is concerned,[34] but with its stereotyped treatment of the language often appears unrealistically stylized as far as the form is concerned. The romance, on the other hand, 'romanticizes' real life to a much greater degree, and in many aspects of its subject matter tends away from reality, but where the form is concerned, with its more flexible and more analytical style and greater emphasis on the 'private' side (e.g., the true-to-life dialogue) it achieves much greater external realism.

As has already been said, the military plots in the romance are not seen in the context of a nation's history and world view – we only have to compare the battles of the Saracens in *Sowdone of Babylon* or *Guy of Warwick* with those in the *Chanson de Roland*: it is futile to look for a rigid religious framework for the battles such as is contained in Laisse 89 of the *Chanson de Roland*.[35] It has also been pointed out that 'private' themes such as love and the adventures of individual knights are given as much emphasis as political and military themes, and are sometimes even more important.

There are also differences in the approach of the two genres to the supernatural: in the epic everything miraculous and outside human experience is part of an 'accepted' mythology, the 'accepted unconscious metaphysic' of the society from which the epic originates, as described by Abercrombie and Tillyard, and the impression of reality is thus created. In the romance, on the other hand, the supernatural is a fairy-tale element, as unreal as time and place. The question of credibility does not arise at all.

Finally the epic and the romance differ – as Dixon and Herford have suggested – in the way the characters are portrayed. An epic figure is characterized almost solely by his deeds, his behaviour in the situations in which he becomes involved, and possibly also by his words. His character is not analysed and his emotions are not described in detail. Thus we find in the epic summaries of character reduced to a single sentence, e.g.,

> Roland est proz et Oliver est sage
> (*Chanson de Roland*, 1,093)

or stereotyped expressions of praise, e.g.,

> ac þaet wæs gōd cyning
> (*Beowulf*, 883)

and brief references to mood or inner emotions, e.g.,

> Dunc ad tel doel pur poi dire ne fent
> (about Ganelon, in the *Chanson de Roland*, 304)

or

> wæs him Beowulfes sið
> mōdges mere-faran, micel aefþunca,
> forþon þe hē ne ūþe, þæt æniȝ oðer man
> æfre mærða þon mā middan-ȝeardes
> ȝehedde under heofenum þonne hē sylfa
> (about Unferð in *Beowulf*, 501 ff.)

By comparison, in the following passage from the *Roman de Tristan* the characters' state of mind is given in much greater detail and subtle emotions are explored:

> Quant il vint enz e vit Ysolt,
> Il vait vers lu, baiser la volt;
> Mais ele se trait lors arere.
> Huntuse fu de grant manere,
> Kar ne saveit quai fere dut
> E trussuat u ele estut.

Tristan vit k'ele l'eschivat:
Huntus fu, si se vergundat,
Si s'en est un poi tret ensus
Vers le parei, dejuste l'us ...
                    (978 ff.)

Here therefore, even with respect to content, the romance is more 'realistic' than the epic with its stylized characterization technique. The real reason for this, as will be fairly obvious, lies in the differing objectives of the two types of poetry; the one portrays a hero as a model that the society concerned should emulate, and the other describes a human fate in such a way that the reader can identify with it.

Are the differences in the ideas and content of the epic and the romance also reflected in tangible formal details to be found throughout the poems? Here one should be wary of generalizations: certain themes and formal influences are to be found in both genres,[36] and the presentation conditions to which both are subject – first those imposed by recitation and then those imposed by written poetry – play an important part. However, there are a few formal tendencies which may tentatively be said to stem from the different character of the two genres. The epic requires an elevated style, while the style of the romance can be pitched at a slightly lower level. The epic has a more archaic tone,[37] while the romance tends to adapt its tone to the content and to contemporary tastes. A sequence of long, evenly constructed, proportionable and resounding verse lines – such as hexameters, blank verse, the decasyllabic lines connected by assonance that are found in the ancient French heroic songs or the long alliterative lines of Germanic poetry – are perhaps more suitable for the epic as an 'evenly illuminated, evenly objective present'[38] than a 'perspectivistic' dynamic metre such as is produced by short rhymed verse lines or in particular by stanzas. In the romance, on the other hand, where solemnity is less important than flexibility of tone, the rapidly flowing story is often divided up into small units such as couplets or stanzas.[39]

After these introductory remarks, it should not be too difficult to define the romance genre applying the methods used for the epic.

Initial situation. A narrator addresses an audience (a public) that sometimes is, but does not have to be, limited to a particular social class or nationality.

Nature of presentation and external form. The romance is sung, recited or written, has a loosely constructed plot and the fixed rhythmic form of a poem, and varies considerably in length. By comparison with the epic it is relatively free from obligatory form conventions.

The ballad

Intended public. Any public looking for high-quality entertainme This was only initially a particular social or national group, e.g., court socie an upper class of conquerors speaking a foreign language, etc., and later included the lower classes who listened to minstrels.

Content. Entertaining themes, with a preference for love, adventure, the miraculous and the exotic and the world of the knights and the court: in other words 'romantic' themes. No merely regional interest; marked emphasis on the 'private' aspect.

Poetic intention. Entertainment and excitement. Frequently also the representation of the life style and moral code of a particular class – the ruling class or aristocracy. Originally describing society as it was at the time the poems were written and later portraying past periods of history. There is scope for symbolic depth, but this opportunity is not always exploited.

Tone and style. In accordance with the content and poetic intention, less elevated than in the epic. Stronger dynamic shading of the story created by stylistic means.

Reality content. While the elements of the plot are remote from reality, the descriptions of human reactions and the behaviour of particular classes (above all the lower classes) are often realistic.

Here the reader is once again referred to the wider definition of the romance in later parts of this book. The above description, which once again tries to combine the timeless and typical with the historical aspects, is more or less adequate as a 'synchronic' explanation of the romantic verse narrative genre provided that the epic, as its opposite and complement, is also brought in for comparative purposes. Since, however, the origin of this 'genre' is being traced from several possible roots and it is important not to leave out any of the factors involved, there is another genre concept that must be described in greater detail: the ballad.

Third genre definition: the ballad

The highest form of ballad requires from a poet at once narrative powers, lyrical and dramatic.
Algernon Swinburne, *Essays and Studies*, London, 1897 (in an essay on
Dante Gabriel Rosetti)

The ballad has something of the mysterious without actually being mystical; the latter quality in a poem results from the subject matter, the former from the way this is treated. The mysterious in a ballad is produced by the manner of narrating, the minstrel having his deeply significant subject matter, his figures, their actions and movements so deeply engraved in his mind that he is uncertain how best to bring it all to light. He consequently makes use of all three basic genres of poetry in his attempt to express, right at the start, the things that will excite the imagination and engage the intellect; he may begin in a lyrical, epic, or dramatic manner, and change these forms at will as he goes on, either rushing speedily toward the close or postponing it for a long time. The refrain, the repetition always of the same concluding burden, gives this genre a decidedly lyrical character.

J. W. Goethe, 'Ballade, Betrachtung und Auslegung' (Ballad, Reflection and Definition) in *Über Kunst und Altertum*, 3, 1 (1821).

Here, as with the epic, there is an authentic form and a literary imitation. In this case, however, the original form has remained binding to such a degree that, at least in England, the art ballad is not so very different from the folk ballad.[40]

The historical origin of the genre need not concern us to any great extent. In order to describe the character of this genre, it is not vital to establish whether the original medieval ballads that we possess are only the few recorded examples of a tradition that goes way back into the dim and distant past, later manifestations of a development that goes back to tribal dances and songs; or whether ballads will always appear anywhere where there is an unsophisticated national tradition of putting current events into song; whether the composition of the ballad was always connected with individuals – minstrels and choir leaders – with 'the people' only supplying stereotyped refrains; whether the genre began with songs connected with contemporary events originating before the appearance of the heroic songs, so that the epic in fact has its roots in the 'original ballad', or whether the ballad as we know it only appeared after the epic, romance and fabliau and is a folk rendering of the same material, repeated again and again in ever new mutations. As John Buchan says in his *History of English Literature* (1933): 'Of no branch of literary art is the peculiar quality more easily recognized, and in none are the sources and ancestry more obscure.'[41]

What then does this 'peculiar quality' consist of, and how does the ballad differ from the romance? First, the ballad always has more of a folk element about it; it originated from the people and was their genre. Even though in later periods there are art ballads written with an intellectual aim, they nevertheless always retain the naive tone of folk tradition. The ballad was also restricted from the start to more rigid musical forms, by contrast with the epic and romance. It is constructed like a song (usually divided up into stanzas) and is much shorter than the other two genres. The refrain is in addition a very common feature. For all these reasons it is on the borderline between narrative and lyric poetry.

By contrast with the epic, the ballad does not describe the fates of nations, but of individuals. It is in any case limited to a much narrower sphere than the epic and the romance. The clan is generally the largest group of people it covers. There are of course occasionally ballads about national events, such as Drayton's *Agincourt* ballad, but even in such cases the horizon of the poem is the horizon of the people. With its smaller number of characters and the emphasis on the individual, the ballad is more like the drama, with which it also shares the restriction to a self-contained plot. It frequently builds up to an exciting climax at the end. Examples of this are the *Edward* ballad with its technique of gradual revelation and stressed final line; *Sir Patrick Spence* which culminates in catastrophe; *The Nut-Brown Maid* written in a form resembling the debate, where the excitement created by the contrasts of the dialogue continues to build up right to the end; or – to cite an example from later literature – the conclusion of Goethe's *Erl-King*. Even this, according to Schiller, is not an epic but a dramatic element, since 'each step of the epic poem is of equal importance; we do not hasten impatiently towards a final goal but dwell lovingly over every development'.[42]

There is further similarity with the drama in that several of the characteristics of tragedy as identified by Goethe and Schiller[43] – 'personal suffering ... introverted characters ... limited scope' – are also characteristics of the ballad. The ballad can thus be described as the most dramatic form of narrative poetry (the techniques of narration detailed below reinforce this) and must, on account of its form and presentation at the same time be termed the most lyrical of the category.

As a genre it also has strong links with tradition, and although this permits a variety of ballad types ranging from the short song to the ballad that is a miniature epic,[44] and several stanza forms as well as a great variety of themes (political events which form the background to the story and their impingement on private fates, historical or semi-historical family tragedies, legendary, romantic, novelettish, sensational and even farcical subject matter; kings, knights, minstrels, sailors, peasants, Jews, pages and robbers, etc.) every one of these poems nevertheless bears the unmistakable stamp of the ballad. The basic elements of this tradition are the particular narrative technique and the retention of certain stereotyped formal elements.

The ballad does not narrate in a broad, epic flow, but achieves dramatic brevity by leaving out almost all the narrative, reflective or descriptive filling. It abruptly highlights particular situations, has dialogues that form part of the plot, and dramatic peripeteias. It thus does not describe developments but individual facts and fully fledged events. Even if the plot develops gradually, this is conveyed by a few meaningful portrayals of the current situation or by dialogue. In the ballad the focus is on meaningful objects and instantaneous illumination of significant scenes. Everything in between is left in darkness.

The form is characterized by the frequency of refrain, indicating the ballad's choral origins, and the stereotyped lines, both aspects which are often to be found in identical form in several ballads. They are sometimes not necessary for the plot and are occasionally not even suited to the poem, or at all events add little to it. Further characteristics are incremental repetition, i.e., the intensification of suspense reinforced by the repetition of a stanza or line, whereby a few important words may be changed each time; various repeatedly occurring features such as the rhetorical question that is immediately followed by the answer, or the frequent commencement of the line (which is usually iambic) with 'and'; and finally the considerable freedom of metre[45] and the preference for archaic and dialectal expressions. All this gives the ballad a rough, unpolished character by comparison with the poetry of the professional poets. The English and Scottish idea of the ballad is in addition closely associated with a particular type of metre that is by no means common to all ballads, but occurs so frequently that it is termed the ballad metre and is always thought to be especially ballad-like. This type of rhythm, or rather of stanza, as is well-known, consists of alternating tetrameters and trimeters with a basic iambic structure and masculine endings; it permits many variations and has also become established in the German ballad.

The ballad's strong links with tradition make it a genre that is easy to imitate, and English poets – even twentieth-century ones such as W. H. Auden and John Betjeman – have always been attracted to this clearly recognizable folk and, in the derivative form of the street-ballad, popular style.

As far as the relationship of the ballad to reality is concerned, its contents, in a similar manner to those of the epic, embody the refreshing closeness to nature and things that characterizes naive human beings, without of course setting out to reveal an essentially 'accepted' relationship to reality and an underlying profound interpretation of the world as the epic does; from the point of view of form, however, it is stylized and stereotyped in the same way as the epic.

Following this brief survey of the qualities of the ballad genre, we can now proceed to a descriptive summary as for the other genres.

Initial situation. 'The people' – in groups or represented by a soloist or main singer, who does not however differ socially from them, and who, even if he is a professional singer, never leaves the folk sphere – sing for their own entertainment.

Nature of presentation and external form. Singing (later only in the reader's imagination) of a coherent, self-contained story in the form of a song with traditional stanzas and rhythms, of brief to medium duration. Highly conservative with respect to form.[46]

Intended public. Listeners and readers who are looking for literature of a less demanding kind.

Content. Dramatic description of an unusual, real or invented occurrence. Historical, heroic (at an individual level), romantic, sensational or farcical themes. There is often local interest, and there are often motifs based on popular beliefs.

Poetic intention. Entertainment, and the passing on of information about unusual occurrences.

Tone and style. Not very elevated, in accordance with the social orgins of the genre, but nevertheless potentially able to convey a natural, naive dignity and a sense of tragedy. There is much that is stereotyped, but in spite of the predominantly traditional tone, the mood can be greatly varied. There are affinities with lyric poetry and drama.

Reality content. The contents are close to reality (even the supernatural or sensational is originally believed possible and considered as part of reality), but the form is stylized.

2 The initial situation

Jeder Künstler findet bestimmte 'optische' Möglichkeiten vor, an die er gebunden ist ... Das Sehen an sich hat seine Geschichte, und die Aufdeckung dieser 'optischen Schichten' muss als die elementarste Aufgabe der Kunstgeschichte betrachtet werden.

Every artist finds himself faced with a number of 'optic' [visual] possibilities to which he is bound ... Human perception has its history, and the disclosure of the historical 'strata of perception' no doubt is and has to be the art historian's primary task.

Heinrich Wölfflin, *Kunstgeschichtliche Grundbegriffe*,
Munich, 1923, introduction.

It would be out of place here to study all the radical changes in the approach to poetry and the new trends in intellectual development which – via various early romantic stages and tendencies – led to English romanticism, and hence also contributed to the rise of the English verse narrative. The literature on the subject would fill a library, and any abbreviated outline would carry with it the risk of simplification and distortion. It is, however, undoubtedly necessary to isolate from the myriad developmental trends those which were instrumental in the creation and rise to popularity of the genre under discussion. In the interests of brevity, the poetological change with which every connoisseur of eighteenth-century culture will be familiar will be given in summary form, indicating the implications for the romantic tale in verse. The following five sections will deal with the role of the medieval revival, the eighteenth century and the epic, the shift from 'design' to 'continuity', the 'theatrical horrors of the German School', and the social changes in the reading public.

The development of new poetological theories

The part this played in the development of our genre is fairly obvious. It is not even necessary to trace the highly complicated history of the concept of imagination (in the sense of literary invention and the creative faculty) if we are aware that as far back as 1659 Henry More, the Cambridge Platonist, opposed Hobbes' disparagement of the imagination as 'decaying sense', i.e., as an ability dependent on what has been experienced through the senses and on memory, and hence vastly inferior to reason, with his idea of 'most free imagination' as a prerequisite for 'Romantick Inventions'.[1] The poetological debate about the concept of imagination that occupied the rationalistic critics of the Augustan Age, who held fast to the Aristotelian mimesis theory, of course shows that it was a long time before More's limiting but positive approach to imagination as against reason resurfaced – although Shakespeare had already anticipated it in the famous passage from *A Midsummer Night's Dream* V, 1, lines 12–22. What was first necessary was the combining of a refined definition of imagination with the emotionalistic theory that art was a spontaneous expression of subjective feeling – in other words with that complex of theories that M. H. Abrams summarized using the metaphor 'the Lamp'.

If we are also aware that the 'primitivistic' theory clearly formulated by theoreticians such as William Duff and Adam Ferguson played a large part in the development of the emotionalistic approach to poetry (according to this theory, when culture was in its infancy poetic imagination originated from natural feelings in a more spontaneous, individual and pure fashion than was the case when culture had become established on the basis of reason) then we already have before us many of the factors that gave rise not only to Wordsworth's but also to Scott's 'invention' of the romantic verse narrative. Even a thinker who placed as much emphasis on reason as Adam Smith was able to say of the early poets (models for both Scott and the authors of the *Lyrical Ballads*): 'As their subject was the marvellous, so they naturally expressed themselves in the language of wonder, that is, in poetry, for in that style amazement and surprise naturally break forth.'[2]

If the revival of narrative poetry developed from these ideas of poetry – which were being widely discussed, particularly in Scotland – it could not then be a logical descendant of the neo-classical epic with its exclusive orientation towards the highly advanced civilization of the classical age, its rationalistic mimesis concept and principle of restraint of the passions by reason and willpower. Instead it drew on the emotionalistic, primitivistic inspiration that the Scot, A. Ferguson, in 1767, described thus: 'Under the supposed disadvantage of a limited knowledge, and rude apprehension, the simple poet has impressions that more than compensate the defects of his skill ... The simple passions, friendship, resentment, and love, are the movements of his own mind, and he has no occasion to copy.'[3]

The role of the medieval revival

A people slowly emerging from a condition of barbarism into civilisation, regards the change it is undergoing with great admiration and pride ... while a sort of feeling, even of hostility, ensues, to that dark and inveterate barbarism from which it is accomplishing its deliverance ... The whole mind of the nation looks forward to futurity ...

But when a nation reaches a high point of civilisation, and when its literature is highly refined and perfect, it must then either turn itself to the study, and consequently the imitation, of the literature of other nations, or it must revert to the ancient spirit of its own ...
Blackwood's Magazine, 21, December 1818, 'On the Revival of a Taste for our Ancient Literature'.

The historical facts concerning the medieval fashion that resulted from the change of attitude just described are well known. Every history of literature contains details of the extent to which the revivers of the ballad (Ramsey, Percy, Scott, T. Evans, Herd, Ritson, etc.), the collectors of romances (Ellis, Scott, Southey), the literature theoreticians (Hurd, the Warton brothers, Thyrwitt), the imitators and fakers (Macpherson, Pinkerton, Chatterton) and the many authors who ventured into this new field (from Gray, Thomson, Beattie and Shenstone to Walpole, Clara Reeve, M. G. Lewis and Scott) were involved in this movement. What needs to be explained, however, is why it was almost fifty years after the first symptoms of this revival before really powerful, exciting, longer tales appeared that held the reader's attention throughout and were written 'in the language of wonder, that is, in poetry'.

Since Percy's *Reliques of Ancient English Poetry* (1765)[4] there had of course been many ballad imitations. Even Bishop Percy, in order to bring the 'artless production of the old rhapsodists' more into line with the tastes of a 'polished age, like the present', 'to atone for the rudeness of the more obsolete poems' and 'to take off from the tediousness of longer narratives', had not only removed the rough edges from authentic ballads and added 'little elegant pieces of the lyric kind' – which shows how far public taste around the middle of the century still lagged behind the aesthetic views of the early romantic theoreticians – but had also, as Scott noted in the 'Introductory Remarks on Popular Poetry' in his *Ministrelsy of the Scottish Border*[5] (1802 – 3), produced a ballad, *The Marriage of Sir Gawein*, in which he had 'given entire rein to his own fancy, though the rude origin of most of his ideas is to be found in the old ballad'. Scott wrote of another of Percy's ballads, *The Child of Ellis*, that 'that elegant metrical tale ... has derived all its beauties from Dr. Percy's poetical powers' (ibid.). With respect to his countryman Alan Ramsey's 'collecting activities', Scott found it regrettable that the latter followed 'the unhappy plan of writing new words to old tunes without at the same time preserving the ancient verses' (ibid.).

The many ballad imitations that fell between old texts with modern additions and entirely original works might to some extent have formed the basis for the romantic narrative literature in verse that came later: they supplied subject matter and established a taste for modern notions of the Middle Ages[6] and swiftly moving plots – which had scarcely existed in eighteenth-century verse narrative. Scott's first verse narrative, *The Lay of the Last Minstrel*, was even originally planned as a ballad imitation on the subject of the gnome Gilpin Horner, and was intended, even after it had been expanded into a 'kind of romance of border Chivalry, in a light horseman sort of stanza', to be included in the third volume of his *Minstrelsy*, just as his edition of the Middle English *Sir Tristrem* (1804) was also originally intended for the *Minstrelsy*.

There are three reasons, however, why the romantic tale in verse could not develop as a natural continuation of the ballad imitations.

1. They were too short to meet the increasing demand for narrative continuity in poetry, and too lightweight and 'primitive' to be able to compete with the genre that was still the yardstick for all literary narrative in verse: the epic, or 'great poem'.

2. As more value came to be placed on accuracy about the past, the 'ballads of modern date' were demoted to the status of pastiches and distortions of history by comparison with the authentic old ballads.[7] This rejection of Percy's approach was a consequence of the passionate polemics of the learned if biased Joseph Ritson, with whom Scott agreed to the extent that in his *Minstrelsy* he made a clear distinction between the modern ballads and the original medieval ones – he put the former all together in a separate volume, Volume III. T. Evans' son R. H. Evans even drastically reduced the number of modern works in order to make room for more old ballads in a new edition of his father's ballad collection that he published in 1810).[8]

3. While the ballad publications of academics and poets interested in antiquity hence bore greater resemblance to the medieval originals, a need for something diametrically opposed to this was being created through social changes in the reading public and the resulting change in taste – a hunger for sensational reading material, tales of wonder, wildness, passion and horror, that was increasingly being met by imported German literature. The conflict to which this gave rise is reflected in the *Edinburgh Review* in a review of Scott's *Minstrelsy* published in 1803, where the critic expresses the opinion that modern ballad poets should not allow themselves to be so blinded by the anachronistic 'refinements' of modern times that they forget the strength of the old ballads; he then goes on to say that Scott's and Leyden's more faithful imitations of the old ballads are not only better than the 'fakes' of Pinkerton, but much better than all the many tales of wonder being produced as a result of the German influence. (This is of course a reference to G. M. Lewis' ballad collection entitled *Tales of Wonder* that appeared in 1801. Here the critic may have overlooked the fact that, with their contributions to Lewis' collection, Scott and Leyden were also subscribers to this, in his opinion, inferior fashion for sensation, or he may perhaps have been trying to attract Walter Scott away from the German trend, to which the latter had paid tribute very openly as early as 1796 with his free renderings of G. A. Bürger's *Lenore, The Wild Huntsman* and later *The Chase*, even if these had not proved very popular.)[9]

However, before we study this change in taste in greater detail, we must go back to the genre that was at least to some extent ousted or replaced by the romantic tale in verse.

The eighteenth century and the epic

> ... we must be satisfied that narrative poetry, if strictly confined to the great occurrences of history, would be deprived of the individual interest which it is so well calculated to excite.
>
> Walter Scott (about Homer's *Iliad*), Introduction to the First Edition of *The Bridal of Triermain* (1813).

As a neo-classical age, the eighteenth century had great respect for the epic, which was considered the sublimest poetic genre. As a non-heroic, often sceptical, rationalistically critical and realistic age, however, it could not convincingly express its attitude to life through this genre. This contradiction dominated the relationship of the whole epoch to the epic. On the one hand there was still a strong temptation to emulate Virgil and Statius, and many lesser poets such as R. Blackmore, Aaron Hill, Richard Glover, William Wilkie, Henry J. Pye, William Sotheby, Joseph Cottle and even Edwin Atherstone succumbed to it and wrote extensive epics in which they kept largely to the classical epic conventions and neo-classical epic rules. On the other hand, almost all the great poets from Pope to Wordsworth and Byron indeed planned such epics in their youth[10] but none of them made the mistake of actually putting such plans into effect. That it would have been a mistake is only too evident from the failure or total obscurity of the lesser poets just named and their epics.

Scott saw this very clearly. In his review of Southey's romantic epic *The Curse of Kehama*, which he wrote for the *Quarterly Review* in 1811,[11] he maintained that these poetasters had only won esteem as a result of the critics' trust in authority, and it was 'needless and invidious' to continue to talk about them: 'They loaded our shelves indeed, and are recorded in our catalogues; but who can say that the learned labours of Bossu, so admirably ridiculed by Pope, have added one readable poem to the literature of France or England? The harp of Mincio has made miserable music in the hands of Voltaire, Blackmore and later worthies.' After quoting a similar judgement from George Crabbe's *The Village* (I, 17 ff.), he continues: 'Here therefore is one road to the temple of fame, not indeed blockaded, but broken up and rendered impassible by the numbers who have trodden it.'

The great neo-classical English poets were satisfied with producing free renderings of the classical epics;[12] or if they did narrate in verse, it was in a form that did not compete with the classical heroic poem, i.e., they limited the scope of their works and wrote mock heroic poems, domestic and idyllic poems, fables or frivolous rococo verse narratives that were modelled on Lafontaine, Grécourt or Crébillon.[13]

When Scott wrote the *Kehama* review from which the above quotes were taken, the epic had of course already been superseded by the romantic poems of Southey and of Scott himself. However, since the mid-eighteenth century there had been increasing signs that the neo-classicists were relinquishing their hopes of continuing the epic tradition, signs which amounted to more than just the tacit avoidance of the genre by the important poets, the occasional complaints about the constricting genre regulations and ridicule of the trivialization of the epic model.[14] Young propagated 'original composition', Fielding usurped the titles epic and poem for his prose novels; Germanic and Celtic history, the Middle Ages and finally even the great narrative poets of the Renaissance – Ariosto and Spenser – whose narrative manner of proceeding differed from that of the classical epic poets, once again came to the fore through the renewed, primitivistic interest in the 'old poets'.

In the *Poetical Epistle on Epic Poetry* that William Hayley addressed to his friend William Mason in 1782, he requested the latter 'to remove all prejudices which obstruct the cultivation of epic writing'; at the same time, admittedly, he also asked him – in vain – to create a modern English national epic, that would perhaps even overshadow Virgil.[15] Homer now ranked higher than Virgil as a 'bard' and Southey found that the *Odyssey* appealed to the heart more strongly as 'a poem of nature' than the heroic *Iliad*.[16]

In his most instructive article about Scott's *The Vision of Don Roderick* in the *Quarterly Review* in 1811[17] Scott's friend Erskine claimed to be speaking for his whole generation when he said that although Tasso's and Lucan's epics had more political and historical weight, he preferred the 'adventurous dreams of Ariosto'; and he ascribed the fact that the reader's attention was not held continuously in Milton's *Paradise Lost* – which was something Dr Johnson had also maintained – to the subject of the poem, in which 'there is no novelty to reward perseverance and no suspense to stimulate attention'.

Even though there are many reasons why it cannot be said that there was a uniform attitude towards the epic in the period from 1780 to 1830[18] this and similar quotations do suggest certain tendencies.

1. There was an increasing preference for the authentic epic over the literary epic but, given this basic attitude, there was a preference for the 'romantic' approach over the 'epic' approach with its adherence to rules.

2. There were two possible courses advocated for the epic, one moderate and the other radical. In the former case the character of the epic poem was maintained, even if it was called by another name, but all the classical rules were abandoned. They were considered to be unnecessarily restrictive, for they did not arise naturally from the subject or from an instinctive feeling about what was right, but were only a pedantic way of stressing certain aspects that had been peripheral even in the works of the classic epic poets. The proponents of the radical course, on the other hand, were convinced that what had previously been understood by the term epic poem could not be achieved

in its natural form, and was unsatisfactory in its 'cultivated' form, and were hence anxious to create something new and different, or at least choose something to imitate that appealed more to their tastes and emotions.

As we follow the history of the romantic tale in verse, we will see how the moderate approach first resulted in works that already had many of the characteristics of the romantic verse narrative genre; how the radical break with the classical epic opened the way for the prototype of the new romantic tale in verse genre; but how even with the most radical transformation of the fundamental epic characteristics, the dream of an epic poem appropriate to the romantic age is still there in the background – and is only finally abandoned, with disappointment, at the end of the period we are dealing with, even though English romantic poetry, as we know today, came very close to realizing this dream with several of its important works – *The Prelude, Don Juan*, and *Prometheus Unbound*.

The shift from design to continuity

Since the eighteenth century was the great age of the novel, it is all the more remarkable that in the rest of the literature written in this period very little interest was shown in continuity or the build-up of excitement in the telling of a story. Even the dramas of the Augustans, which were more marginal products of the age, are structurally more like clocks that can be wound up again and again than inevitable processes. Without wishing to go into too much detail about the reasons for the special position of the novel – the individual authors are too different from one another to make this feasible – the well-known attitude of the reading public to this genre should nevertheless be mentioned briefly. Up until around 1815–20, until, in other words, the Waverley Novels became popular and even after this, the intellectuals looked on the novel as low, inferior, a frivolous diversion, and not really worthy to be called literature. If the educated person did perhaps actually enjoy novels, he read them in the privacy of his room, kept quiet about it and was often secretly ashamed of himself.[19] Around the turn of the century middle-class ladies talked frequently of the thrills of emotion they had felt when reading the latest Gothic or fashionable novel, but they thus laid themselves open to the ridicule of 'stronger spirits' and criticism from the guardians of their virtue.

However, none of the verse narrative forms of the eighteenth century placed great emphasis on excitement, identification with the characters and narrative continuity. In almost all the neo-classical poems of the eighteenth century that have the external form of a story, the plot – if there is a real plot at all – is engulfed in a wealth of descriptive detail, 'classical' embellishments or philosophical and moral reflections and instructions. The only classicist who could really tell a story was George Crabbe, but he only developed this ability in the works he produced after the long period (1785–1807) when he stopped writing, and after that he was strongly influenced by the romantic models that are the subject of this study, as even his contemporaries realized. It would perhaps be unjust to say that the poets of the Augustan age were unable to narrate in verse or arrange interesting plots in verse form. The truth of the matter is rather that they felt no urge to do so, and that their readers – usually educated people with a humanities background, as is evident from the frequent classical mottoes and references to mythology – did not find anything wrong with this.

In the first half of the century, literary critics were still assessing epic poems according to the narrative characteristics that the post-Renaissance epic theoreticians had decided were important: integrity of the action, propriety of the episodes, surprising incidents of a delightful nature and pathetic episodes, etc.[20] In practice, however, these requirements did not have the same sense that they would have today – or since the romantic period – and they were not met in a modern sense either.[21] They were in fact primarily used when a narrative work was being condemned by the critics. Praise, on the other hand, was based on the presence of other qualities such as a high standard of verse, sublime emotion, colourful scenes and an exemplary moral. The whole verse style of this period was in any case not conducive to narrative. In accordance with the contemporary preference for the intellectual approach – the social term for this was wit, the philosophical one reason – verse was written in a sophisticated, antithetical and epigrammatic form, none of which were characteristics which exactly facilitated narration.[22]

Further reasons for the poorly developed ability of the neo-classical poets to narrate continuously and the unsuitability of their verse for this task are suggested by G. Tillotson, who contrasts the emphasis on design in the eighteenth century with that on continuity in the nineteenth.[23] In his opinion this change originated in the fact that, according to the philosophy of the Augustan age, everything that might be material for poetry already existed, had been explored and was well known, whereas later thinkers (even before the turn of the century) considered everything they focused on as new, constantly developing and expanding, with the result that the poetry of this generation resembles continuous progress from discovery to discovery. This change of thinking had a marked influence on the nature of verse composition as well as on the speed with which people read. A. Lovejoy, Morse Peckham, R. Wellek, M. H. Abrams and others have since described in much greater detail the change from the static, mechanistic conception of the world as a 'great chain of being' to the dynamic conception of the world as an organism which was shared by many poets of the romantic age. Tillotson, however, also points out the practical consequences of this change as reflected in the narrative manner of proceeding and in reading behaviour. In his essay he maintains that the great classicists – in particular Pope and Dr Johnson – had very little interest in narrative and supports this with quotes. What he says about Johnson's attitude to the novel and the ballad confirms the conclusions already reached in this section: 'Johnson ... enjoyed reading romances, though uneasily. He read [*Amelia*] ''without stopping'' and with inclination. But he read it doubly fast, because that was all any novel could be worth. As for the ballads ... he disliked them ... they were much too like ''that kind of conversation which consists in telling stories'', and which he did not ''much delight in'': ... there was nothing to them except a hollow continuousness: they had not enough stuff in them.'[24]

The fundamental change that began at the end of the eighteenth century was influenced not only by the medieval revival but also by a special offshoot of German literature, which strengthened and coarsened certain tendencies that had been set in motion by the medievalist trend.

'The theatrical horrors of the German School'[25]

We should submit to carry our own brat on our own shoulders; or rather consider it as a lack-grace returned from transportation with such improvements only in growth and manners as young transported convicts usually come home with.

Coleridge, 'Critique on Bertram' (1817)

The most noticeable of the elements of fictional literature between 1795 and 1830 that were even then being described as 'romantic' are horror, violence and fascination with evil. Studies of the literary influence alone do not of course provide an adequate explanation of this fashion, and political and ideological explanations, which see the phenomenon solely as a manifestation of the latent anxiety of the *ancien régime* as it headed for decline or as the shock-waves created by the revolutionary epoch, also do not tell the whole story. The change in taste started much too early, and was far too extensive and complex to be attributable to a single cause.[26]

Here only two aspects of the phenomenon – 'the German fashion' and, in the next section, 'social restructuring and changes in taste' – will be dealt with, for the following reasons.

1. There is no lack of literature on the subject.[27]

2. A brief description of the way the political situation had brought about a change of mentality would be too speculative, since there would not be enough room for adequate historical documentation.

3. While the fashion for horror and the enjoyment of sensational stories was to some extent responsible for the success of the romantic tale in verse, it was not really an inherent part of the genre.

4. The reasons for participation in this fashion are not only to be found in the receptivity of the public, but also in the individual mentality of each author, and all the poets were involved for different reasons; Byron's reasons for example, were completely different from Scott's.[28]

The ideas that the words German literature, German romance, German drama or simply 'From the German' conjured up in the mind of the English reader in the first two to three decades of the nineteenth century are described by Coleridge in his 'Critique on Bertram', that he added as chapter 23 to his *Biographia Literaria* in 1817. There he proves to his countrymen that the German drama that had attained dubious popularity was basically a reimport or reinforcement of aspects of English literature dating from the mid-eighteenth century, which a few Germans craving for popularity had taken over and mixed together to an *olla podrida*. These aspects were;

1. 'the bloated style and peculiar rhythm of Hervey';[29]
2. 'the figurative metaphysics and solemn epigrams of Young';
3. 'the loaded sensibility, the minute detail, the morbid consciousness of every thought and feeling in the whole flux and reflux of the mind, in short, the self-involution and dreamlike continuity of Richardson';
4. 'the horrific incidents, and mysterious villains (geniuses of supernatural intellect, if you will take the author's word for it, but on a level with the meanest ruffians of the condemned cells, if we are to judge by their actions and contrivances) ...; the ruined castles, the dungeons, the skeletons, the flesh and blood ghosts and the perpetual moonshine of a modern author (themselves but the brood of the *Castle of Otranto*)'.

Coleridge then goes on to say that while Schiller's *Robbers* marked the beginning of these offences 'to good taste' and 'sound morals' in Germany on account of the extreme youth of the author, who in the meantime regretted this piece of youthful folly, it could be classified as a stroke of genius. He also says that Shakespeare cannot be held responsible for this new fashion, and names as the German who was primarily instrumental in making it popular August von Kotzebue.

This virulent criticism of the encroachment of the German *Sturm-und-Drang* excesses on English drama and literature must to some extent be attributed to Coleridge's subjective annoyance over the fact that C. H. Maturin's successful 'Gothic' drama *Bertram* had been put on in the Drury Lane Theatre at the recommendation of Scott and Byron, who belonged to the selection committee, while this same committee had rejected Coleridge's poetic but undramatic play *Zapolyta*. However, his analysis of the reasons why the English public succumbed so easily to this type of literature is probably an objective representation of the prevailing situation. As well as asserting that in England the ground for this change in taste had been prepared for a long time, since all the elements of German fashion were actually of fairly recent English origin, Coleridge also sees the political danger of the success of the German *Sturm-und-Drang* imports, a fact of which, since around 1796, Wordsworth, Southey, the *Anti-Jacobin Review*, *The Meteor*, the whole of conservative England and even the archliberal Jeffrey had also become aware. Coleridge's objections are at first of a general nature: in the creation of their outrageous heroes these authors had abandoned the essential balance between the generic and the individual without which art cannot exist; they were guilty of subverting logical thinking, morals and good taste. But then he goes on to say that all these defects have a political origin:

> the whole secret of the modern Jacobinical drama (which, and not the German, is its appropriate designation) and of all its popularity, consists in the confusion and sub-version of the natural order of things in their causes and effects: namely, in the excitement of surprise by representing the qualities of liberality, refined feeling, and a nice sense of honour ... in persons and in classes where experience teaches us least to expect them; and by rewarding with all the sympathies which are the dues of virtue, those criminals whom law, reason, and religion have excommunicated from our esteem ... The shocking spirit of Jacobinism seem[s] no longer confined to politics. The familiarity with atrocious events and characters appear[s] to have poisoned the taste ... and left the feelings callous to all the mild appeals.[30]

Although Coleridge published this view at a relatively late stage in the general development, he maintained that he had been issuing similar warnings for the last eighteen years.

The battle waged by many critics against this 'Jacobinical depravation of the public mind' in the guise of the German fashion did in fact have a limited amount of success after 1800.[31] (Unfortunately critical assessment of impor-tant German literary works in this period was also tainted by the anti-Jacobinical suspicion of everything that was 'German'). There were also many parodies of the horror fashion.[32] However, public taste was already so strongly infected with it that the influence of this craze could no longer be eradicated.

This subject is of revelance because the important English poets were influenced in many ways by the German fashion;[33] it was responsible for something that the English Gothic novel, which was affected by the general discrimination against the novel, would never have brought about alone, namely the shift in focus of the medieval revival and hence the poetic romance genre revived by Scott to the outwardly sensational and exaggeratedly thrilling, and to admiration for rebellious, amoral 'heroes'; and on closer examination it reveals political connections which enable us to understand why, for example, Byron's oriental tales were so successful. It is probably not pure coincidence that almost all the writers of verse narratives at the time when the genre was popular were either Whigs or Whig sympathizers. We should of course beware of exaggerating the importance of these political connections: the politically progressive Francis Jeffrey often expressed similar reservations to those of Coleridge about these contestable developments in 'romantic' taste,[34] while the much more conservative Walter Scott took over the charac-teristic villain hero in only his second tale in verse, *Marmion* (1808). It is never-theless worth mentioning that in his letter to John Murray of 12 October 1817, in which he mentions Coleridge's attack 'upon the then Committee of Drury

Lane', Byron – whom Coleridge probably had at least as much in mind as the author of *Bertram* with his criticism of the 'depravation of the public mind' – does not take Coleridge up on his arguments. The words 'Putting my own pains to foreward the views of Coleridge out of the question' even imply that Byron to a limited extent agreed with him, which is also evident in Byron's many references to the 'wrong direction' that he and the other modern romancers had taken.[35] In the above letter, however, Byron produces a rather thin excuse for not replying to Coleridge's argument and then has recourse to general invective: 'Mr. Coleridge may console himself with the "fervour – the almost religious fervour" of his and Wordsworth's disciples as he calls it ... He is a shabby fellow – and I wash my hands of, and after him.'[36]

The 'German fashion' thus in the opinion of Coleridge, but also in the opinion of Jeffrey, had a much wider impact than merely providing the English stage with a few successful plays. The public would perhaps have been much more inclinded to reject Byron's or Crabbe's occasionally very harsh portrayal of rebellion, guilt, crime and depravity, and indeed all the 'Satanism' of the younger generation of romantic poets, if the German influence in drama and also in the novel had not extended the boundaries of what was seemly and tolerable in literature.

One thing, however, is certain: ranged alongside the harmless minstrel as a main and indeed culturally established figure of the romantic tale in verse, were now the noble robber, the fascinating rogue, and the rebel against the morals of society, in addition to ghosts, madmen and similarly melodramatic fantasy figures, often presented in a 'medieval' setting that is in reality in an ahistorical no man's land. The interest in ancient and primitive cultures is superseded by a taste for the description of passions and the profound emotions which these produce. Where the same effect can be achieved in another milieu (in the Orient, in America, amongst the buccaneers or even in the poet's own environment) the connection with the medieval romance world becomes unimportant, and is abandoned.[37] The essential features are an exciting, continuous story and the opportunity for the reader to become emotionally involved.

The influence of the 'German fashion' on the romantic tale in verse as a genre should not therefore be underestimated, but the extent of this influence can only be explained if we also take into consideration the way certain social changes amongst the readers affected the literary tastes of that age.

Social restructuring and changes in taste

The craving of the public mind after novelty and effect is a false and uneasy appetite ... A poem is to resemble an exhibition of fire-works, with a continual explosion of quaint figures and devices, flash after flash, that surprise for the moment, and leave no trace of light or warmth behind them.
Hazlitt, *The Spirit of the Age*, 1825 (article about Thomas Moore)

The well-read public who set the tone in the eighteenth century had probably never been blinded by the 'German' fashion. As we saw from the reaction of the Reviews against the German imports around 1800, the influence of those who judged poetry on the basis of good taste, literary tradition and conservative moral standards, which had only been shaken temporarily by the revolution, was still so strong that it was at least able to stop this popular fashion for the sensational in literature and drama from getting completely out of hand.

However, the critics who belonged to the old school and the truly educated public no longer dictated literary taste in the same way as they had in the eighteenth century. The readers of narrative and dramatic poetry were no longer the urbane, literary, educated class on whom Dryden, Pope and even Dr Johnson had been able to rely, but instead belonged in the main to the middle class, which had developed as a result of the industrial revolution and was now trying to attain a certain level of education. Amongst these new readers, women played a large part. They had never ever participated as actively in the development of literary taste, or in literary life at all. The English social novel from Jane Austen to George Eliot provides numerous examples of the role played by women as readers, and we have only to glance at the history of this period to see how many poetesses, from Mrs Radcliffe, Clara Reeve and Mrs Inchbald to Joanna Baillie, Mrs Hemans and Hannah More competed with the poets for public favour.[38]

This section of the public – on account of its size alone – made demands on literature which could no longer be suppressed by the more conservative critics and experts[39] who had up until then dictated taste. And it was the German fashion that to a large extent satisfied these demands. The literary requirements of this class were limited by their intellectual ability: lacking a proper education in the humanities and philosophy they were excluded from more demanding educational literature. Didactic poems, which eighteenth-century readers had still enjoyed even in the absence of any narrative additions, could no longer hold the interest of the new readers. With the shift of interest in poetry from the formal and intellectual aspects to the subject matter there was a demand for excitement, colourfulness and sensation.

The moral standards of this class, which were rooted in puritanism, led them to reject any kind of frivolity, coarseness, or realistic libertinism (such as were commonly to be found in the eighteenth-century novel),[40] but they experienced a thrill of pleasure on reading descriptions of boundless passion and 'poetic' amorality, as long as these were ennobled by high-mindedness and profound emotion, and any threat to their own secure bourgeois atmosphere was avoided by the historical or exotic settings of the poems. By identifying with the adventurers and noble buccaneers (or the beautiful women they loved), upright middle-class men and women were able to satisfy vicariously their longing for a dangerous life and the opportunity to live out their emotions – and at the end the reassuring knowledge that what they had read was 'romantic' and hence unreal gave them back their bourgeois security.

This class was less interested in having the reality of their own daily lives put into poetic form: they did not want to find themselves pictured as they were, nor did they want to be disturbed by a description of the poor who were below them in society.[41] What they wanted was rather to transcend themselves by sharing the fate of high-ranking, important heroes – even if these were passionate characters – without being endangered by the consequences of too much freedom.

The striving for greater things that is common to all rising classes had an important effect on the development of the genre. The more aspiring amongst the new class of readers, as we have already seen, often found the novel frivolous or subliterary. They wanted verse and they wanted instruction; but they wanted the instructional aspects to be in a form appropriate to their perceptive abilities (the commonplace maxim, the simple moral or reflection about human nature, and historical anecdotes), and they did not want these to interfere with the plot and their involvement in it as readers. Verse and instruction thus served as alibis for the enjoyment of what were basically romantic subjects.[42]

What we thus have here are two coinciding developmental tendencies. The limited improvement in the educational level of the lower and middle classes, who up until then had either read nothing at all, or only edifying books and light fiction, coincided with a popularizing of literature which was probably the result of two eighteenth-century intellectual trends: the enlightened mentality and social levelling that were the product of the French Revolution, and the primitivistic *retour à la nature*, the effects of which we have already encountered in the sections dealing with attitudes to the epic and the medieval revival.

In his review of Crabbe's *Tales*,[43] Jeffrey says that around 200,000 members of the English middle class read for entertainment and instruction, whereas not even 20,000 of the upper class are readers. The taste, moreover, of these 20,000 is no more refined than that of the middle class, who while not so correct and selective in their standards, can nevertheless be considered more sensitive and receptive. Jeffrey's opinion may be coloured by his Whig sympathies, but he is almost certainly correct about the basic facts. Scott's review of Byron's *Childe Harold* III[44] also mentions the growth in the number of readers: 'Reading is indeed so general among all ranks and classes, that the impulse received by the public mind on such occasions' – here he is referring to the appearance of *Childe Harold* I and II in 1812 – 'is instantaneous through all but the very lowest classes of society instead of being slowly communicated from one set of readers to another, as it was the case in the days of our fathers.'

There are finally some informative remarks in *Blackwood's Magazine*'s review of Moore's *Irish Melodies*,[45] where the critic says: 'The literary character has in fact extended itself over the whole face of society ... it has spread its fibres through all ranks, sexes and ages.' Everyone today belongs to a literary 'set', everyone tries his hand at writing, and thus feels personally affected by the judgements of the critics. The consequence is a shift of interest from the book to the author. People are interested in the genius behind the work, and not in the quality of the work itself. While previously only the critics pronounced judgement – according to established principles derived from comparison with old or ideal models – and the readers read and were full of admiration, today everyone has his own personal criteria according to which he assesses literature, 'self being the hidden centre whither all the comparisons verge'. (These remarks illustrate the growing awareness of the social consequences of the new expressiveness in poetry, which lies at the heart of the romantic revolution.)

The new class of readers, of whom so many were members of the semi-educated middle class, had now tasted the sweet poison of the 'German romances' (in the form of novels and dramas) and their English imitations. Even if the defenders of good, traditional taste who edited the Tory literary magazines had obtained an official victory over the foreign influence – with the easily swayed masses anxious to be thought well of evidently to some extent going along with this – one thing could no longer be changed: the demand of the public for violent sensation, a coherent, exciting plot, a 'romantic', i.e., melodramatic orientation, wildness and profound emotions and passions.

The ground for this was prepared by the medieval revival and, as Coleridge rightly saw, early romantic English literature. However, it would not have come about without added impulse from outside, and the restructuring of the readership would hardly have produced such a radical change in public taste if all these elements had not been reimported from Germany to England in a combined form. In some cases they were raised to a higher plane by incorporation in such inspired, skilfully written works as Bürger's *Lenore*, Schiller's *Räuber* and *Geisterseher* and Goethe's *Götz*, so that in spite of the official resistance of the old school, even educated people were interested in them, or at least gave them a favourable reception. The new trend was represented to some extent by drama, which is the easiest way of introducing something novel to a wider public: the lucrative import was seized on by theatre managers and clever English dramatists took advantage of the opportunity to achieve instant success.[46] In no time at all prose novels and tales 'from the German' had taken over the market. All this helped not only to stimulate and sanction the taste for melodramatic sentimentality, hollow emotionalism, poison, daggers and horror, for excitement and pleasurable sensations of fear, but also to establish it so firmly that none of the usual dictators of public taste could undo what had been done. And gradually it became evident that the new taste not only had a hold on the semi-educated middle class but was also dominating the literary medieval revival, which up until then had been mainly in the hands of highly educated people of established taste.

Sometimes, it is true, the 'German fashion' was improved as a consequence of conservative criticism and raised to a higher plane by the cultural aspects put forward as a justification for reading this kind of literature – the verse form, historical information and features linking this product of fashion with literary classics (Shakespeare!). Its unhistorical 'romanticism' was also checked by the continuing interest in antiquity, and its moral permissiveness by the strengthening of conservative morals around 1800. However, its influence on taste could no longer be eradicated, and is repeatedly evident, even in important poems. The extent to which all poetry was affected by this trend is reflected in the following remarks made by a critic writing in the conservative *Blackwood's Magazine* in March 1823.[47] 'This is not a time when people are to be put off with sweet and dainty little devices – pretticisms are past – we want food, strong exciting food, and disdain kickshaws – we want rich generous wines, and the nicest negus in the world will not appease our craving.'

Around this time, of course, the taste for excitement that had been generated at a lower level had already risen to the level of great literature. It had not only wrung acknowledgement from the literati and dictators of taste with the triumph of 'romantic' poetry (in particular Scott's and Byron's), it was also explained and justifed *post festum* as some important attempts were made to interpret it as a socially necessary developmental phenomenon. Jeffrey's article on Byron's *Corsair* and *Bride of Abydos*[48] is an example of a review which takes this line. Here Jeffrey gives his interpretation of cultural history in terms of cycles, in the course of which he presents us with the main phenomena of the romantic mentality (political and literary revolution, a return to the poetry of past ages, primitivism, an interest in emotions and passions, individualism, *mal du siècle*, etc.), and attempts to identify their common roots. He sees that his age is completing a cycle: the circle of development is closing and the beginning and end are meeting, closer to each other than to anything that lies in between them.

In more primitive ages passions were intense, and the finer sensitivity through which they were brought under control had not yet been developed. With civilization came an increasing sense of shame, as a result of which primitive emotions were hidden and the passions restrained. The social order protected society from the violent consequences of passion, and the moral code prevented outbreaks of egoism and coarseness. Gradually this produced a situation where all emotion was banned from poetry. It was subdued by a formal, ceremonious politeness and swamped by a passionless lewdness. Thus poetry first became stiff and pompous (here Jeffrey is thinking of the seventeenth century), then exaggeratedly refined and witty (here he evidently has Dryden in mind) and finally amusing, lively, unemotional and intimate (this is the poetry of the eighteenth century from Pope to Cowper).

Now, however, since unbridled passion was no longer seen as a threat to civilization, there was an increasing longing to experience the suppressed emotions to the full. This longing was finally so overpowering that it triumphed over the fear of the possibly dangerous consequences. The masses still found sufficient outlet for their passions in various kinds of collective dissipation which were without risk because they were anonymous. This was not however sufficient for stronger spirits. They sought first to satisfy their intense longing for strong emotion in an epoch of revolutions, great deeds and even greater expectations (here Jeffrey evidently had the French Revolution and the rise of Napoleon in mind) and then followed a second period of fanaticism, when the passions were redirected and focused on self-abasement and despair (here he is referring to the orientation of Werther, Karl Moor and Byron). Poetry then became intense, individualistic and passionate, and all previous literary traditions were found to be too sober, superficial and untroubled. The poets thus returned to the wild lays of poetry's early past: they broke away from classical subjects, which they found too tame and civilized, and seized on the chivalrous deeds and passionate love stories of the old romances, which they rendered with a wildness and intensity that far exceeded that of the originals. Ballads were resurrected and imitated, since their style and the unspoilt naturalness of the events they described were thought to represent true freedom. Finally, in their pursuit of strong emotions, the poets went so far as to depict misery and vice in all its horror. That, said Jeffrey, was what poetry had now come to, and that was why it contained themes and forms which thirty years ago would have been rejected as vulgar and offensive. 'Instead of ingenious essays, elegant pieces of gallantry, and witty satires all stuck over with classical allusions, we have, in our popular poetry, the dreams of convicts and the agonies of Gipsy women, – and the exploits of buccaneers, freebooters, and savages – and pictures to shudder at, of remorse, revenge, and insanity – of low-born affection and the tragedies of a vulgar atrocity.'[49]

This article of April 1814 shows that the many verse narratives that had been written since the beginning of the century (perhaps also with the inclusion of the ballad imitations and the *Lyrical Ballads*) were seen as a separate branch of poetry, which justifies our speaking of a genre, in a wider sense. A few lines later Jeffrey once again refers to the common factor uniting all these poems, which is purely and simply the interest in strong emotions. It is of secondary importance whether the poems feature the barbarians of a past age, primitive people in distant lands or modern desperadoes, or whether, as is often the case, the events related are somewhat unaesthetic, since this was evidently the poets' aim. All that is important is intense passion and the poetic atmosphere. The article also provides an eyewitness account of how the way

in which the genre developed, which is the subject of this study – the
dominance of the narrative forms in poetry that was first noticeable around
the turn of the century, the replacement of the classical epic with modern forms
of the metrical romance, the imitation of ballads and lays and the exploration
of new subject matter that soon followed the initial concentration of the new
genre on medieval forms and themes – was seen at the time as being
consistent with the historico-cultural situation. Jeffrey does not go as far as
Scott, who in the Introduction to *The Bridal of Triermain* of 1813 uses the
expression 'romantic poetry' as a synonym for the romantic verse narrative
genre of which he was one of the founders, and tries to define precisely the
characteristics of this genre.[50] On the contrary, when he speaks of the
uniformity of modern poetry he is not thinking of a genre concept which carries
with it the idea of a particular form, and it is for this reason that he also makes
no distinction between ballads, lays and romances. Nevertheless, he is still
primarily talking about the branch of poetry that is being described in this
book as a genre and is trying to identify its intellectual origins and objectives.

By mentioning on several occasions the popularity of this type of poetry,
Jeffrey betrays the fact that he, the aloof dictator of taste, is always conscious
that this genre had its origins in low-quality sensational light fiction, in spite
of all his references to the 'stronger spirits' who initiated the movement, and
that as a critic he does not give in to the demands being made in his day, i.e.,
the demands of the masses, without a struggle. His justification of the
'terribly romantic' in terms of historical cycles has a certain historical fatalism
about it.[51]

Summary

Let us now look again in brief at the main points which have been dealt with
in this chapter. The initial situation which gave rise to the romantic tales in
verse is as follows. Neo-classical aesthetics no longer dominate poetry. The
principle of *imitatio* is giving way to that of originality, which does not,
however, preclude the basing of works on particular models. The poets are
now largely turning to the Middle Ages instead of to antiquity for their
material although they do not represent this period very accurately, or define
it precisely from the historical point of view. As the interest in the national
past declines, so the revival embraces the emotionalism, primitivism and
sensationalism summed up in the expressions 'Gothic', 'the age of romance',
and 'our old poets', etc. The neo-classical epic has reached the limits of its
possibilities as far as form and content are concerned, and it is only the
medieval verse narrative genres that prevent the longer narrative poem from
dying out altogether. The revival of the ballad, which was originally nourished
by interest in cultural and national history, generates a new narrative manner
of proceeding in poetry, which prepares the way for the shift from design to

continuity. The novel – the one truly 'continuous' genre – attains new popularity with the rise of the Gothic novel, which takes over the subject matter and new sensitivity introduced with the medieval revival, but does not at this stage have a marked effect on higher kinds of poetry, in particular verse narrative, since novels are not yet considered to be literature. The shift from design to continuity, and from interest in the form and intellectual content to interest in the subject matter and emotional melodrama, is accelerated by sociological changes amongst the readers. These in turn open the way for a branch of German poetry and drama which is more sensational, emotional and spectacular than anything being written in England. The immediate opposition to this that is mounted in England by the literary upper class, the Tory press and the critics, and the eagerness of the general public for education on the one hand, make it necessary to raise the artistic and intellectual level of this type of poetry, but on the other hand the need for a plot, passion and a continuously exciting story has now become firmly established.

All these various demands can now only be met by a poetic genre that offers dynamic narrative continuity, interesting new subjects and excitement, while at the same time maintaining a high literary standard.

The genre that proved most suitable for this task was the metrical romance of the Middle Ages. Its rediscovery or resurrection took much longer than the resurrection of the medieval ballad, which of course paved the way for it. Until after 1800 the longer medieval romances were only of philological interest, and it was only with the appearance of new editions and paraphrases (e.g. Scott's *Sir Tristrem* and Ellis' *Specimens of Early English Romances*) that this old form of poetry became popular and bore new fruit. Scott recognized that the metrical romance or lay genre was just what was needed to fill the vacuum left in epic poetry as a result of changing tastes and to fulfil the need for excitement as well as satisfy the aesthetic and intellectual ambitions of a large section of the public. His *Lay of the Last Minstrel*, written in 1805, marked the birth of the romantic tale in verse.[52]

Part II *THE HISTORY OF THE ROMANTIC TALE IN VERSE: POETS, WORKS, CRITICS AND THE PUBLIC*

Narrative poetry flourished in the 19th century as never before ... We perceive that no poet of any eminence forbore to essay the novel in verse, that the whole world was scoured for plot and pattern, all types and modes of narrative exploded.

W. M. Dixon, *English Epic and Heroic Poetry*, 1912, p. 2

In the following discussion of works that feature in the history of romantic tales in verse in England, the length of the poems that serve as examples has not generally been taken into account, since it is considered here to be of little relevance to the question of genre. While the aims and the character of the three genres – epic poem, romance and ballad – undoubtedly influenced the length of the poems, the length does not determine the genre. It can it is true be said that the average length of the ballad is less than the average length of the romance, and that even the longest ballad is still much shorter than the shortest epic. It can also be said that a long ballad with a complex, detailed plot becomes a romance even when it retains certain external characteristics of the ballad (Scott's *Lay* is an example of this). It cannot, however, be said that a verse narrative becomes a ballad if it is short or an epic if it is long.

3   Early forms

The previous chapter closed with a summary of the developments which produced the romantic tale in verse. The discovery of the genre was attributed to Scott, but this interpretation must now be slightly amended.

Scott's *Lay of the Last Minstrel* did not represent something entirely new, it was simply the most exciting and successful product of a tendency that had been developing for a long time. Even before Scott a few poets had attempted a similar mixture of the elements in question, and, although they approached the task from different angles, they achieved similar results. In fact, in the Introduction to the *Lay* in the complete edition of his poetic works published in 1830, Scott refers to some of these early forms and admits the influence they had on him.

The work with which we will begin nevertheless had at the most an indirect influence on Scott. It is W. S. Landor's *Gebir*, a poem that appeared in 1798, in the year of the *Lyrical Ballads*, the year English romanticism was born. It was to have an important influence on Southey and Shelley[1] and occupies a middle position between the epic poem in the classical style and the romantic tale in verse, at the turning point between the tastes of the eighteenth century and those of the nineteenth.

W. S. Landor's 'Gebir'

> in [*Gebir*] ... you can no more separate the manner from the matter, than you can colour from the rainbow. The form seems incapable of subsisting without the spirit.
>
> Letter from Southey to Landor dated 9 February 1812

When *Gebir* appeared in 1798, Landor was twenty-three. It had been preceded by an earlier work in a similar classical style, the epic poem *The Phoceans*, although this did not yet contain any romantic elements; it was never completed and published and only four fragments remain (a total of 1,067 blank verses).

Nothing was probably further from Landor's mind when he wrote *Gebir* than the creation of a new literary genre. He was extremely well read in classical and English literature, had been inspired in turn by Homer, Virgil and Milton, and now wanted to create an epic narrative in verse in which the fruits of his reading would be developed into a personal style and a polished story with a few revolutionary political allusions. He found the material for his story in an 'Arabian Romance' from the book *The Progress of Romance* (Colchester, 1785) by Clara Reeve. The story inspired him because he sensed in it 'magnificum nescio quid sub crepusculo vetustatis' (cf. the preface to the Latin edition, *Gebirus Poema*, 1803). Right from the very beginning, therefore, the concept of romance – only of course in a very vague generic sense – is found in combination with classical epic conventions. Landor does not seek out the past for its familiarity and established literary tradition, but for its mysteriousness and brilliance.

Landor hesitated over whether to write the poem in Latin or English, finally wrote it in both languages and published the Latin version in 1803, five years after the English one. The English version was first published in 1798 in Warwick as a sixpenny pamphlet and attracted very little attention. Landor had it printed at his own expense, but issued anonymously. Among the few buyers was Robert Southey, who was one of the poem's first admirers. Later on, in April 1808, he became friendly with Landor and in 1810 dedicated his *Curse of Kehama* to the 'Author of *Gebir*'. Southey's praise played a large part in making *Gebir* known to a wider public.[2]

Gebir consists of seven Books in blank verse (a total of approximately 1,800 lines). The style is strongly influenced by Milton, as is evident from the metre, the vocabulary and the images used. Landor did not even have any inhibitions about plagiarizing Milton.[3] Talking about his choice of blank verse he says in the Preface to the first edition: 'I have written in blank verse because there never was a poem in rhyme that grew not tedious in a thousand lines. My choice is undoubtedly the most difficult of the two: for how many have succeeded in rhyme, in the structure at least: how few comparatively in blank verse.' Landor openly admits his indebtedness to Milton, when he later refers to his stylistic orientation in his *Ode to Wordsworth*:

> Our course by Milton's light was sped
> And Shakespeare shining overhead:
> Chatting on deck was Dryden too,
> The Bacon of the rhyming crew.[4]

Nevertheless he does make some qualifications on this point with respect to *Gebir*: 'the language of Paradise Lost ought not to be the language of Gebir. There should be the softened air of remote antiquity, not the severe air of unapproachable sanctity.'[5] In his analysis of Landor's style, W. Bradley shows how Landor's verse construction differs from Milton's: although Landor's periods are shorter than those of Milton he writes more run-on lines. And as for metre, Landor's blank verse, in spite of its closeness to Milton, has almost the metrical regularity of the individual line of the heroic couplet in Pope.[6]

At the time it was written the poem was considered very obscure, and it is still hard to understand today (for example the beginning of Book VII). This is partly due to a disjointed narrative technique that leaves many blanks, and to the absence of any kind of preparation or explanation of the subject matter; partly to a style that bears resemblance to Latin (in some places the poem seems to have been written first in Latin and then translated into English), and also partly to another influence that Landor points out himself: 'When I began to write Gebir, I had just read Pindar a second time and understood him. What I admired was what nobody else had ever noticed – his proud complacency and scornful strength. If I could resemble him in nothing else, I was resolved to be as compendious and exclusive.'[7]

This concentration, brevity and sudden illumination of an isolated event while everything else remains in obscurity distinguishes this poem from the epics of its time. This is no panoramic study of a great conquest or of the fate of a hero; here heroic or problematic characters or situations appear briefly for our inspection from out of the darkness of a mysterious former age, only to vanish back into it almost immediately. This darkness is of a completely different quality from the mist from which Ossian's characters emerge – it has much more in common with Dante's darkness which compels us to think about it and interpret it, but it is nevertheless romantic. We thus have the unusual situation of a classical influence producing a poem that anticipates the romantic period. This classical influence also resulted in a poem of shorter length, suggesting a similarity with the romantic tale in verse. The narrowing of the epic framework was not, however, as with Scott, a deliberate ploy to heighten the poem's chances of popularity with the public, nor was it an imitation of the short medieval forms of verse narratives; it arose rather out of a desire for exclusivity and out of the strange combination of an epic subject and a lyrical classical model with extreme conciseness of expression – the model provided by Pindar. It may be that it was the desire to use this style that resulted in the reduction of the content to only a few characters, a few scenes and a meagre plot.

The characteristics of many romantic tales in verse – an exotic landscape, magic and mystery, horror, the supernatural and a great variety of love and death motives – are also to be found here, not of course in the sensational form they took in the later romances, but softened by the basic classicistic tendencies of the poem. Further romantic elements (almost anticipating Shelley) are the revolutionary political allusions in Book III and the moral which shines through the plot, compounded of Landor's own original blend of liberal and Rousseauist ideas. These pacifist and dissident influences led Landor not only to add a contrasting plot involving the brother of the poem's hero, but also to reverse many traditional epic elements: ambitious rulers and heroes are judged negatively, and passive surrender to nature positively; the visit to the heroes of the past in the underworld becomes a criticism of the rulers of the present, and love in a pastoral framework triumphs over heroic love. Wilkie speaks of 'deliberate reversal or inversion' and classifies *Gebir*, together with Southey's *Joan of Arc*, somewhat confusingly as a 'non-comic mock epic'.[8]

Here, therefore – whether it was intentional or an unavoidable historical development – is a highly original work which was in no way conceived from a romantic standpoint but which nevertheless anticipates many elements of the later romantic tales in verse.

There is much in *Gebir* that reflects the normal epic style. There are mythological allusions, e.g., the mention of Acheron and Erebus at the beginning of Book III, or the image of Aurora ascending at the beginning of Book IV. The opening of the individual cantos is often in the epic style:

Book I: 'I sing the fates of Gebir ...';
Book III: a prayer for the spirit of Dante to help the poet succeed with his description of the underworld;
Book VI: a mythological portrayal of morning;
Book VII: a summary of the plot and moral of the poem similar to that found in Milton's *Paradise Lost*, but in an esoteric form.

The miraculous journey through the conqueror's purgatory and the visions of lands that are paraded before Tamar on the journey to his wedding (some of them visions of the future!) are also in the epic style, even though the heroic tendency is not always present. All these elements are of course Landor's own additions to the source. Some of the additions were deleted from the final version of the work: an Invocatio to Milton and Shakespeare, a few political allusions, an apostrophe to Fire in Book III and a 'prophetic' anticipation of the French Revolution. These changes involved approximately a hundred lines, and the gaps thereby created were filled with around fifty new verses.

There is no trace in *Gebir* of the medieval ballads and lays or the works of Spenser that were later to have such an important influence on verse narratives; here it is unquestionably the epic genre that has had the most influence. But *Gebir* is almost as far removed from the characteristic tone of the French School of poetry as from the medieval poets – only the description of Charoba and her nurse bears a faint resemblance to Racine.

The romantic poets Southey, Byron and Shelley referred to *Gebir* sometimes as a poem and sometimes as a tale or an oriental tale, which indicates that they were aware both of its epic origins and its similarity with their own verse narratives.

While *Gebir*, the first of our examples, appears to anticipate the romantic tale in verse by narrowing down the scale of the epic poem and analysing heroic themes, the next group of poems comes closer to the genre that Scott later made popular by expanding the shortest narrative form, the ballad. The ballad, which was discussed in chapter 2 from the point of view of its revival and further development, freed itself – as in Germany – towards the end of the eighteenth century from its ties with the medieval genre model and traditional subject matter. It began to feature newer, contemporary problems and was not solely telling a good story. It was also occasionally expanded to a longer form that was already close to the verse narrative. The change took place with the work of Wordsworth and Coleridge.

The 'Lyrical Ballads' of Wordsworth and Coleridge

> Wordsworth's poetry is not external, but internal; it does not depend upon tradition, or story, or old song; he furnishes it from his own mind, and is his own subject.
> W. Hazlitt, *The Complete Works*, ed. P. P. Howe, after the edition of A. R. Waller and Arnold Glover (London, 1930–4), V, p. 163

It is difficult to define the role played by the *Lyrical Ballads* in the history of romantic verse narrative although today they are usually considered to be the first move of romanticism in England. Since most of the romantic poetry in the style of Scott is meaningless to the modern reader and dismissed as irrelevant, it is easy to make the mistake of overestimating the role of the *Lyrical Ballads* in any study of the origins of romantic verse. They certainly had a significant influence on those works of English romantic narrative poetry which we still consider important today, and represent the founding of romantic poetry in England in the same way as the writings of Herder, Schlegel and Novalis led to romanticism in Germany. They exemplify the new conception of poetry and in particular the new imagery of the romantic epoch.[9] For this reason, however, they seemed to be breaking down the boundaries of a genre rather than creating a new one. With them began the 'struggle [of the romantic poets] to create an alternative system for themselves', of which R. A. Foakes says that the great romantics 'found a new language, but clung to old forms; yet their best poetry transcends the limitations of those forms which conflict with the essential purposes of the poet, and the completion of the ostensible structure ceases to matter'.[10]

This tendency towards the dissolution of strictly defined generic types is a process that will create many problems for us. While it did later have a decisive influence on the fate of our genre (in particular where Keats and Shelley are concerned), before it could dissolve this genre first had to consolidate itself, and here the *Lyrical Ballads* were unable to make much of a contribution. It will thus for the time being suffice to discuss the external, direct influences which this otherwise seminal work of the Lake Poets had on verse narrators after 1805.[11]

These direct influences are not very numerous. One is the verse form that leads from the old ballads, from *The Ancient Mariner* to *Christabel* and finally to Scott's *Lay of the Last Minstrel*, which is reflected in the metre that the

romantic poets most frequently used for their verse narratives.[12] Another is
the effect Coleridge's treatment of the supernatural had on the atmosphere
created in the narrative poems of Keats and to a certain extent of Shelley;
Coleridge had more influence on the second wave of romantic poetry – where
the narrative dynamism becomes less important than the atmospheric,
symbolic and intellectual qualities of the poetry – than on the generation that
made romantic verse narrative popular. Finally there is the influence of
Wordsworth on Crabbe, which, together with the influence of Scott, had the
effect of leading Crabbe to shift from reflective and descriptive village poetry
(in the style of *The Deserted Village* by Goldsmith) to the portrayal of stirring
individual fates and hence the telling of stories. Without the *Lyrical Ballads*
there would probably have been no *Sir Eustace Gray* and no *Peter Grimes*.[13]

   The following aspects of the *Lyrical Ballads* probably also influenced later
romantic narrative verse in a diffuse, indirect way: the colloquialism of the
Wordsworth poems, which undoubtedly helped to loosen up the rigid
schemata of poetic diction, as did also the manner in which the two authors
of the *Lyrical Ballads* drew on the simple language of older English poetry and
yet produced something that went beyond mere imitation;[14] the experimentation with old and new stanza forms and verse types, which were not chosen
out of traditional considerations but according to whether they were suitable
for the material in question; the transformation of ideas into narrative, i.e.,
the creation of continuous, dynamic and easily visualized series of actions
instead of presenting individual facts or reflections; the succinct development
of characters' fates and situations; the feeling for nature and the restoration
of naivety. These and many other aspects may have influenced the tastes (even
if not the genre concepts) of the generation of popular poets whose favourite
genre was the verse narrative. We should, however, be careful not to overestimate their effect on the constitution of the verse narrative as a genre. They
were either already part of an existing tendency, or they were so new and so
bound up with the deeper meanings of the poetry that they could have no
significance for the comparatively superficial school of verse narrative that
was merely concerned with telling a story. It should also be remembered that
the *Lyrical Ballads* were not in fact a success when first published. In his *Lectures
on the English Poets* of 1818, Hazlitt quotes an entire poem of Wordsworth's,
which he justifies by saying: 'Mr. Wordsworth's poems have been little known
to the public, or chiefly through garbled extracts from them',[15] and issue
no.31 of *Blackwood's Magazine* says of Coleridge that in England he is not
understood and in Scotland he is unknown, or ignored by the press.

   It is thus not surprising that one of the most important generic
developments that must be credited to the authors of the *Lyrical Ballads* –
enlarging the scope of the ballad and departing from its external medievalism
by raising it to a higher level philosophically and poetically and by using it
for highly intellectual and up-to-date subjects[16] – had no effect on narrative

poetry for quite a long time. If it had done, it would of course also have made Scott's genre impossible.

The poetic style of the authors of the *Lyrical Ballads*, which set the pattern for all the later romantic poetry, is 'not predominantly narrative', however much they endeavoured to clothe their ideas in vivid pictures and transform their experiences into narrative. They lack the objectivity of the true storyteller towards worldly phenomena.[17] Although they have this characteristic in common and fit together from a philosophical point of view (there is that well-known description of the complementary unity of approach in these poems in Coleridge's *Biographia Literaria*, chapter 14) the *Lyrical Ballads* cannot be considered as all belonging to the same genre. Aside from the fact that quite a few of the works are pure lyric poetry in which the narrative character of the true ballad is missing, there is also a difference in the manner of the two authors if we concentrate solely on the narrative poems. Wordsworth's narrative poetry is more a vehicle for his own philosophical experiences, which are communicated to the reader exactly as they are in order to instruct, enlighten and uplift him. Coleridge on the other hand is not trying to communicate philosophical experience with the content of *The Ancient Mariner* or later with *Christabel* but to convey a higher, i.e., more ideal poetic reality. The poem is not attempting to provide a discourse about the world, it is the world. The philosophical, metaphysical aspect of Coleridge's work lies rather in the act of creation itself and the nature of what has been created, while in Wordsworth it is to be found more in the content of the ideas and their concrete message.

This difference between the two authors merits closer examination. (The following remarks are not limited strictly to the poems selected by Wordsworth and Coleridge for the *Lyrical Ballads* but also include other works composed in the same period with the same basic ideas behind them, such as *Christabel* or *Peter Bell*).

Let us begin with Wordsworth. If we limit ourselves to the external generic aspect, it must be admitted that his development is very much on the edge of the evolutionary process with which we are concerned. He narrates in verse, but the narrative in his work is not an end in itself; it is an example and an allegory that serves to illuminate philosophical and psychological questions. In the events and situations he is describing he attempts to investigate 'truly though not ostentatiously' the basic laws of human nature, and in particular the 'manner in which we associate ideas in a state of excitement'.[18] The aim is thereby 'to excite a feeling analogous to the supernatural by awakening the mind's attention to the lethargy of custom, and directing it to the loveliness and the wonders of the world before us', as Coleridge puts it in chapter 14 of the *Biographia Literaria*.

With this essentially lyrical and philosophical[19] objective all questions of form that do not arise directly from it or contribute to it are of subsidiary importance. The question of genre that in the eighteenth century had largely become a phenomenon of the 'lethargy of custom' is here clearly pushed into the background. Almost all Wordsworth's narrative poems (including the later ones and many narrative passages in *The Prelude* and in *The Excursion*) are first and foremost 'lyrical ballads', or, as Kroeber[20] describes them, 'visionary lyrics', since they are all characterized by the same poetic objective, they are all similarly lyrical, i.e., subjective and philosophical, and thus in fact merit the description ballad in the same way as do the poems in the 1798 volume. In other words, the basic plot is only appropriate for the shorter narrative form and would not be sufficient for the epic or the longer romance, both of which require a more complex, extensive plot.[21] C. H. Herford aptly describes this basic plot as 'single situations of concentrated pathos'.[22]

Although the young Wordsworth's poetic aims inevitably led him away from conventional generic types, he nevertheless did become involved with the question of genre as he endeavoured to find the form most suitable for what he wanted to express, and he also considered the longer types of narrative poem, the epic and the metrical romance, as possible vehicles for his 'unmanageable thoughts' as that informative passage in *The Prelude* Book I shows, where he speaks of the dilemma between his sense of mission – 'a man who would prepare for such a work' – and the difficulty of presenting material poetically:

> Time, place, and manners do I seek, and these
> Are found in plenteous store, but nowhere such
> As may be singled out with steady choice ...
> (158–60)

There follows a list of all the themes and genres he considered that were common in the past and might serve his purpose now:

> ... some British theme, some old
> Romantic tale by Milton left unsung.
> (168–9)

Next come the pastoral and the chivalrous genres with magic events, battles and the trials of the Christian hero, classical subjects and political and historical material, and he declares that whatever possibilities he selects, he is unable to

> ... make them dwellers in the heart of men
> Now living, or to live in future years.
> (164–5)

Wordsworth was clearly dreaming of writing the great contemporary epic poem, and hoped, like many others of his day, to achieve this with a romance. The ideas that have been considered in these lines and then rejected as impracticable

... the unsubstantial structure melts
Before the very sun that brightens it,
Mist into air dissolving ...

(225–7)

are now compared with 'My last and favourite aspiration',

... some philosophic song
Of Truth that cherishes our daily life;
With meditations passionate from deep
Recesses of man's heart ...

(229–32)

This plan too foundered temporarily on the poet's inner unrest and lack of clarity. However, it cannot be disputed that seen as a whole Wordsworth's poetic work was in fact such a 'philosophic song of Truth'. This 'generic description' based on the objective of the poetry renders relatively unimportant distinctions between poems according to whether they are closer to this or that conventional narrative genre. This is the key to his poetic development. From this point on we can follow his progression from the *Lyrical Ballads* via the later long poems *The Prelude* and *The Excursion* to the ambitious plan for *The Recluse*, of which only fragments were completed.

Some of Wordsworth's ballads and narrative poems certainly do come quite close to the romantic verse narrative, which is in any case rather a vague category: *Guilt and Sorrow* (1793–4, originally called *The Female Vagrant* and begun around 1791, incorporated in this form in the *Lyrical Ballads* in 1798 but later expanded to something much longer) has a certain affinity with Crabbe or Byron, *Hart-Leap Well* (1800) with Scott, and *Vaudracour and Julia* (1805, originally part of *The Prelude*) or *The Ruined Cottage* (written from 1795 to 1797 and later integrated in Book I of *The Excursion*) with Campbell's *Gertrude* or *Theodric* and Rogers' *Jacqueline*.

There were also critics who tried to classify Wordsworth with the poets who wrote popular verse narrative by pointing out tendencies they had in common; in addition to the formal break with the eighteenth century, their way of presenting passion and their interest in human failure were for example considered similar and were traced back to German influence.[23] However, even in Wordsworth's lifetime there was a general awareness of the unbridgeable gulf that separates him as an outstanding individualist and true philosophic poet from the school of pure verse narrators that began with Scott.[24] And in the last chapter of the *Biographia Literaria* Coleridge showed more insight into the character of his friend as a poet than all his contemporaries when he wrote: 'What Mr. Wordsworth will produce, is not for me to prophesy: but I could pronounce with the liveliest convictions what he is capable of producing. It is the FIRST GENUINE PHILOSOPHIC POEM.' (Coleridge of course already knew *The Prelude*, that was dedicated to him but had not been published, and knew about the *Recluse* plan).

This broad generic description – which will now be discussed in greater detail – is the only one that fully covers the basic characteristics of Wordsworth's poetry (including the narrative poetry). This area – philosophy or *Weltanschauung* converted into poetry – at first developed separately from romantic verse narrative. It was not until the second romantic generation that 'romantic' narrative and intellectual depth moved closer together and serious syntheses of *Weltanschauung* in poetry and romance were attempted (the Rousseauist and antimonarchical ideas in *Gebir* and the conventional, Protestant and humanistic morals of Southey's epic narratives cannot yet be described as independent interpretative views of the world). The discussion of this particular question will be continued in subsequent sections (pp. 166ff.). For the present it has sufficed to show the real reason why Wordsworth's influence on the fashionable wave of narrative verse literature after 1805 could only be marginal and why his narrative lyrical ballads – whether they are in the 1798 volume or not – are early forms but not, in the opinion of this author, fully fledged examples of the genre of romantic verse narrative.

Indeed Wordsworth himself very soon recognized that the modern romance was of no use to him as a genre, and was even more certain about this than he had been about the other genres mentioned in *The Prelude* I. In Book VI of *The Prelude* he says:

> ... The hemisphere
> Of magic fiction, verse of mine perchance
> May never tread ...
>
> (87–9)

In Book VIII there is also a clear rejection of the sensational plots of romantic narrative poetry:

> ... The history of our native land –
> With those of Greece compared and popular Rome,
> And in our high-wrought modern narratives
> Stript of their harmonising soul, the life
> Of manners and familiar incidents –
> Had never much delighted me. And less
> Than other intellects had mine been used
> To lean upon extrinsic circumstances
> Of record and tradition ...
>
> (617 ff.)

He had in fact always known this; even before the modern metrical romances became fashionable he began the second part of his poem *Hart-Leap Well* in 1800 with the words:

The moving accident is not my trade;
To freeze the blood I have no ready arts:
'Tis my delight, alone in summer shade,
To pipe a simple song for thinking hearts.
                    (97 – 100)

And in the Preface to the *Lyrical Ballads* of 1800 he also gives the theory behind his position. Here he says that the main difference between popular poetry in the 'German' style and his own poetry is 'that the feeling therein [in the *Lyrical Ballads*] developed gives importance to the action and situation, and not the action and situation to the feeling'. The poem *Simon Lee* from the *Lyrical Ballads* is a clear example of the effect this approach, developed to its logical conclusion, has on the narrator's manner of proceeding: here there is no action or story but an attempt to develop the appropriate kind of feeling from a particular concrete situation, leaving the reader to make a story out of it himself.

However, we do once find Wordsworth on Scott's territory. *The White Doe of Rylstone* (1807), obviously inspired by Scott's successes, is the work where the lyrical-philosophical narrative style from the *Lyrical Ballads* and the metrical romance form come together for the first time. The problems involved here will be dealt with in greater detail in the section on this poem (pp. 112 – 19).[25]

Coleridge had scarcely more influence than Wordsworth on the external features of contemporary narrative verse. The main reason for this is almost certainly that his work in this area is neither extensive nor really relevant. Of his narrative poems only *The Ancient Mariner* and *Christabel* can be said to have some generic affinities with the endeavours of Scott and the romantic verse narrative of which he was the initiator.[26] However, *The Ancient Mariner* was too similar in form to the traditional ballad to have any influence on the romantic verse narrative genre, and *Christabel*, although written from 1797 to 1801, was not printed until 1816 (probably partly at Byron's insistence[27]) and was previously only accessible to a few people in manuscript. This enigmatic, unfinished poem could not have affected the genre or narrative techniques of the modern romancers, and could at the most have had some influence on their handling of theme, atmosphere and metre. In addition, as already mentioned, the importance of Coleridge's work was not even recognized by well-meaning critics,[28] and critics who opposed him either ignored him or attacked him violently.[29]

In 1822 the comment could still be made[30] that Coleridge was not well enough known; a few hundred people knew *The Ancient Mariner* and *Love* by heart, and no one else knew anything by him. What makes *The Ancient Mariner* and *Christabel* so outstandingly new and original is thus not that they represented the establishment of a genre in the traditional sense. It is pointless to try and decide whether these are examples of romantic verse narrative or not. In *The Ancient Mariner* there can be no doubt that it is the ballad elements that predominate, so this poem (alongside Keats' *La Belle Dame Sans Merci*) should rather be described as the best of the independent ballad imitations during the romantic period. In the case of *Christabel* it might also be considered whether Coleridge did not have to break off the poem precisely because the content was more than the framework of the ballad could accommodate. The mysterious vision would have had to be developed into a broader-based story, and it would then have been impossible to leave it as unresolved as *The Ancient Mariner*. In the period 1807–25 a longer romantic narrative – as is shown by the Scottish romances – had to identify the good and evil forces clearly if it was to win public approval. It had to be rounded off with deliverance, catastrophe, a wedding or the breaking of a spell if the average reader was to be interested in it or the critics to consider it complete. This would however have destroyed what Coleridge was really aiming at – poetry which operated at many levels and required an understanding of the symbolic, and the higher imaginative reality of the supernatural and the irrational fascination exerted by this higher reality – or degraded this to the status of machinery in the service of a fairy-tale.

In other words, Coleridge's poetic temperament and artistic objectives are also such that his work has only external features in common with romantic verse narrative. He is neither able nor willing to develop his abilities in the area of pure verse romance – all that interests him about the romance is the atmosphere, the poetic intensity and the traditional elements of the imagery and plot that can be expanded to produce an easily comprehensible symbolic structure. Here therefore we have again reached a point where the higher intellectual unity of the work makes it meaningless – and in the case of *Christabel* impossible – to speak of formal generic rules. While it is possible to connect certain poems with particular genres (*The Ancient Mariner* and *Love* are written in ballad form, and *Christabel* is a fragment of a metrical romance which could not be completed according to the rules of this genre) this only tells us something about the superficial characteristics of these works and not about their essential nature. If in Wordsworth it is primarily the philosophical content of his work, and also the general poetic method that renders the generic aspect unimportant, in Coleridge it is to an even greater extent – in fact almost exclusively – his philosophical view of the creation and essence of poetry.

Herbert Read has reduced Coleridge's expressive emotionalistic poetic theory to a brief formula shorn of all metaphysical reasoning, which is worth quoting for the concise, comprehensible way in which it shows why any attempt to confine the great Lake Poets to a genre as we have done with other poets of the time, from Landor and Southey to Scott, Moore and Hunt, is so unproductive.

The form of a work of art is inherent in the emotional situation of the artist; it proceeds from his apprehension of that situation (a situation that may involve either external objective phenomena or internal states of mind) and is the creation of a formal equivalent (i.e. a symbol) for that situation. It resists or rejects all attempts to fit the situation to a ready-made formula of expression, believing that to impose such a generalized shape on a unique emotion or intuition results in insincerity of feeling and artificiality of form.[31]

This is obviously a strong argument against genre. If it really were the basis of all the poetry of the romantic epoch – an opinion sometimes expressed today with the tendency to simplify matters that historical perspective produces – then this entire study would have no point. This is not the case. In the earlier English romantic period only Coleridge and Wordsworth really understood poetry in this way. Even the third Lake Poet, Southey, was hardly influenced at all by this view. He was not nearly philosophical or 'romantic' enough (in the present-day sense of the word) to grasp such ideas (which were also making their appearance in Germany at the same time) with the same acuity as Coleridge, or to experience them as intensely. If he has any subjectivistic, emotionalistic ideas at all, then these appear at most in the watered-down form of reflections about technique, or a self-assured rejection of out-dated conventions, such as occurs with every radical change of style.[32] It is obvious that Scott did not understand poetry in this way at all. Only with the younger romantic poets did this romantic style, in today's sense of the term, become more common, and for them of course it became the essence of poetry and part of their very being.[33]

Aside from the diffuse influences we have already talked about, the only concrete evidence of influence that our two poets had on the fashionable genre developed by Scott is the latter's adoption of the *Christabel* metre or stanza form in *The Lay of the Last Minstrel*. This is indisputable, since it was admitted by Scott himself,[34] but it is nevertheless superficial: Scott could just as easily have found the basic principle of this metre in medieval poetry, or in the work of Spenser or Chatterton.[35] *Christabel* did not have a determining effect on the genre. Scott was not in general able to reproduce the music of Coleridge's verse language and the magic of the atmosphere: what Coleridge saw with his imagination, Scott 'fabricated' as a mere product of fancy. Scott's bright and cheerful style of narrating broke down the magic of the poem he took as his model into powerful 'Gothic' horror and colour effects. He served the public with the colourful externals of romanticism and was rewarded with success after success, whereas Coleridge was concerned with the innermost core and pursued the essence of romantic poetry and the romantic experience of the world to the limits of what could be expressed. Hardly anyone, however, appreciated his achievements or understood the tragedy of the problems revealed by his failed attempt to provide a complete romantic narrative that went beyond mere story-telling and also beyond the balladry of *The Ancient Mariner*.

With the next poet we return to the area of narrative poetry which bears more resemblance to the epic, the category to which Landor's *Gebir* belongs. But while in *Gebir* the romantic element consisted only of a certain softening of the basic classical tone, and the narrowing of the epic framework with respect to scope and content occurred almost coincidentally as a result of the 'Pindaresque' style, in Southey's work the separation from the classic epic type and its infusion with romantic elements is much further advanced. His narrative poems, after his youthful error *Joan of Arc*, represent the qualified renunciation of the conventional epic poem that was mentioned in chapter 2.

Southey's narrative poems

> I have fewer imitators than any other poet of any notoriety; the reason is, that I am less fashionable.
>
> Southey to Landor, letter of 7 May 1819

It is with some reservations that Southey's long narrative poems are here included amongst the early forms of romantic verse narrative. Aside from the fact that they are spread over the whole epoch during which this genre emerged, attained the height of its popularity and finally dissolved, they have, of course, almost all the external features of romantic verse narrative: highly romantic themes, the abandonment of the uniform heroic style of epic poetry, the experimentation with verse forms not found in epic poems, the rejection of the classical epic rules, the adoption of medieval forms and the consciousness of reviving the poetry of romance in a rationalist age. Southey's contemporaries also ranked him without reservation alongside Scott. This is shown, for example, by the fact that both poets were often mentioned in the same sentence in the *Reviews* or were compared with one another.[36] In addition, when the Poet Laureate Pye died in 1813, both were offered the post as representative poets of their day, which indicates that the revival of epic narrative poetry in the romantic spirit was considered the greatest achievement of that time, and that both Scott and Southey were credited equally with it. The reason why Southey's work is nevertheless being dealt with here under the category of early forms of romantic verse narrative is that the objectives and form of the classic epic poem are almost always very clearly visible through the romantic urge for freedom that is displayed on the surface. This can be illustrated in many different ways.

Let us first look at Southey's poetic development, drawing on evidence he himself has provided. The poetic 'genealogy' contained in Southey's description of his poetic development in the Preface to the first volume of the Collected Edition of his works from 1837–8 (hereafter abbreviated to *CE*) is in itself a source of information about his stylistic orientation between classicism and romanticism and the intermediate position of his long narrative poems between the romance and the epic genres. Southey's earliest models were Ariosto and Tasso, whose works he read in Hoole's translation 'for the sake of the plot'. Somewhat later he became interested in Spenser and Chaucer.[37] The revival of medieval and Renaissance poetry through the work of Percy and Warton – with which he now became familiar – strengthened his affinities for the old poets, of whom he said furthermore that they had had the strongest influence on his style. Later he studied Homer and the Bible. As far as verse construction was concerned, he was first influenced by poets who were primarily classically orientated – Gray, Akenside, Mason, Cowper and Bowles – and subsequently developed an interest in new form problems.

After he had composed *Joan of Arc* and *Madoc* in clear, correct blank verse, that was no longer antithetical and epigrammatic but was lacking in originality and density of language, and showed the influence of Shakespeare, Ben Jonson and Milton without any of the genius that characterizes these poets, in 1800 he became interested in the free use of metre and rhyme and found examples of this in the work of Collins and Dr F. Sayers. It was under the influence of Landor's *Gebir* that Southey's verse at last improved considerably 'both in vividness and strength' (but unfortunately not in the direction of brevity): when he was working on *Thalaba* he always had Landor's poem with him (as he writes in the Preface to Volume IV of the *CE*). What he thought of the genre he then wrote in, as a result of all these influences, is indicated in Southey's descriptions of his poetic intentions in the prefaces to his works.

Southey's youthful work *Joan of Arc*,[38] published in 1796, was clearly intended to be an epic. 'In six weeks [I] finished what I called an Epic Poem', he writes in the Preface to this lengthy poem in the *CE*. The Original Preface, dated 1795, which is very informative on a number of points relevant to this study, shows however that he was already beginning to break away from the rules that define this genre.

Southey first emphasizes that the mysteriousness of the fate of the Maid of Orleans renders the material particularly suitable for poetry. He follows on from this to express cautious opposition to the usual mythological framework of the epic poem. The intervention of angels and devils – instead of the intervention of the gods that had once been the norm – would have weakened the strong, radiant, but above all mysterious personality of the heroine, upon which this epic poem depended, and would have reduced Joan to the main character in a fairy-tale. There follow criticisms of the convention that epic heroes are not usually very interesting as human beings and are generally mere symbols of national pride whose fates cannot be expected to fascinate readers in another age when the historical problems being dealt with have lost their significance. Odysseus is the only exception that Southey acknowledges.[39] It is more important to feel love and sympathy for a hero than admiration. He then illustrates this idea with examples from the history of epic poetry, from Virgil, Statius, Lucan and Tasso, and with references to Ariosto, Milton and Camoens. As a result of all these deliberations, Southey expresses the desire to make his *Joan of Arc* 'interesting', and says the way to do this is precisely by abandoning the traditional epic apparatus. Southey wants no mythology, descriptions of weapons, military or geographic catalogues, no animal similia comparing men with lions, tigers, bulls, bears or boars and no lists of the dead and wounded. He goes so far in his rejection of the imitation of the old epic poets that he deliberately does not select material from his own country and chooses a heroine who fought against his own countrymen. The deciding factor is that she stood for justice. The bonds of the epic poem were thus already being loosened, a process which would soon lead in the general direction of the romantic verse narrative. The epic poem itself, however, was not yet being rejected as a genre.

This was the next step, and it was taken in Southey's long poem *Madoc*, which he planned in his schooldays, began in 1794, finished only in 1799 and did not publish until 1805 after thorough revision and the addition of 3,000 lines. In the Preface he introduced it with the words: 'It assumes not the degraded title of Epic: and the question, therefore, is not whether the story is founded upon the rules of Aristotle, but whether it be adapted to the purposes of poetry.' *Madoc* is not headed with the 'degraded' title of epic poem and is free of the bonds of epic theory, as advocated by Southey in the Original Preface to *Joan of Arc*, but the poet nevertheless only detaches himself gradually, and never completely, from the conventional idea of the genre, not only here but also in subsequent poems. Even if we apply the lofty definition of the epic poem formulated in chapter 1 of this book, this work (and, as we shall see, all Southey's other long narrative poems) was designed as an epic, even if the final version cannot be classified as such: he is not satisfied with the more entertaining aspects of the romance and only uses romance elements as a means of enhancing particular effects, and not as an end in themselves.[40]

How then can we recognize this epic design in *Madoc*? Can it not be said that Southey combined historicism (the hero is a twelfth-century Welsh prince) and exoticism (much of the poem is set in America, among the Aztecs) and was thus using exactly the same sort of theme as most writers of romantic tales in verse? The difference lies in the way the later romantic poets and the way Southey actually dealt with such themes. Unlike Scott, Byron or Thomas Moore, Southey does not choose his subjects primarily for their attractiveness or the appeal of a different atmosphere or new, colourful setting (although such considerations will certainly have played a part in his choice). Neither is he, like those same poets, searching for a milieu where the passions have not yet been subdued by the introduction of moral law and the noble simplicity of naivety has not yet been corrupted by civilization.[41] What he is trying to do is to describe a national and a world event, the legendary discovery of America by the Welsh, and to portray this event as a meeting of two great religions, Aztec and Christian. It is nothing less than the moral confrontation of two worlds, whereby the absolute standard is always his own moral and religious standpoint. This is indeed a design of truly epic proportions! In *Madoc*, of course, the description of the heathen religion is still the 'machinery' rather than the 'foundation' of the poem, as Southey himself says in the Preface to the eighth volume of the *CE*. This does not quite fit the requirement that the epic has to offer an interpretative view of the world (here we are only applying this standard to the objectives of the poem, and not the achieved result). However, elsewhere in the Preface it is made clear that there is no contradiction here with the epic poem written according to classicistic rules: Southey writes that if in *Madoc* the mythological machinery is only occasionally linked with the plot, this is in accordance with the general practice of the epic poets.

It is evident from the introduction to Volume V of the *CE* that he wanted his *Madoc* to be considered fundamentally as an epic. There he writes, referring to *Joan of Arc*: 'I pleased myself with the hope that it would one day be likened to Tasso's Rinaldo, and that, as the Jerusalem had fulfilled the promise of better things whereof that poem was the pledge, so might Madoc be regarded in relation to the juvenile work which had preceded it.' Full of confidence, therefore, he does not hesitate to place his second long poem, for which he rejected the 'degraded' title of epic, alongside Tasso's famous epic work. 'Madoc must be my monument', he writes on 30 April 1801 to Wynn, and in the Preface to Volume V of the *CE* he also says: 'Thinking that this would probably be the greatest poem I should ever produce, my intention was, to bestow on it all possible care.'

The reference (in the same text) to the *Iliad* and the *Odyssey* as the justification for dividing *Madoc* into two almost independent parts is yet another indication that Southey considered this work as belonging to the European epic tradition. We can thus exclude *Madoc* from our study of romantic narrative verse, as well as *Joan of Arc*, which after all was still being described as an epic. However, the process of external detachment from the old epic model, the beginning of which was already indicated in the Original Preface to *Joan of Arc*, had continued a step further with the romantic use of remote historic material, some of it set in exotic countries. Foreign mythology subsequently formed the basis of Southey's narrative poem *Thalaba* (1801), his Mohammedan 'epic', and *The Curse of Kehama* (1810), his Indian 'epic'. Two further works in a similar vein were planned, one dealing with Persian and one with Runic mythology, but these were never written.[42] While he never expressly included *Roderick* (1814) among the works that set out to 'interpret' the world's religions in epic fashion, if the fine epigraph from Wordsworth which introduces the poem[43] is assumed to represent its essence, this would perhaps suggest that he saw this tragic poem as the crowning achievement of this series: as the 'epic' of virtue as understood by European Christians.

There thus seems to be sufficient evidence that all Southey's long poems were basically epic rather than romantic, even though we repeatedly find characteristics that belong to the romance genre. If, from *Madoc* on, Southey rejects the classification of epic, he is only discarding the narrow conception his generation had of this type of poem. With each work he noticeably distances himself a little further from the form of the conventional epic model, even though connections with the English epic tradition are still in evidence.

In the first draft *Madoc* was divided into fifteen Books (*Joan of Arc* consisted of ten); when Southey revised it in 1803 he broke it down into forty-four smaller sections with headings which are more like dramatic scenes or chapters of a novel than the sections of an epic poem.[44] Southey retained this form of subdivision in all his subsequent longer narrative poems.[45] The beginnings of this can already be seen in *Thalaba*, which was completed and published before Southey began revising *Madoc*. *Thalaba* is still divided into Books (without headings but with epigraphs[46]), which even number twelve in accordance with epic tradition. These Books however already bear a resemblance to the scenes or novel chapters that we noted in *Madoc*. Like them they also always end with a decisive moment or climax in the plot and this design is more pronounced than in *Madoc*, probably because it was planned from the beginning. Every book in *Thalaba* has an effective, vivid conclusion, and the unequally and arbitrarily constructed, numbered stanzas are rounded off in a similar way. This design developed quite naturally in *Thalaba* out of the narrative procedure, which only partially resembles that of an epic poem. The work has quite a different effect from the great epics of world literature, in spite of its noble feelings and moral: it is not a pure 'romance' but it attempts to clothe an epic idea with the material and style of a romance.[47]

This new style is not only characterized by a verse technique using free unrhymed verse lines with many rhythmic deviations from a basically iambic cadence,[48] but also by the pronounced dynamics of the story, the varying emotional intensity with which the events are presented and which is due to the sensational material of the work. This is alien to the strict procedures of the epic, which deals in detail with every development and illuminates its subject evenly and objectively. Another indication that when he wrote *Thalaba*, Southey's subconscious ties to the classical epic model were no longer as strong as they had been, is the fact that in his prefaces to this work and letters written in connection with it he never refers to the classic epic poets, but he does refer to Ariosto.[49] Ariosto's 'romantic' epic form, however, like Spenser's epic form[50] was increasingly being classified by the romantic poets as belonging to the romance rather than the epic genre. Southey's verse technique in *Joan of Arc* and *Madoc*, as already mentioned, still owed much to the older English tradition. Although in his review of *Madoc* (*ER*, 13, article 1 of October 1805) Jeffrey criticized the poet for his archaisms, unconventionality, prolixity and childish mannerisms, the blank verse of these works is still far from representing a revolutionary renunciation of the epic style of the past. It is only free of the particular polish of the Pope school, and tries in its way to get back to the naturalness of Elizabethan blank verse or the language of the ballad, which was also the aim of the other Lake Poets. Jeffrey's dislike of this style stems only from his reactionary tastes.

In *Thalaba* and *Kehama* Southey then went a step further and radically freed the language and the metre from the conventional characteristics of the epic. The irregular 'pindarics' of these works of course seemed bolder and more original to Southey's contemporaries than they really are, and in fact there was nothing about them that was a new invention. What at first glance appears to be the most unusual feature – the symmetric arrangement of the lines, which are of irregular length and either do not rhyme at all (*Thalaba*) or rhyme freely according to a constantly changing scheme (*Kehama*) – was modelled on Dr Sayer's *Dramatic Sketches of Northern Mythology* (1790), as Southey himself repeatedly emphasized (see Preface to Volume I of the *CE* and the Original Preface to *Thalaba*), but really goes back to the irregular eighteenth-century ode.[51] Southey's boldness consisted only in using this metrical structure for epic poetry. The blank verse of *Roderick*, which is barely distinguishable from that of *Madoc* or *Joan of Arc*, is, as the *Roderick* review in the *Quarterly Review* (25, April 1815) points out, again based on the Elizabethans.

Southey's verse language was also attributed to a wide variety of other influences. In the *Thalaba* review of the *Edinburgh Review* (1, article 8 of October 1802) Jeffrey maintains that Southey's more relaxed attitude to the verse rules and renunciation of poetic diction is allied to Wordsworth's endeavours in this area, and then says that anyone could compose a *Thalaba* after studying the styles of Rousseau, Kotzebue, Schiller, Cowper, Ambrose Philips (here he has this poet's *Collection of Old Ballads* of 1723 in mind), Quarles and Donne. He also finds that Southey's inclusion of old ballads is in particularly bad taste. Jeffrey repeats this criticism in his review of *Kehama* (*ER*, 24, article 11, February 1811), where he also adds Withers and Henry More to his list of Southey's 'ancestors'. Although in these reviews Jeffrey contradicts himself, by accusing Southey of 'babyish gentleness' and then saying that his poems would perhaps be acceptable if their tone were a little more modest but Southey obviously wanted to do better than anyone else and had thus fallen into the trap of rhetorical exaggeration, there is nevertheless some truth in both of these censures. Southey's works do in fact contain two basically irreconcilable elements: on the one hand the attempt to retain the superior form of the epic that is also visible in the language,[52] and on the other the imitation of the ballad tone[53] and the dramatic[54] and lyrical[55] insertions that the poet believed necessary to a romance. Southey allows these last-mentioned stylistic peculiarities, that have nothing to do with the epic, to interrupt the flow of the elevated style just for the sake of their picturesque effect. Strangely enough, however, when the works are read quickly the mixture is not noticeable: the oriental poems seem to have a uniform, personal style.

In *Roderick* these characteristics have almost completely disappeared, and Southey once again writes consistently in iambic pentameters. This does not indicate that Southey had become one of those romantic poets who develop the form of their poems from the material and its emotional value alone, or that he has betrayed romantic freedom and returned to a metre that is more in line with epic conventions; but rather that he proceeded in this way purely out of a sense of fitness or decorum, feeling that where the material is carried by its noble simplicity and greatness, it is unnecessary to embellish it with rhymes and unusual metres, dialogue and lyrical passages.[56] This procedure together with the sober, realistic style has the effect of emphasizing that this tragic poem is closer to Southey's first two epics and hence to the old epic model. Several 'romantic' elements that Southey had been developing since *Madoc*, however, set *Roderick* apart from the heroic poem in the old style both in form and content. Ecstasy and pathos are indicated by the many exclamation marks, breathless excitement or suspense by the pauses marked '...', all of which heightens the drama and passion of the narrative style in a manner that is foreign to the epic. Particularly effective is the use of the verbal echoes as a kind of leitmotif. Southey had already used the leitmotif in the oriental poems: in *Thalaba* the lines 'Blindly the wicked work / The righteous will of Heaven!' occur three times (V, 38; IX, 13 and 26). In *Kehama* the curse is the leitmotif, running through the work in many linguistic variations (II, 14; II, 5 and 10; IV, 5; V, 7; IX, 10; XV, 10 and elsewhere). And in *Roderick* the beginning and end of the poem are held together with a literal repetition (I, 75 ff. and XXV, the penultimate paragraph) clarifying the path of the hero from guilt to deliverance in a manner that impresses itself upon the reader.

The form, content and effect of all these repetitions have of course nothing to do with the stereotyped oral formulas of the Homeric epic; they are determined strictly by the theme. Thus this closer examination of the elements of Southey's style would seem to support the thesis that the work of this poet falls somewhere between the epic poem and the romance, and between the eighteenth and nineteenth centuries. The most important factor that excludes his relevant works – *Madoc*, *Thalaba*, *Kehama* and *Roderick* – from the category of the epic poem as defined in chapter 1 of this book, is that they contain no 'unconscious accepted metaphysic', and neither the world of the plot nor the world the poet lives in is interpreted comprehensively in them. Southey's narrative poems are for this reason in particular not genuine epics.

The focus on the plot, and on adventure, ghosts and 'private' destinies is of course so strong that they are not simply epic poems which have failed to meet the requirements of the genre (the works of Cottle, Sotheby and Atherstone are in this category), but rather romances which strike other chords in the reader and meet other needs. If they had limited themselves to this, it would have been possible to say that they had succeeded. What Southey is aiming at, however, is an epic interpretation of 'worlds' and in this he cannot succeed. In spite of all the historical and ethnographic studies that he pursued when writing his 'epics', as shown by the copious notes to these works,[57] he does not understand the civilizations where his poems are set or the mythologies he is trying to illustrate. He is completely incapable of intuitively understanding other worlds, and is also unable to provide a poetic counterpart to the comprehensive interpretations of historical processes which the German philosophers from Friedrich Schlegel to Hegel sketched out in his time. Even Scott's understanding of the Middle Ages is more adequate than Southey's of the oriental mythologies (see the discussion of Jeffrey's reviews on pp. 80ff.). This is partly due to his limited intellectual horizons, of which there is ample proof,[58] and partly to the fact that historicism and ethnography are by no means a suitable basis for epic poetry, a fact perhaps demonstrated as convincingly here as anywhere.

The present author is thus obliged to agree with C. H. Herford, who wrote: 'Through all the phantasmagoria of oriental adventure we detect the decorous English Protestant, Southey, animating his hero with ideals of virtue caught from Epictetus and the Age of Reason ... He was too "enlightened" to penetrate into the inner genius of the faiths whose picturesque beauty he admired.'[59] What Herford is saying here also implies that Southey was intellectually unsuited to the use of the rich oriental or historic imagery for interpreting the philosophical or social questions of his day, i.e., the use of the romance to create a real romantic epic with contemporary problems, as Wordsworth was to do in his *Prelude* and Shelley partly succeeded in doing in his *Revolt of Islam*. 'He stood on the verge of the two centuries between Rationalism and Romanticism, participating in both, possessed by neither. He toiled before the threshold of Romanticism, while Coleridge stood already at its inner shrine.'[60]

This applies to all Southey's intellectual, poetic and political qualities. This iconoclastic destroyer of classical taste and classical form, this former revolutionary and pantisocrat was basically a conservative, imperturbably moralistic, egocentric and rather simple soul, who, as an author, was strangely unaffected by the changes through which he was living, by his friendship with the other Lake Poets[61] or by the overturning of supposedly unshakeable values by the younger romantic generation. Southey's type of narrative poem should thus be defined as follows. His longer narrative works in verse are epics that do not keep to the epic rules and have been 'painted up' to the status of romances. They deal with idealized heroes set in foreign or former civilizations and reflect the poet's conservative, moralistic attitudes.

The romantic, universal epic of world religions that Southey had originally set out to create in this way thus never came to fruition. Instead he introduced, or was at least instrumental in introducing, two new aspects into English romantic poetry: exciting narrative in verse and a poetic reflection of the oriental world.[62] His works might appear today as faded as theatre sets in daylight. One might, as Byron did, mock this English Poet Laureate who set out to produce works ranking with those of Virgil, Ariosto, Spenser and Milton, but whose 'epics' are little more than moralistic Gothic or historical novels in hastily written verses with a thoughtless mixture of incompatible elements as their only mark of originality; or metrical romances, where the entertainment value and fairy-tale quality have been impaired by the mass of book-learning worked into them and by the lofty ambitions of their author. But he must nevertheless be given credit for those two new aspects.

Southey's poems are being designated in this book as early forms of romantic verse narrative on account of their fluctuation between the epic and the romance. Even if he did succeed in reviving narrative verse and inventing the romantic epic of adventure, he was unable to detach himself so completely from the old idea of the epic as to create something artistically satisfying and, by blending together the elements he had taken over, something genuinely new. He did not see that, in order to put the romantic material into a popular contemporary form, he had to relinquish something, namely the sublime pretension of the epic. He did not see that the epic as a type was dead unless it was completely redesigned by a genius such as Wordsworth.

This conservatism and misunderstanding of the complexities of romantic thinking and of the causes of the changes in taste whereby the epic was rejected in favour of the romance are also the reasons why Southey could not develop as a romantic poet. He only contributed some stimulating works to the genre as it were in spite of himself. However, instead of progressing to the popular form of the verse narrative which made Scott and so many others after him successful, and using it for weightier subjects as Wordsworth (in *The White Doe of Rylstone*), Keats and Shelley did, Southey constantly tried to produce the 'great poem of high imagination' in intellectual emulation of the old epic. There is something quixotic about the eagerness with which this ambitious, industrious, uninspired poet – who was not at all above considerations of public popularity and financial gain[63] – attempted to create the modern epic. His basically unromantic nature actually led him not forwards to meet the new taste in poetry, but backwards. *Thalaba*, written by Southey when he was twenty-seven, possesses the most romantic traits, both in the plot and in the form of the poem. It has something of the freshness of narration that sets Scott apart, and in spite of its considerable length has a clarity and uncluttered quality about it that makes it more readable than *Madoc* or the later works (with the exception perhaps of *Roderick*).[64] In *Thalaba* Southey comes closer to the later verse narrators than in any other poem, and here there are also signs of certain characteristics that were not fully developed in poetry until the second decade of the century.

In *Kehama* Southey has already departed from this promising line of development, and nothing of *Thalaba*'s simplicity of portrayal remains. The 'machinery', which was already heavily reliant on Gothic horrors in *Thalaba*, is reduced here to pure theatricality, the fantasy with which the poem is embellished is as old-fashioned as an eighteenth-century pagoda, and here and there touches of a rococo-like prettiness are added that do not fit in at all with the overall tone of the poem (such as the appearance and flying skills of the Glendoveer *Ereenia* in Books VI and VII, and the pastoral idyll in Book XIII). Everything appears contrived and every detail is described in a laboured fashion so that the lightness of the fairy-tale romance is lost, while at the same time the poet fails to achieve the unity of the complete epic work that he was aiming at.

Roderick, the Last of the Goths is probably the best of Southey's narrative poems, since it has the most mature and humanly appealing plot and a hint of genuine tragedy. However, it is at the same time one of his most traditional poems. Only its verse language, which is entirely free from any influence of the French School, the dramatic narrative intensity and the stronger degree of sympathy the hero awakes in the reader distinguish it from the epics of the classicists. These qualities, on the other hand, draw attention to the unoriginal and 'made to measure' blank verse used for a plot that is half novel, half drama, and to the many opportunities for making the poem more effective that are missed. The character portrayal, that in *Madoc* and the oriental poems was idealistic or black-and-white with no regard to psychology, is better here, but the psychology resembles Corneille's set types rather than, for example, Byron's more empirically conceived character descriptions.

The later works in verse, *A Tale of Paraguay* (begun in 1814, published in 1825), *All for Love, or a Sinner Well Saved* (1823) and *Oliver Newman* (uncompleted, published posthumously in 1845 – of the twenty-one sections planned only nine were written), where the poet might most have been expected to have learnt from Scott and Byron, are the most colourless and old-fashioned examples of Southey's narrative verse. *All for Love* is a weak legend in the ballad metre where the *diablerie* is purely theatrical and the religious tone reflects neither the profound piety of the true legend nor the conviction of a modern religious poem. *A Tale of Paraguay* bears certain resemblances to Campbell's *Gertrude of Wyoming*, which is partly due to the use of the same metre (the Spenser stanza) in both poems, and partly also to the lyrical, sentimental way in which basically idyllic material from the colonial world is given a tragic ending. With its much less polished verse technique and 'sweeter' variation of the theme of the noble savage, which is presented almost like a tract, Southey's poem is however markedly inferior to Campbell's.[65] Here the Poet Laureate sinks to the level of Bowles' *Missionary of the Andes* (1815, in eight books and heroic couplets) or Montgomery's *Greenland* (1819, in five cantos and heroic couplets), both utterly forgotten, equally pale verse narratives dealing with subjects from Christian missionary history.

The completed sections of *Oliver Newman* are equally insignificant. Here Southey returns to the *Kehama* metre and 'dramatic' dialogues worked into the narrative. Such 'free' elements seem completely out of place in this epic dealing with the more realistic, sober world of American Quakers in the seventeenth century. Even in this work Southey had not yet abandoned all thought of the traditional epic and the epic style: when he first planned the poem in 1811 he wrote to the Reverend H. Hill (letter of 5 March 1811): 'The principal personage is to be a primitive quaker – certainly a character new to heroic poetry'; and he was thinking of writing it in hexameters.[66]

As a final quote from Southey himself about his work, the following longer passage from a letter (to Wynn on 30 December 1804) illustrates many aspects of his position in relation to the generic developments of the times. Here he says:

> I wish I could find an English story for a poem, it would make me feel like a cock on his own dunghill – all the necessary or desirable knowledge would be so completely within my reach. Edmund Ironsides ... is the best hero, but though the event is of first-rate importance, being no less than the amalgamation of the Danes and Saxons, it is not of sufficient popular interest; no national string could be touched ... I have great drawings of mind ... towards King Arthur, if his history were not such a chaos; but if we take the Arthur of romance, he is eclipsed by his own knights, of the historical Arthur, his actions are of no consequential importance. Something might be made of the tale of Brutus, were it not for that unhappy name, which would always remind the reader of a greater hero than I could possibly create ... I am afraid there cannot be any worthier hero found for an English poem than Robin Hood, and that lowers the key too much; so I shall go on with 'Kehama'.[67]

After examining the genre of Southey's works on the basis of his own evidence, the form of his poetry and this author's own assessment, all that remains is to look at the opinions of his contemporaries. This will not only reveal more about Southey's own approach, but will also shed light on how his contemporaries viewed the whole question of genre. The material for this section is drawn from comments in the main periodicals and from assessments of Southey made by the romantic poets.

We should commence with the negative review of *Thalaba* by Jeffrey (*ER*, 1, article 8, October 1802). Jeffrey rejects the principle of adapting the style to the individual situation as unsuitable for epic poetry: if the important parts are emphasized by a change of metre it becomes too obvious that the poet is unable to maintain the level of the epic manner. It is precisely the narrative and descriptive sections which need a consistent heroic style. The *Thalaba* style is consistently ecstatic, but this is often much ado about nothing and only achieved by mystical phrases that sound good but say nothing. The plot with its wild extravagances is entertaining, but the 'chaster and severer graces by whom the epic muse would be most suitably attended' are missing. The 'domestic scenes', descriptions of nature, dramatic movement and exciting plot are skilfully created, but the poem is not forceful enough for an epic. The lowly, accidental and imperfect nature of the subject and the language are unpoetic. Naive simplicity, which is pleasing in Burns because it corresponds to his nature, is distasteful in a learned epic poet like Southey. Jeffrey calls *Thalaba* a metrical romance, but does not go into the difference between this and an epic poem. Here he is simply copying Southey, who in the Original Preface called *Thalaba* a romance, a poem and an Arabian Tale without differentiating between them. At the time the article was written, there were no comparable romantic verse narratives. Jeffrey is therefore still judging everything by the epic.[68]

He is even more critical in his review of *Madoc* (*ER*, 13, article 1, October 1805), which opens with a philippic against Southey's ambition to be better than all the great epic poets – and here Jeffrey names Virgil and Milton. In his subsequent criticism of the poem for the improbability of the story, which is in stark contrast to the academic quality of the annotations, we encounter for the first time a comparison with medieval romances. These, says Jeffrey, were naive and could therefore deal with the unreal and the improbable. Southey's approach to his writing, however, is scientific and realistic, which makes the machinery of the epic look childish. All the advantages of the work cannot outweigh this defect or the other basic weaknesses it has.

Here, therefore, a work of Southey's is already being assessed as both an epic and a continuation of the medieval romance genre – and being dismissed as a failure in both cases. As Jeffrey takes up his pen again to pass judgement on Southey after the publication of *Kehama* (*ER*, 24, article 11, February 1811), his attitude to the romance, both medieval and modern, has changed. Scott is the poet he feels the writer of *The Curse of Kehama* should model himself on. Scott has replaced the naivety of the old romances with things that appeal to the mind of the modern reader: he gives his romances historical interest, portrays social forces and an adult, manly world, and has a feeling for variety that the long narrative poem needs. Southey, on the other hand, has composed a fairy-tale characterized by worthless glitter that can only appeal to uncritical young people,[69] but has presented it with the ambition of an epic poet. Epics for men cannot, however, be created out of fairy-tales, especially when the poet does not model himself on the true poets and experts but on the 'tame vulgarity of old ballads'. While Southey does attempt to follow the general trend towards large-scale, all-embracing works dealing with massive problems, man and the universe, in reality his world is artificial and unreal. His heroes appear to live in an age of innocence. Their only passion is love of parents or children and their eroticism is so tame that they always seem to behave as if they are under supervision. The only community that is represented is the family, and there is a complete absence of any social interest or of opposing moral forces in the individual. To use the terminology of this book, Southey is not offering an interpretation of a real world, as in the true epic, but is describing a fairy-tale world. Jeffrey even denies that Southey has succeeded with the fairy-tale: the *Kehama* fable is so untrue and so far removed from all that is human and natural that it is not even as interesting as one of the *Tales of the Thousand and One Nights*; at best it is a yarn.

If we eliminate all the exaggeration due to political opposition, reactionary tastes and personal distaste, there is much in these articles that astutely explains Southey's difficulties and traces them back to their origins. Most important of all is the recognition of the discrepancy between the romantic and epic elements, which is perhaps the key to Southey's failure.

The *Quarterly Review* treats Southey as one of its colleagues and later as Poet Laureate with respect; and as with Jeffrey it is necessary to eliminate the elements of opposition, here we must exclude an over-willingness to praise.

The first Southey article printed in this journal – Scott's review of *Kehama* – and the controversy between the two poets to which it gave rise have already been mentioned (see note 40 on p. 245). Instead of getting annoyed about Scott's disdain of his 'epic' achievement, Southey would have done better to listen to the concealed advice that the clever and successful Scott was giving him under the guise of anonymity. After Scott has paid due respect to the view of the Lake Poets that the poet is driven by inspiration to create and should not create under any other circumstances, he develops his article into a kind of poetological manifesto, which opens with the succinct sentence: 'The object of poetry is pleasure.' For this reason, he continues, poets and critics must adapt to changes in taste. Although this is openly directed against Jeffrey, who had accused Southey of ignoring the rules, it is also directed at Southey, who was still clinging to the ambition of becoming an epic poet. The rest of the text is nothing but a defence of romantic poetry as Scott understands it and of what Northrop Frye calls the 'low mimetic mode' against classical standards. Tasso is best when he does not reflect Homer and Virgil, and Ariosto is even better. The classical epic poets, from Voltaire to the present day, have not produced a single readable poem, so this way is evidently blocked for today's poets. Contemporary painters are also no longer guided by Guido Reni and Raphael but paint peasants, fishermen and smugglers, so why should not poets also try their hand at subjects that are appropriate to the spirit and tastes of the times? Examples of such subjects are Gothic castles, modern peasant cottages and now, in addition, Indian pagodas (these three examples of course relate to the work of Scott, Crabbe or Wordsworth and Southey as representatives of modern poetry). After an approving analysis of *Kehama*, Scott embarks on a cautious criticism of the work: there is such an abundance of fantasy in this poem that Southey has no alternative but to set it in an unreal world. On account of this excessive quantity of subject matter with which the reader cannot identify he loses interest, and 'the object of poetry' is after all 'pleasure'. There follows advice as to how the reader's interest might have been held by shortening the plot and concentrating on just a few motifs. Scott even has reservations about the choice of Indian mythology: only the Greeks have managed to create a poetically viable world of gods.

What this means in terms of genre is simply that if the poem is an epic with a mythological framework then it should be in classical form, otherwise it should be written as a romance with a concentrated plot, human interest and no mythology. This criticism is immediately softened: Scott claims that he does not want to make the same mistake as Jeffrey, who requires a modern epic to have the sublimity of Homer, the majesty of Virgil, the fantasy of Ariosto, the pure taste of Tasso and the awesome seriousness of Dante – in other words all the attributes of the greatest poets put together. Such advice is easily given, but how would it ever be possible to combine all this? We know that Scott himself modified these postulates in order to suit his own character as well as guarantee himself success with the public. His article seems to be trying to advise Southey to do the same. However, the future Laureate did not take it in this way, and was so angry with Scott that the latter apologized. He had written the article in a hurry to make sure it appeared before there was anything in the *Edinburgh Review* and to ensure the public were favourably disposed towards the poem from the beginning; he would, however, in accordance with Southey's wishes, publish an additional paragraph about the high moral quality of *Kehama*. Southey continued undeterred to try and produce Jeffrey's impossible combination of great attributes.

The result was *Roderick, the Last of the Goths*, his last complete poem of epic design. It is hard to judge whether the taut construction of the plot and the absence of any excessive supernatural agency in this poem indicate that Southey had after all taken Scott's article to heart.[70] It is only possible to say that Scott was right to make the suggestions he did to Southey, since *Roderick* is the most exciting of Southey's poems.

When *Roderick* first appeared it was also reviewed in the *Quarterly Review* (25, April 1815). This review is so flattering in the way it confirms that Southey has achieved all he has been aiming for that it might even be thought he dictated it himself. Here is a summary of it.

The dictates of the human heart override the dictates of the theoreticians in all Southey's works. The treatment of mythology is better in his poems than in the *Iliad*, where the gods as all-powerful helpers diminish the greatness of the heroes by their intervention. Since his *Joan of Arc* Southey has planted divinity in the human heart and there is no more inconsistent help from above: while gods, spirits and angels do still intervene, it is man who makes the decisions through his own inner strength. Thalaba throws away the magic ring and cries: 'The talisman is faith!' In *Roderick* the poet has replaced a miracle attributed by his source to the Virgin Mary with a natural event that benefits the hero. This latest poem is completely original and has not been modelled on any other work: with the best will in the world it is impossible to place it in any category. However, it will be of enduring value and occupy a worthy place amongst the famous literature of the world.

This, however, was not to be, and subsequent generations were perhaps even a little too harsh in their judgement. The historical material as adapted by Southey in his own original way offers many possibilities, and one can imagine that a genuinely dramatic poet like Kleist might have made a stirring tragedy out of it.[71] Even Southey possibly saw the dramatic potentiality of this narrative poem: he called it 'A Tragic Poem' and prefaced it with a list of characters as in a play. However, as always with his work, the good in it is reduced to mediocrity as a result of hasty production, a lack of 'modern' psychology and the difficulty he had in reducing a story to its essentials. Mere epic breadth does not make an epic; here it has the effect rather of stifling material that is by its nature romantic and dramatic.

From Hazlitt's remarks about Southey in *Lectures on the English Poets* (1818 – 19) and *The Spirit of the Age* (1825) it is evident that his attitude to the Poet Laureate's long narrative poems changed in the six years that elapsed between the two reviews. In the *Lectures* he ranks Southey without qualification with the epic poets of classicism, the style now on its way out. He speaks of the 'larger epics' of Southey and is reminded of Blackmore, who however, in Hazlitt's opinion, is light, nimble and less mechanical than the ponderous, solemn and phlegmatic Southey. Southey's talent is probably more suited to short forms, since the longer epics contain too much indifferent material. The Southey article in *The Spirit of the Age* contains an excellent character portrait, which in spite of its political bias analyses Southey's personality fairly and attempts to find the origins of the intellectual weaknesses of the poems in the character of the poet. Hazlitt is now more complimentary about the long narrative poems (he does not call them epics this time but 'larger poems'): they are vividly narrated and have a commendable breadth of vision, the imagery is brilliant and the pace and suspense are stimulating. These works may seem startling to readers with refined tastes, but the unlimited freedom from rules that makes them paradoxes as poems must simply be accepted, the good must be taken with the bad. The positive qualities in any case easily outweigh the abandonment of the rules, which in any case only bothers the pedants. With such general remarks one might well wonder whether Hazlitt had read Southey's 'epics' again in the meantime (even in the *Lectures* he admits he only remembers them faintly), or whether he is merely reflecting the changing tastes of the times under the influence of the romantic verse narratives of Scott and Byron. However, it is probably true to say, in summary, that in the *Lectures* Hazlitt does not notice these poems are generically different, and in *The Spirit of the Age* this no longer interests him.

The romantic poets' opinion of Southey's achievement is predominantly positive. While none of them adopted Southey's genre, the epic poem with romantic features, both Scott[72] and Shelley[73] were inspired by the freedom of the metre, the descriptive artistry or the fantastic unreality of the machinery in his works. Scott recognized without envy the importance and seriousness of Southey's intentions with regard to the epic, and believed Southey's epics were of greater significance than his own romances. When the title of Poet Laureate was offered first to him, he passed it on to Southey as the more worthy of it and wrote to him: 'I am not such an ass as not to know that you are my better in poetry, though I have had ... the tide of popularity in my favour.'[74]

In chapter 3 of the *Biographia Literaria* Coleridge paid tribute to the humanity and ability of his friend and also vituperated against the uncomprehending critics (this was of course primarily directed at Jeffrey). Southey had worked in almost every genre and was successful in them all; he had in addition discovered new genres. From the text it emerges that by these genres Coleridge was mainly thinking of the special narrative forms of *Thalaba*, *Kehama* and *Roderick*. In the terminology of this book, we can interpret Coleridge's remarks as saying he considered Southey's synthesis of epic and romantic elements to be successful.

As well as Shelley and Coleridge, Cardinal Newman was also an admirer of *Thalaba*. He described it as the 'most sublime of English poems', adding, 'I mean, morally sublime'.[75] *Roderick* was described by Hogg and Byron as the greatest epic of the age.[76] Byron's other opinions of Southey's long narrative poems – he always calls them epics and measures them against the quality if not also the rules of the great epics of world literature by Homer, Virgil, Camoens, Milton and Tasso – are too numerous and too dominated by ridicule and dislike to be quoted here as serious views of Southey's work. An entry in Byron's diary, made in the year 1813, will nevertheless serve as an appropriate conclusion to this section on Southey's verse narratives since it sums up wittily but accurately the extent to which Southey's obsession with the epic genre was an integral part of his nature. Byron had only made the acquaintance of the author of *Thalaba* in this particular year and was, contrary to his expectations, impressed with him right from their first meeting. A little later he wrote in his journal: 'Southey I have not seen much of. His appearance is epic ...'[77]

4　The establishment of the genre by Sir Walter Scott, its fashionable period, and imitations by other poets

The romances of Sir Walter Scott

And find, to cheat the time, a powerful spell
In old romaunts of errantry that tell,
Or later legends of the Fairy-folk,
Or Oriental tale of Afrite fell,
Of Genii, Talisman, and broad-wing'd Roc
Though taste may blush and frown, and sober reason mock.

Walter Scott, Introduction to *Harold the Dauntless*, 1817

From quite different starting points, Landor, the Lake Poets and Southey came very close to the romantic literary form that was the natural, logical development of the tendencies described in chapter 2. All these poets, however, failed to achieve the breakthrough to the popular romance, for reasons we attempted to define in the section on early forms. It was Scott, finally, who was successful, and who was predestined as no other to discover this genre. He had that combination of qualities that was necessary in order to create the type of poetry that was the 'inevitable' development of what had gone before: he had a deep personal academic and literary relationship to the world of medieval singers and knights,[1] which had to provide the inspiration for a new type of narrative poetry once classicism had lost its validity. Like the old minstrels, he took naive pleasure in the magic, horror and colourfulness of all 'romantic' happenings. He was not so sensitive that he shrank from the savagery of the aggressive world portrayed in the old romances, nor were his tastes so refined that he was repelled by the simple form of most of the old poetry. He was inhibited neither by high intellectual ambitions nor by an exalted sense of mission from exploiting poetry for pure story-telling purposes. He was perspicacious enough to recognize the narrow limitations of what he could do as a poet and also the limitations of what poetry that was aimed at popularity could expect of the reader. In his happy middle position between old and new preferences he was sufficiently confident to shed all regulations that he found constrictive without going so far that the wider public was offended. He was sufficiently original to stamp his own individuality on the material and forms that he borrowed for his poetry from a wide variety of sources. And he also had enough business sense to exploit the mine of ideas he had discovered for exactly the right length of time, i.e., the length of time

86

the public would permit. While Southey was a 'great' poet without being a genius, Scott was a genius but not a great poet.

In our study so far we have followed the epic to the point where a moderate alteration of its basic features, such as Landor and Southey had in mind, could no longer prevent it from rapidly going out of fashion. Only the substitution of a completely new, i.e., popular, form satisfying the needs of a public primarily interested in the story could stop the verse epic from becoming an anachronism, the private enjoyment of only a few isolated individuals with humanistic or literary interests. We have followed the medieval fashion to the point where the ballad imitation became even more popular than the previously favoured genres of serious poetry – the sonnet, the ode and the domestic or descriptive poem, etc. Interest in the longer medieval narrative poems was also awakened by Ritson, Scott's *Sir Tristrem* edition of 1804 and Ellis' *Specimens* of 1805. We have followed the history of the influence of German literature and seen that Tory criticism dealt a heavy blow to the 'German' robber and horror literature that was fashionable in England around 1800, but that it had already had such an effect on the majority of readers that the taste for the sensational remained. We have examined sociological trends in reading and their influence on tastes and literary requirements, and concluded that neither the traditional epic nor the prose novel was the most suitable form for the large new group of readers: the epic could not meet the requirements of a fast pace, excitement, involvement and the opportunity to retreat into a passionately intense world bearing little relation to reality; and the novel was considered too frivolous or looked down on as a mere consumer good by a middle class striving for culture and refinement. The time was ripe for the man who could follow these developments in poetry to their logical conclusion and fill the vacuum that had arisen. That man was Scott. As in the last section, the aim here will be to create an overall picture of Scott's genre from a combination of his own statements, brief examinations of the works themselves and the reactions of his contemporaries, and to underline the most important generic aspects.

In the Introduction to his *Lay of the Last Minstrel* that Scott added in the collected edition of 1830, he only discusses in detail one of the factors leading to the development of the romantic tale in verse that has been mentioned in this text, namely the influence of the ballad, and does not go into any further detail about the verse forms he considered or how he came to write *The Lay of the Last Minstrel*. The article, several pages long, shows that since Scott wanted to give up neither the legal profession as a means of earning money, nor literature, from which he derived much more satisfaction, he attempted to practise both, thus renouncing the highest honours in either which could only have been achieved by making a choice between them. This involved no great sacrifice, since Scott did not overestimate his capabilities either as a judge or as a poet. His previous literary activity – 'a young man who was taken up with running after ballads, whether Teutonic or national', 'my open interference with matters of light literature' – had brought him neither great popularity nor material gain worth mentioning. And since for him 'giving one-self up to literature' and 'pleasing the public' were virtually the same thing, his biggest problem was how to capture the imagination of the readers with some-thing new, since around this time (approximately 1802 to 1804) they were sat-urated with ballads and had had more than enough of the ballad metre 'which had become hackneyed and sickening, from its being the accompaniment of every grinding hand-organ', as Scott wrote in the Introduction to his *Lay*.

A new type of plot had to be found, but one which still lent itself to presen-tation with the 'simplicity and wildness of the old ballads', since Scott, who knew what his limitations were and where his interests lay, valued this aspect as much as his public, which was tired only of the form, not the contents of the ballads and tales of wonder. A metric structure also had to be found which was suited to this type of plot, without resembling too closely the singsong of the ballads.

When Scott attributes finding what he was looking for in both cases to chance, this is something of an exaggeration: he had a likeable tendency to detract from his own achievements and pay a debt of gratitude to everyone who had ever promoted him. He would have probably arrived sooner or later at the form of the longer metrical romance, even without the banal goblin story of Gilpin Horner that a young lady in his neighbourhood passed on to him as a subject for a ballad, and which provided him with the idea for *The Lay of the Last Minstrel*. His enthusiasm for Bürger's *Lenore*, of which he produced a free rend-ering in 1796, and the Middle English *Sir Tristrem*, which he adapted and pub-lished in 1804, must have already pointed him in this direction. Even the in-vention of his 'light horseman sort of stanza', as he later liked to call the metric scheme he used in the *Lay* and four of his other eight verse narratives, is as much due to his extensive reading of ballads and romances as to the recital of *Christabel* he once heard and which he claimed had given him the idea for it.[2]

Whatever the case, the *Gilpin Horner* ballad grew with his treatment of it. Around it he constructed a fable of duels, magic and love which made it too long for use in the *Minstrelsy* as originally planned. Finally, after rejecting explanatory headings to the individual cantos in the style of Spenser's epigraphs as being 'too oracular', he created the framework story of the old minstrel, 'who, as he is supposed to have survived the Revolution, might have caught somewhat of the refinement of modern poetry, without losing the simplicity of his original model'. He narrates the actual story, set in the sixteenth century, to a seventeenth-century duchess. The above quote is taken from the short prose Preface to the first edition of the *Lay*, where he also writes: 'As the description of scenery and manners was more the object of the author than a combined and regular narrative, the plan of the Ancient Metrical Romance was adopted, which allows greater latitude in this respect than would be consistent with the dignity of a regular Poem.' This model also permitted Scott to use a freely changing metre and machinery adopted from popular belief, which 'would have seemed puerile in a poem which did not partake of the rudeness of the old Ballad, or Metrical Romance'.[3]

This attempt to define the genre of something that originally amounted to an expansion of ballad material in a probably rather unplanned way, and justify it by comparison with the epic, shows that Scott did not dismiss the ordered generic ideas of the older generation in the same way as Wordsworth or Coleridge. However, the fact that he himself saw – probably at an early stage – the similarity of the narrative structure he was developing with the romances and lays of the late medieval minstrels is easily explained by his particular familiarity with this genre through Percy, Ritson, Ellis and his own studies.

It would seem from this description of the origin of the *Lay* and what Scott was saying about it in the 1830 Introduction that this poem was not intended to be a slavish imitation of the medieval romance genre but a new creation in the original spirit. Scott, who was an ardent admirer of all medieval poetry, was still attempting to make the 'rough' art of his forefathers 'palatable' and improve their 'undeveloped' poetic art with modern refinements much in the same way as Percy. He did not want to copy and he did not want to ignore developments in poetry; he wanted to work all the literary achievements and ideas of the intervening period into the old generic model, so long as they were in accordance with his essential objectives and had not recently become stale through overuse. Hence we find in his work many echoes of classicism as well as details from the Gothic novel and German *Sturm-und-Drang* poetry.[4]

The extensive deliberations about verse technique that form part of the 1830 Introduction show even more clearly than the remarks in the short Preface to the *Lay* of 1805 the extent of Scott's independent artistic achievement. Scott thought very carefully about which verse form would be most suitable for the 'extravagance' he was planning. The ballad metre and the popular couplet consisting of two tetrameter lines would have been most suitable from a historical point of view. However, the common ballad measure was out of the question since it had, as already mentioned, been used too often in the numerous ballads written in the decade preceding 1805. And with the tetrameter couplet, the traditional verse of the original romances and a form characterized by 'extreme facility', there was a danger that the dignity of serious poetry would be lost and a poet like Scott in particular, who did not pay such precise attention to form, would run the risk of writing hastily and carelessly.[5] A further argument against the ballad stanza was that it imposed too many limitations and constraints on the accentuation of the sentence which Scott also felt was the case with the heroic or elegiac stanza in which Gray had written his well-known *Elegy* and Davenant his *Gondibert*. The heroic couplet, the conventional type of epic verse[6] since Dryden, was of course even less suitable than any of these metres, since it lacked the simplicity and naturalness that the subject demanded. It was reminiscent of neo-classical epic poetry, which in any case was to be replaced with something new, and the public was at least as tired of it as it was of the ballad verse.

We have already seen how Scott's acquaintance with the *Christabel* metre suddenly resolved all his doubts about form. But while the poet of the *Lay* avoided the over-used verse styles by employing this metre, he did not avoid the carelessness in his verse technique which he had hoped to prevent by staying away from the short tetrameter couplet or common measure. The verse style of the *Lay* (and of Scott's other romances) bears no resemblance to the consistently 'heroic', exalted style which dominates Southey's poems in spite of characteristics suggestive of the ballad. Scott's verse is never distinguished but it is pleasant, easy to understand, lively and swift-moving; it varies according to the subject it is dealing with and is seldom so good or so dull and unpoetic that it draws attention to itself and away from the story. It is just as foolish to measure Scott against Homer[7] as it is wrong to say that it is only the lack of consistency and exquisite qualities in his style that prevent him from being one of the greatest epic poets in the world, as W. M. Dixon does.[8] In spite of any weaknesses it might have, Scott's verse is surprisingly effective considering the class of literature to which his works belong and the poetic objective that motivated them.

One can of course criticize Scott for his thoughtless, eclectic mixture of the widest variety of hackneyed characteristics from classicistic and pre-romantic poetry, from the ballad and romance tradition, *Christabel* or Bürger's German ballad style, for the scant attention he pays to subtleties and overtones when he adopts these features and for the extent to which they make his style sound affected by their dependency on rhyme and the frequency of their occurrence.[9] To criticize in this way, however, is to forget that Scott had voluntarily and quite deliberately chosen a level of poetry where the originality and subtlety of style that characterizes the great romantic writers were unnecessary and even out of place. Scott gives the details of the verse language sufficient attention and endows it with sufficient variety, colour and musicality (or rather rhythm, since Scott was completely unmusical and lacks a finer feeling for the sound of language in spite of his frequent use of alliteration and other features based on sound) so that the verse form never gives the impression of being a trivial addition or something that is even foreign to the narrative. It does not intrude and after a time is no longer noticeable; it is simply part of the poem and in its own way serves the story as a whole.

More poetic structuring would have been wasted effort, not only because the public he was aiming at was neither particularly aware of differences of this nature nor very interested in form, but also because chamber-music nuances cannot be heard in a loud piece for a large orchestra, which is what all Scott's verse narratives are. Less attention to the poetic form would have

reduced the whole verse structure to a superfluous addition. Here the middle
road was the only road that led to Rome, and it is both wrong and anachronistic to dispute this.[10] If on account of Scott's carelessness and poetic eclec-
ticism the formal structure of the verse was not quite satisfying to the
contemporary critics, who judged everything from a classicistic standpoint,
and is not quite satisfying to us today, since we have experienced an escalation
of the cult of form to the point of *poésie pure*, this does not mean that it is totally
unattractive and adds nothing to the content. While it is true that the rhythmic
effect of his 'light horseman sort of stanza' is coarse and often achieved by
some rather dubious rhymes, it is nevertheless the appropriate accompaniment
to the knightly and martial themes.[11]

More important than the verse language for the analysis of the genre are
the other means whereby Scott attempts to avoid both the uniformity of the
old romances and the monotony of the conventional epic style. While with
the division of the stanzas a remnant of the 'design attitude' that characterized
eighteenth-century poetry has been retained as fitting for the 'description of
scenery and manners', the dynamism of the plot at the same time carries
everything on without lingering over individual images. We cannot go into
detail here about Scott's skill at linking events and maintaining suspense or
the balance he instinctively achieves between description and narrative, and
in the *Lay*, in any case, these things have not yet been fully mastered. Nevertheless they were responsible to a large extent for the success of the poem,
as will be seen from comparison with different manners of proceeding in later
verse narratives, and were even more important than the vital functional
connection of all details with the main plot, which Scott sometimes omits to
make. The contemporary critics were only too keen to find Scott, the darling
of the public, guilty of such offences. Jeffrey established, for example, that
large sections of *The Lay of the Last Minstrel* were unimportant for the plot.[12]
He admits that in *Marmion* the plot is handled better, but here he reprimands
the poet for many insertions that cannot be classified as 'relief' but 'almost
as substance'.[13] These offences are of no consequence and no longer
noticeable when we read the poems today. Everything that Scott writes is
designed to grip the reader – the consumer of literature and not the specialist
– as he reads but not to make him think much about what he has read
afterwards. Hazlitt criticized Scott for this,[14] but it was precisely what Scott
intended: he wanted to be a minstrel and not a divinely inspired prophet or
an alchemist in search of the exquisite form. When the minstrel has sung for
the public before him, he has achieved his goal. He must know how to grip
his audience as they listen to him, and this is something Scott knows how to do.
The suspense of the main plot, created through obvious, established methods,
acts as a strong draw, but only while the reader is in the midst of it. However,
when Scott wants to interest the reader for a while in a detail that does not
belong to it – a subplot, a description of scenery, a pageant – the main plot

is interrupted without any difficulty and with no damage to the overall effect. These diversions are brief and skilfully produced, so that the reader is immediately enticed to follow them. So one reads on, drawn from subject to subject, never led away for long from the main story and always eager for the next development, and never bored or retreating to a critical distance even while one is being diverted from the main story. One also reads quickly: all Scott's works are designed for fast reading where the reader becomes deeply involved with the story, rather than looking at it from the outside.[15] In all of them continuity is what counts, and this is the main difference between the poetry of Scott's generation and that of the previous one.

For this reason it was neither painful nor difficult for Scott to make the transition to the prose novel: interest in the form and the detached examination of the artistic design or pattern became even more subsidiary to involvement in the story in prose works than it had been in the verse narratives. This was seen very clearly by Christopher North in 1827[16] when he listed the advantages of prose for Scott: it was faster to write, and hence could contain more material; it was less exclusive so that subjects and characters could be included that were ruled out in poetry; and it was more suited to Scott's realism (i.e., interest in every kind of real-life material) than verse. North did, it is true, regret the loss of intensive passion and vivid imagination, for which there is more scope in poetry. However, it may be added that since Scott did not possess great quantities of either the one or the other (a shortcoming that, as he best knew himself, excluded him from the highest poetic achievements) the prose novel was best suited to his talents. From 1814, therefore, he wrote prose.

The individual scenes or images in Scott's romances are lovingly and artistically drawn within the dynamic framework to which they are subordinated. For his descriptions of landscapes he makes do with very little space, always of course using the same simple means. But when E. M. Forster says that Scott's 'rocks are of cardboard' and 'the tempest is turned on with one hand while [he] scribbles away ... with the other' working in some erudite association,[17] this might perhaps be true of the passage from the *Antiquary* that Forster has before him; for the verse narratives (at any rate the early ones up to and including *Rokeby*) it is unfair. To judge Scott thus is to forget that he was no literary revolutionary like Wordsworth or Coleridge, and therefore felt he should put in erudite comparisons to satisfy the classic tastes of the most literate of his readers. This is one of the ways in which he attempted to refine the 'rough' old romance material. This judgement of him also unjustly focuses on the few obligatory, fashionable Gothic landscapes and ignores Scott's many descriptions of nature, so fresh that they are obviously drawn from the poet's own experience and observation,[18] accustomed as he was to hunt and ride in the woods and mountains where his ancestors the Scotts of Buccleuch, whose story the *Lay* tells, fought their border battles.

The weakening of the dividing line between the narrative and the dramatic and lyrical in the interest of greater variety and shading in the story occurs in Scott's works as it did in Southey's. In the first canto of the *Lay* there is a 'dramatic' dialogue between two spirits of the elements which is not far removed in type from the conversation of the spirits in *The Ancient Mariner* and the dialogues in *Thalaba* as well as similar situations in the poetic dramas, that came later and were related to the verse narrative, e.g., in *Manfred* or *Prometheus Unbound*. In the fifth canto the calls of the heralds and the two army commanders for a duel are given dramatic emphasis, and in the sixth canto the ballads sung by the knights in the singing competition and the *Dies Irae* of the choir (translated) are lyrical intervals in the plot. These non-narrative passages are often so tenuously linked with the main plot that there is a temptation to wonder whether they are not remnants from some of his earlier poetry that the poet has worked in. The last canto even gives the impression of having been tacked on, as the material has nothing to do with the actual story. Later on, with the songs in *The Lady of the Lake* and *Rokeby* such insertions are blended in much better and made more rigorously subservient to the narrative.[19]

By calling his poems metrical romances, Scott was able to introduce all these changes of form, as well as a lot of subject matter that had not previously featured in epic poetry, without laying himself open, as Southey had, to constant accusations that he was ignoring epic rules. Only later, in the Introduction to the first edition of the anonymously published *Bridal of Triermain* in 1813, does he let it be known that even he had a revival of the epic in mind with his 'Romantic Poetry'.[20] In the meantime of course the *Lay* had been followed by other works which were better entitled to be called 'combined and regular narrative' than his first poem of this type, which, as Scott clearly emphasized, could not be measured by such a standard.

The phenomenal success of the *Lay* – over 30,000 copies in eight editions were sold within five years – showed how correctly Scott had assessed the poetry situation and the needs of the English reading public. The subsequent history of Scott the 'Romancer' is nothing but a repetition or expansion of this same generic formula, a repetition of the same attempt to win the approval of the readers, for whom he supplied exactly what they expected of him, and of the same enthusiastic response – until the day, eight years later, when his sales went down as a greater poet drew the crowds: Byron. For eight years Scott held the English in his thrall with a form of poetry that they would have rejected only forty years earlier as being primitive, written with little regard to form, and trivial in its content. For eight years he proved to literature specialists and critics, who were expressing cautious reservations, that with the radical political and economic changes a new age had also dawned in literature, where it was not the voices of a few experts that counted, but the support of the masses. For eight years almost all the poets in England attempted to profit from Scott's success or at least improve their own less successful works a little with gleanings from his style. There were hundreds of exact imitations, and there were a few original syntheses of his type of poetry with other elements: classic verse forms or genres, exotic, Italian or contemporary material and messages of deeper significance. All of these developments show that literary tastes at the beginning of the century were dominated by two diametrically opposed principles: a tendency towards fashion, with an attendant loss of individual, artistic profile, and a constant demand for something new and original.

And at the end of these eight years the genre split into two separate branches according to these two prevailing tendencies, an 'original' branch, whereby the genre was dissolved and the positive qualities it had introduced developed into new forms and objectives (which naturally often entailed sacrificing popularity); and an 'unoriginal' branch, that modified the genre without changing its basic structure until the public had had more than enough of it, and it too became unpopular. The first of the two alternatives was beyond Scott's capabilities, and he abandoned the second after a few increasingly timorous attempts, because he saw it would not last. He went where success was already beckoning and began writing novels.

A more exact explanation of these processes will have to wait until the last chapter, and the closer examination of developments within the genre itself. For the present we will return to our account of the external developments. Scott knew only too well the limitations of what he had launched with the *Lay*. Even in the Preface to this poem he had already mentioned the 'plan of the Ancient Metrical Romance' and the historical and descriptive aspects it involved as an alibi for the lack of taut and strictly functional handling of the plot, a sophisticated poetic technique and serious machinery.

The critics accepted this special pleading: in his review of *The Lay of the last Minstrel*[21] Francis Jeffrey is kindly disposed towards Scott and confirms that he has succeeded in refining the old generic model. His imagery is more compact and more appropriate, his material finer, his taste better, and his feelings more worthy than those of the original romancers. The longer descriptions – which Jeffrey is not so comfortable about – are at least rendered interesting by sentimental associations and finer feelings and the romance genre has in any case been in general 'greatly improved in point of brevity and selection' by Scott. Individual passages are quoted as 'illustration of the prodigious improvement which the style of the old romances is capable of receiving from a more liberal admixture of pathetic sentiments and gentle affections'. Comparison with the conventional epic and the assessment of the new genre according to epic rules are missing entirely from this first review. When Jeffrey calls many things ludicrous and uninteresting as well as superfluous to the plot, he is not defending any Aristotelian rules but rather an absolute standard of values for narrative poetry. Individual aspects do of course make him uncomfortable about this all-too-carefree 'romantic' versifying: he criticizes Scott for the unclassical verse, the careless style, the regional aspects and in particular the machinery (this word is in fact taken from the terminology of the epic theoreticians). The gnome story is a constant hindrance to the plot and to the poet. It is vulgar and the reader is given the impression that the minstrel only worked it into his lay when he left the castles to go to the peasants.

Three years after the *Lay* Scott presented his next romance to the public: *Marmion – A Tale of Flodden Field*. It can be seen from the Introduction to the First Edition (1808), and from the verse epistles to his friends with which he introduced each of the six cantos, what he had been praised for and what he had been criticized for in the meantime: 'The present story turns upon the private adventure of a fictitious character; but it is called a Tale of Flodden Field, because the hero's fate is connected with that memorable defeat, and the causes which led to it.' Had the recollection of Goethe's *Götz* encouraged him to give the historical framework of this second verse narrative more general interest? Had he been told that a fairy-tale like the *Lay* was too lightweight as reading for adults? Had he been referred to Homer, Virgil, Spenser and Milton or had he been persuaded that as an epic poet he should stick to true and important historical data? All of this was probably the case in some way or another (the clearest evidence of such advice is contained in the warnings of his friend W. Erskine, quoted in the introductory letter to Canto III).

Scott rejected these attempts to influence him. He was clever enough not to let himself be led astray by well-meaning friends and the uncertain prospect of higher honours: the special pleading of the *Lay* Introduction is repeated in the Introduction (1808) to *Marmion*. 'Any historical narrative, far more an attempt at epic composition exceeded [the author's] plan of a romantic tale.' However, he took what he could use and considered likely to increase his success from the advice given him: 'yet he may be permitted to hope ... that an attempt to paint the manners of the feudal times upon a broader scale and in the course of a more interesting story, will not be unacceptable to the public'.

The dangerous label epic, which would immediately bind the poetry to very specific requirements, is thus once again firmly rejected, and again it seems to be the description of historic customs that Scott wants to place in the foreground. He is nevertheless no longer content to present a general picture of a society in the guise of a fairy-tale, but wants to focus on a particular national historical event – the victory of the English over King James IV of Scotland on 9 September 1513. The framework is to be expanded and the 'private' plot given more weight.

In three of the six introductory letters to the cantos (Cantos I, III and V), Scott protects his poetic method and hence his modest genre from judgement by standards that are too high and outlines its field: it ranks far below the epics of the classic age,[22] also the works of those great English poets who transformed 'romantic legends' into immortal poems – Spenser, Milton, Dryden (who would have written a great work based on the Arthurian legend if a corrupt court and foolish king had not forced him to choose more transitory genres such as satire, licentious songs and comedy). He leaves no doubt in the reader's mind that he considers the romance a more modest form of poetry than the genres which have as their aim the portrayal and extolment of exciting national events and personalities of ancient and modern history. He mentions the death of the Duke of Brunswick in 1806 at Jena as a subject for an elegy in the classic style and the deeds of the crusaders, Charles XII of Sweden and Nelson as subjects for epic or encomiastic poetry.

In each of the three letters mentioned, he also puts forward his own arguments in defence of his poetry: in Canto I he cites Spenser, Milton and Dryden as examples of the fact that even the great poets did not think the world of romance was unworthy of them. In Canto III (to William Erskine) he refers – as do the Lake Poets – to the driving force of inspiration, for which, however, he offers no philosophical and metaphysical interpretation, but attributes it to his natural disposition and the habits of youth. Moreover, the minstrel who entertains us has as much right to exist as the great poet, in the same way as there is a place for both wild flowers and garden flowers. In Canto V (to George Ellis, whom he greets as someone who shares his ideas and thanks for being his guide, pattern and friend) he attempts an apology for escapism – the political troubles of the present (i.e., the threatened invasion of Napoleon) are perhaps as illusory as the magic of the old lays in which he takes refuge from the present – and compares his stories with the medieval stained-glass windows, which were also not designed according to any fixed plan, but nevertheless glow with colour and have a greatness of their own.

How then does *Marmion* differ in type from the *Lay*, i.e., in what way is it broader in scale, as Scott himself described it? As promised in the Introduction of 1808, it always remains within the scope of a romance, and Scott almost systematically avoids those features that might bring him close to the old epic. It is assumed that readers know the historical situation with respect to England and Scotland in the year 1513 and hardly any further light is shed on it in the poem. For Scott it is only of value as background that gives his 'private' story a stronger definition than the fairy-tale atmosphere of the *Lay* and involves the hero in a political event that leads him to be justifiably punished, but at the same time allows him to die honourably. This hero is at the centre of the plot (this was not the case in the *Lay*). In this way a greater unity is achieved than in the *Lay*, although this unity of course bears more resemblance to an adventure novel than to an epic or a court romance: Marmion is not virtuous like Aeneas or generous and chivalrous like Arthur, he is not a great lover like Tristram or Launcelot and not pure like Perceval.

Marmion is rather a combination of the sinister fascination of the demonic lord in the Gothic novels and the daredevil amorality of the heroes of the 'German' robber dramas.

This is the first time in the history of the romantic verse narrative that what was to become the fashionable male character of this period makes its appearance. The figure is still naively drawn with no psychological foundation, but it already has the main characteristics of the hero burdened with guilt and the noble criminal which was later to become the central figure of Byron's works. The personality traits of a Werther or a René are still missing, as well as the psychological, even autobiographical reality which in Byron's work gives this character greater depth; we are still closer to Mrs Radcliffe than to *Manfred* or *Cain*. The unreality and melodramatic portrayal of this hero is particularly noticeable in the inadequate, psychologically unbelievable causes given for his criminal behaviour. Although he is introduced as being of noble birth, brave, rich and proud, and is all the more attractive for his grimness, it emerges that he is guilty of malicious slander, political intrigue, and forgery of documents, unscrupulous greed and highly dishonourable behaviour towards the two ladies of his choice. Scott himself very soon noticed that such crimes were not characteristic of the feudal age.[23] It was not, however, in his nature to rework something he had already completed, and *Marmion* was thus issued without revision, to delight a public that was offended neither by inconsistent psychology nor such subtle historical anachronisms in literature of this type. Even in the unscrupulous Constance de Beverley (who is nevertheless pardonable by virtue of her love and dependency) it is pointless to look for more complex personality traits.

With *The Lay of the Last Minstrel* Scott succeeded in reviving the medieval romance and at the same time introducing elements of popular Gothic literature of English and German origin into good poetry. He had thus successfully avoided the danger of being automatically labelled an epic poet at a time when poems were being judged and analysed according to classic definitions of genre, which would have been to his disadvantage. Although in the Introduction and the verse epistles of *Marmion* he had taken the same precautions, in this second work he was unable to prevent the expansion he had risked for the sake of greater success with the public – in addition to the greater emphasis on historical aspects and concentration on the hero, the greater length of the poem, the more considered and more unified plot, the somewhat more refined language[24] and the greater seriousness of the work might also be included here – from producing precisely that reaction from the critics that he wanted to avoid: Francis Jeffrey attacked the poem and the whole 'genre' summoning the laws of good, i.e., for him, classical taste to his aid.

In his review (*ER*, 23, article 1, April 1808) Jeffrey initially concedes that *Marmion* is certainly not worse than the *Lay*, which he had praised.

He immediately adds, however, that in this second work, that claims to be 'more ambitious', does not have the same sweetness and has a better plot and stronger characters, the basic defects of Scott's type of narrative poetry are more obvious. He then goes on to list these defects:

1. The plot is interrupted too often by tedious descriptions, which lack the freshness and true-to-life nature of the old romances, and instead sound very dry and academic.

2. The poetry is not all of the same level but is in general lacking in delicate taste and elegant fantasy. Even the high points are of very uneven merit.

3. The material would perhaps be sufficient for a ballad, but is not sufficient for such a long narrative poem. It is in addition unpoetical and is twisted at the end to bring it to a violent conclusion. The sentence: 'The events of an epic narrative should all be of a broad, clear and palpable description' is obviously directed at the method of creating suspense which leaves the resolving of all mysteries – the appearance of ghosts, disguise, the return of someone believed dead and criminal intrigue – to the end of the poem. This reminds Jeffrey of a bad German novel. Such things as the crimes of Marmion and Constance are not just anachronisms (as Scott had himself admitted) but altogether unworthy of poetical treatment, and so also are the details about medieval life that even extend to the kitchen boys. Unworthy of poetical treatment, as it becomes clear from the context, means not suitable for an epic.

4. The style bears resemblances to Schiller, to the weakest poetasters of the sixteenth century and (which for Jeffrey is just as bad) to Wordsworth.[25] It is low and vulgar and the speed with which it has been written is unpleasantly obvious.

5. A further criticism is directed at the Introductory Letters, which Jeffrey does not think are a success partly because they are too dependent on the period in which they have been written (and in fact, as C. H. Herford very correctly says,[26] their Biedermeier tone exposes the melodramatic unreality of the plot's sinister elements as a concession to current literary fashion) partly because they express political opinions contrary to his own, and probably partly because to him as a purist the insertion of subjective, informal poetic epistles dealing with private matters into an objective, epic story is absurd. It cannot be denied here that while the letters may be of interest to us as historical and biographical documents, for the majority of readers all they do is underline the discrepancy in Scott's poems that Hazlitt described as follows: 'The forms are old and uncouth; but the spirit is effeminate and frivolous.'[27]

Even more interesting than this reaction, which is not just born of a classicistic taste but evidently also of a feeling for 'epic' traditions, is what Jeffrey says at the end of this review. Here he extends the discussion beyond the individual poem and expresses his fears that with his works Scott might start a new school of poetry which would cause a lot of problems. In his opinion this type of 'historical' poetry was still only a fashion amongst fine ladies and gentlemen, comparable with the nature poetry of Dr Erasmus Darwin, that had soon faded out. However, Scott would one day no longer be the only writer of this type of poetry as he was now with no one daring to imitate the person who was well known as its inventor, and it was then that English poetry might be in great danger, with the English public overlooking the obvious weaknesses and developing an unselective taste for 'chivalrous legends' and 'romances in irregular rhymes'. Then Scott would certainly be imitated as much as Mrs Radcliffe and Schiller, resulting in a split in poetic development which would not be healed until the extravagances of the worst imitators had revealed just how inferior this new branch was. 'We admire Scott and all the others who may fall prey to this modern sect, but we rue the day when such talents were corrupted by nonsense about magic and knights of bygone days.'

After the *Lay* Jeffrey had hoped that the next time Scott would progress to a worthier form of poetry. Now he feels compelled to rally him and all the other contemporary poets back to the standard of a classical or at least neo-classical style. He fought a losing battle. In spite of his protests, and in spite of a general tendency of those in literary circles to look for defects in *Marmion*,[28] in spite of the mockery of Byron, who in *English Bards and Scotch Reviewers* (1809) called *Marmion* 'A mighty mixture of the great and base' and a 'stale romance' (V. 166 ff.)[29] and like Jeffrey complained about the decline of public taste and the poets' business orientation, in particular Scott's, 36,000 copies of *Marmion* were sold between 1808 and 1825. In view of this resounding success, Jeffrey was obliged to be less harsh in his judgement of Scott in his later reviews, and the fact that he did not include the *Marmion* review in his collected *Contributions to the Edinburgh Review* of 1844 almost amounts to a capitulation. The envious literary experts who had picked holes in *Marmion* were forced to acknowledge Scott as England's leading poet. Byron too, who was still expressing his displeasure at the current developments:

> These are the themes that claim our plaudits now,
> These are the bards to whom the Muse must bow,
> While Milton, Dryden, Pope, alike forgot,
> Resign their hallow'd bays to Walter Scott
> (*English Bards*, V. 181 ff.)

was soon to till the soil of the 'stale romance' himself, although not without revolutionizing it first. Much of his fame was in fact to come from his works in this sector, and his attitude to Scott's poetry therefore also very soon changed. In a letter to Murray on 3 February 1816 he called *Marmion* inimitable and at the same time admitted that in *Parsina* (stanza 14) he was guilty of unconscious plagiarism from *Marmion* II. In his famous pyramid of poets[30] he put Scott at the top and in 1821 dedicated his poem *Cain* to him.

Can Scott be blamed if he continued as he had begun? Can it be denied that in his next work, *The Lady of the Lake* (1810), he excelled himself and produced perhaps the best example of his own romance form that was possible without drastically altering its basic design? He took Jeffrey's *Marmion* review badly, and this was what first prompted the founding of the *Quarterly Review* (1809), the idea of which was to introduce a more moderate, politically less partisan and from a literary point of view, more progressive tone into the assessment of newer poetry than was customary in the *Edinburgh Review*. In spite of this he erred neither in the direction of a lifelong passionate hate of his critical opponents, nor in that of exaggerated self-confidence: in the Introduction to *The Lady of the Lake* of 1830 he declared that he still refused to be drawn into literary feuds about his works, since his popularity had never deceived him into thinking his style of poetry was more than just an 'amusement' with which he sought to stay in favour with the public purely by giving it what it obviously wanted.

It is not possible here to go into this and Scott's subsequent works in greater detail, and it is also not strictly necessary, since they introduced little that was new into the genre. The only exception is *The Vision of Don Roderick* (1811), which must be dealt with separately. In the other metrical romances – after the *Lady* came *Rokeby* (1812), *The Lord of the Isles* (1815) and the two smaller, anonymously published epyllions *The Bridal of Triermain* (1813)[31] and *Harold the Dauntless* (1817) – there are no major deviations from the generic type established in the *Lay* and *Marmion*, although small innovations are often introduced. In *Marmion* the cantos have headings which indicate where the action is taking place. In the *Lady* where, as in the first two poems, each canto covers a day, the headings are related more to the plot than to the scene, and in *Rokeby* they have been abandoned again. In the *Lady* and *Rokeby* the *Christabel* verse is replaced almost throughout by more regular iambic tetrameter couplets. In *The Lady of the Lake* the framework story of the *Lay* and the dedicational epistles of *Marmion* are replaced by two apostrophes to the 'Harp of the North', which Scott probably inserted instead of the call upon the Muses traditional in epic poetry and which open and close the story (he may have wanted to give his poem the dignity of the epic without being caught in an obvious imitation of classic models). While these two apostrophes each occupy three Spenser stanzas, the cantos are always begun with one or two Spenser stanzas which either reveal the time of day in an image from nature or contain a reflection (as in Canto III). In *Rokeby*, where the division into days is retained, the images from nature or reflections introducing the cantos are, however, written in the same metre as the rest of the text.

For *Rokeby* Scott leaves the Scottish Highlands and Lowlands where his previous poems were set, and the sixteenth century, and chooses material from Yorkshire at the time of the battle of Marston Moor. This gives him the opportunity of introducing new but just as fashionable and interesting characters: in addition to the lovers, with whom, as usual, he has unlimited sympathy, and the obligatory sinister villain, Oswald, there are also the former pirate Bertram and the lovesick young singer Edmund who has joined the pirates in his desperation and who is the vehicle for a wealth of varied songs (the two latter are variations of the usual brave scoundrels of the Marmion kind); and above all there is the noble but weak and melancholic Wilfrid, who sings to the moon of his love and who has to die at the end, to atone for the deeds of his villainous father and to set the beautiful Matilda free to marry her more manly and of course preferred admirer Redmond.[32]

According to Lockhart[33] Scott himself maintained that in each of his longer poems he had focused on a different aspect: in the *Lay* on the style, in *Marmion* on the descriptions, in the *Lady* on the plot, and in *Rokeby* on the characters. This is not at all obvious from a comparison of the poems, since the main ingredients of Scott's poems are always the story, the setting, a particular historical epoch and the unmistakable Scott style; and his characters are always effective although flat, even when they are intended to be complex. Slight changes in the quantities of these ingredients are of no consequence. Scott's claim once again shows the extent to which this poet tried to meet the contradictory demands of his public, who wanted works that followed the established fashion in poetry but at the same time wanted constant variety, novelty and originality, and how he manoeuvred between them. (He later proceeded in a very similar way with his novels, constantly changing the themes.) According to this principle, which had the public eagerly awaiting every new work by Scott even though he basically always offered them the same thing, he selected for *The Lord of the Isles* an episode in history that was well known to every Scot and satisfied Scottish national feeling without being unacceptable to the English reader: the return of Bruce to Scotland in 1307.[34]

In *Harold* he goes even further back in history to the invasions of the Danes in the ninth century. The *Bridal* on the other hand combines a legend of Arthur and Merlin with a framework plot set in more recent times; this gives Scott the opportunity of occasionally introducing an ironic tone, which is not at all successful. In general there is a noticeable loss of naivety and enthusiasm in the later verse narratives (after *The Lady of the Lake*) and in the form there is evidence of either repetition or even greater carelessness. When Scott tries to extend the scope of the poems he sometimes goes beyond the limits of his capabilities and no longer has an instinct for avoiding this.

These lapses had notable consequences: while *Rokeby* is still almost on the same level as *The Lady of the Lake* – it is only less attractive because it is not set in Scotland, which is Scott's true domain, and because of the strong 'German novel' elements – *The Lord of the Isles* is the first obvious failure. George Ellis, who reviewed it in the *Quarterly Review*,[35] got to the heart of the matter when he said that Scott's basic mistake in this work was to graft a 'domestic plot' onto heroic material: the return of Bruce. The reverse procedure was possible and even desirable: 'private' episodes could and should occasionally be inserted into epic material. But to use heroic material as a peg to hang a romance on was not done: in tales of heroes private fates aroused little interest. If Scott had written an epic poem about Bannockburn and merely woven in the story of Edith of Lorn, he might have been successful; but to make Bannockburn an episode in the private romance of a few fictional characters was impossible, and one level of the plot destroyed the other. In generic terms what this means is that Scott tried to flirt with the heroic epic for the sake of popularity, and his failure demonstrated conclusively that an alliance between the epic and the romance was out of the question.[36]

In the *Bridal* and in *Harold* Scott flirts with the salon and is equally unsuccessful. We have already spoken of the ironic tone of the first poem, which was probably an attempt to imitate the elegant Italian school that was then becoming fashionable (imitations of Ariosto, Pulci and Berni) and was later to have a strong influence on Byron and Hunt. Scott sets the rough story of *Harold the Dauntless*, 'Count Witikind's Son', in the framework of an apostrophe, written in Spenser stanzas, to the fashionable illness 'Ennui, or, as our mothers call'd thee, Spleen'. In both cases the illusion created in the reader's mind of the naive world of the old romance is unpleasantly shattered by the sudden intrusion of the modern mentality, and the story is revealed as 'rubbish masses of colossal trifle', as the review in *Blackwood's Magazine* (1, article 1, April 1817) called the two poems, while conceding that the art of grouping figures in landscapes or rooms that brought to mind Murillo and Caravaggio, did to some extent save the works. It was clearly beyond Scott's capabilities to make capital out of such clashes as did the German masters of romantic irony. The decline of the later Scott romances as a result of unsuccessful expansion of the generic framework was accompanied by an increasing lack of discipline in the form.

In the *Bridal* and *The Lord of the Isles* there is a return to the *Christabel* metre, probably because Scott could write it faster and better than the couplets of the intervening works. *Harold*, however, is the untidiest metric jumble he ever produced: the first canto is written throughout in anapaestic tetrameter couplets and the following five mix this rhythm with the old 'light horseman' metre and an arbitrary number of Spenser stanzas (three to twelve), at the beginning of all the cantos except the second one, which are sometimes used as a reflective introduction and are sometimes part of the story. To complete the mixture there is a heroic couplet at the close of Canto III which describes the curtain falling at the end of the previous scene and the scene change for the next episode of the story. In order to make the poem look at least as if it has been rounded off, the last couplet of the story (before the resumption of the apostrophe to ennui) takes up the anapaestic rhythm of the beginning of the story. All of this indicates that Scott's pleasure in his genre declined in the same measure as his success. The first signs of this were in 1812 when *Rokeby* was published; it was coolly received by the critics and only 1,500 copies were sold. When the attempt to boost the metrical romance by superimposing heroic interest failed in *The Lord of the Isles*, Scott no longer took the genre seriously: *Harold* is almost a parody of Scott's previous works with its unsystematic form and narrative, its cheap horror effects, consciously trivial ending[37] and, as *Blackwood's Magazine* described it,[38] 'very affected and unnatural [device], now rendered trite by repetition, of making his hero wed his page, who turns out to be a lady in disguise'.

Scott attributed the decline of his popularity in part to the fact that the public were satiated with his own poems and even more with the many imitations, which, when they were good, showed how easy this type of verse narrative was to produce, and when they were bad exaggerated the weaknesses to such a degree that the whole style was exposed to ridicule, as Jeffrey had already predicted in the *Marmion* review of the *Edinburgh Review*. He did to some extent see that the free rhyming system that he had introduced into English poetry had caused the correctness of the language to be badly neglected, particularly with respect to word order, on which correct grammar depends, so that the public were now demanding greater discipline with respect to form.[39] However, he primarily ascribed his waning popularity – with good reason – to the arrival on the scene of Byron, who possessed the same talent for success as he did, but in addition offered the reader more profound ideas, a more disciplined form, original new subjects and more opportunity for involvement in passions and psychological problems.[40]

One of Scott's 'narrative poems' has been left to the end of this brief survey of the generic aspects of his verse narratives because it is different from the others: *The Vision of Don Roderick* of 1811. This also represents an attempt by Scott to enlarge the scope of his metrical romance and use his special form of verse narrative for something that amounted to more than mere 'amusement'.

The relatively short work – it consists of three parts and comprises a total of ninety-three Spenser stanzas – is actually an occasional poem on a political theme, the earnings from which were to go to needy victims of the Portugese war. Descriptions of events in the history of Portugal and Spain from the time of King Rodrigo, who had also featured in works by Landor and Southey, up until the time Scott was writing, are presented in the guise of a vision of the future, of which examples are to be found in epic poetry, from Virgil's *Aeneid* (Book 6) to Ariosto's *Orlando Furioso* (Bradamante's vision at Merlin's grave in the third canto) and Milton's *Paradise Lost* (Adam's vision of the future in Books 11 and 12). Even Gray used the basic structure of the epic vision in his *Bard*, as did Landor in *Gebir*, and in political poetry a variant of it had been employed since the Middle Ages.[41] In Scott's poem the vision takes on a very romantic form (according to legend Roderick opened an old vault and saw there a vision of his own downfall); towards the end, however, when Scott has arrived at the present, it is discarded in favour of a homage to Wellington, the victor of Talavera.[42]

Here we see once again that the Scott type of romance does not tolerate the introduction either of lofty, epic-style elements or of any modern theme. For the former combination it is too light and for the latter it is too dependent on the illusion of naivety and remoteness of time and place. In both cases therefore there is a discrepancy that threatens both the attractiveness of the 'romantic' aspects and the purpose of the poems. If it was going to offer some kind of interpretation of the contemporary world, the romantic verse narrative would have to drop the entertaining, exciting and sensational element, the one basic characteristic which in Scott's work dominates all the others. The 'romantic' side had to acquire more depth and the whole idea behind it had to change from the way Scott interpreted it to the way we interpret it today. When Scott combines romanticism with topical subjects, the romantic element is reduced to a mere external structure.[43]

The contemporary reviews of Scott's verse narratives, which have already been quoted extensively, are among the most interesting to be found in the old periodicals. They frequently anticipate future developments and are often very perceptive about historico-cultural trends. Unfortunately it is not possible to give more than a summary of their content here.

Three of Jeffrey's Scott reviews have already been dealt with: his review of the *Lay*,[44] of *Marmion*,[45] and of *The Lord of the Isles*.[46] The most important is the review of *The Lady of the Lake*.[47] He is obviously trying to be very just to Scott after the aggressive *Marmion* review, and indeed the way he tries to understand Scott's position and attributes all his characteristcs to the two basic requirements of the day – popularity and overcoming the difficulties arising from the over-use of all poetic material and forms – could not be fairer. Equally admirable is the analysis of the ways in which, according to Jeffrey, modern poets have tried to resolve these difficulties, by resorting to greater exactness in the description of scenery and characters, more courageous analysis of the passions, and distortion of nature and passions according to some fantastical theory of their own. With these four manifestations Jeffrey is of course thinking of specific contemporary poets: Crabbe, Byron and the Lakers. Here he very cleverly spotted in the cultural situation of his day the beginnings of major lines of development which were to continue through the nineteenth century. He sensed the connection between the focus of the story[48] and the increasing departure from natural and habitual experience in romantic poetry. On the other hand he sees how Scott, by his very nature and his striving for popularity, is prevented in his treatment of sensational material from going beyond what the general public can comprehend and identify with (Jeffrey had quite often criticized Scott for offending against this law of popularity). He recognizes the necessity of satisfying specific tastes which led Scott to write in the way he did and also the attractions of this kind of poetry that is not seeking to be great. At the same time, however, he also laments the decline of form and the tendency to want to dazzle the reader with facile and false splendour, things he feels are consequences of the exaggerated interest in the story.[49] He excuses Scott's thoughtless borrowing of material that has already been used – Shakespeare's careless richness, the harshness and antique simplicity of the minstrel romances, the homeliness of the ballads and the sentimental glitter of modern poetry – by saying that this talented poet, born later into an age when the poetic means had been exhausted, was forced to borrow what, had he lived in the time of the minstrels, he would certainly have given away generously and of his own accord. Where Jeffrey can praise, he does so unstintingly; he praises the brevity of the descriptions, which are not just lists of things like Crabbe's, but are sketched with few strokes and illuminated with moral aspects; the characters, which are fresh and pleasing and not imbued with false eminence through an excess of seriousness (here he is obviously thinking of Southey); the originality and the 'finish' Scott gives all his popular material. Where be believes that criticism is due, he is merciless. He draws attention to the unrealistic concentration on 'poetic' figures (kings, knights, damsels in distress, warriors and magicians, etc.) which excludes other important areas of human life such as the lives of the poor or the family. He also declares that it is a myth to believe that there is an abundance of important ideas concealed beneath Scott's easy style, as people were inclined to do, and he makes the devastating observation that the examples of bad taste are not so noticeable simply because there are so many of them.

The only contemporary critic who resembles Jeffrey in his assessment of Scott is Hazlitt. In *Lectures on the English Poets* (1818 – 19) he calls Scott's verse narratives 'history or tradition in masquerade', distinguishes between success and true worth and attributes Scott's popularity to the fact that he 'has just hit the town between the romantic and the fashionable'. He closes with the remark that this poet lacks the greatness that would transform other minds: 'The notes to his poems are just as entertaining as the poems themselves, and his poems are only entertaining.'[50]

While in the *Lectures* Hazlitt had acknowledged many aspects of Scott's romances under the influence of their huge success, when he wrote about him in *The Spirit of the Age* (1825) the situation had already changed: Scott's verse narratives had in the meantime gone out of fashion, or rather been put in the shade by his novels. In Hazlitt's view they would have lost popularity even without this substitute. They lacked the creative impulse of great poetry and had translated truths about feelings and life situations 'into a tinkling sound, a tinsel commonplace'. His assessment culminates in an important though terminologically confusing observation about the genre of Scott's works: 'The Epics are not poems, so much as metrical romances.'[51]

If these two important critics judged Scott as a poet much as we do today, the reviewers of the *Quarterly Review*, in particular his friends Ellis and Erskine, were naturally over-enthusiastic about his work. G. Ellis' review of *The Lady of the Lake*[52] consists not only of praise of his friend but also of an apology characteristic of the writer of *Specimens of Early English Metrical Romances* for the romance as a special genre with its own laws, and a defence of the modern examples of this genre against judgement according to the standards of epic poetry, which, although Jeffrey evidently does not see this, are not applicable here. The whole controversy revolves around the crucial question of whether the medieval romance genre is a poetic form at all suited to modern times – even if it belongs to a 'subordinate class of literary honours' – or whether it is too primitive, improbable, unplanned and absurd. Ellis' thoughts on this subject slightly resemble Schiller's aesthetic theories.[53]

The most important points in the other Scott reviews in the *Quarterly Review* have also already been touched on, as also Southey's and Byron's attitude to Scott.[54]

Two more pieces of writing by Scott himself will serve, finally, to round off this study of the true founder of the romantic tale in verse; both examples show clearly how he saw the origination of his genre and the situation that gave rise to it. One is his review of Jane Austen's *Emma* in the *Quarterly Review*, written in October 1815, one year after the appearance of *Waverley*.[55] In addition to the discussion of the bad reputation from which the novel as a genre was still suffering that was quoted earlier in this book,[56] the article defends the entertainment and compensation aspects of novel literature and lists the different functions of the novel of manners and the novel of adventure, but above all firmly establishes the novel genetically as the modern form of the medieval romance. He then considers in some detail the parallels between the romance and the novel in the narrator's manner of proceeding: the necessity of creating ever new suspense in the limited area between the possible or ordinary and the improbable is given as the reason for the abundant material and variety of the novel. As far as sacrificing the unity of the plot was concerned, the romance and the novel were to the epic what the Elizabethan history play was to the tragedy. The generic similarity between the romance and the novel also extends to the sentiments: both portray nature, but it is always *la belle nature*. Hero and heroine, although not idealized, must at least awaken sympathy and admiration in the readers.[57] Recently a kind of novel appeared to be developing that no longer employed the device of creating suspense by alternating danger and rescue in the framework of an adventure; the excitement and edifying effects this produced had worn off as a result of overuse. Scott now gives a detailed description of the wearing-out process of a literary form, in which, in addition to the frequent repetition that leads to over-familiarity, the follies of the bad imitators also play an important part. He speaks from experience – his own experience with his metrical romances, which was also described in the Introduction to *Rokeby* of 1830.[58] He points out that the 'surprise and horror' possibilities of modern material have been used up: there are few enough of these in normal life and what there is (here he lists all the features of German literature, 'robbers, smugglers, bailiffs, caverns, dungeons, and mad-houses') has lost its interest owing to excessive repetition in recent literature. Novelists today are thus turning to material which has not previously been thought at all likely to result in success and profit, or at least not without a great deal of effort and skill on the part of the writer. This explains the origin of Jane Austen's novel of manners.

It is not necessary to describe in detail the relevance of these comments for the verse narrative. The connection with the historico-cultural and sociological aspects of our generic history is obvious. Here Scott is describing the matter-of-fact, almost businesslike adaptation of literature to a social structure changed by the economic and political upheavals of the eighteenth century. Here – when one also bears in mind that the great romantic poets were not very popular – the division of art into consumer goods and interpretations of life, into popular, easy-to-understand works and esoteric works that has continued in an intensified form to the present day is made plainer than ever before. While in Scott's time it was still relatively easy to bridge the gap (the verse form and the historical erudition in his romances are an attempt to take the cheapness from works written with nothing but entertainment in mind), and the two kinds of literature still overlapped,[59] the division had appeared and was soon to become permanent.

The 'market research' slant is less in evidence in the discussion of the generic questions raised by the modern revival of the metrical romance in the Introduction to *The Bridal of Triermain* of 1813. It has already been mentioned that Scott adopted the style and manner of arguing of his friend Erskine in order to pass the anonymous poem off as his own work. This is the same William Erskine whose exhortation to return to the classical genres Scott answered with a defence of the romance in the third verse epistle of *Marmion*. Now he, as it were, puts an apology for this genre in Erskine's mouth and even lets him defend it as the more modern form of the verse epic by comparison with the classic epic poem.

The 'few remarks on what has been called Romantic Poetry' that are made in this Introduction are once again an outline of the history of a particular aspect of literature, similar to the discussion of the novel in the *Emma* review or the discussions of the history of literature in terms of cycles in some of Jeffrey's and Ellis' articles. It is more than likely that this form of critical essay on literature displays the same kind of 'continuity' thinking as the poetry of this period.[60] With the help of the historical outline, Scott clearly establishes how the genre he inaugurated is to be interpreted and in which aspects it differs from the classic epic model. In the Introduction the word romantic is to be understood purely as it was defined in Walkers

Dictionary in 1791: 'Resembling the tales of romance, wild ... fanciful, full
of wild scenery.' Romantic poetry is quite simply the genre of the medieval
-minstrel verse narrative, 'the popularity of which has been revived in the
present days under the auspices, and by the unparalleled success of one
individual' – the words reflect both the pride and the modesty of Scott. The
original purpose of poetry, he continues, was religious or historical, or both.
The epic poets of former times should primarily be regarded as historians
recording the early history of their people, and only later was there a differen-
tiation between the poet, who narrated material of his own invention in verse,
and the chronicler, who handed down facts in prose. The restriction to
historical material was, however, a disadvantage for the early epic poets, since
this material – for example the Trojan Wars – often had a less exciting plot
and even less opportunity for poetic creativity. The duty to be faithful to
history was thus gradually sacrificed by the epic poets to the need for gripping,
colourful narratives and the traditional chronicle of the epic became the
romance.

What Scott-Erskine sees as a hindrance to the epic poet – namely being
bound to specific historical, genealogical and military facts – had, however,
repeatedly been insisted on as an obligatory characteristic of the genre by the
epic theoreticians, who based all their standards on Homer. Scott thinks it
would now be more logical for the present-day narrator, who no longer has
any obligations to fulfil as a chronicler, to liberate himself from these bonds
and take advantage instead of the boundless possibilities of free invention.
If the modern poet could not hope to achieve anything like the artistic quality
of Homer, he should nevertheless not sabotage his own poetic endeavours by
taking over the encumbrances resulting from Homer's mission to record
history, in other words the conventions that, according to the literary critics,
were the essence of the epic. This also always exposed him to comparison with
Homer, which no modern poet could withstand. Here Scott in typical fashion
mixes two crucial reasons for the romantics' dissociation from the epic – their
rejection of the restriction of the epic genre by the neo-classicists and their
awareness that they could produce nothing to equal the achievements of the
classic epic poets. What was described earlier in this book, using W. Kayser's
expression, as the 'world containing' aspect of the great epic, by which was
meant that totality of the beliefs and preferences of its age which nourished
a true epic, is presented here with rationalistic simplification as a mere consequence of the poet's duty as a chronicler, a duty which leads to a stifling
of the imagination, and is rejected as a relic of classicism unsuitable for the
modern poet. While he does see the strong connection between the loss of that
'universal significance' and the narrative poets' descent to the level of
romancers, he regards this descent (in the sense of poetic elevation, not of
quality) as representing progress and as an increase of poetic possibilities.
Although Scott frequently finds the modern poets inferior by comparison with

Homer,[61] he offers no explanation why modern poets cannot hope to equal him. The *mediocritas* of the modern poets is vaguely ascribed to a lack of 'rapture', poetic inspiration and enthusiasm, but the *mediocritas* of the age is noted without explanation.

How then should the romantic poet distance himself from his epic origins? Here Scott gives precise instructions. He should choose simpler and 'more interesting' material. A few characters suffice, since the fate of three or four people, skilfully grouped, has a more penetrating effect than the fate of a society, whatever the level of the problems involved. Scenes between only a few people have more effect on the imagination and emotions of the reader than political conflicts and upheavals which influence the fates of kingdoms. Everyone can become involved with individual fates when they are vividly described, but the fates of great societies of the past, even if this is superior material, are not something the reader can identify with so closely and are thus vaguer and harder to imagine by comparison. This general material also has no effect on the emotions, and this is after all the object of poetry. The poet who generalizes makes no appeal to the emotions and hence deprives himself of his best effects. Scott is not interested in investigating why the fate of an individual is more moving than that of a society. However, in order to defend himself against the accusation of bourgeois narrow-mindedness and egoism, he draws a comparison with moral philosophy, which shows the extent to which certain philosophical attitudes basic to romantic thinking were current in his day: if the fortunes of an individual soldier or two lovers arouse more concern than the life-and-death struggle of whole peoples, this is parallel to the contrast between (to put it in modern terms) 'material value ethics' as interpreted by Herder and the abstract, formal law of virtue of the categorical imperative: the latter may be on a higher plane, but the former provides people with guidelines for use in their daily lives.

While the section of the Introduction to *The Bridal of Triermain* just described contains a highly interesting blend of rationalism and pre-romantic ideas, of a lofty view of poetry and an all-too-human ambition for success with the public, of modesty and self-confidence, and of concise arguments and superficially thought-out consequences, the rest of the text is somewhat disappointing. The further definition of the ways in which 'romantic poetry' differs from the epic should in fact be the most important part of the article, but all it amounts to is a claim for unlimited freedom. Romantic poetry features fictional stories dependent solely upon the tastes and preferences of the poet and beginning and ending where he wants them to. It is neither obliged to deal with supernatural subjects, nor does it reject them. It is free from the technical rules of the epic, since the only laws it obeys are those dictated by clear meaning, good taste and healthy morals, and is conformable to all forms of poetry. The material is not bound to any particular time: it can be set in the past or present, and the characters must not belong to any particular social class; they can be princes or peasants.[62] The author is therefore absolute master over his material, and everything is permissible except offences against art in general, such as ponderousness or unpoetic treatment of the material.

Scott closes with the following remarks. This is what romantic poetry is like, and if today people make unpleasant remarks about it and talk of bad taste, they should first try to understand the basic principles described above. People either complain about the lack of sieges, battles and military action in romantic poems – here it must be said that the current campaigns and heroes are so constantly, vividly present in everyone's thoughts that no help is necessary from fictional poetry (Scott thus gives another, more modern reason for the separation of historical and romantic poetry[63]) – or they complain about the poets' lack of skill: and here one should be fair and acknowledge the modesty of these poets, a modesty which limits them to subjects which always have the charm of novelty about them however differently they are handled, thereby assuring that they at least avoid staleness if not the other weaknesses of this type of poetry that are harder to prevent.

Scott's immediate successors

> The present author, like Bobadil, had taught his trick of fence to a hundred gentlemen (and ladies) who could fence very nearly or quite as well as himself.
>
> Walter Scott in the Introduction to *Rokeby* (1830)

From everything that has been said here about Scott, it is clear that his poetry was considered as something radically new. With, in addition, his great popularity and financial success, it is not surprising that he had a swarm of imitators. In the Introduction to *Rokeby* of 1830, written a number of years after the work was first published, he himself said that the many imitations had harmed him, and that because of them, 'the popularity which once attended the School, as it was called, was now [i.e., 1812] fast decaying'.

Here, as with all literary 'imitations', we must distinguish between poets who processed Scott's ideas in their own individual way, and poets who just copied him. The stimulating effect that Scott's verse narratives had – primarily on the genre itself – and which was noticeable everywhere, both in the works of the older school (Campbell, Rogers, Crabbe, etc.) and in those of his 'modern' contemporaries (Wordsworth, Byron, Keats and Shelley, etc.) will be dealt with in detail: this is indeed the most interesting part of this study. The works we will be discussing are all syntheses of one aspect of Scott's work with other, older or newer elements and objectives, in other words original processing of his ideas.

In addition a proper Scott school developed, with a large number of imitators slavishly following his example or, at least, if they did alter form, material or style independently, remaining close to his original idea in that they attempted to produce popular verse with the aim of entertainment or historico-cultural education based on romantic themes, i.e. adventure or events set in a past age. As already indicated in the Introduction,[64] it is neither possible nor necessary to examine in detail this second group of poets and their works. In order to do justice to this 'school', it will suffice to look at the reviews in the three main periodicals to see what effect it had during its brief history.

Even when Jeffrey expresses the fear, in April 1808, that Scott's work might start a school (in the *Marmion* review in the *Edinburgh Review*) he is still of the opinion that Scott is for the time being the only representative of this modern romance form that he dislikes so much.[65] It is significant that he does not regard the early, freer imitations of Scott's genre, such as Wordsworth's *White Doe* (1807), Campbell's *Gertrude* (1809) or Montgomery's *Wanderer of Switzerland* (1807), as direct consequences of his work.

Only two years later, on the occasion of the publishing of an anonymous metrical romance – *Wallace: or the Fight of Fallkirk* – there is a complaint in *Quarterly Review*[66] about the many bad imitations of Scott. When Scott later says, in 1812 after *Rokeby* was only nominally successful, that the 'school' has already had its day, this is not quite correct. Even in 1817 his anonymous 'self-imitations', the *Bridal* and *Harold*, were very successful, and still later, in 1821, his friend, the dramatist Joanna Baillie, published the popular *Metrical Legends*, of which she says in the Preface: 'The manner and rhyme I have in some degree borrowed from my great contemporary Sir Walter Scott; following, in this respect, the example of many of the most popular poets of the present day.'[67] However, when Scott made the above remark, the flood of fashionable Scott copies – mainly written by women, among whom contemporary reviews mention Miss Holford, Miss Davidson, Miss Mitford and Miss Francis in particular – had in fact begun to abate.

From the mass of 'pupils' only two stand out, whose works even the great Jeffrey reviewed favourably:[68] James Hogg, the friend and discovery of Scott, the Ettrick Shepherd immortalized in North's *Noctes Ambrosianae*, whose ambitions to be the Burns of the nineteenth century were never realized; and the learned Scottish schoolmaster William Tennant. Of all Scott's works, it was the *Lay* that had the strongest influence on Hogg's *The Queen's Wake* of 1874. The framework story of Queen Mary of Scotland, who organizes a three-night-long singing competition, is rather weak and with its iambic tetrameters in couplets does not possess the vigour of Scott's 'light horseman' stanzas. But it does allow many ballads to be inserted – seventeen in all – among them *Bonnie Kilmeny* that features in many anthologies. While this poem achieved a certain popularity that even continued into this century, Hogg's numerous other attempts in this vein – *The Hunting of Badlewe* (1814),

The Pilgrims of the Sun (1815), *Mador of the Moor* (1816) and *Dramatic Tales* (1817), among others – have been rightly consigned to oblivion.

Similarly Tennant's *Anster Fair* of 1812 (in six cantos) is the only work by this author that is occasionally mentioned today. With its mixture of elements from *A Midsummer Night's Dream*, Burns and Pulci,[69] it is much less dependent on Scott than Hogg's *Queen's Wake*; at any rate the Scott traits are harder to detect. It can only be said that in general this poem, like Hogg's, could not have been written without Scott's development of the verse narrative and his continuation of Scottish poetry where Burns left off.

We now leave Scott's closer followers and turn to the more general effect that he had on important contemporaries. First we once again encounter Wordsworth.

Wordsworth's 'The White Doe of Rylstone'

> He said he considered the 'White Doe' as in conception the highest work he had ever produced.
>
> Grosart, *Prose Works of Wordsworth*, III, p.430

Up to now we have dealt with two forms of the romantic tale in verse: the 'early forms' represented by *Gebir* and Southey's narrative verse which were more closely related to the epic, and the metrical romances of Scott, which were bound equally to the ballad and the medieval romance. What both types have in common is that at a time when the poetry that was to have a significant effect on future developments – i.e., the works of Wordsworth and Coleridge – was increasingly becoming dominated by ethical, epistemological and metaphysical ideas, they concentrated instead on colourful stories with a great deal of action, a supernatural element, romantic descriptions, traditional heroes and a commonplace moral without touching at all on deeper intellectual problems (the Rousseauist and political elements in *Gebir* and the Protestant humanism in Southey's poems cannot be considered to be serious philosophy).

In the first decade of the nineteenth century, therefore, it appears that after the *Lyrical Ballads* of 1798, which do not entirely belong to the same category, the development of the verse narrative proceeded quite separately from the philosophical stream of English romantic poetry as represented by Wordsworth and Coleridge. Nevertheless, the success of the *Lay* seems to have attracted Wordsworth's attention. His own poetic endeavours had various points in common with Scott's: both were trying to appeal to the reader with poetic descriptions of human fates and passions; both replaced the detailed, descriptive analysis typical of eighteenth-century poetry with an overall picture of the personalities created, in all their dynamic range, by recounting how these characters behave in a particular situation. Both were influenced by the form of the ballad, and both attempted to get away from the urbane poetic techniques of the Pope age. And like Scott, although he did not just theoreticize about it but actually put it into practice, Wordsworth tried out all kinds of metres and stanza forms in his verse narratives: Spenser stanza in *Guilt and Sorrow* (1793 – 4), modified ballad metre in *Peter Bell* (1798) and *The Idiot Boy* (1798), blank verse in *Margaret, or the Ruined Cottage* (1795 – 7), *The Brothers* (1800), *Michael* (1800) and *Vaudracour and Julia* (1805), and very free tetrameters with varying rhyme schemes mixed with a few lines in a different rhythm in *The Waggoner* (1805).

It is almost by chance that Wordsworth did not arrive at the romantic tale in verse at more or less the same time as Scott; all the above-named longer poems are extended *Lyrical Ballads* rather than metrical romances. But what looks like chance is, as we have seen, a highly significant indicator of the poetical character of Wordsworth.[70] If he had carried out his plan to write epics, of which he spoke in the first book of *The Prelude*, with his unconventional literary style they would most probably not have been epics in conformity with the traditional rules, but would have been closer in form to the verse narratives of Southey and Scott, albeit with one difference: Wordsworth would never have written in the same popular, sensational and effective style.

Using quotes from *The Prelude* in particular it has already been shown how Wordsworth gradually came to the conclusion that he was not born to be a romantic story-teller.[71] The prologue to *Peter Bell* in 1798 should also be mentioned in this connection, since in it he dismisses the dream ship of fantasy that is about to bear him away to the stars, to the universe, to the Orient, the medieval fairy-tale world and the world of ancient magic (realms that Shelley, Byron, Southey, Scott and Moore were later to make their own) in order to write the 'philosophic story' of the donkey that softens a man's hardened heart with its faithfulness.[72] Finally we should also remember the poem *Simon Lee* in the *Lyrical Ballads*, which leads the reader to expect a story and then says:

> O Reader! had you in your mind
> Such stores as silent thought can bring,
> O gentle Reader! you would find
> A tale in every thing.
> What more I have to say is short,
> And you must kindly take it:
> It is no tale, but, should you think,
> Perhaps a tale you'll make it.
>
> (Ninth stanza)

This is basically true of every 'tale' that Wordsworth wrote: the most important part about a tale is not, as far as he is concerned, the action but the meaning. His dislike of the external features of plot and events, and his inability to narrate them vividly when he cannot avoid them, are so great that he always fails when the material requires a description of fights and battles, sinister misdeeds or passionately sensuous love,[73] and he leaves out altogether the ghosts and spirits that feature in the works of Southey and Scott. These were the elements that made the romantic verse narrative successful, at least in the first decade of the century. This 'new' form of narrative poetry needed a dynamic narrative technique which excluded longer reflective passages and it needed 'romantic' events: the gentle, inward-looking, mystical approach or the revelation of the deeper meaning of everyday events were out of place. It was thus a sound instinct that kept Wordsworth away from the romance and led him to the 'philosophic song/Of Truth that cherishes our daily life': both *The Prelude* and *The Excursion* are weighty works of literature. What Wordsworth's verse narratives on medieval or 'romantic' subjects might have been like can be seen in the work he wrote in this vein under the influence of Scott's *Lay* of 1807 but did not publish until 1815: *The White Doe of Rylstone*.[74]

Like Scott's first verse narratives, *The White Doe* is set in Scotland in the sixteenth century. It also bears similarities to the ballad, and even uses a ballad, *The Rising of the North* from Percy's *Reliques*, as a source.[75] As in the *Lay* the plot is a mixture of political conflict, feudal family history and a traditional story about a miraculous event. The form is also close to that of the *Lay* without copying it exactly. *The White Doe* consists of seven cantos in tetrameters. Only three lines are in trimeters: one in Canto I when the doe makes its first appearance, one in Canto II with the first appearance of Emily and one in Canto VII as the doe recognizes Emily and moves her to tears. All these are important moments in the story, so the metric change is strictly functional. The basic rhythm is iambic, but is often mixed with anapaests and trochees. The rhyming structures vary, but the rhyming couplet is dominant. The Dedication to Mary Wordsworth, recalling how they read Spenser's *Faerie Queene* together and referring to Spenser's gentle but steadfast Una as the forerunner of the heroine Emily, is written in Spenser stanzas and was not added until 1815.

The framework of the actual story which is provided in the first canto is interesting, since Wordsworth underlines once again that even this tale in verse influenced by *The Lay of the Last Minstrel* is not a

> tragic history/Of facts divulged, wherein appear/
> Substantial motive, reason clear.
>
> (199 ff.)

On the contrary, the harp is called upon:

> To chant, in strains of heavenly glory
> A tale of tears, a mortal story.
> (Conclusion of Canto I)

The first, introductory canto tells of a white doe that for longer than anyone can remember has been appearing in the churchyard of Boston monastery every Sunday during the church service and going to a particular grave, next to which it peacefully lies down, and after a certain time returns to the woods. The church-goers make various conjectures about this phenomenon, and the individual explanations are all material from which a real ballad or romance in Scott style could be developed. Wordsworth rejects them all as 'fancies wild' and stresses that the interpretation he is going to provide is something quite different: it has nothing to do with the founding of the monastery as the old man interested in local history thinks, nor is it a family history involving murder and guilt, as imagined by the arrogant aristocratic lady, nor the romance dreamed of by the Oxford student featuring fairies, magic and readings of the stars.[76] Instead it is a fable full of deeper meaning about a beautiful soul to which nature, in the form of a pure and gentle animal, communicates the knowledge of man's duty to submit himself to his fate and thus cure the world of its ills.

This introduction thus makes it clear that this 'Scott imitation', *The White Doe of Rylstone*, is also in the final analysis a 'philosophic song / Of Truth that cherishes our daily life', like the *Lyrical Ballads*, *The Prelude* and *The Excursion*, and is not a story for its own sake like *The Lay of the Last Minstrel* and the other verse romances of Scott. On closer examination of the actual story, the details also reveal how different this poem is from Scott's work: while Scott's narrative technique involves drawing the threads of the plot together to produce a happy or a tragic ending, according to the requirements of poetic justice, so that the story does not in any way lead away from itself, Wordsworth's *White Doe* is so to speak left open: the gradual inner liberation of the heroine has steered the reader away from the story and on to an intellectual subject that is intended to leave him with something to think about afterwards. Emily's death is almost casually recounted and appears inconsequential by comparison.

While pugnacity is a noble, natural male quality in Scott's estimation and he cannot indulge often enough in battles or tournaments, Wordsworth regards war as something tragic and lamentable and the enthusiasm of the participants as gravely misplaced. In Scott the supernatural appears naive because it is described by an enlightened poet as one would describe a superstition in which one did not believe, even though he uses all the right props and a 'real' setting. In the best of his verse narratives it is also explained rationally (*Marmion*) or left out altogether (*The Lady of the Lake* and *Rokeby*). In Wordsworth, on the other hand, although the supernatural element is based on folk tradition, the question of whether it is 'true' or 'untrue' has been rendered irrelevant since it is given its own reality by the poem: the white doe is the symbol and poetic equivalent of 'the great social principle of life / Coercing all things into sympathy' (*Prelude* l. 389 f.) that is the real subject and message of the poem, and also the symbol of the strong and enduring healing power which flows from nature to the imaginative spirit.[77] Here we are once again confronted with the same problem that was examined in the earlier section on Wordsworth's work:

is romantic verse narrative possible without strong dramatic accents, a certain naive dynamism of narrative, action, suspense and theatrical effects?

We can learn much from the contemporary reviews of *The White Doe*, since they revolve primarily around this question. The *Edinburgh Review* and the *Quarterly Review* reviewed the poem in the same month, October 1815.[78] The review in *Blackwood's Magazine*, which had only been founded in April 1817,[79] appeared in July 1818. It is not a criticism but a polemic defence of Wordsworth in reaction to the above two articles, in particular Jeffrey's in the *Edinburgh Review*. *The White Doe* appeared at a time when the romantic tale in verse was considerably more developed as a genre, and Scott's most important works and Byron's first had already been written. Jeffrey's criticism must be understood in this historical context. After analysing Wordsworth's poem in a thoroughly negative manner, he gives a brief but convincing reason for his rejection. The material is at the most sufficient for a ballad.[80] It has possibilities that could have been developed by Scott or Byron into very pretty images and descriptions, but what Wordsworth had taken over from the old historic ballads of the North was purely the negative characteristics: uneven verse techniques, a vulgar style and narrowness of outlook, while the positive qualities – the vital energy, bold simplicity and occasional aptness of expression – had been lost at his hands or suppressed by his metaphysical sentimentalism or his torrents of mysticism. In this article Jeffrey is at his most vituperative about Wordsworth.[81] While his attack is one-sided, we must ask ourselves whether it is completely unjustified.

The review in the *Quarterly Review*, which also covered the first collected edition of Wordsworth's poems up to that date (with the exception of *The Excursion*), has little time for this 'out-of-the-way production' and 'ballad sort of poem' by the Lake Poet. It is not very interesting as a story, is disjointed and in places incomprehensible. Instead of a dénouement, the reader is offered only an explanation of an unusual phenomenon, which provokes amazement rather than excitement. Certain positive qualities, in particular the gratifying delicacy of feeling and occasional simplicity of expression, are acknowledged, but in general the criticism that the naivety is affected and the language, unpolished, flat, obscure and unnatural, in fact meaningless verbiage, outweighs everything else.

The man who three years later in *Blackwood's Magazine* passionately defended Wordsworth against these antagonistic reviewers was Christopher North, alias John Wilson, who as a poet followed in the footsteps of the great Lakers and as a critic was mainly responsible for the fact that, as from 1817, Wordsworth's poems were regarded less and less as modernistic absurdities and gradually assumed the status of great contemporary poetry. North also begins his review by citing Wordsworth's comparable contemporaries, Scott and Byron. If, however, Wordsworth is different, he is certainly not worse. North praises his moral qualities, his natural piety and the musicality of his

language. He particularly stresses the absence of all artificial social distinctions: this poem is not dealing with man as a product of society, but with
the psychological make-up of the individual, which is natural and constant.
For this reason the emotions and truths represented in *The White Doe* go
deeper, in a manner comparable only with the Bible. Wordsworth is the
poet who has best captured the sensuous beauty of the natural world and
reconstructed it for the reader in an ennobled and ennobling fashion. The
critic of the *Edinburgh Review* paid too little attention to the individuality
of this poetry, which stimulates the imagination and thereby arouses emotion
and sympathy. While there is a lack of strong passion and excitement,
it is one-sided and lacking in imagination on the part of the critic to overlook the true beauty of the poem by focusing on these externals.

The opposing views of these critics oblige us to try and draw some kind of
conclusion: on the one hand we must decide which of the two positions we
consider to be the correct one, and on the other we must establish what is to be
learned from them about the history of the verse narrative, its success and
its reception.

The aesthetic ideas on which Jeffrey's literary opinions are based and the
real reasons for his rejection of Wordsworth will not be discussed here: they
have been dealt with in detail by René Wellek in his *History of Modern Criticism
1750–1950.*[82] On the subject of the review we have talked about, Wellek
writes: 'Especially inexcusable is the jeering review of *The White Doe of Rylstone*,
because it completely misreads the tone and theme of a simple and grave
poem.' He thus fully endorses the view of Christopher North, which on the
basis of today's definitive opinion of the value of the statement the poem
contains, the quality of the form and Wordsworth's poetic standing, is
perfectly correct. However, Jeffrey's objections are not entirely unfounded.
When a story embodies important ideas, then however symbolic the external
elements of the fable, this does not exempt the poet from the rules of story-
telling, i.e., from telling his tale well, making it gripping, involving and
dynamic and using good narrative technqiues, and not limiting all this to the
'business parts'. Scott and Byron were without a doubt better at this than
Wordsworth.

Here we encounter an important question with respect to the assessment
of romantic verse narrative: can the depth of thought and the basic subjective
attitude of romanticism – whereby every work tries to express something
essential about the self, the artist, man, life, nature, existence or the transcendental – can this great European intellectual, philosophical movement
be combined with anything but lyrical, symbolic, mythical or fairy-tale poetry?
Are the objective realistic epic and dramatic genres still possible? The answer
will have to be postponed until later, and for the time being it should merely
be noted objectively that Wordsworth's contemporaries evidently found
it hard to understand this first piece of concrete evidence of the change

from, as McFarland put it, the mimetic to the 'meontic'[83] mode of narration and accept this symbolic product of the subjective imagination as a story.

Thus in the review of *The White Doe* in the *Quarterly Review* the fact that he always writes about himself is given as the reason for Wordsworth's unpopularity. While this was also true of other poets, they were convincing because they were like other people, but Wordsworth always wrote about those aspects of his personality which differed from the ordinary. One criterion of a good story, however, was that the reader must be able to relate to what was going on. This idea is also the basis of the article on *The Excursion* in the *Quarterly Review*.[84] Even Wordsworth's admirer North, in his essay 'An Hour's Talk about Poetry'[85] in which he is seeking the 'Great Poem' of the romantic age, does not consider that *The Excursion* qualifies for this title, since it is a long story (or rather a series of stories) without an epic plan. A poem of this nature cannot be called great, unless artistic standards change. Artistic standards have changed: in our present age, when – as a consequence of Wordsworth's introduction of the emphasis on ideas – T. S. Eliot's *Waste Land* or Ezra Pound's *Cantos* are considered 'great poems', Wordsworth's *Excursion* or *White Doe* would not be excluded from this category because of their disjointed narrative technique or their subjective ideas. If however by the term 'great poem' one understands the platonic idea of the epic, liberated, of course, from the strict rules established by centuries of literary criticism, one has to include convincingly mimetic narration in the qualifications for epic greatness (as North, like everyone else in his day, evidently does), and then Jeffrey's objections cannot be completely overridden. *The White Doe of Rylstone* is then, while not a failure, a slightly perplexing work that has not fully achieved its aims and is hence not a 'great' poem.

We will still have to ask ourselves whether there is such a thing as a 'great' romantic tale in verse, whether it is not a utopian idea or whether, because the word 'great' can apply to the statement or the story, it is not a generic paradox since it is not possible to combine objective narrative and the ideas of the romantic movement. This will be dealt with in greater detail in the final chapter of this book.

Wordsworth's attempt to expand Scott's genre by adding depth of thought was thus for the time being the only one of its kind. The group of strongly classicistically orientated poets who will be dealt with in the following section expanded Scott's genre by combining it experimentally with formal elements derived from the aesthetic ideas of the second half of the eighteenth century, and by using different material. They in some ways diverged so far from Scott's model, and from Southey's 'romantic epics', that the influence of the previous romantic verse narratives is noticeable only in the selection of the short narrative form with a clear emphasis on the plot, rejection of the epic rules and the use of 'private' topics to make poetic statements. Since these are the main characteristics of the vaguely delineated romantic verse narrative genre, and since the origins of these works are so closely connected with the roots of that fashionable genre (influenced by Scott and influencing later verse narrators, especially Byron) that contemporary reviewers measured them by the same standards that they used for Scott and Wordsworth, they must not be omitted from this generic history.

5 'The postscript of the Augustans' and the opposite of romance

> In the field of aesthetics historic necessity, the 'fury of extinction' (Hegel) strictly forbids compromise of any kind.
>
> T. W. Adorno, *Philosophie der Neuen Musik*, 1949, p. 3

Thomas Campbell

> Polished, worked up, touched and retouched into sweet and artificial beauty ... simple – but insipid.
>
> *Blackwood's Magazine*, 96, January 1825 (review of Campbell's *Theodric*)

In 1809, when Campbell brought out his first tale in verse, *Gertrude of Wyoming*, he already had a significant reputation as a poet. He was Scotland's prince among poets until Scott took over from him with his *Lay*. Byron, however, still placed him among the top contemporary poets in his famous pyramid of poets,[1] and even in 1829 Goethe considered him to be the most important modern British poet after Byron, although he also stressed that he (Goethe) did not feel at home with the newer English poetry.[2] This fame was established by several lively ballads full of national spirit and empire sentiment and in particular by *The Pleasures of Hope* (1799), a reflective poem in pure neoclassical style, and a successor to Akenside's *Pleasures of the Imagination* (1744, 1757) and Rogers' *Pleasures of Memory* (1792) with echoes of Pope, Thomson, Cowper, Johnson and Goldsmith.[3]

When in 1809 Campbell produced a proper verse narrative that was more like the works of Scott – he actually began *Gertrude* in 1806, a year after the *Lay* appeared, and rumour that he was working on a tale in verse spread before its publication[4] – it was clear how much tastes had changed and how the poets of the old school had to fight to stay in favour with the public. *Gertrude of Wyoming* also illustrates another important point, namely the gradual realization that the new genre Scott had created with the *Lay* and *Marmion* permitted not only close imitations (which is what Wordsworth's *White Doe* was as far as the type of poem was concerned, in spite of the completely different intellectual basis) but also rich variations of subject and form and combinations with a great variety of influences and models. Thus Campbell and other poets who already had a reputation to defend, such as Rogers, Bowles, Crabbe and later Byron and Moore, could follow the path Scott had so successfully trodden before them without having to give up their claim to originality. This also meant that the 'genre' was constantly being extended and becoming vaguer in definition. We must therefore always examine the verse narratives that are the subject of this section from the point of view of what they owe to Scott and in what way they are original or involve other influences.

In *Gertrude of Wyoming* there are many examples of other literary influences. With his *Atala*, written in 1801, Chateaubriand had already made America popular as a colourful background for a sad plot full of feeling. We can therefore be certain of the fact that Campbell borrowed a number of elements from this poem.[5] The creation of the couple that grow up together and later fall in love, roaming with paradisiacal innocence through the wild countryside, sparing the animals and taking pleasure in nature, probably owes as much to the tradition of the pastorals and idylls as to Bernardin's *Paul et Virginie*, a work that had also influenced Chateaubriand. Of course, direct borrowing can no more be proved here than it can from Goethe's *Hermann und Dorothea*, a poem that with its mixture of idyllic, realistic, classical and romantic characteristics also bears a faint resemblance to Campbell's work, even though it is much more 'tangible' than *Gertrude of Wyoming*. Campbell, who was familiar with Germany, would certainly have known *Hermann und Dorothea*. He was, however, without a doubt inspired by another German work, the novel *Barneck und Saldorf* (1804) by August Lafontaine, the founder of the lachrymose family novel in Germany.[6] It should also be said that Hazlitt called *Gertrude* 'a kind of historical paraphrase of Mr. Wordsworth's poem Ruth',[7] although in this author's opinion one can scarcely even speak of similarity, let alone influence.

The model that inspired the use of the Spenser stanza was Thomson's *Castle of Indolence*, which Campbell greatly admired. Campbell did not in general adopt Thomson's archaisms, but his manuscript does contain some of Thomson's obsolete spellings such as *gulphs*, *groupes*, *controul*, etc. as well as one verbal echo. Campbell was not only influenced by other literary works, in a way that illustrates his position between neo-classicism, pre-romanticism and romanticism, but also by circumstances in his personal life that led him to choose this almost contemporary subject (the story takes place in 1778). Before his marriage, Campbell's father had lived for some years as a trader in Virginia, and later maintained trade relations with that state from Glasgow. An uncle of the poet, who was a clergyman, and two brothers emigrated permanently to Virginia and in 1797 Campbell briefly considered following them.

That the intermediate position of the author of *Pleasures of Hope* and *Gertrude* between neo-classical form and romanticism with its abundance of feeling is due not only to the times and changing fashion but also to his character and tastes is confirmed by much that was written about him by his contemporaries.

Leigh Hunt reports that in addition to the poets of the eighteenth century

Campbell particularly liked Virgil and Racine, and adds that this preference together with his liking for old ballads, 'may serve to shew both the natural and artificial bent of his genius'.[8] Hunt supports this general opinion with analyses of passages from Campbell's two main works. He shows how Campbell's own feeling, his naturalness, originality, imagination, emotionalism and dynamism – all characteristics which are expressed without inhibition in his battle songs and ballads – are constantly suppressed by his admiration for elegance, urbanity, refinement, artificiality or anything sanctioned by classical example. This criticism and the accusation of exaggerated self-criticism appear in almost all the contemporary reviews.

From Scott we have both an official and a private view of Campbell. The former – the article on Gertrude in the Quarterly Review – had already been mentioned.[9] It says what a disappointment the poem was to an eager public, and attributes this to the selection of a subject that embarrassed British national feeling, to the much too personalized framework and the bad narrative technique. Scott, the experienced writer of verse narratives, competently shows his fellow poet where the weaknesses of his plot lie, and how unnecessary or even damaging to popular verse narrative too much attention to the verse construction is. Scott's private opinion of Campbell is known from a conversation with Washington Irving.[10] There he called Campbell's poems 'real diamonds of the first water', compared with which his own poems were 'smoky topazes'. But even on this occasion he accused Campbell of a lack of spontaneity and reprimanded him for his self-criticism that made him hold back and prevented him from the outset from blossoming as a poet: 'He is a bugbear to himself ... He is afraid of the shadow that his own fame casts before him.'

In Jeffrey's review of Gertrude of Wyoming[11] he characteristically plays off Campbell against Scott. Nature and truth were today obscured by the 'splendour, bustle and variety of the most popular of our recent poets', in whose verse narratives there was, however, evidence of genius made for higher things than coarse effects. There was nothing noisy or stormy about Campbell's work, and even if he told his story badly and was often obscure because of excessive attention to the verse construction, his manner of narrating in verse was closer to perfect poetry than the 'babyism' of the Lakers and the antiquarianism of Scott. Jeffrey's favourable review of Campbell's poem at the expense of Scott's achievement at least partly explains Scott's adverse critique of Gertrude in the Quarterly Review a month later (see above).

Hazlitt's comments on Gertrude in his Lectures on the English Poets of 1818[12] are predominantly negative: Campbell seems to him to have been thinking with every line how his poetry would look when it came off the press printed on the finest vellum. His main criticism is of the lack of spontaneity and the bad narrative technique. In 1825, in The Spirit of the Age,[13] Hazlitt has considerably altered his opinion, to the extent that he now praises Gertrude extravagantly: 'the scales and crusts of formality that fence in his couplets in *Pleasures of Hope* ... fall off, and he has succeeded in engrafting the wild and more expansive interest of the romantic school of poetry on classical elegance and precision'. Hazlitt now places Campbell between Byron and Rogers: he has something of the dynamism, brilliance and romantic subjects of the one and something of the exaggerated elegance of the other; but he has none of Byron's extravagances nor Rogers' effeminacy.

The bad narrative technique, which bothers us less today and occasionally has an almost impressionistic attractiveness about it like *Gebir*, was something Campbell admitted to himself. In a letter to Scott in 1805 he confesses that he was by nature 'always a dead bad hand at telling a story' (and we must remember that his work had its origins in eighteenth-century reflective poetry). It also cannot be denied that the Spenser stanza, which tends to divide the narrative into a sequence of pictures rather than produce a continuous flow of narrative, accentuated this weakness of Campbell's.

Of the younger romantics, Keats appears to have thought highly of *Gertrude*. He mentions the work in a letter to his sister-in-law Georgiana Augusta Keats dated 13 January 1820 and calls it 'poetic'. Byron, otherwise an admirer of Campbell's, was evidently not very impressed by the latter's attempt at a romance. In a note in the M(urray) manuscript of the *Hints from Horace* (1811)[14] he vents his feelings about Jeffrey's good review of this 'mediocre work of Campbell's' and then says: 'It is fortunate for Campbell that his fame neither depends on his last poem, nor the puff of the Edinburgh review.' There follows a typical Byronesque criticism, not to be taken too seriously, of the catachresis in the last couplet of *Gertrude*:

> Because I may not stain with grief
> The death-song of an Indian chief.

Finally he uses a quote against Campbell from the poet 'for whom [Mr Campbell] and his school have no small contempt' (meaning Pope):

> E'en copious Dryden wanted, or forgot,
> The last and greatest art – the art to blot.[15]

This is most informative: after the appearance of *Gertrude* Byron evidently viewed Campbell as a defector to the camp of 'romantic' poets, hostile to Pope, and as far as Byron was concerned, it was unpardonable to be against Pope. Ten years later his opinion of Campbell is quite different. In his notes to Bacon's *Apophthegms* written in Ravenna on 5 January 1821, which follow a note on *Don Juan* V, 1. 147,[16] he is full of praise for Campbell's 'classical, honest, and triumphant defence of Pope', of which he says in his *Journal* of 10 January 1821 that 'it is, to be sure, in his own defence, too – but no Matter, it is very good and does him great credit'. The following day, however, he censures *Gertrude* for its inaccuracy with respect to costume and description: it 'has no more locality in common with Pennsylvania than with Penmaenmawr'.[17]

In order to give some idea of the style of *Gertrude* it will suffice to select at random one of the ninety-two stanzas:

> So finish'd he the rhyme (howe'er uncouth)   [1]
> That true to nature's fervid feelings ran;   [2]
> (And song is but the eloquence of truth):   [3]
> Then forth uprose that lone wayfaring man,   [4]
> But, dauntless, he nor chart nor journey's plan   [5]
> In woods requir'd, whose trained eye was keen   [6]
> As eagle of the wilderness, to scan   [7]
> His path, by mountain, swamp, or deep ravine,   [8]
> Or ken far friendly huts on good savannas green.   [9]
>   (*Gertrude of Wyoming*, Part I, stanza 27)

Here what Campbell's contemporaries described as his 'fastidiousness' is clearly in evidence. Preceding this passage is the song that the Indian Outalissi sings to the child he has brought to the European Albert. Campbell does not call it a song but uses the refined word 'rhyme', just as in the next line he chooses 'fervid' in preference to a simpler word for the sake of alliteration with the word 'feelings'. As Scott often does, he describes the song he has inserted – the song of a primitive, uneducated singer – half apologetically as 'uncouth'. However, while such an expression in Scott's work always seems justified by a change of metre and style and the ballad-like traditional or martial character of the inserted song, here the word 'uncouth' is not justified: Outalissi's song is also in Spenser stanzas and is in the same refined eighteenth-century poetic diction as the rest of the poem. The effect of line 2, where he professes a Rousseauist, primitivistic faith in poetic spontaneity, is weakened by the reflection in line 3, where a commonplace is expressed in a classical, sententious manner, and, like the first parenthesis in line 1, unnecessarily interrupts the flow of narrative which the reader expects to be continued after the song. As if to compensate for his delay, Campbell now compresses two actions into one expression – 'forth uprose' instead of 'he stood up and went forth'; we are familiar with such practices from the ballad, e.g., 'Up and spak an eldern knicht' in *Sir Patrick Spence*). However, the pace is not speeded up, as Campbell cannot refrain from affectedly calling the Indian a 'lone wayfaring man', whereby a classicistic epithet is introduced that is more suited to Ulysses than to an Indian returning to his forest. The remaining lines, which do not continue the plot but turn a comment about the Indians' sense of direction from a travelogue into verse,[18] also contain nothing original: the syntax is latinized as in Milton, of whom the pronounced use of *enjambements* is also reminiscent. The eagle's eye as a simile for good eyesight may perhaps be appropriate for an Indian, but appears artificial and outdated owing to the choice of words, 'whose trained eye' where a relative pronoun, 'whose', opens a main clause and the vowel in the last syllable of 'trained' is not elided; and 'As eagle of the wilderness', where the article is omitted, and 'to scan his path', which is too refined an expression. Line 8 is pure classicism with its division into three parts with the stress on the last one and the omission of the articles. Line 9, finally, with the archaic word 'ken' is only an alexandrine because of the two uninspiring and unnecessary adjectives placed in a mannered fashion before and after the word 'savannas'.[19]

It might be objected that original verse language does not have to be a criterion of quality for a poet who still has close links with the Augustan tradition, and that neo-classical clichés are even to be found in Scott's and Byron's work. All that can be said in answer to this is that Scott and Byron are more skilful at mixing the old with the new, reflections with narrative and design with continuity, and that their gift for narrative compensates for much that in Campbell's work shows up as artificial and clumsy. There is no doubt that *Gertrude of Wyoming* nevertheless contains some memorable lines, such as the final alexandrine of I, 12 that was praised by Hazlitt in *The Spirit of the Age* as an 'ecstatic union of natural beauty and poetic fancy'[20] – 'Till now, in Gertrude's eyes, their ninth blue summer shone' – or the image that is often praised of the dark-skinned Indian who leads the white boy by the hand 'like morning brought by night' (I, 13). There are some impressive passages, such as the description of Gertrude's childhood (I, 11–13) that Hazlitt also admired,[21] the melodious stanza II, 25 or the song of Outalissi that brings the poem to a close (III, 35–9). Even in the case of the stanza quoted in full above it can be said that at the end of it Campbell nevertheless succeeds in conjuring up the Indian's environment in a few words, even though the America Campbell describes is as unreal as the fourth continent of the Baroque painters and, in spite of ethnographic notes, so artificial that in places it is more like an Augustan's Arcadia. All these positive traits are individual details that do not suffice to make this a great narrative poem. Almost no stanza stands up to exact analysis: the poem is beautiful but not great; charming but not effective, as Hazlitt says in his *Lectures on the English Poets*:

> Of outward show
> Elaborate; of inward less exact.[22]

Campbell's later verse narratives, e.g., *Theodric, a Domestic Tale* (1824) and *The Pilgrim of Glencoe* (1842), have today rightly been consigned to oblivion and play no significant role in the history of the genre. In *Theodric* the clumsy narrative and Campbell's insipid, rather feminine tone that he only managed to rise above in his ballads and battle songs stand out to such an extent that the poem, only 500 lines long and in heroic couplets, was unanimously rejected as soon as it appeared by critics used to the highly successful works produced by Scott and Byron;[23] and *The Pilgrim of Glencoe* was written at a later period which no longer concerns us here, when readers had no time for this weak rehashing of the turn-of-the-century poetic spirit.

Samuel Rogers

> Then was thy cup, old man, full to the brim
> But thou wert yet alive ...
> Rogers, *Italy* ('Foscari', l. 145)

There are so many similarities between Campbell and Rogers that in histories of literature they are always dealt with together. In spite of an age difference of fourteen years (Rogers was born in 1763, Campbell in 1777) they belong to the same literary generation, the generation that grew up under the influence of Samuel Johnson, Goldsmith, Cowper and Akenside, and had their first successes emulating these poets, but then after 1800 suddenly found themselves obliged to adapt to a young, revolutionary type of poetry which had captured the imagination of the public in a relatively short time and fundamentally altered contemporary tastes.

We have often spoken of the vacuum that was left after the gradual retreat of Augustan classicism, making the appearance of the romantic verse narrative as a new type of poetry almost inevitable.[24] The actuality of this vacuum can be proved with data from the lives of the poets: before the appearance of their first verse narratives, which were always in some way or another inspired by Scott's first successes, many of them in this generation had had long periods when they produced little or nothing. Between Campbell's *Pleasures of Hope* (1799) and his *Gertrude* (1809) ten years elapsed during which he wrote only prose works and a few poems in ballad style. After his *Pleasures of Memory* (1792) Rogers wrote only a poetic *Epistle to a Friend* (1798) in the same neo-classical style, and twelve years then passed before he attempted to imitate the younger poets with *The Voyage of Columbus* (printed privately in 1810, with the first public edition in 1812). There was an even longer break in the work of Crabbe (born 1754): there were twenty-two years between *The Village* (1783) and *The Parish Register* (1807), during which time he had published nothing. Although *The Parish Register* was not directly influenced by Scott, we will see that Crabbe too wrote more narrative than reflective poetry after this interval and endeavoured to develop an unromantic alternative to Scott's romances. With Bowles (born in 1762) the break occurred at a slightly different time, but he too had a silent period; nine years elapsed between his topographical poem *Bowden Hill* (1806) and his first verse narrative *The Missionary of the Andes* (1815).

What was the cause of this phenomenon? It cannot be a coincidence. Was the disruption of European culture by the French Revolution and the Napoleonic Wars also having repercussions on English literature? Was the vacuum due to the fact that classicism had died out before romanticism had fully emerged? Was this a national, politically motivated reaction against the French School of poetry, leaving a gap that was only filled when the Lakers and Scott founded a type of poetry that had a specific English style? Can this interval in the creativity of a whole age group be explained by the technical difficulties that the lesser poets, who were in no way inclined towards poetic innovation, experienced when they had to adapt to a new type of poetry for which there was already a high demand (how this came about was discussed in chapter 2) but which they were ill equipped to produce themselves? Or is the main reason the psychological resistance that had to be overcome when literary conventions that had been sanctioned for over a hundred years suddenly had to make way for a new trend popular with the non-literary public that was even suspected to have intellectual and moral links with the violence of the political revolution?[25]

There is probably something to be said for all of these hypotheses and together they give us the true picture of the problems of this generation. A small amount of basic data from the lives of a few lesser poets has revealed some important aspects of contemporary intellectual developments which in more than one way enrich our understanding of the history of that period.

Like Campbell's *Gertrude*, Rogers' *The Voyage of Columbus* also represents an attempt by a neo-classically orientated poet to compete with the popular authors of romantic verse narratives. And like Campbell, Rogers also fails to produce a true romantic poem: his attempt founders on his attachment to the old school with its particular way of seeing and describing things, and the clumsy narrative technique which is partly a consequence of this. Rogers' failure is more obvious than Campbell's, since the discrepancy between the conventional and 'modern' components is even greater.

In Campbell's *Gertrude* the romantic influence is not very pronounced; from its basic structure the poem is a sensitive, idyllic domestic poem, which only has a tragic ending because of the intrusion of war into the idyll. Something similar (even if interspersed with reflections and with less weight attached to the plot) would not have been unthinkable in the late eighteenth century, for example in a poem by Goldsmith or James Beattie. The romantic traits *Gertrude* does contain – the emphasis on the plot and the idealized exoticism – do not clash with the characteristics typical of domestic poetry, but on the contrary enhance the work's dynamism and interest. The rather careless form that characterized Scott's early romantic verse romances also underwent a change at Campbell's hand owing to this fusion with the idyll: there was a refinement of both the language and the external machinery, with a resulting gain in human depth. The fact that the work remains colourless in spite of this is due rather to Campbell's limited ability than to the incompatibility of the various elements. A glance at Goethe's *Hermann und Dorothea* shows that such a combination was possible.

The components that Rogers assembled in *Columbus* are much less amenable to synthesis, and in fact rule one another out. What he is namely trying to do is turn a classicistic epic poem in heroic couplets into a Scott-style romance by only developing fragmentary sections and imposing on the resulting 'broken' epic form a framework of irregularly rhyming eight-syllable stanzas such as were typical in Scott's work, and which he even mixes with prose at the end; the fragments of the story are supposed to be remnants of an old manuscript that he had translated.[26]

There are a number of factors which indicate that when Rogers wrote this 'romantic' poem he had only very incompletely detached himself from the classic idea of the epic poem:

1. He justifies the selection of material by saying that in Spain there is no national poem about Columbus. Since no Camoens had devoted a work to this figure, he was doing it himself.

2. He feels it is most important to include those aspects of the event that impinge on world history. For this reason he pretends that his poem is from the time 'when the great consequences of the Discovery were beginning to unfold themselves'.[27]

3. He doubts whether the event and the machinery go together in the form he has chosen, and wonders whether Columbus is not too modern a hero for a poem which features angels and evil spirits. He then justifies this infringement of the epic tradition on the one hand with his pretended discovery of the authentic old manuscript on which his poem is based – 'I found them [event and machinery] together' – and on the other hand with his pretence that he used supernatural elements in the interest of the deeper meaning of his *Columbus*: even today angels and devils must be enlisted if one is trying as a poet 'to clear up the Darkness, / And justify the ways of God to Man'.[28]

4. The fragmentary narrative is written in the epic metre of the Augustans, the heroic couplet, and in spite of its 'broken' form is divided into the twelve traditional cantos.

5. The poem ends in Canto XII with the conventional vision of the future, although this is shorter than one would normally expect: an angel prophesies to Columbus that he will be driven out of his paradise, America, will suffer and be glorified by posterity.

A number of other factors however show that Rogers was trying to forge a link with the new school:

1. Just as Scott might have done, he justifies his adherence to the spirit of the old Spanish chronicles by the attraction that their 'simplicity' and 'sensibility to the strange and wonderful' and even their weaknesses possessed, a charm that was as refreshing as clear spring water.

2. According to Rogers, the narrative sections of these chronicles provide an interesting picture of the clash of two civilizations that might add to the attractions of his poem.

3. The material is recommended as being particularly poetic because of its warm colour and the wildness of its imagery.

4. The leisurely pace and cohesion of the epic poem is abandoned in this work. It is not, as in Scott's *Lay*, broken up by a romantic variety of events – for which Rogers did not have sufficient imagination – it is torn apart by the fragment form. Rogers speaks of 'sudden transitions' and shows a somewhat romantic attitude when he justifies dissolution of the form by saying he wants to stimulate the reader's imagination.[29] The introduction of a dramatic persona, who tells or writes the story as his own experience, the monk who left the manuscript and who had accompanied Columbus as a sailor, is reminiscent of *The Lay of the Last Minstrel* and anticipates *The Giaour*.

It is not necessary to examine in detail the style of this poem and the other works that will be named below in this section on the four more conventional poets, Campbell, Rogers, Bowles and Montgomery, since the result would always resemble the analysis of Campbell's *Gertrude*: remnants of Augustan poetic diction, some more clearly recognizable than others, and the antithesis technique of the French School of poetry are mixed with a variety of other literary influences or borrowings and occasional attempts at an insipid romantic style.[30] The poet's own stylistic abilities are so poor that the borrowed aspects often look as if they have been added on as ornaments, and the contrast between the great poetry of which they remind us and the poet's own standard only serves to emphasize the meagreness of his own achievement.

The Voyage of Columbus was not a great success with either the public or the reviewers. The *Edinburgh Review* criticized the choice of subject, but was otherwise quite positive.[31] The article in the *Quarterly Review*,[32] written by Rogers' friend Ward, was much more critical and even led to a temporary estrangement between the poet and the critic. It is witty and objective and brings out the main narrative defects of the work and the disadvantages of the material in a manner that indicates how the principles of exciting story-telling, after having been established again by Scott, were now slowly resurfacing in the public consciousness. The main ideas of the review, which shed further light on the historical development of the genre, are as follows. Ward considers the Columbus material unsuitable for heroic poetry: the hero is serious and scientifically minded, not a dreamer or a visionary but a clear thinker, nor is he a decorative, active fighter like Achilles, Orlando or Marmion (here the difference between epic and romance has already disappeared completely). He may in the estimation of an enlightened age be superior to those heroes 'of epic or romantic song', but for poetry he is too unromantic; 'fiction' about him only serves to reduce the admiration one has for him. In addition, the historical facts about him are so well established that there is no room for fantasy. The central event is equally unpoetical: the antecedents to the story which take place in Spain are unsuitable for descriptive writing; the sea voyage is too static (nothing spurs it on or holds it back); since the outcome is known there is no suspense. When there is an opportunity for poetic writing, with the description of the American landscape, the plot has in fact come to an end. Rogers' attempt to turn this subject into poetry has not in Ward's opinion succeeded: the machinery (the interference of the evil spirits that instigate the mutiny) produced nothing more than a few troubled hours for Columbus. Divine intervention through angel messengers does not go with the down-to-earth hero. The framework is not exploited, since the narrator who took part in the voyage has no individual character and no history. Since it is therefore only put in to justify the disjointed narrative technique, it must be described as an unfair means of disguising incompetence on the part of the poet. The little love story of Cora does not carry enough weight to arouse interest by comparison with the world-wide significance of the discovery of America. The entire work is in Ward's opinion lacking in 'variety of incident' and 'display of human characters and feelings, which form the great charm of narrative poetry'. Ward advises his friend to stick to what he can do so well and continue with his defence of the Goldsmith-Pope school. He does not have the greatness of spirit and the boldness required for the epic form. With *Columbus* the poet was probably trying to experiment with the 'new style' – 'stimulated by the astonishing success of some later writers he has tried to equal their fame ... tired of pleasing he is ambitious to astonish and transport his readers' – but he is not capable of such a radical change and a mixture of his previous affected style with the modern school can only fail: the elements are incompatible.

Columbus was soon forgotten, with many romantic verse narratives that were now appearing every year. Hazlitt, who found Rogers' effeminate *Pleasures of Memory* affected and commonplace, only mentions this poem in his *Lectures on the English Poets*, and in *The Spirit of the Age* he leaves Rogers out altogether. Even the articles in *Blackwood's Magazine* towards the end of the 1820s which attempted to give a résumé of the whole epoch[33] only include Rogers as the author of *The Pleasures of Hope*. This shows that his second attempt to win public favour with a verse narrative, the short, more idyllic romance *Jacqueline*[34] that was anonymously published in 1814 together with Byron's *Lara*, also enjoyed only a fleeting success, aided by the mystery as to its author.[35] Even Byron, who had a disproportionately high regard for Rogers and in his *Gradus ad Parnassum* of 1813 ranked him as the second greatest contemporary poet after Scott, had to admit in 1817 that 'Rogers the Grandfather of living Poetry – is retired on half-pay (I don't mean as a Banker) – since pretty Miss Jacqueline.'[36] He did not live to see the complete edition of what is probably Rogers' best poetry, the blank-verse travelogue *Italy*.

William Lisle Bowles and James Montgomery

Stick to thy sonnets, man!
John Hobhouse, from some satirical lines about Bowles that he wrote for
    the first edition of Byron's *English Bards and Scotch Reviewers*

... he had an intermittent streak of talent for verse.
    O. Elton on Montgomery, *Survey* II, p. 264

The two literary figures who will now be discussed in brief are, like Campbell and Rogers, the kind of poets who would never take part in a poetical revolution themselves, but who, once it was over, would try and adapt to the new style in as far as they were able. In the work of Bowles, the older of the two (born in 1762), the neo-classical traits are more in evidence than in the work of James Montgomery, who was born in 1777, but the latter also has a conservative rather than a romantic temperament.

W. L. Bowles is the prototype of the minor poet who with his technical skills and natural sensitivity is occasionally successful with short works but can only fail with more ambitious projects. In 1816, when he had already had a good name for thirty years as a writer of sensitive nature sonnets and longer landscape poems as well as extensive reflective works but had latterly been pushed into the background with the wave of romantic poetry, he published a verse narrative featuring 'romantic' events: *The Missionary of the Andes*, in eight cantos and heroic couplets. This work suffers to a much greater extent than Campbell's *Gertrude* and Rogers' *Columbus* from the inadequate synthesis of classicistic style and romantic content. Bowles' pensive and sentimental temperament is reflected in the narrative sections, that are totally lacking in dynamism, conflict and the suspense that this creates, and tragedy, although the material requires all of these. The reflections that the poet inserts slow down the action even more. The few attempts at 'romantic spirit machinery' do not fit in with the rest of the poem, and contribute as little to the atmosphere as the unoriginal descriptions of nature, that are not based on the poet's own experience. Romantic poetry as Scott had invented it, exoticism and the motif of the noble savage are all present here in a watered-down form; all this has become merely a fashion, and its inner intellectual origins and principles have not been comprehended.

The Missionary caused no great stir, but was nevertheless quite well received. *Blackwood's Magazine*[37] discussed the poem in detail three years after its publication without being strongly for or against it, and Byron, who was full of derision for Bowles' *Sonnets* in *English Bards*, l. 34 ff., and later (1819) carried out the famous Pope feud with him, wrote with condescending benevolence in the *Versicles* of March 1817:

I read the Missionary:
Pretty – very.

However, this edifying type of romantic verse narrative that appealed to conservative, bourgeois readers was to have no lasting significance.[38] *The Missionary* is also the only verse narrative with a plot running through it that Bowles, who lived until 1850, ever wrote: like Rogers, he returned in his later poems more to the style of his earlier works.

While Bowles is still remembered today as the poet whose sonnets inspired the young Coleridge, Montgomery has been completely forgotten: hardly anyone still knows that this writer of several well-known English hymns was a popular poet in his day, and hardly anyone can understand the passage about him in Byron's *English Bards*, ll. 415 ff., without recourse to the explanatory footnote. Between 1806 and 1827 Montgomery produced five longer poems, of which only three are relevant here: *The Wanderer of Switzerland* (1806), *The World before the Flood* (1813), *The Pelican Island* (1827). The two others – *The West Indies* (1807) and *Greenland* (1819), both in heroic couplets – belong to the category of the purely reflective poem on a topical theme. They deal with subjects which in those days were considered to be unromantic and even unpoetic: the abolition of slavery and the Christian mission in Greenland.

The three poems that do have a certain limited relevance to our subject are interesting not because of their artistic value (which is not very high)[39] nor because of any influence they might have had in the development of the verse narrative (Montgomery incorporated other influences into his work but was not a source of influence himself), but because of what they tell us about the way tastes in poetry were changing, adding significantly to our picture of the ways in which the lesser, unoriginal poets of the older romantic generation – the generation of Wordsworth and Coleridge – were influenced by contemporary trends. None of these three poems by Montgomery can be directly related to the work of Walter Scott. *The Wanderer* was planned before *The Lay of the Last Minstrel*, and the two other works are in a quite different class of poetry from Scott's romances. However, the story behind the creation of *The Wanderer* is remotely similar to that of the *Lay*, and all three poems contain elements that are also to be found in other verse narratives of the period.

In the Introduction to *The Wanderer* which he wrote for the complete edition of his works in 1841, Montgomery reports that in 1803, after reading a newspaper article with a friend about the freedom-hungry Swiss emigrants ('the unconquerable offspring of Tell') who went to America after Napoleon founded the Helvetian Republic, the friend suggested to him that he should write a poem on this theme. It was at the time when the 'postscript to the Augustans', Crabbe, Campbell, Rogers and Bowles, had become confused about their aesthetic views and were not writing. It was also at the time when the ballad and the German robber drama were at the height of their popularity. Montgomery's friend was probably thinking along the lines of a didactic poem on the subject; but Montgomery, who had already written 'imitations of Fielding and Smollett' and tales in prose and 'in the strange style of the German plays and romances then in vogue' of which he was later ashamed,[40] answered not without some uncertainty that the material 'might be made the burden of a ballad'.

Montgomery soon set to work on the poem. He assumed from the beginning that the dialogue style in which certain folk ballads are written would be most suitable for his purposes, but he tried out many ideas before he arrived at the poem's final form. The work, in tetrameter trochee stanzas four lines long with alternate rhyming, grew at his hand (as did *The Lay of the Last Minstrel* that Scott was writing at approximately the same time) to a length that exceeded that of the traditional ballad and finally consisted of six parts with a total of 198 stanzas (792 lines). Thus parallel to Scott, Montgomery had created his own form of verse narrative, and like Scott and the Lake Poets, Montgomery also developed his new narrative style from the ballad and the literature imported from Germany in that period. With *The Wanderer* he wrote the kind of poem that Southey had already planned in 1799 and had occasionally also attempted: 'Treating an heroic subject in lyric measure and upon a dramatic plan.'[41] Montgomery in fact made a principle out of that mixture. The direct model for this form which he refers to in the Introduction to *The Wanderer of Switzerland* is the ballad of *The Friar of Orders Gray* in Percy's *Reliques*.[42] Montgomery goes much further and *The Wanderer* is not just a dialogue ballad but a dramatic scene in which five persons participate, and there are occasional details about the facial expressions and gestures of the people speaking. The epic part – the wanderer's report of the battles in Switzerland – naturally takes up so much space that it is made to seem like the actual story, with the dialogue parts merely forming the framework.

The novelty of the form and the topical interest of the subject explain why this poem, in places unbearably sentimental and overemphatic with its abundant tears, swoons, Ahs! and Ohs!, at first caused a stir and was praised by the critics. But in January 1807, when the third edition had already appeared, Jeffrey discussed *The Wanderer* in the *Edinburgh Review*[43] and this time Montgomery fared badly. The whining, overemotional tone is attacked as an example of proletarian tastelessness, and the many repetitions exposed to ridicule. As far as Jeffrey was concerned, the whole thing was a bad 'pantomime ... more insipid and disgusting than any tragic ballad either ancient or modern, that we recollect to have met with'. At a time when new works by Scott, Campbell, Rogers, J. Baillie, Sotheby, Wordsworth and Southey were appearing every day,[44] it was incomprehensible that the public could tolerate a third edition of a poem like this. In three years *The Wanderer* would be consigned to oblivion, but there was a danger that other untalented young people would be encouraged to copy this example and ruin the public for classical poetry.

The public did not fulfil Jeffrey's prophecy. In the Introduction to *The Wanderer* written for the complete edition in 1841, Montgomery expresses his great satisfaction that the poem had lasted eleven times longer than Jeffrey thought it would, and had since run to thirteen editions. However, there had been no imitations of Montgomery's own original form of verse narrative: he himself did not risk continuing along these lines and nor did anyone else. This new idea, which was in any case doomed to failure on account of a metre unsuitable for narrative, thus went no further whereas Scott's verse narrative form became more and more popular.

Jeffrey's basic assessment of the poem was never publicly contradicted. In 1809 Byron wrote in *English Bards and Scotch Reviewers*, ll. 148 ff. the following comic obituary to Montgomery's first volume of poems, of which the main attraction had been *The Wanderer*

> With broken lyre, and cheek serenely pale,
> Lo! sad Alcaeus wanders down the vale;
> Though fair they rose, and might have bloom'd at last,
> His hopes have perish'd by the northern blast:
> Nipp'd in the bud by Caledonian gales,
> His blossoms wither as the blast prevails!
> O'er his lost works let classic Sheffield weep;
> May no rude hand disturb their easy sleep![45]

The World before the Flood represents an attempt by Montgomery to approach the verse narrative from a completely different angle: it is a short epic on a biblical subject, the story of Enoch, to which Milton had referred in *Paradise Lost* XI, 664 ff. He naturally takes great pains not to follow too obviously in Milton's footsteps as the Wieland translator Sotheby did in his epic *Saul*, since, as the *Edinburgh Review* said in its review of Sotheby's poem[46] 'A scriptural subject treated in blank verse unfortunately brings Milton to the thoughts of most readers'; and Montgomery knew only too well that he could not stand up to such comparison. He thus wrote in heroic couplets (though of course with pronounced run-on lines) and in his handling of the biblical theme followed the example set half a century before by Gessner, who in his *Tod Abels* (The Death of Abel) reduced Milton's 'heroic' grandeur to the scale of an intimate story by including pastoral and sentimental elements. In this poetic prose poem the Miltonian model, which in German had already been watered down in Bodmer's *Noah*, was completely dissolved in moods, emotions, a soft elegiac tone and idyllic descriptions of nature. *The Death of Abel* became so popular in England that towards the end of the eighteenth century it was competing with Bunyan's *Pilgrim's Progress* and Defoe's *Robinson Crusoe* as one of the most read books. Between 1761 and 1811 six translations appeared, of which four were in prose and two in blank verse.[47] Montgomery, educated by the Moravian brothers at Fulneck near Leeds, was also familiar with Bodmer's and Klopstock's work in translation. However, the heroic style did not suit him and in addition, as we have already said, was always reminiscent of Milton, so that for *The World before the Flood* (in ten cantos) Montgomery chose to follow Gessner's model as far as narration was concerned. He used no epic apparatus and described the pastoral, patriarchal world of the Old Testament in sentimental rather than heroic cantos. Although the story was not written as an entertaining, exciting tale or romance but as a religious parable – 'Fiction though it be, it is the Fiction that represents Truth; and that is Truth in the essence, though not in the name' he writes in the Original Preface of 1813 – it has more suspense in its plot and more of the character of a poetic religious novel than Gessner's *Death of Abel* and the tone is less sentimental. The extravagance of *The Wanderer* has disappeared, and this work is on a higher plane, in calm and classical style. However, for precisely this reason it is particularly colourless and impersonal: sentiment was the only thing Montgomery had to offer; when it was suppressed, all that remained was 'a Prize Poem'. The review in the *Quarterly Review*[48] discloses the connection with Gessner and describes the sector of society to which this type of poetry appealed: uneducated people who love 'an abundance of emotion and flowery language and aquatint reproductions'. Even the puritans could enjoy such fiction, since it dealt with biblical subjects in an innocent pastoral setting. The educated person might be irritated by the inclusion of romantic fiction in a biblical story, but the common people are not offended by it: what they like, they like, and they do not seek reasons for it.

The Pelican Island was written at the end of the period we are studying. In this work Montgomery has got away from the ballad and the sectarian Bible stories of the late eighteenth century and is attempting in part to be modern (his work shows the influence of Shelley) in part to create something timeless. He finally writes in the blank verse that had been recommended to him in all the above-mentioned reviews as being the most suitable form for his subjects. The poem (in nine cantos) is not a proper story but a poetic allegory: the spirit of the poet, thirsting for the society of a like-minded being, wanders the world from the beginning of time and experiences the stages of the Creation, from the appearance of the stars to the appearance of life and the creation of man, who even after the Fall is conscious of the bountifulness of his Creator and the indestructibility of the spirit. The title is based on the poetic description of natural processes in the sections on the formation of a coral island where the life of the pelicans first gives the poet an idea of the bliss of a communal society.

The Pelican Island is included here because of what Montgomery's change from the purely classicistic, didactic poetry of his early period – such as *The West Indies* of 1807 – to this poem tells us about the development of the genre. Here it becomes evident that the way the reflective poetry of the eighteenth century developed to become the reflective poetry of the nineteenth century can only be understood if we remember that this took place during the period when the verse narrative held sway. Only in this context did the reflections turn into visions: the ability to create a vivid, dynamic vision was learned from the example of the verse narrative, the revival of the art of poetic narrative initiated by Scott and Southey. Seen in this light the change in meaning of the term romantic poetry from 'revival of the medieval romance' to 'the poetic style of the post-1800 generation' has a deeper significance. This is also a key to Shelley's work.

Montgomery is no visionary like the poet of *Alastor* and *The Triumph of Life*, and his *Pelican Island*, even though applauded by Christopher North,[49] is so far removed from any work of Shelley's that the latter's influence was not even detected by his contemporaries;[50] however the examination of this, his last long poem has revealed important lines of development the relevance of which will be even more apparent in the subsequent sections of this chapter.

George Crabbe's verse narrative: the opposite of the romance

> Ah! happy he who thus, in magic themes
> O'er worlds bewitch'd, in early rapture dreams,
> Where wild Enchantment waves her potent wand,
> And Fancy's beauties fill her fairy land;
> Where doubtful objects strange desires excite,
> And Fear and Ignorance afford delight.
>
> But lost, for ever lost, to me these joys,
> Which Reason scatters, and which Time destroys,
> Too dearly bought: maturer judgement calls
> My busied mind from tales and madrigals,
> My doughty giants are all slain or fled,
> And all my knights, blue, green, and yellow, dead.
>
> G. Crabbe, *The Library* (1780), C. 573 ff.

> Crabbe's long career reflects more clearly than any other the progress of what has been called the *epic revival*.
>
> C. H. Herford, *The Age of Wordsworth*, p. 184

The most unconventional and gifted poet of the generation born after the middle of the century, four representatives of which were discussed in the previous section, is George Crabbe. This 'Pope in worsted stockings', as Horace Smith called him in his *Rejected Addresses* of 1812, this creator of 'poetry without an atmosphere', as he himself described his work in the Preface to the *Tales* of 1812, should not be viewed too one-sidedly as a descendant of the French School of poetry, as the last consistent upholder of the classicistic heroic couplet, who never became infatuated with romanticism of any description, as the last Augustan. He is without a doubt all of these things, and in their reviews of his work the contemporary critics seldom omitted to confront him with Wordsworth or the poets of the Scott school and then either praise him for his greater realism or reproach him for his neglect of the ideal aspects of life: imagination, fantasy, the idyllic joys and hidden virtues of the simple life and the portrayal of the noble soul and the enchanting atmosphere. It should not, however, be forgotten that the effect the works Crabbe wrote after 1807 had on the public was largely due to the romantic poets.

By calling his type of tale in verse the opposite of the romantic verse narrative, the idea is not to exclude him from this generic history as being absolutely incompatible with the other poets, but to show that he in fact has much in common with them. Crabbe is not, as is often maintained, an eighteenth-century man who experienced the new age without being affected by it; he is an artist who confronted the problems of his day – both social and aesthetic – like Wordsworth or Byron. But his very different character and lack of illusions made him distance himself from the 'romantic', i.e., idealistic, trends of the times. His keeping to the poetic forms of the previous epoch was a very personal way of maintaining his position as an already famous poet when the current literary fashion was one which was contrary to his tastes. In spite of this he differed just as much in his approach from the eighteenth-century way of looking at things[51] as from that of the early romantic period.[52] Like Jeffrey he is an unromantic figure without as a consequence being reactionary.

The fact that he mixes elements from both intellectual worlds, the eighteenth and the early nineteenth century, in a highly individual, objective manner, looking back to the past and ahead to the future and as it were building a bridge from Pope to Thomas Hardy, makes him a more original post-classicist than the four poets discussed in the preceding section. The members of the romantic generation in England (they did not, after all, consider themselves a single exclusive school) thus for all their cautious criticism always treated him as a contemporary of great stature who had something new and original to say and who was one of them as far as the topicality if not as far as the aims and structure of his poetry was concerned. As late as 1822, an article in *Blackwood's Magazine*[53] describes Scott, Crabbe and Byron as constituting the 'top class' of modern poets and puts them on a level with Dryden and Pope, while Wordsworth, who had always been praised by this journal, is relegated to the class below. Wordsworth, Coleridge and Byron had the highest respect for Crabbe all their lives and Scott and Jeffrey were friends of his.

It is certainly not the purpose of this account to rank Crabbe with the poets just named as one of the greatest poets of the epoch: he does not have sufficient breadth of vision for this. He is blind to many of the metaphysical and aesthetic discoveries of his time. When presenting social problems he merely records without offering any elevated poetic or philosophical interpretation such as we find in Wordsworth's work or scientific interpretation such as that which featured later in the work of the naturalists of the Zola school. His verses have no aura of deeper meaning about them and seldom involve the reader emotionally or stimulate thought; at the most an overall meaning or personal interpretation of the facts is suggested through the formal and rhetorical clichés of neo-classical verse technique such as puns, antitheses, parallelism, semantic zeugmas, epigrammatic aphorisms and satirical irony, etc., but the intellectual brilliance of Pope is not thereby attained. He is a metrical historiographer of the poor and also the frustrated petty bourgeois. Beyond this there is virtually no attempt to explore new areas of the emotions or of aesthetics, which were what gave the works of the great romantic poets their enduring value. In his criticism of life he does not come to any conclusion about the problems he raises. The basic moral concept of his poems, where deterministic pessimism and strict, conventional moral demands exist side by side, is particularly unsatisfactory. Questions such as the responsibility of a person who is the product of a particular milieu or the theodicy problem are left open in all his works. The one is never satisfactorily answered and the other never directly dealt with. Equally unsatisfactory, particularly by comparison with Wordsworth, is his attempt to solve the problem of combining 'pleasure in poetry' and 'the truth of painful subjects' in the Preface to the *Tales* of 1812.[54]

However, among the poets who do not qualify for the 'top class' he is one of the greatest. He not only outshines the late classicists, who flirted with romanticism, but also the romancers who closely followed Scott and whose sole aim was sensation and entertainment, and the 'epic' Laureate Southey. Although he did not aim as high as Southey, he achieved what he set out to do. In our day a Crabbe renaissance would be more appropriate than a Scott, Campbell or Southey renaissance.

It is not all that easy to prove that Crabbe was not merely a descendant of the French School of poetry but also shared many of the interests and problems of the romantic generation. The heroic couplets in the style of Pope and Goldsmith are too strongly reminiscent of the eighteenth century, and even in the alternately rhyming tetrameter stanzas of *Sir Eustace Grey* or *The Hall of Justice* (both dating from 1807) the disparity between Crabbe and Wordsworth or Shelley is noticeable in spite of the similarity of theme.[55]

Crabbe's affinities with the earlier romantic verse narrators become more apparent if we study the genre to which his works belonged. Although between his early works (such as *The Library* of 1781 and *The Village* of 1783) and his last publications (*The Tales of the Hall* of 1819 or *The Posthumous Tales* which appeared in 1834) he scarcely moved out of his chosen field, in this he reflected the spirit of his age: he gradually changed from an observer to a narrator or, to use Tillotson's terminology again, in addition to his Augustan interest in design, he increasingly began to share the interest of members of the early romantic generation in continuity. It is both exciting and instructive to see this process in a poet whose way of thinking differed so radically from that of the romantics. *The Library* and later *The Newspaper* (1785) are pure reflective didactic poems on current topics. They could even be called essays in verse, which was how Pope also described some of his own poems. *The Village* is very much the same type of poem: where individual fates are singled out they serve to illustrate general observations and theses and are no more than short descriptions of a particular situation.

This is followed by the long interval in writing of twenty-two years, and when he reappears on the scene in 1807 with *The Parish Register* it is evident that he has been influenced to a certain extent by the Scott type of narrative poetry. Here he is beginning to develop his examples as independent entities and his descriptions and reflections are no longer the most important part of the poem, illustrated by short, tangible examples, but have now become the additional details that shed light on the stories. The lives of the characters that serve as examples are predominant. While Crabbe gives only a brief outline of their personalities and fates, *The Parish Register* can nevertheless be said to contain material for a dozen socio-critical novels.

The 'sallies of Crabbe into romantic verse'',[56] *Sir Eustace Grey* and *The Hall of Justice* written in the same year, are already polished verse narratives in the characteristic tetrameters of romantic poetry. They even push out the boundaries of the genre in a manner typical of the romantic period in that the story is told in dramatic dialogues and monologues, while the metre and verse form resemble the lyrical style. The poet must nevertheless have felt that this 'passionate' genre with its affinities with the *Lyrical Ballads* was not right for him. These were thus the only two poems of this type that he wrote, even though both of them – provided they are not compared with *The Ancient Mariner* or Wordsworth's *Female Vagrant* and *Her Eyes are Wild* – can be considered successful, and Crabbe was repeatedly encouraged by the critics, in particular Jeffrey, to continue in this vein.[57] He then went back to the heroic couplet and his earlier objective, aloof type of report. It is typical of him that he left several poems in a similar style unpublished, e.g., *Hester* (1804), *The Insanity of Ambitious Love* (1816), and *Joseph and Jesse* (1822 ?). They first appeared in A. Pollard's edition of the *New Poems by G. Crabbe* (Liverpool), in 1960.

In *The Borough* (1810) he nevertheless attempts to develop his own form of the tale in verse based on his earlier style. In the course of this work there is a noticeable change from discursive writing to narrative and fictional writing. Some sections revolve around abstract collective concepts selected mainly for the opportunity they provide for reflection and description – such as sects, the legal and medical professions, schools and the church, etc. – and in which the description of the situation is only occasionally interrupted by short narrative passages. Others, in a similar manner to *The Parish Register*, contain sketches of fates illustrating a particular theme (e.g., those of the actors and the prison inmates), then fuller character portraits (e.g., the vicar and the curate) and finally – after the transition from the character portrait to the life, still rather lacking in action, in the three stories of the poorhouse inhabitants – proper verse novellas with peripeteias and catastrophe (e.g. the four stories of the poor of the community), which are rounded off perfectly with the best and most famous story of *The Borough: Peter Grimes*. Owing to the non-narrative framework, the individual stories are of course always a little like the examples given in a sermon, as they are told not for the sake of the story itself, but because they are supposed to be typical of an overall general theme: an institution, a particular vice or a section of the population.

After the *Tales* of 1812 the non-narrative framework was abandoned even though the emphasis on the moral tended to increase.[58] The *Tales* are a series of unconnected verse novellas, and could be described as a conduct book for the lower and middle classes consisting solely of examples. The moral is not necessarily spelled out in each story, and is sometimes only clarified by a motto at the beginning. *The Tales of the Hall* of 1819 once again have a framework, but this is now itself just another story.[59]

Crabbe's clash with the principle of continuity popular in his day is brought out even more clearly in the comments of his contemporaries, in particular in the advice that Francis Jeffrey gave his friend about his narrative style and choice of material, and in the arguments with which the poet defended himself. Jeffrey had at first resisted the romantic trend, but had been swept along by the popularity of this shift in focus from discontinuous and abstract poetic reflection to exciting plots, and as we have said, like the *Quarterly Review* critics repeatedly encouraged Crabbe to continue with the type of poem represented by *Sir Eustace Grey* and *The Hall of Justice*, i.e., instead of dividing his poems up into short examples as in a novel, making them exciting by means of drama, imaginative and meaningful subject matter, narrative unity, peripeteias and catastrophes and a modern metre. Jeffrey was thus evidently trying to persuade him to combine his style of writing with the romantic narrative style of the Scott 'school'. While this detailed advice was not published until after the appearance of the *Tales* in 1812,[60] Jeffrey's earlier reviews were also really saying the same thing; and from Crabbe's counter-arguments in the preface to the *Tales* it can be concluded that the critic also frequently gave him similar advice in person. Jeffrey specifically wanted Crabbe to include more action and fewer details, and also to drop the 'jocularity', as he called the superior, aloof tone that ran through Crabbe's works – partly an expression of the poet's sceptical temperament, partly an echo of Pope's satirical tone and partly a traditional characteristic of the heroic couplet – and repeatedly broke through the gloom and the naturalism of his descriptions. Jeffrey also wanted him to write a long coherent story rather than a loose sequence of individual anecdotes. His requirements are summed up in the following sentence: 'We do not want him to write an Epic; but we should have liked a little more of the deep and tragic passions – of those passions which exalt and overwhelm the soul.'[61] This brings to mind Scott's objection to the demands Jeffrey makes of the modern poet according to his review of *The Curse of Kehama*, where he apparently expects a synthesis of the sublimity of Homer with the majesty of Virgil, the fantasy of Ariosto, the pure taste of Tasso and the awesome seriousness of Dante: in other words something quite impossible to produce.[62]

Crabbe's defence against Jeffrey, and any other critic who required similar things of him, is to be found in the preface to the *Tales*, and extends over a number of pages. It can be summarized approximately as follows: it was easy, as Crabbe saw it, for people to recommend him to write a work that, if not strictly speaking an epic, was nevertheless a long narrative poem with unity of action, a coherent plot, subordination of the details to the overall design, which consisted of a build-up to a catastrophe or climax, and the grouping of the characters round the hero or heroes as in the epic. He would gladly follow this advice, but the characters available to him and the adventures and passions that were all he was able to write about were totally unsuitable for this kind of treatment. While his works were not completely disjointed, his previous poems bore a relationship to the heroic epic genre somewhat similar to that of a loose association of people such as a group of pilgrims or party of tourists to a well-ordered army. His material did not however permit the unity of design and grand-scale treatment the proper epic poem required. He hoped that what was lacking would be compensated for by the greater variety of action, scenes, characters and tone and the reality and precision of the details. In addition, with the epic a poet could only either completely succeed or completely fail. His poems, on the other hand, were not dependent on one thing for their success, since they offered something for everyone. It was not a question here of whether his method was better than that of the true epic poets, he only wanted to point out that his previous route to literary success was the only one possible for *him*, and declare himself incapable of following any other.

In the subsequent detailed discussion Crabbe deals with another question he had obviously also been asked: why could he not have joined the individual stories with a framework story? He names Chaucer and Boccaccio as poets who provided models for this method. He finds Chaucer's solution too difficult and says that in spite of his basic success even this great poet had been unable to avoid grouping the representatives of the various classes, who are the vehicles for the tales, in a rather arbitrary and improbable fashion as a single band of pilgrims. How then is a modern poet supposed to create a framework story that successfully fulfils the same function? Boccaccio's solution he declares to be useless: there is no connection between the novellas of *The Decameron* and their narrators, so that the unity is only imposed in a very superficial fashion. (It has already been mentioned that Crabbe did later on think of a framework for *The Tales of the Hall* which, even if it does not have all the advantages of the framework of *The Canterbury Tales*, nevertheless unites the individual stories.

Crabbe concludes by defending his own type of poetry against the accusation that it is not poetic, since it is neither 'lofty' nor 'heroic' nor does it fit Shakespeare's well-known definition of the poet in *A Midsummer Night's Dream* V, 1, 12 ff. Here he refers to the great representatives of satirical and realistic poetry in England, Chaucer, Dryden and Pope, saying that they have a completely different idea of poetry, but one which, after all, is also accepted as valid. He thus also differs considerably from the romantic poets, in that he consciously distances himself from the expressive idea of poetry of the early romantic and romantic period. This gives us a more detailed idea of how Crabbe saw his own work and how he classified it, clearly allying himself with the great representatives of the Augustan Age but also with Chaucer. The fact that Crabbe in addition found many ideas similar to his own in Shakespeare is demonstrated by the many Shakespearean mottos that are scattered throughout his works. He was probably conscious of his distance from the type of poetry characterized by abundant imagination and 'fine frenzy', but unquestionably concerned with those things that were important to the verse narrators of the Scott school: a *variety* of action, a narrative technique adequate for the material – and popularity.

Even Jeffrey, in his review of Byron's *Corsair* and *Bride of Abydos*[63] indirectly admitted that Crabbe did have the ability to portray 'passions', which was the main characteristic of modern poetry as far as the romantic critics were concerned. When in this article Jeffrey, with his cyclical interpretation of the history of civilization and literature,[64] says that today's poetry, in search of strong emotions, is sinking to the depths of misery and vice, he is of course thinking primarily of Byron, about whose *Corsair* he is writing. However, it is not hard to see from the text that he also has Crabbe, Wordsworth and Scott in mind. In his list of the subjects of contemporary poetry it is sometimes possible to identify the work that is meant: 'the dreams of convicts' refers both to the man sentenced to death in Crabbe's *Borough* (Letter XXII) and Byron's *Corsair*; with the 'agonies of Gypsy women' he has Crabbe's *Hall of Justice* in mind; 'the exploits of buccaneers and freebooters' is a reference to Bertram in Scott's *Rokeby* and Byron's Conrad in *The Corsair*; 'pictures to shudder at of remorse, revenge and insanity' fits almost all romantic verse narratives, but is also certainly an allusion to Crabbe as well (particularly with respect to the last point); of the 'triumph of generous feelings in scenes of anguish and terror' there is scarcely a better example than Crabbe's *Ellen Orford* (*The Borough* Letter XX) and 'the heroism of low-born affections and the tragedies of a vulgar atrocity' seem to have been included with Crabbe specifically in mind.

Although he names no names, this article of Jeffrey's would seem to prove fairly conclusively that Crabbe's contemporaries saw more connections between him and the romantic verse narrators than we do today, and that as far as they were concerned he was also a modern romancer, even if he was a rather special kind of romancer. A small detail in the Preface to *The Borough* shows that Crabbe himself was not basically opposed to being classified in this way: here he draws the reader's attention to the similarity of his *Peter Grimes* with 'Mr. Scott's ruffian' Marmion.

Contemporary critics always pointed out the ways in which Crabbe differed from the romantics (particularly Wordsworth) but also occasionally confirmed that there were certain similarities between his endeavours and those of the other 'modern' poets. In his review of *The Borough*[65] Jeffrey emphasizes that, like the romantic poets, Crabbe meets two of the public's requirements: the desire for sensation, which is a very fundamental one, and the desire to witness need and suffering, that by a strange psychological mechanism gives the reader more enjoyment than the portrayal of purely pleasurable things, precisely because such descriptions of pain are more sensational than an idyllic representation of life, and because impressions in poetry are always measured according to their intensity and not according to their pleasantness (in works of fiction the reader is after all spared the unpleasant consequences of need and danger while he can still enjoy the sensational aspect[66]). Crabbe only offends now and then against the first principle of all art, which is that it must please: he cannot help describing need in such a way that it has a repulsive effect instead of arousing pity and admiration.

The *Quarterly Review*'s review of *The Borough*[67] begins by accusing Crabbe of not lifting the reader out of his everyday life to the dream world of fantasy, and then continues with a detailed apology for escape in poetry.[68] At the end however it is admitted that Crabbe has already been influenced by the spirit of romantic poetry: some of his work (the reviewer is almost certainly thinking of the two poems *Sir Eustace Grey* and *The Hall of Justice*, of 1807, and perhaps also the narrative pieces from *The Borough*, in particular *Peter Grimes*) no longer appeals just to reason but also to the imagination. Here he has put down the deadly weapon of his previous manner – a 'satirist of low life' was what Jeffrey had called the poet in his review of *The Borough*! – and wielded a magic lance instead.

The clearest definition of Crabbe's connection with the romantic movement is provided by Christopher North. In his 'Preface to a Review of the Chronicles of the Canongate' in *Blackwood's Magazine*[69] he maintains that Crabbe should not be contrasted with the Lake Poets, since he owed 'much of his best inspiration' to them and since without the model of the Lake school the best things in *The Borough* would never have been written.[70] He calls Crabbe's works 'an incongruous mixture of romance and the news of the next Parish'. The main difference between Crabbe and the romantic poets of the Lake school, as he sees it, is that Crabbe, with his bold descriptions of human beings, only gives an outline of their external characteristics, instead of exhausting the human content of his subjects like Wordsworth. His framework is the earth not the universe; his stories contain no poetical causes of the events but represent 'the fortuitous concatenation ... of downright reality'.

Among the many factors that have motivated this criticism, some in all probability political, is an instinctive reaction against Crabbe's view of humanity and resulting narrative technique. When the writer of *The Borough* describes a life, what is almost always lacking is a comprehensive view of the individual as a whole personality whose fate is developed from his basic character. His people are either types – the old farmer, the rake, the thoughtless youth, the weak-willed, fallen girl, etc. – or, if their psychological make-up is described in all its complexity, as in the later works starting with *Peter Grimes*, they are portrayed as almost passive victims of their own disposition and the prevailing social influences. Only rarely does one of his characters exert free will over the adverse circumstances and triumph morally, and even in such cases, for example in *Ellen Orford*, it is more a question of the person concerned clinging to the faith of their childhood and the security this gives them than of inner freedom and strength of personality. This deterministic view (together with the factual outlook of the social critic) has an effect on the narrative style. Crabbe does not usually narrate dynamically in the manner of the writer who shares his characters' experiences and wants the reader to do so too, but for all his skill with the narrative structure produces a sequence of situations described with a certain aloofness. The life of the poorhouse inhabitant *Clelia* (*Borough* Letter XV), for example, is presented in short sections, each summarizing the events of a ten-year period. The slow decline of this cocotte is thus broken up into a series of disconnected, static pictures.

Most of *Peter Grimes* also consists of a series of situations picked out of the continuous story. Here, of course, the monologue of the hero at the end, when he has gone mad, does shed light on his inner development between the episodes and on the psychological background. The later stories are in general more fluently narrated, which is certainly in no small part due to the influence of the many romantic verse narratives that were now being written. However, in these stories too the narrative technique not infrequently consists of a series of situations, e.g., in *Arabella* (*Tales* No. 9) or in *Edward Shore* (*Tales* No. 11). Oliver Elton compares this narrative technique with Hogarth's cycles of pictures entitled *Progress*,[71] contrasts it with the free, continuous style of Balzac and points out the suitability of the heroic couplet for Crabbe's 'curious habit of marking out uniform stages'.

He thus accurately describes Crabbe's position in the literary process that we are following here: this poet too is on the threshold between the design perspective of the eighteenth century and the continuity perspective of the nineteenth century.

When Hazlitt, in *Lectures on the English Poets*, wittily calls Crabbe the poet of the 'still life of tragedy'[72] and elsewhere says[73] that 'He rivets the attention by being tedious' this summarizes what has been said here about Crabbe's characters and verse technique. A further remark of Hazlitt's about Crabbe from *The Spirit of the Age* is worth mentioning, because it refers once again to the genre of his works: Hazlitt calls him a 'Malthus turned metrical romancer'.[74] We have already seen from Hazlitt's criticism of Scott that his generic classifications do not prove very much, and we can deduce from all his remarks about Crabbe that he certainly did not put him in the same category as Scott, Southey, Moore or Hunt. However, the expression 'a Malthus turned ... romancer' and the concluding words of the same essay[75] show that he did classify him with the many narrative poets of his day, not as a representative of the fantastic, exciting and unrealistic romantic genre but of its 'opposite'.

6 Ramification and dissolution

> To keep the literary kinds severely apart is one of those classicist precepts
> of which the breach and the observance are (in right hands) equally to the
> advantage of literature.
> C. H. Herford, Introduction to his edition of the *Narrative Poems of Shelley*,
> London, 1918

The poets and works discussed thus far are a representative selection of the
mass of narrative verse literature that began with Scott. The purpose of
examining them more closely was to show how Scott fulfilled the demand for
an epic form suited to the times; how Scott's model inspired a large number
of rather unoriginal imitators; how Wordsworth tried to exploit this romance
form for his own poetic purposes; how the new type of poetry became so
fashionable that even the representatives of conservative taste succumbed to
it or at least attempted syntheses between the old and the new, which was
naturally not a very promising line of development; and finally how Crabbe
in his later works produced something that was the complete opposite of the
'genre', and that, although the mentality behind it was entirely different,
would scarcely have been possible without the existence of Scott's form of
literature and the success this had had.

In the preceding discussion of the works of individual poets it was
sometimes necessary to abandon the chronological order and move ahead of
events. We will now return to the situation in 1812 and 1813.

Scott's retrospective report about this period in the Introduction to *Rokeby*
of 1830[1] shows that now, for the first time since 1805, public interest in his
form of romance was beginning to wane. The structure, style and form had
been reproduced three times by Scott himself and prolifically copied by others,
and a saturation point had been reached. The reviewers seemed to be
unanimous in their advice that Scott should produce nothing more in this
vein.[2] Jeffrey's prophecy made after the appearance of *Marmion*, namely that
the fashion for modern romances would one day die out as a result of the gross
incompetence of bad imitators, thus seemed about to be fulfilled. Then came
Byron, the first representative of the younger romantic generation, and the
situation changed overnight: the romantic tale in verse was once again a
resounding success and was avidly cultivated by the poets, proof enough that
its possibilities had not after all been exhausted.

146

The genre naturally underwent increasing alterations at the hands of the younger generation. If the works named thus far had already deviated from the original type as far as themes, metre and style were concerned, so that Scott's model was only recognizable as a distant influence, the boundaries of what has here for the purposes of discussion been called a genre were broken down even further in the verse narratives of the younger romantic poets. Scott's type of romantic poetry, which represented a revival of the epic forms of the Age of Romance, was slowly merging into the complex of romantic poetry where there was no exclusive assignment to a specific genre. Here every work is basically so individual that conventional classification is no longer possible and generic distinctions become increasingly vague and, because of more and more new admixtures, difficult to define. Before this dissolution process is discussed in greater detail, the characteristics of the 'genre' established between 1805 and 1812 should be summarized once again.

1. The romantic verse narrative was the modern equivalent of the medieval courtly or minstrel romance. It has important generic elements in common with these forms.

2. These elements are: (a) an exciting story, entertainment, emotion, strong appeal to a wide sector of society through a plot full of human interest but extending beyond everyday reality and adventurous in the widest sense, whereby the reader is encouraged to share in the hero's fortunes and identify with them; (b) a loose framework and relatively free approach to metre and structure; (c) no attempt to offer lofty historical, metaphysical or ethical interpretations; strong emphasis on the material itself.

3. This type of poetry was eminently suitable for the constant introduction of new material, forms, themes, statements and levels of style. It was this flexibility that finally undermined the character of the genre completely, and together with the striving for the new and original that is also an inherent characteristic of such poetry, was responsible for its dissolution.

When we come to analyse the works of the great poets who gave the Scott genre its finishing touches and finally destroyed it – Byron, Keats and Shelley – the generic elements that have been identified and described so far are no longer adequate. Each of the three poets added something substantial. The fates of the heroes, that had previously been objectively portrayed and were in no way linked with the poet,[3] are transformed by Byron into subjective descriptions of his inner life, analytical self-portraits. He thus expands the genre by adding a confessional tendency that had not been encountered in it before, but that in the age of *Werther*, *Obermann* and *Adolphe*, an age also marked by an increasing subjectivism in philosophy, was already in the air. The consequences of this development for the generic form and the problems it gave the reviewers will be discussed below.

Keats transfers the interest from the plot to the form or rather the purely poetical aspect, and in so doing becomes an early English forerunner of the nineteenth-century poets, whose key concepts were symbolism and *poésie pure*. In Shelley's work, finally Scott's genre was transformed into philosophical or political allegory.

This, in very rough outline, is what happened to the genre between approximately 1813 and 1823, and the works of the three great younger romantic poets will now be examined in this light. The poems that will be discussed will be those where the requirements named under points 1 and 2 above are still more or less met, or there is clear evidence of the poets having been influenced by this genre. Here too the focus of the discussion is on the historical process, on the blend of influences, and on comments on what was happening by the poets themselves and by the reviewers. There are no descriptions of the content or analyses of the form of these well-known works.

Lord Byron

> Well now, I must say ... there is no doubt that Lord Byron is very much to blame, if it really be so, which I am no judge of, that he was the first who wrote in a personal manner. It was introducing a dangerous – a deadly trick. There is no saying where it may end yet ...
>
> *Noctes Ambrosianae* III (May, 1822)

> We care less for Byron's stories, as stories, than for Scott's and he might have said, like Maturin, 'emotions are my events'.
>
> Oliver Elton, *A Survey of English Literature 1780–1830*, II, p. 149)

Of all the many possible angles from which Byron's poetic tales can be approached, three are of relevance for this genre history. We will look first at Byron as the poet who developed to their full extent the possibilities of the popular genre of romantic verse narrative as initiated by Scott; second we will look at him as the poet who carried the genre further, as a narrator who explored new forms, styles and effects and thus contributed to the dissolution of the initial type; and third we will look at him as a critic of the genre, and indeed of romantic poetry as a whole, who realized sooner and with greater perspicacity than Jeffrey, Hazlitt or Christopher North that the possibilities of the romantic verse narrative as a genre were limited and foresaw the disadvantageous effects that the romantic 'fashion' would have on the tastes of the following generation, although or precisely because he had contributed to this decline in taste.

The fact that he can be described as having completed the development begun by Scott is in itself proof of his popularity,[4] which superseded and even overtook that of Scott[5] and which, after *Childe Harold's Pilgrimage* I and II had made him famous overnight, was based on his tales in verse.[6] In these Byron provided readers with everything that had also contributed to Scott's success: excitement and continuity, romantic events and characters, which on the one hand were remote from the readers as far as time, place, social class or daily experience were concerned, and on the other could awaken their sympathy, and even, in the case of many of his contemporaries, a strong sense of identification. In addition there was passion and sentiment, violence and sensational horror effects, all of which was packaged in flowing, spirited, but stylistically traditional verse.[7] Like Scott, Byron did not go beyond the level of education and intelligence of the average reader[8] in spite of the wealth of information contained in his tales, but to a greater extent than Scott he met the general demand for 'romantic' intensity of feeling.

When the critics of his day praised him – and they were agreed that he ranked alongside Scott, Wordsworth and Crabbe as one of the greatest poets of the epoch, and indeed even overshadowed his famous contemporaries – then it was always for those qualities that they admired in Scott and his imitators.[9] The reviewers even occasionally discovered details in Byron's metrical tales where they felt he had plagiarized Scott,[10] and Byron once caught himself unintentionally imitating Scott's *Marmion*.[11] He felt he fully belonged to that 'school' or 'system' of poetry that he had thought wrong since at least 1817,[12] the most important representative of which he considered to be Scott. Although he did occasionally emphasize his distance from Scott and the different nature of his work[13] (he saw Scott as the 'Ariosto of the North'[14] who, while not concentrating solely on Scotland, did limit himself to 'all countries that are not the South', and dealt mainly with 'Chivalry – war & love'[15]) he was nevertheless well aware of his rivalry with Scott and of his position as the latter's successor as far as the public were concerned).[16]

And the public as well as the reviewers took Byron's affinities with the founders of the romantic verse narrative, Scott and Southey, so much for granted that although he was occasionally accused of deviating from these genre models – with for example the lack of plot in *Childe Harold* and *Lara*,[17] the similarity of his heroes, his constant gloom and depravity which, as an adoption of the German fashion, was associated with Jacobinism, his emphasis on 'metaphysics', i.e., the analysis of emotions that was an attribute of the pessimism then fashionable instead of on a gripping plot – he was still also repeatedly bracketed with Scott and Southey as an 'abductor into the kingdom of romance', the only difference being that he was ranked above his predecessors on account of this 'orginality'.

What was meant by this key word 'originality' that appeared in almost all the reviews? Evidently this concept summed up everything that made Byron's metrical tales superior to those of the other 'romancers', everything that widened the previous scope of the genre and finally led to its dissolution. It was less the external differences, such as Byron's skill at unearthing exciting material, his preference for shorter forms, and for geographical rather than historical distance from the everyday world, his more intensive treatment of erotic themes or his adherence to the 'criminal hero' whose resemblances to

Scott's *Marmion* and naturally to the attractive villains of the German fashion was seen but whom Byron transferred to another milieu and made more interesting than his predecessors, precisely through that analysis of the passions that was found to be original and 'metaphysical'.

These things alone, however, were not so new in 1813 – 20 as to explain the intense fascination of the public with Byron's poetry. The poetic form can also scarcely have given Byron his reputation for originality, since he used the same metres as Scott, Crabbe, Rogers and Campbell and also, in spite of his *al fresco* metrical technique, which he shared with Scott, repeatedly defended the Augustan standards.

Although in his review of *Childe Harold* II[18] Jeffrey speaks of the strong influence of the Lake Poets on Byron's approach to poetry, style and manner, he also says quite clearly that Byron's originality does *not* lie in differences in the poetic form or the details. Byron is on the contrary, like all people who are quick to respond in matters of aesthetics and are confident enough of their own originality not to fear plagiarism, 'a great mimic of styles and manners, and a great borrower of external character'. What his contemporaries understood by the catchword originality and what was repeatedly mentioned by all reviewers of his works were two characteristics of his poetry which are in the final analysis only two sides of the same coin: his constant portrayal of himself beneath a mask or in the guise of the 'criminal hero', and the suffering at the hopelessness of existence that was recognized as the common denominator of all these fictionalized self-portraits. In other words, Byron combined the subjective, confessional tendency which had entered European poetry with Rousseau with a view of or feeling about the world that a whole generation found highly topical, whether the readers reacted with fascinated horror or an irresistible sense of identification.

It is possible to justify the assertion that Byron's work constantly circles in the manner of a confession round his own self and his own experience of the pointlessness of existence simply by comparing the content of the works with his biography, as his contemporaries and earlier biographers frequently did. It is also possible, in line with Byron's frequent denial that his heroes were identical with him, to modify the thesis of the confessional and subjective tendency in his protagonists (as was often done in the later Byron literature) usually with reference to the literary roots of the Byronic hero, to Byron's tendency to assume poses or to those sides of his character which were not reflected in his 'romantic' poetry. This whole topic is only of relevance to this study in so far as it concerns the works belonging to our particular genre and Byron's own attitude to his metrical tales.

The work which made him famous, *Childe Harold's Pilgrimage*, is today only categorized with many reservations as belonging to the romantic verse narrative genre since it has almost no story at all,[19] but the fact that he used a mixture of literary traditions as vehicles to express the problems *he* had with life and impressions from *his* travels – travelogue, descriptive and reflective poetry of the kind that followed on from the later eighteenth century, Spenser pastiche (with a hint of biography) in the style of Beattie's *The Minstrel* – tells us a great deal about what it is that distinguishes all Byron's subsequent narrative poetry, what is the basis of his success as a narrator and what finally made him step outside the limits of the romantic verse narrative as dictated by fashion: about his lifelong conflict between the poetry that was a personal confession and his many attempts to conceal the person he was by means of changing literary strategies.

In his letters from the *Childe Harold* period this paradoxical attitude is already quite plain to be seen. On the one hand he repeatedly stresses, in particular when writing to R. C. Dallas, his literary agent at the time, the authenticity of the experiences described in *Childe Harold*,[20] inserts elegies to his own recently deceased friends Wingfield and Edlestone into the poem, i.e., puts them in Harold's mouth,[21] describes his private melancholy and loneliness in a letter in such a way that it reads like a prose version of a passage from *Childe Harold*,[22] uses the name of his protagonist to refer to himself,[23] and indeed traces with Harold's whole journey his own route through the Mediterranean countries.[24] On the other hand he never stops battling against the identification of his hero with himself: 'I much wish to avoid to identify myself with Harold, but to deny all connexion with him ... I would not be such a fellow as I have made my hero for the world.'[25] In the Preface to the first and second cantos in the Addition to the Preface he also defends himself against any identification of Harold with his creator and refers to literary models such as Shakespeare's *Timon of Athens* and Dr J. Moore's scoundrel *Zeluco*.

All these endeavours were in vain. The public did not read Byron's 'Romaunt' as an objective piece of fiction. They did not read it as any of the traditional models that Byron had tried to suggest: neither as a mere travelogue of a primarily descriptive nature[26] nor as an imaginary story of a fictitious character from traditional misanthropist literature or the fashionable Gothic villain mode (who was allegedly only incorporated 'for the sake of giving some connection to the piece',[27] nor as a pastiche of Spenserian vagrant knights embarking on their adventures (in other words as a pure study in stylization), nor as a philosophical study of the sentimental humour with an objective moral anatomy of its passions.[28] They read this poem first and foremost as a revelation of the author's character, as his *Confessions* and *Rêveries du Promeneur Solitaire*.[29] Here it is symptomatic that as early as 1808, Byron, when his mother compared him with Rousseau, denied that there was any similarity between himself and that 'illustrious madman'[30] and that he repeated this denial again in the *Detached Thoughts*, but that in the third canto of *Childe Harold* he paid his respects to Rousseau, the

> apostle of affliction ... who threw
> Enchantment over passion, and from woe
> Wrung overwhelming eloquence
>> (stanza LXXVII)

which made every reader aware of the denied similarity and hence the fact that *Childe Harold* was a piece of confessional literature:

> 'Twas not for fiction chose Rousseau this spot
> Peopling it with affections ...
>> (stanza CIV)

Although these circumstances are in fact well-known, they have been described again in detail here because of the light they shed on many important aspects of our genre.

1. After the publication of *Childe Harold* I and II, the much-famed originality of Byron was repeatedly considered to lie in the subjectivity or confessional character of his poems that shone through all the literary guises.

2. *Childe Harold* did not only make him famous, it also created the requirements for all subsequent metrical tales: the Byronic verse narrative, which – in addition to all the poetic attractions that had been valued in this type of poetry but of which the public was growing tired by 1813 – offered the attraction of personal feelings and experience, the hallmarks of the confession genre, gave the genre we are studying a fresh impetus and greater popularity than it had achieved even with Scott's romances.

3. Many literary developments had of course paved the way for the subjectivity of romantic poetry, not least Wordsworth's 'egotistical sublime'.[31] However, in Wordsworth's work this subjectivity was either expressed symbolically or intellectually abstracted from his private personality, as a result of which the tangible events and plots were weakened and the 'I' of the poems came through neither as a forceful character nor as a fascinating private person. In Byron's verse narratives after *Childe Harold*, on the other hand, the private person is at the centre of exciting plots, and is not the clichéd idealized hero of most previous romances (although there was still an element of this), but his moral opposite; and this *persona* is nevertheless (or for precisely this reason) an 'interesting' personality who in addition has a variety of different external experiences, and is extraordinarily active and vital and hence arouses the sympathy of the reader as much as the traditional 'good' romance hero.

4. With his ready, even if only partial confessions, this Byronic hero is also a figure who excites the readers' curiosity with the possibility of scandal, particularly since he is usually, like the author, a man from the upper classes.

The result of all this was such a novel mixture of fiction and reality, that the equation of romantic invention with factual biography was not limited to Byron's contemporaries, who felt they had been taken into the confidence of this unique personality; even now it still seems almost impossible to separate studies of Byron's works from his life and psychological make-up.[32]

Byron's originality as defined under the four points listed above, and hence the originality of his narrative poetry, also made him appear modern to his contemporaries. The key factor here was of course that with the antiquarian ballast of the Scott romance type he also threw out the ill-fated longing for a revival of the epic, which played an all too obvious part in the case of Landor and Southey, and a less generally acknowledged one in the case of Scott and Rogers.[33] And here too of course the political and geographical reality of *Childe Harold* and the Eastern Tales set the tone for the later metrical tales.[34] But what above all classified Byron's productions as modern were the emotions of the Byronic *persona*, together with that pessimistic attitude to existence which was later defined as *Weltschmerz* but also in moral terms as 'Satanism'. Elements of this had, it is true, featured in early romantic poetry: in melancholy ruin, night and graveyard poetry, and in the gloom in which Gothic villains at the end of the century were enveloped. The *vanitas vanitatum* had been lamented in poetry ever since Ecclesiastes, decorative villains had been in existence since the Elizabethans and Otway, and 'Satanic' protest against suppression and unjust rule was widespread in the literature of Blake's and Godwin's age. In Byron all these attitudes appeared together for the first time, and since they appeared as it were spontaneously, independently of the Christian and also of the classical tradition of scepticism, Pyrrhonism or mechanistic materialism, they were felt to be a direct 'metaphysical' expression of the *Zeitgeist*. Many found them eminently relevant at a time when so many political hopes were crumbling and so many old bonds had proved fragile.

When Walter Scott summed up *Childe Harold* IV,[35] in what Byron in acknowledgement of Scott's fairness called 'the review of a poet ... on another',[36] he said of the novel emotional world in Byron's poetry that it was not like an imaginary feast but more like the loneliness after the feast, when the lights had been extinguished and nothing was left but a lonely ruin, peopled by one man full of cares, he was probably thinking first of the Lara/Byron who roams through Newstead Abbey and of Harold who roams through the ruins of ancient Rome until 'His shadow fades away into Destruction's mass' (*Childe Harold* IV, 164), but at the same time he provides an almost emblematic formula for the feeling of cultural decline and existential depression which is reflected by so much of what Byron and the other younger romantic poets wrote.

In *Childe Harold's Pilgrimage* I and II Byron wrote in this key for the first time. The expectations that he thus raised were great. On the other hand, there was no lack of reviewers who criticized this, his first great work, for its 'want of story'. Perhaps it was as a consequence of these reactions that Byron subsequently wrote shorter narrative poems; perhaps he also felt instinctively that a more condensed story would fulfil his need to reveal as well as his wish to conceal himself. In any case, during the next two years he published, in rapid succession, *The Giaour*, *The Bride of Abydos*, *The Corsair* and *Lara*.

In addition to enthusiasm, there was a reaction amongst the public that was of particular significance for the history of the genre. It is expressed by George Ellis in his review of the *The Corsair* and *Lara*.[37] Although he fully acknowledged Byron's 'originality', he took the expectations of the reading public with respect to all longer romantic poems since Southey and Scott and applied them critically to Byron's works, thereby arriving at the following conclusion: the character of Childe Harold was too dramatic for him to be portrayed merely as a passive traveller. This suggested that Byron's verse narratives were written as sequels to the first two books of his 'Romaunt', since his heroes – Harold, the Giaour and Conrad, the Corsair – were otherwise too homogeneous and too similar to one another. In the second canto of *Lara*, which Ellis like Jeffrey, Sir Egerton Brydges and many others saw as a continuation of *The Corsair*, Byron had in the same way disappointed all the expectations that he had raised in the first part. And Ellis closes by offering suggestions as to how the plot might have been concluded in order to make a decent story out of it.

This attempt to apply the same criteria by which the earlier romantic verse narratives were judged successful to the popular poems that Byron published between February 1812 and August 1814 confirms once again that his works were seen as a further continuation of the Scott – Southey – Rogers – Campbell line. However, what to begin with in Ellis' (and also Scott's) opinion restricted the effect of these Byronic poems (or threatened to restrict it if Byron continued in this way), namely the Byronic hero with his consistently gloomy attributes, presented as a self-portrait of the author himself, was in fact to prove the secret of his success. It was not only his trademark – what was acknowledged as the mark of his originality – but it was what Jeffrey had correctly identified from the beginning as the element which raised Byron's poems far above the tales in verse that flooded the market every month.

In *Childe Harold* Byron had already, as Jeffrey remarked,[38] dispensed with almost all the usual 'ingredients of poetic delight' but nevertheless created something that Jeffrey found 'infinitely refreshing after the sickly affectation of so many modern writers' and that he felt to be important on account of the 'tone of self-willed independence and originality' and 'a certain manliness and strength of manner'. Even at this time – 1812 – Jeffrey had also recognized Milton's 'fiend' as the spiritual ancestor of the Byronic hero, in other words Satan, who 'sees undelighted all delight'. Nevertheless, at this stage he still ended his review with the succinct remark: 'Its chief fault is the want of story or object.'

However, in Jeffrey's review of *The Giaour*[39] his interest in the story, which was in fact criticized by some of the other reviewers for being obscure as a consequence of the fragmentary form and the long confession of *The Giaour*, has already become secondary to his fascination with the description of the hero's inner life. Jeffrey even welcomes the trick of the fragmentary narrative technique, which would confuse other critics, since they could now no longer write about the structure of the story. However, only the inexperienced could speak of obscurity here; the experienced would be grateful, since 'the greater part of polite readers would now no more think of sitting down to a whole Epic, than to a whole ox'. What made Byron's poems beautiful – and 'This, we think, is very beautiful' – was the originality of the character analysis: it transformed a normal story of a marauder into great poetry.

In his review of *The Corsair* and *The Bride of Abydos*,[40] Jeffrey takes what he has written only about Byron up until now and turns it into a general principle. He describes western cultural history broadly in terms of cycles and in this context defines the Regency period, the later romantic period, as the second age of fanaticism to occur in modern times, as the poetic revolution that followed on from the political one. And he explains the historical inevitability of this poetic revolution as a reaction to the suppression of emotion and the over-refinement of the Augustan period and as a return, resulting from this reaction, to the crude genres and subject matter of earlier cultural periods. The wildness of the early genres would, however, be exceeded as a consequence of the collective hunger for real passion. The generalized examples from contemporary literature that Jeffrey gives as proof, without stating their authors' names, are not hard to identify as references to works by Crabbe, Scott, Wordsworth and Byron.

What was special about Byron, however, and put him above the other contemporary romancers, was that he did not look to the past for his models of unsuppressed passion, but to the Turkish and Arabian East. This was more poetic than going back to the Middle Ages. What also distinguished the modern romantic poets, and Byron more than all others, from the old romancers was the way strong passions were presented. By contrast with the old romances, one was not primarily given the *results* of the passions but a *description* of them: not therefore facts and deeds, but what lay behind them. The analysis of the unbridled emotions themselves had become the main object: 'The minds of the great agents must be unmasked for us – and all the anatomy of their throbbing bosoms laid open to our gaze.' From this Jeffrey draws two conclusions: one relating to the reader's response and one to a special problem of the romantic poet. Both are significant with respect to the development of the genre.

As far as the response to the works was concerned, this focus on the analysis of emotions leads readers to identify more strongly with the characters portrayed. They suffer, with a kind of vicarious suffering, the emotional turmoil of the fictitious figures and in this way are able to work off their own feelings, experiencing a modern kind of catharsis.

As far as the production of romantic poetry was concerned, however, Jeffrey sees the danger of a marked discrepancy arising between the milieu in which the poems are set, which is generally historic, i.e., barbaric, and the modern sensitivity of their protagonists. The examples he gives are again from verse narratives by Campbell, Scott, Southey – and Byron, who had given the public a 'merciless corsair with every virtue under heaven except common honesty'.

Jeffrey's observations indicate a significant awareness – not yet quite put into words but unusually astute – that the subjective or philosophical analysis towards which romantic poetry was now tending was basically no longer compatible with Scott's type of 'romantic poetry'. If descriptive analysis of feelings resulting from the modern-day refinement of sensitivity replaced facts and deeds, in other words the ingredients of a solid narrative plot, the tale in verse in its previous form would be left without its basic foundation. The genre would then have to change, or rather the elements of straightforward narration and the analysis of subjective passions or states of mind would find their way into other genre forms, the former into realistic fiction genres, the latter into lyric forms of expression. This was in fact, as will be seen in the final chapter, the eventual fate of our genre.

In his review of *Childe Harold* III[41] Jeffrey called it an unavoidable consequence of Byron's interest in the analysis of passions 'that his scenes should be narrow and his persons few'. He added that in this respect Byron often seemed to be closer to the Lake Poets than to any other school of poetry, whereas in his style and description of manners he was, like Scott, 'a great borrower of external character'. There could be no better definition of Byron's position between the traditionalist Scott and the 'real' romantics, between the tendencies of the 'Ariosto of the North', which were still 'epic' and objective (and were eventually to result in Scott's turning to the historical novel) and the 'lyrical' and subjective tendencies of the authors of the *Lyrical Ballads*. And nothing could better account for the historical necessity which led not only to the definitive disappearance of the epic in the classical mould but also to the shift – within the romantic verse narrative genre – from the comparatively long romances of Southey and Scott which still featured crowded scenes and interest in ethnic or national collectives[42] to such shorter forms as the (lyrical) ballad, the fragment, or the dramatic monologue, which became increasingly popular in Byron's generation.

In Byron's case there are further complications, since other methods or models are superimposed on his contribution to realistic fiction, *Don Juan*: echoes of the exotic romantic verse narrative of the type that he had written earlier; satirical conventions; the Italian burlesque epic; modified mock-heroic elements and the relaxed way of telling a story of the Italian *improvisatori*.

In addition he had seen what was happening to the epic revival of the narrative poets of romanticism, an insight which was incorporated in the parodic characters of *Don Juan*, but he arrived at this, his own true domain, via a detour: previously he had resorted to the lyric drama and to the neo-classical tragedy of the type written by Alfieri in order to try and escape his dissatisfaction with the romantic verse narrative. It may be remarked here that Jeffrey's *Corsair/Lara* review had ended significantly with his advising Byron to write a drama in the old, i.e., Elizabethan, style.

There are of course connections between Byron's metrical romances and his poetic dramas. It was not after all without reason that he called his *Manfred* 'A Dramatic Poem'.[43] Since the poetic or lyrical dramas are intended for reading rather than watching, the plot – if it can be called that at all – can be transposed to the characters' inner life and thus become an expression of romantic subjectivity, as is frequently the case with the dramatic monologue in Byron's poetry after 1816, which takes the place of the 'objective' narrative form.[44] As in the romantic verse narrative, in the dramatic poem the genuine drama's exciting interaction between characters can be replaced with a basic monologue structure and overlaid with lyrical elements. Byron saw clearly the similarities between *Manfred* and his own metrical romances: 'It is too much in my old style ... I certainly am a devil of a mannerist.'[45] The emergence of this mixed, romantically inspired genre loosely connected to the verse narrative should be looked at in the wider context of the disappearance of normative genre rules and ideas in the romantic period. There will be more to be said on this subject in connection with Shelley's *Prometheus Unbound*.[46]

Thus far an attempt has been made to elucidate Byron's development as a verse narrator primarily with reference to his early work, *Childe Harold*, and also to the change reflected in his late works, the dramas and *Don Juan*,[47] in order to find the key to his role in the history of the genre and show the extent to which he contributed to the continuation, expansion and resounding success of the tale in verse, but also at the same time to its dissolution. The framework thereby created, consisting primarily of a study of works outside the genre and the critical reactions to them, must now be filled in.[48]

The most important addition that has to be made to the previous discussion concerns Byron's own statements about the origin of his tales in verse. Here the characteristic Byronic dichotomy between the subjective description of experience and attempts to be objective or distance himself comes over particularly clearly. *The Giaour* was probably inspired by a personal experience, but Byron has surrounded it with mystery and made it impossible for us to see what was really behind it.[49] The fragment form was fashionable[50] and Byron himself admitted that he had been inspired by Rogers' *Voyage of Columbus*.[51] However, one of the original reasons for his selecting it was probably that on the one hand it lent itself particularly well to indirect narrative distributed between several fictitious narrators and could protect Byron from his own penchant for emotional confessions, and that on the other it conferred a certain authenticity on the story being told.[52] However, the urge to reveal his own emotional state was far stronger than all his attempts to distance himself from his story. The story, brought back by Byron from Greece, which closed with 684 lines (at first only about 344) of accounts by 'objective' if also critical narrator figures, and which Murray – after Byron had abandoned the idea of publishing it together with *Childe Harold* I and II – published in this length in June 1813, grew until it was about twice as long by the eighth edition, which was also published in the same year as the first edition, 1813; and the additions were nothing but a confession of the hero. As early as September of the same year, Byron wrote to Lady Melbourne: 'you ... will perhaps perceive in parts a coincidence in my own state of mind with that of my hero – I have tried & hardly too to vanquish my demon – but to very little purpose'.[53]

We can only give an outline of Byron's continuing dilemma. The conflict between personal confession and concealment of his own self endured for much longer and became the real reason his tales were so successful.[54]

The Bride of Abydos (1813) was written on Byron's own admission in flight from his own reality, i.e., from his pangs of conscience about his relationship with Augusta.[55] However, in this poem, in spite of all the personal traits it contains – sibling love in the first draft, Harold-like pride and contempt for the world in Selim's speech in Canto II[56] – there is in fact less evident personal confession and dissection of character than in *The Giaour* and the first *Childe Harold* cantos: Byron prevents Selim from opening his heart in a great deathbed confession by allowing him a quick death – 'a quicker fate' (II, 578); and

> If aught his lips essayed to groan,
> The rushing billows choked the tone!
> (II, 581 f.)

However, the scene in which the lovers are surprised on the point of flight,

> 'Oh! fly – no more – yet now my more than brother!'
> (II, 502)

is not by coincidence one of the most impressive: at the time he was writing this poem Byron must have been constantly tormented by the thought that his forbidden love might be similarly discovered.

In *The Corsair* (1814) the motto (from Tasso), 'I suoi pensieri in lui dormir non ponno', is already a description of Byron's state of mind rather than that of his hero. The public immediately identified the pirate with the author, and in his *Journal* Byron played with the idea of this identity:[57] even in the dedicatory letter to Thomas Moore[58] he looks at the question of the 'drawing from self' from so many angles that it is impossible to decide what he really meant, as Scott stated in his *Quarterly Review* review of *Childe Harold* III.[59]

In *Lara* (1814), the continuation of *The Corsair*, Byron makes his hero even more openly similar to himself: even to the extent of physiognomical resemblances such as the arrogantly pursed upper lip or the diet he describes – and naturally also to the extent of Lara/Byron's confrontation with his terrible guilt, 'If yet remember'd ne'er to be reveal'd' (*Lara* I, 248), where the verse is like an echo of the tormented line from his *Journal* written on 14 November 1813, in which he tries to come to terms with his own reactions of horror to his incestuous relationship with Augusta Leigh: 'Dear name, rest for ever unreveal'd.'

It was after this tale that Ellis suggested, as already mentioned, that all Byron's verse narratives to date were probably sequels to the first two *Childe Harold* cantos[60] – which, if seen as emotional autobiography of the disguised author, they in fact are.

We cannot know whether Byron took pleasure in the wild conjectures of the public and critics about the reality represented by his heroes; whether he was continuing, because of the success it brought him, to play the role the world had imposed on him and in which, for all he showed of himself, he always portrayed only his feelings and not their cause, or whether his own character had already changed to such an extent that the Byronic hero was already an objective figure as far as he was concerned and no longer a true self-portrait when he retained it in his work even after *Lara*.[61] In any case the Adriatic renegade Alp in *The Siege of Corinth* (1816) and both the Renaissance tyrant Azo and the remorseless marriage breaker Hugo in *Parisina* (1816) are still variations of this type, which Byron then also transplanted into his dramas, using it (still with a confessional element) for political purposes as in *Marino Faliero* or for philosophical or negative theological self-clarification as in *Manfred* and *Cain*.[62]

Once Byron finally left England for good and particularly during his long period in Italy, he did then of course begin to look critically at what he understood by romantic poetry, of which the passionate Byronic hero with his personal confessions was a part. This process of dissociation from romanticism that comes over particularly clearly from Byron's letters has been described elsewhere by the present author[63] and will thus merely be given in summary form at this point, together with a study of the ways in which this dissociation also affected the verse narratives written between 1816 and 1824.

In September 1817, around sixteen months after his departure from England and a good year after the summer spent in Shelley's company by Lake Geneva, Byron came to the conclusion 'that ... all of us – Scott – Southey – Wordsworth – Moore – Campbell – I – are all in the wrong – one as much as another ... we are upon a wrong revolutionary poetical system – or systems – not worth a damn in itself ... and ... the next generation will finally be of this opinion'[64] ... 'from the quantity and facility of imitation they will tumble and break their necks off our Pegasus, who runs away with us; but we keep the *saddle*, because we broke the rascal and can ride'.[65] Four months before this he had completed *Manfred*, and a month later he wrote *Beppo*.

The list of names in the passage from the first letter suggests that, similarly to Scott in his Introduction to *The Bridal of Triermain*, what Byron is referring to with the 'wrong revolutionary system' is the 'romantic poetry' that is the subject of this book, i.e., the romantic tale in verse. The addition of 'or systems', the inclusion of Wordsworth in the list and many passages in the letters written from 1817 to Byron's death, however, also indicate that his criticism of the 'wrong revolutionary system' is to be more widely interpreted, not merely, as frequently happens, in terms of a return to the gentlemanliness of the Augustan standards in style and verse technique and not merely, as the letters of 1820–1 and the dramas of those years suggest, in terms of the introduction of a new dramatic classicism characterized by 'suppressed passion'[66] based on Alfieri, but in terms of general criticism of the subjective, emotional basis of all romantic artistic production. Incapable of accepting the idealistic or transcendentalist positions of other great romantic poets and disgusted by the shallowness and vanity of the imitators of Scott and himself, what Byron now wanted to see was a type of poetry which, in as far as it was not purely comical or satirical, would still have to be 'the expression of violent passion',[67] but should above all be a true 'reflection of the world'[68] and not be inspired by mere imagination or a vague enthusiasm – 'entusymusy'[69] – that had little to do with real experience. What was crucial to this poetry was the factual experience of having lived in more than one world.[70] With this commitment to realism and experience Byron now saw his Eastern tales as 'exaggerated nonsense'[71] and expressed his indignation at 'the deluge of flimsy and unintelligible romances imitated from Scott and myself'.[72] This is also reflected in gradual changes in his narrative verse after the 'fatal separation'.

It is often pointed out[73] how in Cantos III and IV of *Childe Harold* the narrator/hero has developed away from the stereotype of the earlier Byronic hero and acquired a more pronounced interest in modern life and modern politics. In the third canto his ability to analyse the world and his own ego objectively is still inhibited by the influence that his association with Shelley had on him, but in the fourth canto he has largely abandoned the fiction of the 'sinner and outlaw persona' which featured previously, so that the pessimism about life expressed in this canto is less egotistic and more general than the *Weltschmerz* of the earlier cantos. Hand in hand with this development goes a change in Byron's treatment of the tale in verse genre.

The fact that after *The Siege of Corinth* (1816) his romances were already much shorter than the earlier tales – the late poem *The Island*, written in

1823,[74] is an exception – and that at least *Parisina* and *The Prisoner of Chillon* (both 1816), but with some reservations also *Mazeppa* (1819) tend more in the direction of the ballade as written by Goethe and Schiller, may have something to do with Byron's judgement of the change in public taste; but it may also be a consequence of the poet's growing distaste for 'romantic' poetry and the verse narrative genre. He has had enough of the tale[75] and he shows increasing reserve when speaking of his earlier romantic works.[76] After 1816 his own very special problem, the tragic tension between himself as a poet and society, only appears in dramas, shorter dramatic monologues or works in the prophecy genre, and Byron hides his subjective perplexity behind that of older poets: Tasso in *The Lament of Tasso* (1817) and Dante in *The Prophecy of Dante* (1821).[77]

Byron again takes the opportunity of repressing the romantic fantasy content together with the subjectivity in *The Prisoner of Chillon* and in *Mazeppa*: both poems are the dramatic monologues of historic figures whose experience is, as it were, only metaphorically similar to Byron's. Although Bonnivard's frame of mind on attaining freedom –

> It was at length the same to me,
> Fetter'd or fetterless to be,
>   I learn'd to love despair ...
> My very chains and I grew friends,
> So much a long communion tends
>   To make us what we are: – even I
> Regain'd my freedom with a sigh.
>   (372 ff.)

– is unmistakably Byronic, because of the person who is speaking it is less intertwined with Byron's private fate than similar, earlier *Weltschmerz* passages, has a better foundation created by the events of the story and is more complex as a consequence of the Wordsworthian 'friendship' with the spiders and mice of the dungeon and, combined with this, the isolation of the 'lord of creation', who, as 'monarch of each race/Had power to kill' (380, 384 f.)

Like Byron in Italy, Mazeppa is a daredevil beginning to grow old who looks back at the adventures of his youth in the same way as the narrator of *Don Juan* and sees in his own fate the absurdity of human existence:

> Thus the vain fool who strove to glut
> His rage,[78] refining on my pain,
>   Sent me forth to the wilderness
> Bound, naked, bleeding, and alone,
> To pass the desert to a throne; –
>   What mortal his own doom may guess?
>   Let none despond, let none despair ...
>   (848 ff.)

The irony which comes through in these lines and occasionally elsewhere in *Mazeppa*, has often been noted. It is not the tragic irony of *Manfred* or *Cain*. Although in true Byronic fashion it remains the reaction of the 'derelict' person to the irony of the world as a whole or of existence or of the impassive creator, it is full of a gusto that entitles it to be described as 'humour'. One is reminded that *Beppo* had already been written and that Byron had established this new style with the first canto of *Don Juan*. With these two works Byron had, as already described, put the romantic tale in verse behind him: generically *The Island* (1823) – whether one views it with Andrew Rutherford[79] as a 'rag-bag of old Byronic themes' or with Paul Fleck[80] as Byron's *Prometheus Unbound* – is certainly not an exploration of new possibilities for the metrical tale that are no longer romantic, as in the case of *Beppo*, or an attempt to create a new realistically ironic and sceptical epic as in the case of *Don Juan*. In spite of this final return to the metrical romance that was part of the already fading 'romantic' fashion, Byron had basically long since dissociated himself from the old genre and its style as a wrong track, a stylistic Babel, and 'uttermost decline and degradation of literature',[81] for which he himself felt partly to blame.

In 1817 he had prophesied that its popularity would last only one generation.[82] By then this 'Claudianism'[83] would cease to have any further effect and poetry would have to return to more rigid standards of language and versification and a more empirical content. In Byron's own case, in the last months before his departure for Greece, the desire to write left him altogether – and his opinion of 'rhyming' and 'scribbling' and 'sweating poetry' had anyway never been very high. He was tired of writing and publishing. There were personal reasons for this: bitterness over the poor reception of his later works;[84] a feeling that his 'stimuli of life' had begun to peter out[85] and that he only wrote out of habit;[86] but also a long-felt distaste for the whole 'garrison'[87] of contemporary poets who, as he had already felt in 1813, were only useless 'spectators' of the events of the day,[88] who arrogantly viewed their activity as a profession rather than an 'art' or an 'atttribute'[89] and who, instead of being leaders and actors in the struggle for greater freedom, showed 'no sympathy with the spirit of this stirring age'[90] but were full of self-love.[91] Byron also to some extent (and influenced particularly by the feeling that the poetry of his generation was ineffective) began to have fundamental doubts about poetry; '*who* [was] ever altered by a poem?';[92] 'things *all fiction*' were hateful[93] by comparison with active involvement in the tackling of current problems;[94] poets had for a long time no longer been *vates* but 'a marked race',[95] people with over-exaggerated sensibility or imagination[96] whose productions were 'the result of an uneasy mind in an uneasy body': 'their insanity effervesces and evaporates into verse'.[97]

Is all this only the legendary irritability of the poet – and particularly of the exiled poet, who realizes that he is beginning to lose his public?[98] Or is it a very modern outlook, where Byron not only foresees the educated readers' rejection of the 'romantic' narrative fashion as compensatory self-deception lacking in substance, which was to become a *fait accompli* at the latest with Dickens' death, but also recognizes the hollowness and the end of the romantic cult of the genius, a cult which in its exaggerated form was a concomitant of the literary romantic movement. Did Byron not in fact see that his world-weary literary *persona* would be a dangerously suggestive model inviting imitation by 'uneasy minds in uneasy bodies' and poets who would put forward their allegedly highly pronounced sensibility 'as an excuse for all kinds of discontent'?[99] Did he not foresee that untalented imitators of the 'exaggerated nonsense' of his earlier narratives in verse would produce quantities of tasteless melodrama and thus in the future finally reduce 'romantic poetry' to the level of trivial literature, in the form of Victorian melodramas, the often very weak opera libretti of the nineteenth century[100] and the pseudo-romantic kitsch of many novel passages?

Byron may have underestimated the positive consequences of the romantic period, but he predicted with great confidence its awful degeneration to a subliterary form. The possibilities of the romantic tale in verse, which he brought to the height of its popularity and later discarded as 'exaggerated nonsense', were exhausted with his death, but the negative effects of this kind of poetry and romantic aesthetics as a whole, when not based on a serious intellectual foundation, were anticipated by almost no other English poet with as much foresight as Byron.

John Keats

Das Sinnliche des Kunstwerkes soll nur Dasein haben, insofern es für den Geist des Menschen, nicht aber insofern es als Sinnliches für sich selber existiert.
... In jedem Fall, wenn der Inhalt auch geistiger Art ist, wird er dennoch nur so ergriffen, daß er das Geistige, wie menschliche Verhältnisse, in Gestalt äußerlich realer Erscheinung darstellt.

The sensuous element in a work of art should only exist in so far as it appeals to man's intellect, and not for its own sake.
... In any case, even when the content is of a spiritual nature, it is only understood thus if the spiritual, like human relationships, appears in a tangible form.

G. W. T. Hegel, *Ästhetik*, ed. G. Lukács, Berlin, 1955, pp. 79 and 84

In a letter of 8 October 1817 to his friend Benjamin Bailey, Keats, who was not yet twenty-two and was in the middle of his first long poem, wrote the following:

I have heard Hunt say and [I] may be asked – why endeavour after a long Poem? To which I should answer – Do not the lovers of Poetry like to have a little Region to wander in where they may pick and choose, and in which the images are so numerous that many are forgotten and found new in a second Reading: which may be food for a Week's stroll in the Summer? Do not they like this better than what they can read through before Mrs. Williams comes down the stairs? a Morning work at least? Besides a long Poem is a test of invention which I take to be the Polar Star of Poetry, as Fancy is the Sails, and Imagination the Rudder. Did our great Poets ever write short Pieces? I mean in the shape of Tales – This same invention seems indeed of late Years to have been forgotten as a Poetical excellence ... I put on no Laurels till I shall have finished Endymion.[101]

These lines reveal much about the situation that had arisen as a result of the general flooding of the market with tales in verse since 1812 or 1813 and about the reason why Keats embarked on his *Endymion* project.

Since several new tales in verse appeared every month and poetry lovers had to read them in order to keep up to date, and since all that really mattered to the readers was that plots and subject matter were always different and that the poets were constantly producing something new and original, the romances grew shorter and shorter by comparison with the works of Scott and Southey. Instead of the many-stranded, loosely constructed, adventurous form reminiscent of the medieval romances, Ariosto or Spenser, the shorter tale, which could be fragmentary, in novella form, or even – more in the manner of a classical drama – have a unity of plot resembling that of a ballad, gained increasing ground. The role that Crabbe, Rogers and Byron played in this development has already been touched on, and we will find further illustrations of this tendency when we come to Hunt and Moore. In his review of *The Giaour*,[102] Jeffrey bluntly describes the reasons, as he sees them, for the reduction in length of the popular verse narratives: 'Since the increasing levity of the present age ... has rendered it impatient ... of the long stories that used to delight our ancestors, the taste for fragments ... has become very general, and the greater part of polite readers would now no more think of sitting down to a whole Epic, than to a whole ox ...' With a hint of irony he then condescends to set his seal of approval on this development: long poems are in any case never read again in their entirety once one knows the plot: so it is after all quite in order if the poets merely string the highlights together and spare the reader the connecting passages.[103]

In the letter quoted above, Keats is evidently stating his opposition to 'this increasing levity of the present age'. Other passages in the same letter indicate that he was having a battle on this account with his mentor Leigh Hunt, who was an advocate of cutting and brevity. By the 'long Poem' he obviously means something that is much longer than the many tales in verse that were being produced in abundance. The phrase 'a Morning work at least' is a very vague indication of length, but it means at least 3,000 verses, which is not so very different from the length of Scott's and Southey's works. (*Endymion* has 4,050 verses.) Keats did not consider the verse novella to be a 'long Poem',

as is confirmed by his classification of *The Eve of St Agnes* as a 'little Poem'
in a letter to George and Georgiana Keats of 14 February to 3 May 1819.
Lamia too is described by him as 'a short poem' in another letter to the same
recipients (from 17 – 27 September 1819).

However, he was not only planning something longer, but also something
more ambitious than a Scott/Byron-type romance, even though he was also
very positive about using the term romance in his subtitle.[104] He talked in
plain, if unphilosophical terms of the three poetic abilities, the possession of
which he wanted to prove by means of this work to real lovers of poetry, and
above all to himself; and of these he placed invention first, as a gift that had
declined amongst contemporary poets. By this he probably meant independence, originality and ingeniousness in creating and arranging poetic images
and an expressive fable that does not depend on mere observation of reality:
in other words a quality which is essential for the full development of the other
two requisites, fantasy and imagination, as it serves to focus their activity on
a particular objective and contain it within a meaningful plan. He was hence
not aiming at a romance as his contemporaries understood it.[105] Did he –
in spite of the designation 'A Poetic Romance' – have a new form of the epic
in mind, in the way Southey thought of the epic, in spite of rejecting the
'degraded title of epic'? He never called *Endymion* an epic, either in his letters
or elsewhere. He never even used the word for *Hyperion*.[106] He already
belonged to a generation to which this generic term was strictly limited to the
classical epics from Homer to Tasso and Milton and to the neo-classical epics
emulating the classical form. (Hazlitt, who was seventeen years older than
Keats, still called all longer narrative poems written in verse epics.) As far
as young Keats was concerned, the epic was

> ... of all the King
> Round, vast, and spanning all like Saturn's ring
> (*Epistle to Charles Cowden Clarke* of 1817, V. 66 f.)

This is very different from the description in his letter to Bailey of what he
was aiming at with the 'long Poem' *Endymion*. This 'garden full of images',
this 'summer walk', seems further removed from the epic than the 'heroic'
romances of Southey, which, after all, are still 'heroic' and, it might even be
said, further from it than Scott's poems of Scotland's past.[107]

Endymion is thus not an epic, nor however is it a verse novella or a romance
in the Scott sense. Generically speaking it marks a significant step forward,
blending as it does, epic-like, romance-like, lyrical and pastoral elements into
a new form, the 'generic character' of which merits our closer consideration.
Keats frees the concept of the poetic romance even more definitively than
Byron from its poetic origins and the new meaning it acquired in the narrative
revival of the day. His idea of the romance is not a shallow, narrative poem
with martial and historical themes, sensational adventures and passions and

a superficial interest in the outward fate of individual people; not an exclusively plot-orientated poetic genre with a highly varied form based on 'primitive' models, and not 'fiction for fiction's sake' verging on popular light fiction. It also has little in common with the definition in chapter 1 of this book, of which only a few elements apply to Keats' 'Poetic Romance': the 'unheroic' style by contrast with the epic, the tendency to move away from reality and the exclusive focus on more 'private' subject matter interwoven with erotic plot elements rather than on the objective interests of a historical community. The 'private' matter is of course dealt with differently and at a more profound level than in the old minstrel romances or the work of Scott and his successors – differently and more profoundly also than in the work of Byron. It is raised to an importance which allows us to refer to it – making use of Northrop Frye's terminology – as the 'central episodic theme' of nineteenth-century poetry, as the 'analysis or presentation of the subjective mental state' of the poet,[108] as the 'Growth of a Poet's Mind'. In *Endymion* this no longer appears in an autobiographical, philosophizing form as in Wordsworth's *Prelude*, nor in an autobiographical, egocentric form as in Byron's works, but in a symbolic, mythological form. With the poetic use of symbols and myths the romance goes back to the poetic sphere from which it had its origins; a sphere with which even in the late Middle Ages it had little contact, and which only reappeared as a result of comparative myth research in the nineteenth century and the discovery of the collective unconscious in the twentieth century: a sphere that had to be left out of the definition in chapter 1, since the aim there was to define the romance as a historical, formal type taken over by Scott and not as a poetic archetype. Now this omission must be remedied, bringing in as for previous more comprehensive genre questions the theories of Northrop Frye.

We have said that in Keats' work the romance returns to the sphere of symbolism which is related to a mythical view of the world. Of course in his case the symbolism assumes a modern form, which is no longer a religious but a poetic philosophical form;[109] it does not have a cult orientation but an individual and sentimental orientation. According to Frye[110] the mythical element of the romance (it should be noted that he is using the term romance in the sense of an archetypal mode of poetic expression, not in a generic sense, and is thus referring to medieval *and* romantic poetry) is not the immanence of the divine in this world, which in early legendary periods was expressed through oracles, prophecies, commands, Orphic mysteries and sacred writings (all things that still play a large part in the 'natural epic') but the myth of the Absolute which has vanished from the earth and which man tries to approach by ardent searching, purposeful journeys and 'remembering'. This is what originally produced the poetic phenomena of the romance. 'Its typical episodic theme [i.e. its thematic development in "works of fiction"] is perhaps best described as the theme of the boundary of consciousness, the sense of the poetic mind as passing from one world to another, or as simultaneously aware of both.'[111] Hence the contrasts between the romantic 'memory' of the supernatural and mythical, and real 'experience' of actual events; between dream and reality; between the distant goal and the laborious journey; between the Utopian or lost homeland and exile which occur in romantic plots and can assume the following forms: the elegiac reminiscences of an 'exile' – *Widsith*, *The Wanderer*, *The Last Minstrel*;[112] a lover hero separated from his lady, an adventurous journey in quest of the Holy Grail or in the service of the 'princesse lointaine', the May-morning vision, the revelation of the *Vita Nuova* through female or divine grace, etc.

In Keats' ingenious interpretation of the myth of *Endymion* an unconscious transition from the metrical romance as the imitation of a historical generic form to a revival of the romance in its archetypal form has taken place. Here again is what Frye has to say: 'With the low mimetic, where fictional forms deal with an intensely individualized society, there is only one thing for an analogy of myth to become, and that is the act of individual creation ... In this age the thematic *poet* becomes what the fictional *hero* was in the age of romance, an extraordinary person who lives in a higher and more imaginative order of experience than that of nature. He creates his own world, a world which reproduces many of the characteristics of fictional romance.'[113] In this sense *Endymion* – and as we will see, *Hyperion* too – is a romance.

This explains why it was inevitable that Keats and Shelley would turn away from the superficial and comparatively 'realistic' world of the merely narrative and descriptive romances of Scott to an idealistic world removed from reality, where the poet appears 'in a state of pantheistic rapport with nature' and 'curiously invulnerable to the assaults of real evil'.[114] According to Frye the 'encyclopaedic' tendency of the romantic epoch[115] led to the construction of mythological epics 'in which the myths represent psychological or subjective states of mind'.[116] These states of mind are nothing but the modern equivalent, secularized as 'philosophy', of the mythical (or myth-seeking), 'thematic' content of the old romances, and they at the same time constitute the core of the 'episodic themes' of the modern romances. When these themes are expanded encyclopaedically, i.e., when they move out of the 'private' sphere (which for example characterized much of Byron's work) and are generalized to produce a more comprehensive meaning, what we have are the 'mythological epics' of the romantic period.

This brings us to the achievement of the young poet Keats, which is nothing short of unbelievable from a literary historical point of view, an achievement of which, of course, as is evident from the letter quoted earlier and other comments of his, he was not fully conscious, and which, as we will see, also lies perhaps to a greater extent in the root idea of *Endymion* than in the effusiveness of the finished poem itself. In order to put the 'episodic themes' of 'romantic' poetry (romantic in the above sense) on a higher mythical plane, he creates an important cultural synthesis by blending them with ancient mythology. Here however the Greek myth, the myth of the god present in the poet, is reinterpreted as a romantic myth consisting of 'memory', longing and dreams, the climax of which – the union or final sameness of the divine and the human – is not the guaranteed tenet of the myth but a Utopian vision.[117]

After a period when ancient mythology had been increasingly rejected since, after centuries of use as a mere element of education and decorative element in poetry by a religious civilization which no longer had its foundation in myths, it had lost all its mythical content; after a period of concentration on the romances of the Christian medieval period, the 'mythical' undertone of which was not however revealed by this 'Medieval Revival'; after an epoch which had nothing to do with myths, when only the visionary Blake managed to create his own mythology, which, however, since it was purely personal, remained a complete mystery to his contemporaries; in the middle of a period of historical and philosophical research into the mythologies of the past and of distant cultures (one has only to think of the endeavours of German scholars from F. Schlegel and the Grimm brothers to Hegel); only twenty-five years after Southey's 'epic project', in the realization of which the poet had not even begun to understand the mythical content of the foreign religions which he was making the subject of his romances – the young poet Keats felt that he had to create a true romantic myth in order to give the 'modern' themes with which he was preoccupied a symbolic framework. And his sense of belonging to the European cultural tradition is as marked as the vividness of the ancient myths with which this tradition began, with the result that the romantic themes fuse as if of their own accord with the figures from the Greek world of gods, and what he writes is an archetypal romance in imitation of classical antiquity.

Keats' highly original achievement is not diminished by the fact that Hölderlin, Goethe, Shelley and Byron succeeded in approaching the ancient world of myths in a comparably 'modern' fashion at around the same time. He did not know the German works, and Shelley's and Byron's attempts at an ancient Titan myth (in their Prometheus poems) came after *Endymion* and are along different generic lines. These poems – like Byron's versions of the Satan myth – do it is true qualify as 'fictional romances' with their archetypal episodic themes, which Frye summarizes as 'exile' and the contrast between 'the worlds of memory and of experience'.[118] They are also ultimately based on the idea of the gods having withdrawn from the world. However, they are tragic and egocentric forms of this idea and these basic themes, and the poets hence selected or created formal generic types that have less in common with the narrative metrical romance than with drama: Shelley's *Prometheus Unbound* is a dramatic poem and Byron's *Prometheus* a dramatic monologue. Keats, on the other hand, the least egocentric, heroically and titanically orientated and dramatic of the English romantic poets, does not use the dramatic side of the ancient mythology (dramatically preformed by the ancients) but the romantic side in the story of the love of the mortal youth Endymion for the gentle moon goddess, with its idyllic and bucolic setting, a story already romanticized by Ovid. Here he found the contrast between the world of experience and that of 'memory' already existing in mythical form, and by coupling this myth with the narrative subject of the purifying journey which archetypally belongs to the romance – and is after all closely bound up with the theme of exile – he effects a perfect transformation of the myth into a romance.

This explanation of the historical generic context – or the unconscious forces and ideas which form the background to the poem – sheds much more light on its intellectual and historical roots than the usual hunt for sources and models that characterizes conventional genre research, and which in the case of *Endymion* seized on its relationship to Drayton's *Endymion and Phoebe* (1595) and Wieland's *Oberon* and other possible models,[119] relationships that are difficult to establish. Great romantic poetry cannot be understood from normative and purely formal generic standpoints: the archetypal mode theory of Frye is one approach which helps us to discover more about the real nature of the genre it represents. Later on we will find a second approach.

How then is all that we have talked about reflected in the assessments of Keats' contemporaries? While they did not see the deeper significance of the poem – even Keats himself was probably only barely conscious of it – they did register the poetic consequences of the unusual synthesis of ancient myth and modern romance.

The hostile *Blackwood's Magazine* critics objected to the 'great craze of the Cockney to be Greekish', maintaining that the Greek mythology only came to life in the works of Homer and Milton (thus only in works belonging to the heroic epic genre). Any attempt to revive it now was doomed to failure, and only a very powerful 'Promethean' spirit might be able to achieve the impossible. In the opinion of the *Blackwood's* critics, the Cockneys could not bring about a renaissance of the Greek myths because they understood nothing of Hellenism: Hunt allegedly knew no Greek tragedies and Keats could only read Homer in Chapman's translation.[120] The notorious *Endymion* review in the *Quarterly Review*[121] flatly declares the story to be completely incomprehensible (the author, Croker, of course admits that he only read Book I, since he considers the poem unreadable).

In spite of its inevitable prejudices, Francis Jeffrey's review in the *Edinburgh Review*[122] is much more understanding. Here Jeffrey analyses with great interest the use of 'heathen' mythology in *Endymion*. Since Keats does not adopt the usual mythological apparatus but only the general 'conditions and relations' of the gods, in order to give them an original character and a distinct individuality, he adds the merits of his own invention (!) to the attraction of the fictions of the old world. The ancients – probably for religious reasons – had as good as never described and analysed the feelings of the gods, and,

as they had never revealed their passions, had failed to give them a recognizable identity,[123] but Keats had invented and described the 'loves, sorrows,
and perplexities' of beings with whose names and supernatural attributes
people had always been familiar. Jeffrey doubts whether this will hold
permanent interest for a modern public, but, he adds somewhat patronizingly,
'since it is done well and heightens the grace and attractions of the fictions on
which it is engrafted, it may have a chance of enduring'. He no more attempts
to interpret the 'allegory' of *Endymion* than did those reviewers who dismissed
the poem as unreadable and incomprehensible.

Here too a detailed discussion of how the symbolical or allegorical meaning
of *Endymion* is to be interpreted must be omitted. Aside from the fact that it will
have to be clarified a little further on whether interpretation in the conventional sense, i.e., breaking down the vivid symbolism into logical discursive
units of meaning, is at all adequate to cope with Keats' art, this question goes
beyond the scope of this study of the generic context. All that will be said for the
time being is that most well-known interpretations in the literature about Keats
concentrate solely on what Frye calls the typical episodic and encyclopaedic
themes of the 'fictional romance' as well as on the 'comprehensive intellectual
tendency' of the romantic period towards common 'themes, modes of expression and ways of feeling and imagining' studied by M. H. Abrams.[124]

As far as the assessment of Keats' objective poetic achievement is concerned, we can also refer to the words of the young poet himself – in the
Preface he calls his first narrative poem 'a feverish attempt rather than a deed
accomplished' – and to the opinions of the critics from Shelley and Jeffrey to
present-day literary experts.

We come now to a point of much greater relevance to this genre history: the
question of the narrative qualities of *Endymion*. Here all the contemporary
reviewers are united in their opinion that in this poem the narration is not
Keats' strong point. Even the benevolent Jeffrey cannot avoid noting the
'interminable wanderings and excessive obscurity' and the lack of the usual
ingredients of narrative literature: 'interest of story ... vivacity of characters ...
engaging incidents ... pathos'.[125] But he does in part ascribe these defects to
the youth of the poet and in part turn them into advantages: the sole purpose of
the plot in this work of Keats' was to serve as a framework for 'ornaments' and
poetic 'enchantment lavishly presented'. Thus *Endymion* became a measure of
whether a person had a feeling for the pure essence of poetry. Other great poets
had so much with which they could hold their readers' attention that even
those readers who had little understanding for the poetic side, and in fact only
saw it as an obstacle to their enjoyment of the other attractions, found their
works fascinating.

It is only where those other recommendations are wanting, or exist in a weaker
degree, that the true force of the attraction, exercised by *pure poetry* ... can be fairly

appreciated – where, without much incident or many characters, and with little wit, wisdom or arrangement, a number of bright pictures are presented to the imagination and a fine feeling is expressed of those *mysterious relations by which visible external things are assimilated with inward thoughts and emotions, and become the images and exponents of all passions and affections* [this author's emphasis].

This ingenious apology cannot conceal the fact that the narrative qualities that are essential for a poem which is designed as a story are nevertheless missing. It does, however, help explain why this is so and sheds some light on the relationship of Keats and Shelley and the romantic period in general to poetic narrative.

Jeffrey puts the matter brilliantly, even though there is much he has not understood about *Endymion*. He recognizes clearly and to some extent prophetically the elements in this type of poetry that produced a line of poetic development which subsequently gained the ascendency in the nineteenth century and for a third of the twentieth century.[126] He not only anticipates the idea of *poésie pure* that was later to become so important, but also explains the internal mechanism of this concept in a manner which would have done credit to Baudelaire or Mallarmé and would probably even have met with the approval of T. S. Eliot, the theoretician and practician of objective correlatives in poetry. However, he also sees two aspects of this 'pure poetic art' which make it questionable whether it is suitable for all kinds of narrative poetry: its esotericism – 'To the unpoetical reader such passages always appear mere raving and absurdity' – and its slender connection with reality, which makes it unfit for longer works such as epics and romances – 'besides the riot and extravagances of his fancy, the scope and substance of Mr. Keats's poetry is rather too dreary and abstracted to excite the strongest interest or to sustain the attention through a work of any great compass or extent'.

It is perhaps necessary to look more closely at the words 'dreary' and 'abstracted'. Jeffrey does not say that the substance and scope in this work of Keats' are limited or insignificant (as did the critics who wanted to brand him as a poet who merely specialized in sensuous beauty).[127] He only says that they are of such a nature as to make Keats unsuitable as an author of long narrative poems. 'Too dreary' probably means: not varied, colourful or adventurous enough, not enough changes in the tone and the events to hold the attention, little the readers can identify with and not enough activity – too uniformly 'nostalgic and elegiac'.[128] And 'too abstracted' is aimed at a new element in this poem, the definition of which (in addition to the archetypal viewpoint) leads us to a second important generic aspect of Keats' work and also of all the other great highly romantic narrative poems: the relationship of the poetically represented world to reality, i.e., the fact that these works are predominantly metaphysical and symbolic and concentrate less on the telling of a continuous story. Let us now look at the narrative poems of Keats from this angle.

We have already encountered the question of the relationship to reality of the narrative poems (Aristotle's *mimesis praxeos*) in our general definitions and also in discussion of individual works. It was shown, for example, that the epic is essentially close to reality in the sense of the total historic reality of the community which produced it, and also in the sense that certain trivial circumstances of life which it takes seriously are described realistically, but is remote from reality as far as the highly stylized form is concerned. The romance was distinguished from the epic by showing that while the subject matter can frequently be classified as unreal, its flexible adaptation of the style to the situation often makes the narrative seem close to reality. Realistic characteristics were also occasionally found in the romance when the lower social classes were represented with scenes in the camp and the bar.[129]

In the discussion of narrative verse literature in the eighteenth century and the individual romantic tales in verse we were also repeatedly confronted with the question of the relationship of the poetry to the social or political realities of its day. Here the last point to be noted was the distance between the symbolic mythological 'epics' of Shelley and Keats and the external realities of life.[130] In order to understand this distance and hence the historical importance of these two poets for the romantic tale in verse, we will trace how the relationship between literature and the reality it portrayed, between the self-contained form and the 'imitated' real object changed in the course of this genre's history.[131]

Let us begin, with reference once again to Frye's essay, with Hamlet's statement to the actors that poetry holds the mirror up to nature. This does not mean that the literary work reproduces 'the shadow of nature', but rather that (like every language form) it 'causes nature to be reflected in its containing form'.[132] Mimesis is thus not pure reflection. An exact 'semantic' congruence of the poetic description with the real object that it is describing is unthinkable. Reality and language are different, incomparable media. Every conversion of real facts into linguistic units is in itself an interpretation of these facts; and in the process of being converted into the word pattern of a literary work they acquire in addition numerous intellectual and emotional aspects that they do not have in reality. The reality of a poetic work is thus something basically more meaningful and wider in scope, and hence basically different from the reality of nature to which it refers. This is noticeably the case in the poetry of epochs characterized by a strong, consistent style, and it is particularly pronounced in the 'classical' and 'neo-classical' phase of Western European culture, i.e., in the epoch from the Renaissance to the romantic period.[133]

In this genre history a number of phenomena have been established that indicate the breakdown of the division between the reality that enters the work of art and the semantic potential of the representative form. This breakdown may be interpreted as a dulling of the artistic instinct that produces a clean separation between the two. Here we can only recapitulate in summarized form some of the points that illustrate this process.

There is the slowly dawning consciousness of the remoteness from reality of neo-classical poetry (in particular the epics) which favoured the development of the novel as well as the romantic tale in verse.

There is the constantly increasing emphasis on 'nature' and 'heart' in poetic theories since the early romantic period and the development of these two aspects at the expense of the 'unnatural' rules that can no longer be considered an intrinsic part of the poetic form.

There is the suppression of the principle of design, with its emphasis on the form, by the principle of continuity, with its emphasis on content.

There is the increasing interest in the subject matter at the end of the eighteenth century. It brought with it a demand for historical and ethnographic precision; a hunger for sensation; enjoyment of the identification of the reader with the fates portrayed; growing interest in the (real) personality of the poet as reflected in the work; retention of the traditional verse only out of habit (e.g., in the neo-classically orientated tales in verse) or with laborious substantiations (as in Wordsworth's famous Preface)[134] or put in as historical 'colour' (e.g., in Scott's works) or as an alibi for the reader anxious to appear educated who would not admit he was enjoying the works for the story alone (this also applies to Scott and to the popular verse narratives).

There is, as a consequence of all this, a tendency towards prolific, undisciplined writing and an increasing deterioration in the formal qualities of the poetry, from Southey's 'radical' but in practice half-hearted attempt at an 'epic' *vers libre* to Scott's careless 'light horseman stanzas', and finally the official rejection of 'refinement' in the reviews already quoted of Campbell and Byron.[135]

There is Wordsworth's early theory of the basic similarity of the language of poetry and the language of prose as spoken by ordinary people, and his practice of including the colloquialisms of country people in his poems.

There is Crabbe's reduction of the distance between 'nature and art' with respect to the subject matter of his works by photographic reproduction of the social realities, which to Jeffrey, writing with the best of intentions, made the neo-classical focus on formal elegance, an approach that was basically unsuitable in this context, and therefore struck him as 'frivolous'.[136]

And finally there is the even greater reduction of this distance in Scott's *Scottish Novels*, which people still called 'poems', even though they were written in prose.[137]

The intention here is not of course to try and deny the fact that narrative prose is also a 'verbal pattern' that interprets and transforms, but its closer contact with factual experience, by comparison with verse language, is nevertheless obvious.

When we look at the above list – and it could be extended[138] – it becomes clear what an important influence Keats and Shelley had on the romantic tale in verse and beyond it on English poetry in general: they re-established the distance between poetic and actual reality, or rebuilt the glass wall between 'art and nature'.[139] Wordsworth and, in particular, Coleridge may have paved the way for this with their idealistic poetical theories and symbolic use of images and incidents, but Wordsworth's emphasis on everyday experience and Coleridge's limited production and 'weirdness' counteracted the effect described above.

In Keats England had a poet who, as it were, produced naturally what these thinkers and poets only achieved by means of a strong rational synthesis of their poetic or aesthetic experience with philosophical theories. Is this not part of what the famous saying 'Beauty is truth, truth beauty' really means, that the beauty of the perfect cosmos of words and images represented by the poem has become a tangible truth, a truth which, though in a 'fragmentary' mode, renders the meaning and the glory of the 'hyperouranic realm' accessible to human experience, a truth moreover which is 'understood' by the recipient and receptive imagination of the reader in a process of identification with it, i.e., of absorbing it as part of his own intuitive, imaginative, intellectual and sensual experience and not merely reflecting on it?

It is no coincidence that in the chapter entitled 'The Concrete Universal' of his *Verbal Icon* W. K. Wimsatt used a narrative poem of Keats as an example when explaining what we have been talking about here. What Wimsatt generalized as the features of all good narrative poetry are not felt by this author to be really applicable to the classic epic poem, the medieval ballads and romances and the narrative poems of the classical period from the Renaissance to the end of the eighteenth century, and his opinion that this is the main criterion of whether a 'story poem' is good or not certainly cannot be supported here. Wimsatt evidently failed to subject his own prejudice as a critical theorist to 'deconstructing' criticism. However, applied to Keats, his theory sums up the matter exactly. He writes:

The best story poems may be analyzed ... as metaphors without expressed tenors, as symbols that speak for themselves. 'La Belle Dame Sans Merci' for example ... is about a knight, by profession a man of action, but sensitive, like the lily and the rose, and about a fairy lady with wild, wild eyes. At a more abstracted level, it is about the loss of self in the mysterious lure of beauty – whether woman, poetry, or poppy. It sings the irretrievable departure from practical normality (*the squirrel's granary is full*), the wan isolation after ecstasy. Each reader will experience the poem at his own level of experience or at several. A good story poem is like a stone thrown into a pond, into our minds, where ever widening concentric circles of meaning go out – and this because of the structure of the story. – 'A poem should not mean but be'.[140]

This last sentence is taken, as will be well known, from A. MacLeish's *Ars Poetica*. It appears in various formulations in many studies of Keats' work (and word for word, for example, in Cleanth Brooks' *The Well-Wrought Urn*, in the chapter significantly entitled 'Keats's Sylvan Historian: History without Footnotes').[141]

Keats himself probably had more or less the same thing in mind when he wrote to Reynolds on 3 February 1818: 'We hate poetry that has a palpable design upon us.' Wimsatt's brief reference to MacLeish's sentence, applying it not only to the image and word structures of lyric poetry but also to the structures of narrative poetry and using it to sum up the effect of the narrative in Keats' work is so appropriate to our discussion that the relevant passage has been quoted at length. All narratives by Keats are indeed 'metaphors without expressed tenors' like *La Belle Dame Sans Merci* and this is also the main point to be taken into consideration when studying their generic nature.

Keats' works could be classified according to sources, length, type of plot, metric form, influences, tone or the themes they deal with, conceivably with the following result: epic-like romances (*Endymion* and *Hyperion*),[142] short epics (*Lamia*), verse novellas (*Isabella*), lyrical romances (*The Eve of St Agnes* and *The Eve of St Mark*), allegorical dream visions (*The Fall of Hyperion*) and ballads (*La Belle Dame Sans Merci*). But these classifications say nothing about the basic generic character of the works and what they have in common; they are based solely on formal externals. Is *Endymion* less a dream than *The Fall of Hyperion*? Is not *Lamia* just as much a novella as *Isabella*, and *Isabella* as much a romance as *Endymion* or *The Eve of St Agnes*? And is it not both right and wrong to call all these poems allegories? It is wrong if this term is used in the old sense, to mean a message that can also be understood as an abstract idea, presented in the form of images, whereby the reader is obliged to deduce the abstract content from the images. And it is right when the meaning of the term is expanded in Wimsatt's sense of a 'metaphor without expressed tenor', a 'symbol that speaks for itself' – which of course makes the idea of the allegory less precise and inapplicable as a term in the old sense, something that was already clear to Coleridge, Goethe and Schelling.[143]

Since all the narrative poems of Keats are the same as far as their 'metaphorical' or 'symbolic' nature is concerned, paraphrases of the 'meaning' at various levels of experience can be attempted for each of them along the same lines as Wimsatt's paraphrases of the levels of *La Belle Dame*. It should not however be forgotten that such explanations in no way cover every aspect of the poems, and that the belief that such an interpretation in terms of rational abstractions is the only 'right' one is just as inadequate an approach as concentrating on the external story alone.

Endymion is a poem about the ardent love, finally returned, of a mortal for a being from a higher, numinous category of existence; about the possibility of the union of the ideal world and life, beauty and truth, art and reality, and the conflict this involves; about the poet's passage through the stages of the beauty of nature and art, friendship, pity and love to the peak of fulfilment, the 'chief intensity'; about man's hope of bringing about harmony in the world through purification and love; about the 'circuitous journey through alienation to integration'.

Isabella is a poem about joy and suffering, the 'luxury' and tragedy of love; about the way the joys and horrors of existence are inextricably entwined ('there is richest juice in poison flowers', Stanza XIII); about ugliness that changes into beauty in a mysterious way and about pleasure that blends with sadness to form a bittersweet melancholy; about the gulf between the 'poetry' and the 'prose' of existence, that can be bridged aesthetically, through the ability of poetry to blend tones and colours and fuse the negative aspects of reality with the positive ones, and psychologically, through the death-seeking sensual pleasure of pain.

The Eve of St Agnes is a poem about the triumph of love, telling the story of a Romeo and Juliet couple who find one another in spite of all obstacles and dangers, and now through the inner flame that has aroused their love are able to flee from the world of menace and terror, which they leave frozen into powerlessness behind them; a poem about the warmth, light, magic, sweetness and hidden strength that can grow in the midst of cold, darkness, hatred and decay when omnipotent love raises its sceptre and makes the 'chief intensity' a reality; a poem, finally, where the contrasting factors are resolved not by means of a melancholy synthesis but by the natural triumph of one principle over the other, and hence a poem about the influx of 'hyperouranic' or absolute essence into our 'disparactic' reality, a theme which is basic to an understanding of the romantic poets' faith in the value of symbols.

Lamia is a poem about a 'dreamer's' love of what is magical and beautiful, and his disillusionment as a result of the realistic world view which his understanding is forced to accept; about the tragic contrast between the illusion of all sensuous and aesthetic bliss and the chilling disillusionment resulting from the sober vision of reality; about the death that threatens the poet when philosophy destroys his imagination; about the central problems of the poetic calling – the doubts about the absolute value of imagination for the world: the poet believes that he can only create true poetry when the drunken 'dreamer' dies in him to allow the 'philosophic mind' to grow instead, but he knows, on the other hand, that his genius and his life are inextricably bound up with the sensuous dreamer; and finally it is also possible that the poem has an autobiographical connection with Keats' relationship with Fanny Brawne;[144] at this level of experience it would be a parable about sensual love, which also belongs to the sphere of the thyrsus-crowned 'dreamer' and has disenchantment and death to fear from the cold eye of the 'thinker'.

Hyperion is a poem about the fall of a race of gods brought about by the new god, who is greater and more worthy than the old gods, because in addition to the gift of the greatest beauty (which, since the opening lines of *Endymion*, Keats equates with a right to power) he is also blessed with a fuller grasp of the tragic sides and dire necessities of existence; about the law of eternal change; about the French Revolution and all revolutions; about the triumph of the new kind of art over the old; about Keats' painful struggle to extend his poetic vision to the historical and political reality of the world, i.e., to the problems of human society; and it would perhaps have been the poem of triumph over the (tragic) *Lamia* theme if Keats had been able to complete the work: Lycius succumbs to death as he is given sight, when the magic of the beautiful dream is dispelled and reality dawns; Apollo however 'dies into life' when he receives 'knowledge enormous' of

> Names, deeds, grey legends, dire events, rebellions,
> Majesties, sovran voices, agonies,
> Creations and destroyings ...
>
> (III, 113 ff.)

from the face of Mnemosyne, i.e., from the memory of the historical reality of the world.

These poems mean all this and a very great deal more besides. They may differ from one another to varying degrees as far as their formal generic appearance is concerned, but these are external, accidental differences. The mode in which the message is translated into symbolic imagery, the basic structure of the themes and the mechanism of the effect on the reader are always the same: Keats' poems represent the 'analysis and presentation of [his] subjective mental state' and at the same time provide an insight into the deep-seated problems of romantic world experience. They are symbolic or metaphorical renditions of existential experiences, which, since they have been turned into experiences of the creative poetic mind, become universal and communicable in the poetic form of images, parables, narratives and 'verbal icons'. The reader – provided he is gifted with imagination himself – can 'appropriate' the experience of the poet: the work stimulates his imagination and he has a subjective experience, which is probably not identical with the poet's, but is in accordance with his own experience of life and with the source of all poetic imagination, whether it is envisaged psychologically (as sensibility) or metaphysically (as transcendence or universal truth).

Here we thus have the second main generic aspect, after the archetypal aspect, of this and indeed of all great highly romantic poems. They are romantic not in Scott's sense but in the modern intellectual historian's sense of romantic poetry as something which replaces the old genres: a meta-physically and epistemologically revolutionary concept of poetry.

The question of the external genre type is hence scarcely of any importance at all. Every work that is romantic in this way is unique and incomparable in that it is based on a unique, subjective experience of the poet that can only be transformed into a unique and incomparable subjective experience for the reader too. And it is comparable, even identical, with other works from the same era in that it is of a similarly metaphysical and symbolic nature.

In the opinion of this author it is wrong to extend this critical or, rather, negative approach to genres outside the romantic period, i.e., to the literature *before* the romantic period, since it is born of a critical attitude that is bound up with the after-effects of the romantic period and a particular time, and cannot be generalized. It has been seen in the course of this study that a more formal and conventional approach to genres, as long as this is not too narrow or normative, can provide us with a great deal of information about the nature of the poetry and the intentions of the poet. However, when romantic poetry was at its peak, as with Keats and Shelley, only the two systematic approaches that have been used here for Keats' poems produce really useful, in-depth information about the way the genre was developing: the 'archetypal' approach which sheds light on the content and the 'metaphorical and symbolical' approach, which covers the formal aspects of the genre in the widest sense.

One question nevertheless still remains to be dealt with in connection with Keats' narrative work, as for the work of the preceding poets, since only this can determine the extent to which a tale in verse is in line with the principles of its genre: the question of whether the narrative gifts of the poet match his intellectual gifts or his ability to interpret a 'world'. This too will provide valuable information about Keats' works and the romantic period, information that will contribute to our understanding of the genre in general.

With the narrative poems of Wordsworth and Coleridge it was seen that the philosophical concern and philosophical approach to poetry that formed the background to their entire work were incompatible with the long narrative form. In the case of Keats, the situation at first glance appears to be different. While he always wanted to be educated in philosophy and thought this would enhance his poetry, his work is not primarily the outcome of philosophical inspiration but of an indisputable gift for portraying the tangible and the sensuous. Because of this gift his narrative fulfils many of the necessary requirements that Wordsworth's and Coleridge's do not. His relationship to nature is, as has already been said, more sensuous and 'tactile' than that of the Lake Poets (and of Shelley). He counters Wordsworth's 'egotistical sublime' – which is without a doubt unfavourable to narrative, unless it is used autobiographically as in *The Prelude* – with his 'objective' idea of the 'poetical character', his view that 'A Poet is the most unpoetical of any thing in existence; because he has no Identity – he is continually ... filling some other Body.'[145]

While he does not have the gift of a true romancer like Scott or Byron of propelling the reader with tempo through a story and immediately redirecting his interest with every interpolation and digression, change of scene or subject,[146] to compensate for this defect he has Spenser's (and Homer's) gift of clearly visualizing individual scenes, sensing their aesthetic *valeurs* and portraying them in a manner that speaks to the senses; and this is not a bad gift for a narrator of symbolic and mythical events. Thus while the plot in Keats' works is not constantly progressing as it should do in a romance, it does have the continuity of a sequence of organically linked images, as in Spenser. This may not match up to Scott's and Byron's externally dramatic, exciting narratives from a purely technical point of view, but it would suffice as a narrative principle both for the shorter form of the 'poetic tale', for which the attraction of a few individual situations and changing colours are perfectly adequate to hold the interest of the reader to the end, and for the long epic form, which does not depend for effect on an exciting narrative, and which even at the time of Homer was tending towards the elaboration of detail. It is difficult to come to any conclusions about Keats' narrative gifts in such a general way. In order to investigate this point properly, his development must be taken into consideration.

In *Endymion* the external plot is admittedly confusing, obscure and undisciplined. If Keats had learnt anything from Leigh Hunt when he wrote this work, then it was certainly not the latter's clear manner of telling a story. The reflective passages seem occasionally superimposed, and the hunt for rhymes and the many descriptions of beautiful things swamp the thin plot so that in places it almost disappears altogether. The verse technique with its exaggerated use of *enjambements* simulates the narrative continuity that is missing in the plot. We have already heard what Jeffrey has to say on this subject. The adverse review by Croker also takes exception not only to the neologisms, the unusual syntax and the 'bad' prosody ('hardly a couplet that contains a complete idea') but also, and in particular, to the 'immeasurable game at bouts rimés', where not the idea but the sound of the rhymes determines the progress of the poem.[147] *Endymion* flows along, but the flow is not checked by the story elements and the 'invention' is not yet precisely focused and maintained in a consistent direction. In the three shorter tales in verse, the narrative technique noticeably improves. In *Isabella* the fable itself, taken from Boccaccio, gives the poem a firmer plot structure. However, here Keats undermines the externally dramatic moments in the plot with the underlying subjective psychological themes to such an extent that even he later found the events bore too little relation to reality and thought they would be hard for the public to identify with, and hence did not want to publish it: 'It is too smokeable ... There is too much inexperience of life and simplicity of knowledge in it.'[148] He had similar, if not quite as strong objections to *The Eve of St Agnes*, but he was unreservedly positive about *Lamia*.[149] And indeed, this marks the peak of his achievements as far as the narrative is concerned, given the limitations of his temperament and of romantic poetry as we have already described them. After using the stanza form for the other two tales, which inhibited rather than facilitated the flow of narrative, he goes back to the heroic couplet, which he now handles in a more disciplined fashion, adapting its structure flexibly to the story and not just using it to produce continuity with respect to the sound as in the *Endymion* verse. This tale in verse probably represents the most successful synthesis of the continuity of Scott's type of romantic poetry with the expressiveness of the true romantic imagination. In spite of all the magical, supernatural elements, it unites a genuine relationship with reality, that is contained both in the symbolically expressed meaning and in the sensuousness of the images, with a truly poetic transformation of the mimesis into an autonomous cosmos of images and symbols. It combines focus on the subject matter and narrative continuity with formal design (and it is a very significant irony of literary history that Dryden was a model for this, the poet who in his *Fables* also succeeded brilliantly in producing exciting tales though using the poetic style of a period that was detrimental to narrative).[150]

La Belle Dame Sans Merci, that successful synthesis of ballad narrative with the poetry of the romantic imagination, was composed a few months earlier. If by today's standards *Lamia* is the best romantic tale in verse – since it is lacking neither in a deeper level of ideas, nor perfection of form, nor excitement and skill in the way the story is told, three things that have seldom been found together in the verse narratives studied up until now – then for the same reasons *La Belle Dame Sans Merci* is the best romantic ballad alongside *The Ancient Mariner* (although of course its concise narrative technique with all the attributes of the true ballad or song is not comparable with that of Coleridge's longer 'Rhyme'.

This brief survey has shown us what Keats was capable of as a narrator. It was enough for him, and it was enough to allow him now to write the romantic epic about Hyperion, Saturn and Apollo that he had been planning since 1817. In that spring of 1819 when he was freed of his anxiety about his dying brother, when he succeeded with *La Belle Dame* in writing a romantic ballad and with *Lamia* in writing a romantic tale in verse, the stage seemed set for the project of writing, with *Hyperion*, the romantic epic, the dream of a whole epoch of poets.

Since October 1818 his imagination had been crowded with epic figures. On 16 October he wrote to his brother and sister-in-law in America:

I feel more and more every day, as my imagination strengthens, that I do not live in this world alone but in a thousand worlds. No sooner am I alone than shapes of epic greatness are stationed around me, and serve my Spirit the office which is equivalent to a king's bodyguard ... according to my state of mind I am with Achilles shouting in the Trenches, or with Theocritus in the Vales of Sicily ...

The first two books were written in spring and summer 1818 – visions of a grandiose world of gods, the prelude to an important poetic presentation of current but also timeless problems, an improvised portico to a truly interpretative poem. A third book was also begun, that raises the central theme of the romantic poet ('the making of a poet's mind') to the level of a myth, and then embarks on a synthesis of the two problem spheres – at which point Keats had to break off the work. What was the reason?

His own explanation, that Milton's model had become overpowering,[151] is obviously not the whole story. This author does not share the opinion of H. W. Garrod that Keats' exclusive talent for 'poetry which proceeds from an exquisite sense of the luxurious' and his philosophic dilettantism were responsible for his breaking off the poem.[152] Our study of the shorter tales in verse and the development of the poet in this area have shown that the reason cannot be a basic lack of narrative gifts. What then led to this strange abandonment of such an important undertaking?

What we are seeing here is the effect of a more basic law that overrides the individual case, or turns it into an instructive model case for this whole genre history. Keats breaks off *Hyperion* at the decisive point where romantic poetry is endeavouring to enter an area which is in fact inaccessible to it on account of its transcendental structure, its 'inward tendency', its subjectivism, its alienation from society,[153] its lack of an 'accepted unconscious metaphysic', its dream character, its idealism and its longing for myth but lack of a direct and immediate relationship to it: the area of commitment to the realities of politics and history, to the need in the world and what to do to remedy it. In fact, inaccessible. This does not mean that these things lie outside the romantic poets' sphere of interest or cannot be used by them as subjects of poems: the best proof of this is provided by Shelley, and also by Blake, with all the problems his work poses; and also by Byron, who was sceptical about anything that was transcendental. All that it means is that the relationship of the romantic poet to this whole area can only lie in the sphere of the idea and the universal and must thus be of a Utopian nature by comparison with concrete reality. The literary exponent of the 'collective unconscious metaphysic' in the romantic age, the person gifted with Coleridge's 'secondary imagination', can produce great intellectual ideas about the past history of mankind and great poetic Utopias with respect to the future, but he cannot in practice bridge the gulf between the area of ideas and the area of reality, between the world of dreams and the world of deeds. Keats himself knew this, but in a well-known passage from a letter[154] spoke of the 'irritable reaching after fact and reason' that was incompatible with the 'negative capability' of the poet.

This applies to Keats and Shelley, Wordsworth (in those works where he achieves greatness) and Coleridge. Keats differs from the other poets only in that he is aware of the Utopian character of the unity of ideal and reality. He cannot get away from his consciousness of this Utopian character by escaping into the 'egotistical sublime' like Wordsworth; he cannot transfer it intellectually to the highest being in which existence and knowledge coincide like Coleridge, and he cannot convince himself with rapturous poetic idealism like Shelley, that what he longs for has become reality once he has succeeded in implanting it in the shape of poetic visions in people's minds. Poetic rapture is suspect to Keats (Lycius wears the thyrsus wreath!) and he experiences the gulf between reality and the dreamed-of ideal as a tragic dilemma. (Lycius dies when the realist Apollonius opens his eyes to the dual nature of what he in poetic blindness worshipped as ideal and real; he cannot bear the revelation that the reality to which he has devoted himself is composed of beauty and horror, joy and suffering, the ideal and the real, woman and snake.) The parable of Adam's dream is not resolved. What should the dreamer do when he awakes to find an unbridgeable gulf between dream and reality? Apollo, in *Hyperion* III, is a further illustration of the same problem. He too is confronted with the problem of the synthesis of the ideal world and reality when he sees in the face of Mnemosyne the requirement reality makes of the poet to identify with the interests of society, with need and the necessity for action. Keats embarks on a paradoxical (and Utopian) poetic solution: Apollo 'dies into life'; the dreamer becomes a god and a true poet, who forces the unity of ideal and life, dream and deed by evoking it poetically. But Keats is not content with Utopia, because he is too deeply convinced that it does not exist anywhere and never will. He cannot ignore the fact that the poetic evocation of a solution to the all-embracing, real problems of mankind is an abstraction – and a piece of self-deception. He knows that he is Lycius and that the 'life' into which Apollo 'dies' is impracticable for the romantic poet. For this reason he cannot complete a poem that is trying to interpret this life.

Byron dwells only in the sphere of 'real' life, and as an egocentric confines his poetry for a long time to that part of it that revolves around him – until he finds the only means of access to real life in all its fullness, through a commitment that lies outside poetry. Shelley only lives in the 'ideal' life of the imagination and considers the evocation of the idea itself to be action – hence his disapprobation of physical violence.

Keats knows about both areas, and when he recognizes their irreconcilability he considers the solution of the problem to be impossible and leaves *Hyperion* unfinished. His final words on this question appear in the letter to Shelley of 16 August 1820, where he accepts the separation of the imagined and the ideal from the hurly-burly of the real world: 'My Imagination is a Monastery and I am its Monk.' The author of the odes had recognized that the domain of his poetry cannot be brought down to the level of actual existence.

In terms of the extended genre doctrine that has been developed by combining our genre definitions with the archetypal genre concept, the conclusions that can be drawn from the case of Keats and *Hyperion* are as follows. The true epic, the interpretation of the total reality of an epoch in the form of a poem, that must be based on the 'accepted unconscious metaphysic' of the historic community to which it refers and from which it comes, canot be produced by the romantic poet. His 'metaphysics' are the problems which were the primary concern of a whole generation of poets and thinkers, but they are neither rooted in a historical community (because they are purely subjectively experienced), nor 'unconscious' (because they are the metaphysics of the longed-for, intellectually postulated ideal myth, millenarian hopes of a 'new heaven and a new earth' or of the 'earthly paradise', of 'something ever more about to be', of the final reunion of all that is divided – an 'apocalyptic marriage'[155] and not the metaphysics of a real myth present in and supported by a whole society).

This general ideological background is the common denominator of all partial explanations that may be given (and have been given) to account for the fact that all attempts to write a romantic epic failed. The phenomena adduced in such explanations are only the practical consequences of the wider context as we have described it.

First there is the lack of action. The epics of the romantic period are 'histories of souls'. They are not, like the true Heroic Poems, stories of 'souls coming into action', nor are they 'that clash of souls which exhibits not them alone, but a whole of spiritual forces, appearing in them, but spreading into the visible society to which they essentially belong, and into invisible regions which enclose it'.[156] Second there is the absence of an unproblematic and unquestioning relationship to reality, which the subject-matter of the epic has even in Milton's work and which alone can turn it into a mirror of genuine world theatre, 'huge, multiform, ponderous, yet quivering with an inward agitation which explodes into violent bodily expression and speaks to the eye of imagination'.[157] Third there is the lack of objectivity, which is unavoidable with the basic epistemological, i.e., subjective, interest of the romantic epics. And fourth there is the lack of narrative continuity and dynamism, which can never be as pronounced in the description and analysis of the mental states and gradual evolution of a particular character or even of this character's inner conflicts as in the real conflicts between historical powers, national parties and flesh-and-blood warriors.

We are not trying to say here that valuable longer romantic poems in narrative form are in general condemned to failure. Even North qualified his assertion that Wordsworth's *Excursion* was not a 'great poem' since it had no central narrative plan with the words: 'unless the principles of art should be changed'.[158] The principles of art have changed, and today we consider if not *The Excursion*, then many of the other long poems of romantic inspiration – including *The Prelude*, *Endymion* and the *Hyperion* fragment, *Alastor* and *The Triumph of Life* – to be 'great' poems. The intention of this author is solely to prove that the idea that the epic could be reborn out of the romantic spirit was Utopian.

In the sections on the narrative poems of Shelley and Keats, our genre study is extended to include both new and perhaps controversial approaches and poems which are not strictly speaking in the line of narrative poetry inaugurated by Scott and Byron. This had to be done for the sake of the deep historical insight this methodical approach provides. It is believed that it can promote a better understanding of the poetry, its aims, successes and failures. More of this, however, in the *Conclusion*.

Going back, finally, to Jeffrey's *Endymion* review, it can now be seen that his objections to Keats' first long work – that it had too little 'interest of story ... vivacity of characters ... engaging incidents ... and pathos' and that its symbolistic style was too 'dreary and abstracted' to appeal to a wider circle of readers and maintain their interest all through the story – do not just represent the dated opinion of a defender of superficial, fashionable romances, but contain a core of objective historical truth about the genre. In the same review (of August 1820), Jeffrey warned Keats against completing *Hyperion*, 'for though there are passages of some force and grandeur, it is sufficiently obvious ... that the subject is too far removed from all the sources of human interest, to be successfully treated by any modern author'.

Keats had no need of this well-meaning advice (he could not in any case have responded to it, as in August 1820 he was already seriously ill). When he ended *Hyperion* with the shriek of the god Apollo as he was given sight, he was already much more deeply convinced than Jeffrey could have suspected that the romantic epic was Utopian. With *The Fall of Hyperion* he had nevertheless made another attempt to create a poem out of the subject-matter that was unsuitable for an epic by clothing it in an archetypal romance form, the dream.[159]

This was in principle a clever decision, and an extremely instructive one. It would in fact have been able to help him overcome some of the above-mentioned difficulties. But there were other obstacles: 1. The new version required complicated machinery because of the dream, and this made it unwieldy from the point of view of narrative technique. 2. The melody of the Miltonic language was so bound up with the subject-matter as far as Keats was concerned that it was not possible to exclude it; its epic sublimity, however, gave the romantic dream something heroic that was no longer quite suited to its basic nature. 3. Here too Keats could not escape the problem that had already led him to break off the first fragment, the incompatibility of dreamer and poet. The lavishly described dream atmosphere of *The Fall of Hyperion* had now however rendered it even more insoluble. 4. As R. A. Foakes correctly observes,[160] Keats had already included in the fragment everything that had interested him in the subject, i.e., everything that could be developed introspectively, subjectively or symbolically and used as a commentary on the idealistic problems of the romantic poet; for this reason he could not have been interested in completing the external mythological story. 5. Finally the onset of Keats' illness and the tormenting hopelessness of his love for Fanny Brawne could also be listed as reasons for his breaking off work on *The Fall of Hyperion*. The poem of Hyperion and Apollo, which could have become the greatest epic of the romantic period – if a romantic epic was at all possible – remained unwritten.

In the light of these background factors, there seems to be no reason to regret that Keats abandoned his plan. There is rather reason to be glad that he did not waste all his remaining strength and time on this hopeless undertaking, but gave the world that which will make him live eternally, that to which his gifts most inclined him and which corresponded from the point of view of genre to the 'pure poetry' which Jeffrey so aptly defined: the Odes.

When Jeffrey said in his review of *Endymion* that the 'scope and substance of Mr. Keats' poetry ... [were] rather too dreary and abstracted ... to sustain the attention through a work of any great compass or extent' and then concluded by saying that Keats could probably produce very beautiful poetry if he did not abuse or misuse his rich imagination and his 'familiarity with the finest diction in English poetry' and avoided 'intractable themes' and exaggeratedly lavish descriptions, he was uttering a more profound truth than he could have been aware of. It does not apply only to Keats, but to the nature of romantic poetry (in today's sense romantic) in general. It explains why the Odes were Keats' best and greatest poetry and it says what has been confirmed by the history of attempts at romantic epics and of the long narrative poems of the nineteenth century: that the romantic imagination is lyric and not epic. The case of Keats is the best illustration of this, which is why it occupies a central place in our history of the dissolution and ramification of the romantic tale in verse genre.

Percy Bysshe Shelley

Avia Pieridum peragro loca, nullius ante
Trita solo; iuvat integros accedere fonteis;
Atque haurire: iuvat novos decerpere flores.
Lucretius, *De rerum natura, Liber IV*, quoted by Shelley as the epigraph of
Queen Mab

Mr. Shelley is too fond of allegories.
Review of *Alastor* in *BM*, 32, November 1819

In Shelley's work the boundaries of the genre of 'romantic tales in verse' are exceeded as never before. A broadly positivistic interpretation of the genre must of necessity lead either to the reaction of many of his contemporaries, which was to judge almost every fictional work of Shelley's in verse as an unsuccessful attempt at the type of poetry under consideration here (which would be absurd), or to the exclusion of the work from the genre altogether. In the latter case one would be reduced to applying a remark of F. W. Schlegel about poetic mythology – 'Each truly creative individual must create his mythology for himself'[161] – to genre: '... must create his genres for himself'. This is also in line with the tenor of a great many aesthetic theories of the period. All the 'new' tendencies were bound to lead to subjectivism and emotionalism in the theory of poetry, to an interest in the contribution of the unconscious to the creative process of imagination, a call for the ideal and the symbolic in poetry, the cult of genius, the belief in perfectibility, the rejection of all regulations that inhibit spontaneity, and the universal desire for liberty, etc., etc. The resulting indifference towards the traditional idea of the genre is expressed effectively if not in a particularly philosophical manner in the words of the minor poet Barry Cornwall, quoted as the second epigraph of this book.

In the Introduction to his edition of Shelley's *Narrative Poems*,[162] C.H. Herford attempted to characterize Shelley's type of verse narrative and classify it as belonging to the epic revival at the beginning of the nineteenth century. He had of course no option but to define each of the approximately twenty-five poems by Shelley that can in some way be described as narrative separately according to genre, i.e., to connect them with genres that might have been direct or indirect models.[163] Herford too finally came to the conclusion that a comprehensive, traditional genre classification of Shelley's narrative poems is in fact impossible. Shelley is too far removed from the 'Homeric' objectivity that distinguishes the true narrator. His poetry – even when in semi-dramatic or epic guise – is always inspired by subjective visions and Shelley's desire to convert the reader to his own philosophical and political view of the world through poetry or, what in his opinion is its equivalent, feeling. For this reason Herford finally rejects any kind of general formula: 'Shelley's complete work is an ocean that washes away all boundaries between genres.'

Here we must thus once again enlarge our concept of genre if we are to make any progress. But there is another step that must be taken first, namely the exploration of Shelley's own references to his relationship to traditional genres or his conscious though selective use of traditional genres in each of his narrative poems.

Even the epigraph of his first long 'Philosophical Poem' *Queen Mab* (1813) – from Lucretius and quoted as the epigraph of this section on Shelley – indicates that he has followed paths 'untrodden by anyone before him'. This may primarily be a reference to the ideas of the poem, which expresses radical political and philosophical views and has extensive notes that are highly didactic, but it is also almost certainly a reference to the novelty of the genre and verse form. However, instead we find here an obvious similarity to Southey's *Thalaba* with respect to metre and style; and it is also reminiscent of the traditional vista of the epic poem, or perhaps of a didactic version of it, with the ride in the chariot of the Fairy Queen, whereby the present state of mankind and its future is revealed to the heroine Ianthe. Desmond King-Hele calls it 'the well-worn eighteenth-century artifice of the conducted tour' and indicates 'Volney's once-famous book *The Ruin*' as a possible model.[164] In Landor's *Gebir* the conducted tour of Tamar is probably based primarily on Milton, but the didactic version of the vista mentioned above is also a possible model. But as we have already seen, Landor's use of the device for didactic content or prophecies did not exclude certain elements that heralded the romantic tale in verse. In Shelley's *Queen Mab* the romantic aspect is considerably reinforced by his own symbolism and imaginative myths so that there is more resemblance to the typical romantic dream journey in Keats' *The Fall of Hyperion* or Shelley's own *Witch of Atlas*. Of course the genuine romantic dream journey in its archetypal form is an odyssey involving a series of trials undergone by the hero in his quest for the transcendental, symbolized by some concrete or anthropomorphized form. Ianthe's dream journey, on the other hand, in spite of its Utopian vision of the future, has no transcendental goal, it is not a journey motivated by longing, nor is it a quest. It would not alter in nature if the narrative structure were reversed, i.e., if the history of mankind were paraded past the observer in the form of a pageant – as in *Paradise Lost* or, in a very superficial form, in Scott's *Vision of Don Roderick*. The dream of Ianthe is hence in fact much closer to the vista, the epic or allegorical and didactic vision, than to the 'archetypal' romantic narrative myth of the quest. In addition, the dream itself is not yet developed as the special power of the romantic psyche to perceive the essence of things, but is an allegorical cliché. It may be that Shelley was thinking of this 'defect' in particular when he wrote to the editor of the *Examiner* from Pisa on 22 June 1821:[165] 'I have not seen this production for several years. I doubt not but that it is perfectly worthless in point of literary composition.' It is also probable that Mary Shelley, with the knowledge of her husband's later works, did not mean the ideas of the work (which she after all shared) when she wrote in 1839 of 'defects that escape the ordinary reader', nor did she mean the style (the originality of which she praised) but rather the continuing uncertainty as to the genre of *Queen Mab*. It is interesting to note that, while firmly denying that Shelley imitated anyone else, she lists non-classical works that had had a combined influence on him when younger, in particular German literature depicting the 'wonderful and wild', but also the works of Wordsworth that expressed his love of nature, Coleridge's verse music with its 'mysterious beauty', Southey's highly romantic fantasies and Landor's *Gebir*. At the same time she acknowledges almost with regret that it was to these sources that Shelley went to satisfy his taste for the wonderful and wild and not to the 'true' sources that had originally inspired Scott and others: the romances of medieval times.[166]

When at the beginning of this 'Note on Queen Mab by Mrs. Shelley', written for the complete edition of Shelley's poetry published in 1839, Mary says that Shelley's 'severe classical taste, refined by the constant study of the Greek poets' might have protected him from certain defects in the composition of his poetry,[167] this is not a plea for adherence to classicistic rules and genre orientation, but rather a censure of the heterogeneous mixture of these neo-classical elements and of that type of poetry free of generic conventions that was later to become Shelley's strength. There is perhaps also a hint of regret here that Shelley, while writing a type of romance, could not bring himself to follow the line of Scott, Byron or Southey and write in such a way as to appeal to a wider section of the public.[168]

Although the Preface to *Alastor or the Spirit of Solitude* that was written a few years later in 1815 begins with a sentence that contains the word 'allegorical', it nevertheless makes a precise distinction between this poem and the much more traditional allegorical formula of *Queen Mab*: 'The poem entitled *Alastor* may be considered as allegorical of one of the most interesting situations of the human mind.'[169] Here in a nutshell are the two elements that also feature in Keats' poems *Endymion* and *Hyperion*: a theme based on the thinking of a man endowed with a poetic imagination and a form based on symbolism. Where content is concerned, *Alastor* already has all the characteristics named by Northrop Frye in his definition of 'archetypal romance' in the literary epoch of the 'low mimetic mode': the poet is the only possible hero because of his greater powers of insight; the 'myth' is 'intensely individualized'; the poet hero is 'in a state of pantheistic rapport with nature' and his spirit is 'simultaneously aware of [two] worlds'.[170] The Utopian 'myth of longing' that the absolute and ideal world and the real world might become one remains tragically unfulfilled in *Alastor*, by contrast with Keats' *Endymion*. In Mary Shelley's opinion, Shelley's illness and nearness to death when he wrote it were responsible for this. Earl Wasserman on the other hand is of the view that it is Shelley's affinity for the sceptical philosophy of Hume that lies behind the tragedy of *Alastor*, or rather behind Shelley's ambivalent attitude towards the persona of the speaker of the Preface, who didactically warns the poet of his 'self-centred seclusion', and the persona of the protagonist, who embodies the tragic lot of the poet, likened later by Shelley in *The Defence of Poetry* to the nightingale singing alone in the dark, and described here with a strong sense of identification on Shelley's part.[171]

The Revolt of Islam (1817) has already been dealt with in detail as a romantic epic by Brian Wilkie[172] and Stuart Curran[173] and I will hence limit myself here to a brief enumeration of the most important facts. While the subtitle 'A Poem in Twelve Cantos' refers to the sacred number of books in the epic poem, the subtitle of the first version *Laon and Cythna*, 'A Vision of the Nineteenth Century' tends more towards Blake's apocalyptic visions, written in defiance of all genre regulations. Shelley's Preface[174] gives the reason for his choice of the narrative genre, to which, by contrast with Blake, he pays tribute with a promise of a story told in a very direct way, using emotionalistic and Rousseauist or Wordsworthian arguments in support of his approach, 'a story of human passion in its most universal character diversified with moving and romantic adventures, and appealing, in contempt of all artificial opinions or institutions, to the common sympathies of every human breast'. He states firmly that he has not attempted to influence the reader 'by methodical and systematic argument' even 'in the cause of a liberal and comprehensive morality', nor does he presume to compete with the leading contemporary poets or imitate earlier poets or poetic systems.

This text also contains some reasons why Shelley is so concerned to avoid the systematic adoption of particular models or conformity with the contemporary literary scene. Here we have his belief in 'perfectibility in works of fiction', whereby he accepts the almost unconscious absorption of the achievements of the great poets, historians and metaphysicians, which exert a cumulative influence on the poet, but rejects the use of forms and systems of thought that are connected with specific periods. Here too he distances himself from the literature of despair of the day which had resulted from the failure of the French Revolution and was evident both in poetry (whereby every contemporary reader would have realized that Shelley had the 'German' horror literature, Scott's *Marmion* and in particular Byron's entire production since 1812 in mind) and in political theory (here Shelley mentions the disheartening population prognoses of Malthus). The Preface culminates in a rejection of all the rules and regulations from the past that dominate criticism – and hence also a rejection of the inherited generic traditions: 'This system of criticism sprang up in that torpid interval when Poetry was not. Poetry, and the art which professes to regulate and limits its powers, cannot subsist together.'

Before we finally reject altogether the classification of *The Revolt of Islam* as an epic poem on the basis of the above considerations, we should however examine some of the remarks made by Shelley in *The Defence of Poetry* and the accompanying letter to Peacock of 21 March 1821.[175]

T. L. Peacock's Essay *The Four Ages of Poetry*, against which Shelley's *Defence* was directed, is a cyclic account of the history of Western literature such as was typical of critics of the period. Peacock's arguments amount to a condemnation of all modern poetry with its back-to-nature tendency as 'disjointed relics of tradition and fragments of secondhand observation' or as 'a modern – antique compound of frippery and barbarism, in which the puling sentimentality of the present time is grafted on the misrepresented ruggedness of the past into a heterogeneous congeries of unamalgamating manners, sufficient to impose on the common reader of poetry'.[176] This is clearly directed at the modern romancers; later this becomes even more obvious when Peacock mentions Scott, Byron, Southey, Moore and Campbell. The new age, concludes Peacock, should stop continuing to want to produce great poetry; in this scientific and 'prosaic' epoch, this age of reason, they should leave the interpretation of the historical process to the historiographers and sociologists.

In answer to this attack, Shelley states his opinion that great poetry can still be produced, but he does not defend the writers of romantic tales in verse. In his letter to Peacock he admits that his prolific contemporaries irritate him as much as they do his friend Peacock, and that he would also much rather devote his time to reading scientific or poetic works of prose than to reading all this 'stuff in terza, ottava, and tremillesima rima, whose earthly baseness has attracted the lightening of your undiscriminating censure upon the temple of immortal song'.[177]

In *The Defence of Poetry* Shelley makes no attempt to discuss individual modern poets (it was his intention to do this in a second section, which however was never written). However, he immediately gets to the heart of the problem: he separates the reason of the scientist and technician from the very different imaginative activity of the artist, and he places the latter far above the former. In other words, he contrasts the achievement of romantic philosophy, the discovery of creative, poetic, emotional, image-laden, symbolic reason with Peacock's superficial rationalism. As regards the assessment of the epic poem and the narrative poetic genres in general – the question which concerns us here – Shelley scarcely differs from Peacock. The requirements he makes of the great poem are even more stringent than those made in *The Four Ages of Poetry*: for him the true epic has only been produced by Homer, Dante and Milton. He excludes Virgil as an imitator of Homer, and the works of Lucan, Statius, Ariosto, Tasso, Camoens and Spenser are in his view much too involved with material reality to merit the 'title of epic in its highest sense'. All the other epic poets are mere 'mock-birds'. The definition of the 'epic in its highest sense' that follows repeats the ideas in the Preface to *The Revolt of Islam*: 'the laws of epic truth, that is … the laws of that principle by which a series of actions of the external universe and of intelligent and ethical beings is calculated to excite the sympathy of succeeding generations of mankind'. An epic poet in the highest sense of the word can only be someone whose work has a particular, intelligible relationship to the knowledge, feelings and religion of his own age and subsequent ages. The ideas and work of the true epic poet run parallel to the historical process. The temporal and worldly distortions of the eternal, absolute truth in such works are only a mask that falls away with the passing of time, without detracting from the beauty of the inner message.

From the similarity of many of these ideas with the general tenor of the Preface to *The Revolt of Islam* it becomes clear that Shelley must have considered this earlier work to be 'an epic venture'[178] – and none of his poems are in fact as close as this one to the epic tradition. It features a genuinely active heroic couple, even if this activity is mainly verbal owing to the pacifist tendency of the poem; there is a historical interest over and above the individual interest, there are struggles and suffering, there is heroism – naturally of the non-military kind – and there is an optimistic belief in the future of post-revolutionary society, for which the poem speaks out. Nevertheless, *The Revolt* is still not a true epic. Herford describes it as 'rather a romance than an epic, of revolution',[179] and Baker calls it a 'pseudo-epic' or 'this essentially abortive epic'.[180]

The external romance elements cannot be overlooked. The original incorporation of the names of the heroic couple in the title – *Laon and Cythna* – and the central position of their love in the narrative are deviations from the traditions of the heroic poem. The same is true of the basic emotionalism, the sensational adventure, exotic colour, choice of the Spenser stanza and many other features of the poem. Given in addition the general tendency towards unreality, as evidenced in the magic landscapes, the historically and geographically unreal world of the poem, the wonderful deliverances from danger and journeys to fantasy kingdoms, the visions in dreams, the spirits and fantasy animals, I am inclined to agree with Herford's verdict as quoted above from the point of view of the external features alone. This is not the machinery of the epic poem, it is pure romance pointing more in the direction of the *Arabian Nights* (and *Thalaba*) than of Homer and Milton.

If however we examine the work more closely with reference to the archetypal genre, as in the preceding study of Keats, it becomes clear here too that these 'romantic' narrative phenomena are only external elements, the means of narrating the 'myth' that is the heart of the poem and is a myth of longing, remembrance and the quest for the ideal. The significance of the 'Golden City', enshrined in the millenarian hopes of many of Shelley's contemporaries, is as obvious as the origin of the incestuous relationship of Laon and Cythna in the *animus/anima* dilemma of many romantics; equally evident is the connection of the Platonic, Utopian conclusion – the removal of the two heroes in their hour of need to the Temple of the Spirit – with the political powerlessness of the radicals in the years of the Holy Alliance.

While not presuming to dismiss Shelley's attempt in this great romantic work to produce the ultimate in fictional poetry, the epic poem of mankind of the nineteenth century, it is my contention that no true epic can be produced from a speculative political Utopia and private myths: the *Revolt* remains a romance, and there is a significant ambiguity in this in the light of Malcolm Kelsall's assessment of the politics of the English romantics.[181]

After completing *The Revolt of Islam*, Shelley on the one hand vigorously defended the ambitious intentions of this poem in twelve cantos but on the other had become increasingly uncertain about the genre of his longer poems. The work provoked many negative reactions, not only from the official critics[182] but also from people well disposed towards Shelley such as William Godwin. In the letter that he wrote to his father-in-law on 11 December 1817, Shelley's defence, with its interesting mixture of modesty and self-confidence, is a revealing picture of the difficulties he encountered when writing the *Revolt*: 'it grew ... from "the agony and bloody sweat" of intellectual travail ... I felt that it was in many respects a genuine picture of my own mind ... I never presumed indeed to consider it anything approaching to faultless'.[183] He excuses the weaknesses of the work with the 'absence of that tranquillity which is the attribute and accompaniment of power'. He also emphasizes, however, that this poem with its oppressive premonition of death is a 'record of myself' and has strengthened his self-confidence in that it compares favourably with contemporary works. 'I felt', he writes, 'that the sentiments were true' referring, as he does in the Preface, to his true strengths: 'sympathy, and that part of the imagination which relates to sentiments and contemplation'.

It was nevertheless more than a year before he felt strong enough to produce another major vision centred round an interpretation of the nature of the world. The longer poems written in the intervening period are, however, of considerable interest for this study of genre, even though they do not belong to the mainstream of romantic tales in verse.

The symbolic tale of *Prince Athanase* (in tercets), in which Shelley attempted to return to the material and form of *Alastor*, is no more than a fragment. We know from Mary Shelley that the hero is disappointed and soon deserted by Venus Pandemos, following which he dies like Alastor; but as he dies he is kissed by Urania, 'the lady who can really reply to his soul'.[184] As Shelley himself wrote in a note, the reason for breaking off the work was the morbid direction in which it was going.[185] Fulfilment only in death was not in accordance with Shelley's secular hopes.

We do not know when Mary first attempted to persuade her husband to write a poem 'of more human interest' and thereby gain the popularity and self-assurance that Scott, Byron and others had acquired in this way. He himself first answers her reproaches in the poem to *The Witch of Atlas* (1820),[186] but her Note on the *Cenci* in her edition of Shelley's *Poetical Works* of 1839[187] suggests that she had probably tried to influence him with advice of this nature at an even earlier stage. She appears in any case to have been quick to contradict his opinion that he could not write a dramatic work because he had no 'capacity of forming and following up a story or plot' and was 'too metaphysical and abstract, too fond of the theoretical and the ideal' to be a tragedian, even though for a time she also shared his assessment of himself as a result of one or two unsuccessful attempts 'to give a specimen of his powers in framing and supporting the interest of a story, either in prose or verse'.

Shelley's difficulty in finding a suitable genre, a difficulty that is noticeable in the longer poems written between December 1817 and August 1818, is perhaps to be attributed not only to the poet's poor health (see Mary's Note on the Poems of 1818) but also to the uncertainty into which he had been plunged by the cool reception of his *Revolt of Islam* by Godwin and others, perhaps even including Mary. He was unable to complete *Prince Athanase* (December 1817) and the verse narrative *Rosalind and Helen: A Modern Eclogue* (summer 1818) was preceded by an 'Advertisement'[188] opening with a *captatio benevolentiae*: this story was 'undoubtedly, not an attempt in the highest style of poetry' and was 'in no degree calculated to excite profound meditation'. While in the middle of writing it he put it aside, and only took it up again after an interval to please Mary. Even when he was already working on *Prometheus Unbound* (begun in October 1818 and finished at the end of 1819) he still occasionally interrupted this, his greatest poem, in order to compose poems which by comparison had a much stronger, more direct relation to reality. These were the tale of *Julian and Maddalo* (autumn 1818), described as 'A Conversation' and clearly a reflection of the time spent by Shelley with Byron in Venice and his dispute with him, in spite of the freedom with which he handles his subject, and the drama *The Cenci* (May – August 1819), which he himself describes in his 'Dedication to Leigh Hunt'[189] as 'sad reality' by comparison with his earlier 'visions which impersonate my own apprehensions of the beautiful and the just', and his 'dreams what ought to be or may be'.

Shelley's dilemma is significant of his position in the history of the genre. It indicates that he had to fight hard for freedom from traditional ideas of genre, which was already hinted at in his comments on *Queen Mab* and *The Revolt of Islam* and which was given a firmer theoretical basis in *The Defence of Poetry*; it also explains why he still made use of traditional genre models – the eclogue, the dialogue poem and the Renaissance tragedy – adapting them for his purposes, and why he was attempting to introduce a new distinction of his own between the genre of 'visionary poetry' and that of 'sad reality'.[190] This distinction is pregnant with meaning in that the works classified as 'visionary poems' are more lyrical, while those classified as 'sad reality' are more dramatic. The lyrical tendency is continued in a more pronounced form in the longer poems that Shelley wrote towards the end of his life – *The Sensitive Plant* (1820), *The Witch of Atlas* and *Epipsychidion* (1821), while the dramatic tendency leads via the two poems in dialogue form, *Rosalind and Helen* and *Julian and Maddalo*, directly to the great drama *The Cenci*.

While it would be interesting to discuss whether Shelley was ever able to look critically at what he was doing, in the manner of Keats, this would lead us too far away from the subject of genre. In the well-known 'Gradus ad Parnassum altissimum' letter to John Taylor of 17 November 1819 Keats wrote: 'As the marvellous is the most enticing and the surest guarantee of harmonious numbers I have been endeavouring to persuade myself to untether Fancy and let her manage for herself. I myself cannot agree about this at all. Wonders are no wonders to me. I am more at home amongst Men and women.'[191]

The maturity that Shelley had attained in his work in 1818 is evidenced by the fact that he had not only overcome the old genre conventions that inhibited creativity, but that he was also able to bridge the gulf of his own making between visionary poetry and sad reality, lyrical and dramatic inspiration. This he achieved with *Prometheus Unbound* and would probably also have achieved with *The Triumph of Life*, had he lived to complete it.

Prometheus Unbound is not a romantic tale in verse, but it is *the* romantic poem that contains all the new characteristics which distinguish the great romantic poem as we understand it today from the romantic tale in verse as conceived by Southey, Scott and Byron. In order to preserve the continuity of this study, the same terminology will be used as in the preceding chapters. *Prometheus Unbound* is a romantic poem according to W. K. Wimsatt's definition of the term – a complex metaphor without expressed tenor, i.e., a long symbolic poem. According to Northrop Frye's definition of the term it is an 'archetypal romance', i.e., it takes its inspiration from the feeling of dualistic separation between the absolute and ideal world and the real world and is basically concerned with 'the sense of the poetic mind as passing from one world to another, or as simultaneously aware of both'.[192]

The objection that since Shelley is an atheist, the divine or absolute is only present in a metaphorical sense, appearing in his work as the human spirit or human thought, is as irrelevant here as the objection that there hence cannot be two worlds. The utlimate goal portrayed in this work is Utopian and therefore transcendent, since mankind continually reverts to blindness and inflexibility. The myth is a 'myth of desire' and also a subjective myth in spite of its resemblances to Aeschylus and its obvious origins in radical-liberal party ideology. All the narrative characteristics of the 'archetypal romance' are present here, as in Shelley's earlier works: exile or imprisonment, the dream, the journey, the Utopian union with the loved one, the revelation of a 'new' life, the supernatural life of nature and much more besides. Finally, *Prometheus Unbound* also contains the 'encyclopaedic tendency' towards the mythological epic that Frye ascribes to the romantic period. Here the unimportance of the formal generic character by comparison with this higher generic classification is convincingly demonstrated by Shelley's choice of the dramatic-lyrical form, which removes the gulf between the 'genres' of vision and sad reality as well as that between the fundamental poetic genres. If we construct a diagram to illustrate the complex and problematic generic nature of this example of 'pro-gressive universal poetry' as defined by Schlegel it will look something like Fig. 1.

But something should also be said about the poems Shelley wrote that are closer to the fashionable genre of 'romantic tales in verse' than the grand culmination of his development we have just been discussing, and have up to now only received mention as stepping stones in this development.

Rosalind and Helen is, as we have seen, a step backwards after the higher aspirations of *The Revolt of Islam*. In this modern eclogue, Shelley came closest to the merely narrative romantic verse novella. Here, in spite of the un-mistakable Shelley pathos and Godwinism, he is nearer to those romancers typical of English domestic poetry, with their gloomy and sentimental idylls

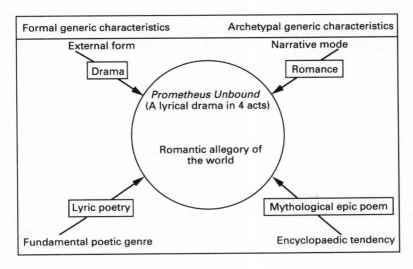

Figure 1

(here I am thinking of works such as Campbell's *Theodric*, of some narrative poems by Crabbe and above all of the works of Wordsworth). While Shelley's revolutionary side is still very much in evidence in this eclogue, it has lost some of its force; his belief in a Utopia has given way to a self-pitying, melancholy tone, a tone which is occasionally present in other works as the psychological opposite of revolutionary optimism. In the foreground is the story or rather the two stories of the heroines and the plot that links them. The poem demonstrates Shelley's inability to make a narrative fable exciting without supernatural visions and the radiant lyricism of his romantic imagery. As the critic of *Blackwood's Magazine* had already established,[193] he was trying to produce something approximating the gentler pathos of the Lake School, but he was not a gentle poet; and the narrative quality here is 'no better than of a weak romantic novel'.[194] He admits in the Advertisement preceding the poem[195] that this verse narrative is 'undoubtedly not an attempt in the highest style of poetry' and that he would be satisfied if the mere story prepared the reader through its 'ideal melancholy' for 'the reception of more important impressions', by which he probably meant the Godwinian revolt against marriage as an institution. In the Advertisement Shelley also supports the emotionalistic view of poetry, a view shared by writers from Southey and the Lake Poets to Scott and Byron, according to which the metre and external form of a poem are determined not by fixed genre rules but by the feelings that inspired the poet to compose a particular narrative. Of course, by using the loose tetrameter verse of Scott and Byron with its free rhyming schemes and many rhythmic freedoms he was signalling to the contemporary reader the proximity of the work to the fashionable tale in verse.

Julian and Maddalo was also influenced by the epic revival of the romantic period: here we find the linguistic informality of Byron, the free verse form of Leigh Hunt and the *italianità* of both, plus the (probably unintentional) similarity of the motif to that of Crabbe's *Sir Eustace Gray*. Similarities with Byron's *The Lament of Tasso* have also frequently been pointed out. These influences are, however, offset by Shelley's originality and exploitation of symbolic means, to such an extent that the work appears as uniquely his own. The same applies to any other contemporary influences on his subsequent work.

In *The Witch of Atlas* we have the reverse of the situation in *Rosalind and Helen*. In both these poems the balance between imagination and reality which is essential for all longer verse narratives is disturbed. The 'modern eclogue' is too close to reality for Shelley and is hence poetically flat at his hands;[196] *The Witch of Atlas* is pure imagination with no obvious, concrete relationship to reality and hardly any story, and hence presents itself to us as merely a flight of fantasy.[197]

The Sensitive Plant and *Epipsychidion* are difficult to place in any particular genre,[198] but pave the way for *The Triumph of Life*: in this, his last long poem, Shelley reverted to the traditional form of the allegory which he had used in *Queen Mab*, even though there it was partly out of a sense of obligation to the eighteenth century and the early romantic mode. In these last years of his life he seems to have realized that it was not the romantic verse narrative with its varying degree of allegorical ambiguity that was most suited to his purposes, but the Italian genre of the allegorical triumphal procession or pageant. Although *The Mask of Anarchy*, *Adonais* and *The Triumph of Life* differ greatly from one another in tone, style, theme and their handling of the basic romantic problems, they are very similar in their use of a sequential structure and their allegorical presentation of the *trionfo*. We shall never know whether Shelley sensed that the romantic tale in verse was on its way out or whether he resorted to this allegorical form from a lack of the 'capacity of forming and following up a plot': whether he was stimulated by his Italian exile to adopt the Italian model or whether he succumbed to the inclination for the pageant that was already evident in *Queen Mab*. We should, however, take a closer look at Shelley's general affinity for the allegory, a term that has occurred repeatedly in this section and should be distinguished from the romantic use of symbols that we find in the work of Coleridge and Wordsworth, and in particular in the work of Keats.

The word allegory was used tentatively in the section on Keats but only to refer to his romantic-symbolic narrative structures when the usual terminological association of 'allegory' with the use of traditional images – at least in the medieval sense – did not apply, for which reason the term was finally abandoned altogether. It is certainly applicable to Shelley's *The Triumph of Life*, since the central picture is in the European allegorical tradition, but it can also be used for many of Shelley's other narrative poems with more justification than for poems by Keats in the same genre. The images created by Shelley are just as subjective as those created by Keats even though they are seldom without literary inspiration (as Baker and Curran have frequently pointed out). However, they do have something else in common with the bulk of traditional allegory, something that is lacking in Keats: they could not exist as narrative structures alone without their symbolic meaning, lacking that 'superficial' human interest and worldliness that Keats' verse narratives almost always have. The romantic-symbolic narrative genre, which was so suitable for Coleridge with his *Ancient Mariner* and for Keats, is not quite adequate for Shelley's philosophical and ethical aspirations. In short: the imaginative process that has already been described, whereby Keats converts his philosophy into concrete experiences, automatically makes his poems romantic-symbolic narratives. Shelley's more abstract and much more intellectual philosophizing is adequately expressed by the subjective allegory, which is rich in meaning but poor in human characters with whom it is possible to identify – unless the imaginatively gifted reader is able to identify with the poet-hero, or rather the problems of a creative person.

If therefore we want to define the genre of Shelley's narrative poems, it is probably correct to say that while Keats wrote symbolic romantic tales in verse, Shelley wrote allegorical romantic fictions in verse. The common denominator is the term 'romantic', and in both cases we are dealing with extended metaphors without explicitly stated tenors. The difference between the two, on the other hand, is expressed by the terms 'symbolic' and 'allegorical'.

The critic of *Blackwood's Magazine*, who is quoted in the epigraph of this section on Shelley ('Mr Shelley is too fond of allegories'[199]) said something perfectly correct in our sense of the term without being aware of such a distinction between 'allegorical' and 'symbolic' as we make today. *Prometheus Unbound* has already been described above as a universal romantic world allegory, and newer interpretations of *The Cenci* (Wasserman, Curran, etc.) have even shown how close the basic thematic structure of this work is to the allegorical structure of *Prometheus Unbound*. As we see from Shelley's firm rejection of didactic poetry[200] and from his 'cosmic syntax',[201] the removal of all conceptual differentiations such as 'equality, diversity, unity, contrast, mutual dependence',[202] the allegorical mode was his way of playing the part of the 'unacknowledged legislator of the world', and not betraying the imagination and feelings to the 'cold, forced, unimpassioned ... cramped and cautious' strategies of rationalistic thought exposition. In his writings on contemporary politics, as he confessed to Godwin in the above-mentioned letter of 11 December 1817,[203] he had often done this. The allegorical mode was for him inalienably linked with 'poetry in its most comprehensive sense', just as he also considered all religions to be allegorical in origin.[204]

In this discussion of the genre of Shelley's longer poems, it has been necessary to apply a very broad interpretation of the terms 'romance' and 'narrative verse'. Any other approach to Shelley's work would have been irrelevant and inadequate. It has nevertheless been possible to trace some important connections to the more traditional verse narratives of his predecessors, in spite of the general tendency of the younger romantics to move in new directions and step outside the delineations of genre.

7   The subsequent fate of the genre

The best of romantic narrative poetry, i.e., the poetry written between 1815 and 1825, has been preserved in the works of Keats, Byron and Shelley, who were discussed in the previous chapter. However, neither the dissolution nor the spiritual elevation of the original generic type that are evident in these works (least in the case of Byron and most of all in the case of Shelley) are general characteristics of those years.

Many of the poets around those great figures continued to cultivate the initial type of the 'romantic' metrical tale of which the main features were a primarily narrative focus, sensational or sentimental subject matter, a free range of metre, a wealth of colourful description and an obvious striving for popularity. Although around 1812–13 there had been signs that the public were becoming tired of it,[1] it was in fact given a new lease of life through the enormous success of Byron's oriental tales. We have already seen that the large-scale format that Southey and Scott had originally developed went out of fashion in 1812. Southey's manifest and Scott's rather more covert ambitions in the direction of the romantic epic were quite alien to the minor poets of the younger generation; they wanted to write popular romances or tales in a pleasing verse language, with no attempt at heroic sublimity. For this they took material from the great poets that they thought suitable and likely to be successful, and then mixed these elements to produce a great variety of works that all fit into the broad general heading of romance as that genre was defined in chapter 1 of this book. The sentence that Byron passed on Barry Cornwall's narratives in a letter to Murray, written on 4 January 1821 (Postscript) applies to almost all of these works: 'they are quite spoilt by I know not what affectation of Wordsworth – and Hunt – and Moore – and Myself – all mixed up into a kind of Chaos'. If they were sufficiently original, i.e., capable of finding some new 'trick of fence',[2] they created new 'schools', but if on the other hand they were conscious of their lack of artistic independence, they faithfully copied a pattern someone else had already established.

Among the more original contributors to the minor poetry of this period are Thomas Moore and Leigh Hunt.

Thomas Moore

Nec lusisse pudet, sed non incidere ludum
Horace, *Epistolae* I, XIV, 26, used by Thomas Moore as the motto for the
volume of poems written in his youth, *The Poetical Works of the Late Tom
Little* (1801)

You have caught the colours as if you had been in the rainbow, and the tone
of the East is perfectly preserved ... I suspect you have written a devilish
fine composition ...
Byron in a letter to Moore of 10 July 1817

Thomas Moore, the 'Irish Anacreon', as his contemporaries called him, or
Tom Little, as he called himself, already had a somewhat dubious reputation
as a writer of *risqué* love poems, an Anacreontic poet and young author who
had challenged the almighty Jeffrey to a duel, when in about 1812, on the
advice of several friends, he embarked on a great verse narrative. Apart from
a few works in a vaguely ballad-like style, he had written no narrative
poetry.[3] When in 1817, after five years' intensive study of all the available
oriental sources, he published his 'Eastern Romance' *Lalla Rookh*, he was
acknowledged all over Europe. The poem was translated into many languages,
and not only Byron[4] and the English reviewers but even Middle Eastern
critics confirmed that he had created an authentic atmosphere commensurate
with the best oriental originals. The public bought the rapid succession of
editions faster than they could be printed and members of the Russian Tsar's
family and the Prussian royal family presented tableaux vivants from *Lalla
Rookh* at the Berlin court in 1822, which inspired the Baron de la Motte
Fouqué, who was present on this occasion, to produce a German paraphrase
in the same metre. In other words, the poem was successful to a degree
comparable only with works by Scott and Byron.

What was the secret of this popularity that to us, not two hundred years
later, appears incomprehensible? What made Moore's contemporaries devour
a work that, as T. S. Eliot points out, hardly anyone in England today has
read?[5] To put it briefly, Moore combines in his *Lalla Rookh* all the popular
characteristics developed by his great predecessors. He melts down the gold
– or perhaps we should say with Thomas Love Peacock the brass – that
he has extracted from Scott, Southey and Byron into pennies for distribution
amongst the people. With great skill he takes advantage of the fact that the
framework story with built-in stories is popular in the Orient. This enables
him to present the public with a voluminoous work, that is bound to attract
attention on account of its length alone (*Lalla Rookh* is as long as *Marmion*,
Scott's longest romance), but still meets the popular demand for the shorter
narrative form. The insertion of four different tales into a prose framework
also has the advantage of enabling Moore to demonstrate what he is best at:
clever displays of many different moods, verse and narrative forms.

In the first and longest of the stories, 'The Veiled Prophet of Khorassan', Moore combines a subject which has something of the 'painted horrors' of Southey's *Kehama* about it with Byron's flowing narrative technique and gloomy passion. The heroic couplet is used in much the same form as in Byron's *Corsair* and *Lara*, although the excessive showiness of the language and imagery of course prevents Moore from ever achieving the narrative dynamism of Byron. The inner distance of the poet, who never quite takes the horrors he describes seriously, but clearly relishes them, produces a similar tone to that of Beckford's *Vathek*, although Beckford's caliph betrays the decadence and tendency towards sadism of his author, while the reader immediately knows that Moore's disguised prophet, the personification of cruelty, is the creation of a healthy, jovial person.

As well as this long tale, the next story, entitled 'Paradise and the Peri', that is short in the manner of a ballad and by today's standards very sentimental, was also extremely popular with the public. Here the verse form is an effeminate version of the irregularly rhyming tetrameters of Byron's *Giaour* and *Bride of Abydos*, the metre found in Scott and originally going back to *Christabel*. The subject matter and the way it is handled have overtones of kitsch that have not been encountered in any of the works dealt with so far. As Hazlitt says in *The Spirit of the Age*, one has to go back to the now forgotten Della-Cruscan School at the end of the eighteenth century to find anything as mawkish as this.

The third story, 'The Fireworshippers', is without a doubt the best.[6] Here Moore comes closest to Byron, not only in the way he handles the verse, which according to T. S. Eliot[7] makes it almost impossible for even the connoisseur to decide whether a passage selected at random is by Moore or Byron, but also in the character portrayal. The lively narrative technique and the more robust emotional tone, by comparison with *Peri*, are also reminiscent of Scott.

The final story is the extremely lyrical 'Feast of the Roses at Cashmere', which is more descriptive than narrative, and here Moore indulges in an excess of luxurious colours, perfumes and sounds to an even greater extent than in the preceding tales. His roses, however, exude no natural fragrance, but a sweet synthetic perfume; and the verse music of the tetrameter passages, that are interspersed with anapaestic stanzas, is analogous to the tinkling of a piano in the drawing room rather than the sound of a full orchestra. (This is also true of the songs that are scattered throughout the work.)

Moore himself was aware of the weaknesses of his poetry, and appeases his readers by making fun of these weaknesses in the prose framework story, thereby also taking the wind out of the critics' sails. For this he uses the character of Fadladeen, the harem chamberlain and travelling companion of the beautiful Lalla Rookh, who is a great *arbiter elegantiarum* and *litterarum*. This character, a mixture of a nazir from *The Arabian Nights* and a 'Scotch Reviewer' of 1817, is too harmless and lacking in specific characteristics to be a deliberate satire on a particular critic,[8] but in slightly euphuistic, arrogant and affected prose he voices the main objections to the inserted tales, objections which are no less than justifiable. This ironic vein makes up, as we have just said, for certain offences to taste committed in this once so popular work.

The critics had no option but to praise in general terms the poem that had had such instant success. Jeffrey[9] diplomatically limits his acknowledgement to the points he genuinely approves of: he praises the accuracy of the local colour, the clear-cut moral attitude that had been absent from the poems of the poet's youth, the avoidance of the 'childishness, cruelty and profligacy of Asia', the richness and brilliance of the imagery, the 'wit' and the original-ity. Then come his criticisms: he finds in *Lalla Rookh* a wealth of individual beauties, but no overall beauty; the poem is a bizarre pagoda but no temple where the beauty lies in the unity of the whole; everything is too rich, too poetic and too exalted. Jeffrey criticizes the first tale for its 'theatrical horrors of the German School', a direction in poetry that he has never been able to tolerate. At the close of his review he contrasts the 'brilliant falsetto' and the 'excessive finery' of Moore with the 'homeliness' of his friend Crabbe: modern poetry lies between these two extremes, which represent the limits of what can be called poetry. Hazlitt's review in *The Spirit of the Age* is very similar, even though it is more superficial and written more with an eye to the reviewer's own stylistic brilliance than the subject in hand.

Two articles in *Blackwood's Magazine*[10] illustrate the position in which the reviewers found themselves with respect to this work. The first article is objective. It defends Moore against the criticism that he has plagiarized Byron, Scott and Wilson. The critic emphasizes the good points of *Lalla Rookh*: however, for the next issue of the journal he promises a list of its faults and indicates that Moore cannot be spared the criticism that he has anticipated with Fadladeen's objections. But when six or eight weeks have passed and the August number appears, the critic admits that he no longer dares say anything negative about *Lalla Rookh* because the public has reacted so enthusiastically: so he lets the matter rest with a mild rebuke with respect to the fourth tale, which he personally finds 'too trifling and sickly' and otherwise surpasses himself eulogizing Moore and his poem.

In spite of the great success of *Lalla Rookh*, Moore only wrote one more work of the verse narrative type: *The Love of the Angels* published in 1823.[11] This poem, a little over 1,600 verses long – also a framework story, this time containing three tales – is in irregularly rhyming tetrameters throughout, and was originally planned as part of a more extensive work. However, while it was still being written, it was destined to suffer an unusual fate: Moore learned that Byron was also working on a poetic rendering of the same subject.[12] In order not to be overshadowed right from the start by such an invincible rival, Moore hastened to publish his *Love of the Angels* before Byron's *Heaven and Earth*. But he did not quite succeed. Byron's 'Mystery' appeared in 1822 in the second issue of the *Liberal*, while Moore's poem was not published until January 1823, in an illustrated deluxe edition in purple linen. Comparison was unavoidable, and of course to Moore's disadvantage, which was doubtless why he did not continue work on the longer poem of which *The Love of the Angels* was only intended to be a part. Byron too never wrote the second part of his lyrical drama *Heaven and Earth* as he had originally planned.

The appearance of these two poems on the same subject reveals much about the state of the genre, and for this reason it is worth studying the reaction of the critics at that time in greater detail. The relevant articles by Jeffrey[13] and North[14] are both in the same vein. Both works are compared with one another irrespective of the fact that there is a generic difference between them. This is further confirmation of this author's opinion that the lyrical drama or dramatic poem does not differ very much from the epic forms of romantic poetry. Jeffrey and North naturally concentrate on the difference between the two authors with respect to temperament and quality. Moore, says Jeffrey, is the poet of the happy and carefree for whom life poses no serious problems and who make up the majority of the reading public. Byron on the other hand is the poet of the afflicted, the small minority who suffer because they cannot be satisfied with life's beautiful, sensuous surface, but are impelled to dwell on its insoluble problems.

Christopher North also very cleverly sums up the difference between Byron and Moore, but then goes on in his reviews to discuss basic questions of approach to poetry. He feels the subject that has been chosen is too sublime and too tragic to be dealt with as a pure romance. In his review Jeffrey contented himself with saying that only a genius could write poetically about this subject – the love of the sons of God for the daughters of men according to Genesis vi, 2 – but was prepared to concede that both poets had sufficient genius to accomplish this. North is much stricter and more precise in his judgement. If the subject, he says, is not dealt with in the spirit of Milton, it is in danger of becoming blasphemous. For all his talent, Moore's poem is embarrassing and even ungodly. It does not endeavour 'to justify the ways of God to men', but does rather the opposite. The character of the angels is completely humanized; they love the coquetry in the daughters of man and all that is specific to their sex, and come over as more Irish than the Irish with their fiery, sensual love ('love so furious was never made out of the land of potatoes'). Byron's work is dominated by emotional need and tragedy which causes heaven and earth to tremble, while Moore's has more the air of a honeymoon. The unintellectual approach is even reflected in the imagery, which is full of 'sighs, tears, kisses, shiverings, shrillings, perfumes, feathered angels on beds of down' and the ultimate in bad taste is a comparison between a snowy white and feathers shed by the Holy Spirit. All this indicates that Moore, as he himself admitted, did not base his account at all on the biblical reference, but on Muhammadan romances from the legends of Hārūd and

Marūd. (In fact the presumably false interpretation of the Genesis passage goes back to rabbinical legends.)

Translated into genre theory, the implications of North's criticisms are as follows. Moore has devalued a subject to which justice can only be done with a poem that offers an interpretation of the 'world' contained in it to the level of a superficial and externally romantic story, and has degraded a myth by turning it into a 'private' romance. A similar objection could not be raised to Southey's 'mythological' epics, as no objective value was attached to the foreign myths, and the reviewers were even grateful that Southey – and Moore too in *Lalla Rookh* – had adapted the dissolute, exotic myths to European tastes and Christian morals. Even when Jeffrey established that in *Endymion* Keats had moved the Greek myth into a private, psychological sphere, he saw it as a welcome enrichment of poetry with a new subject. Here, however, he finds that with the 'private' treatment of a mythological subject from the Bible, turning a myth into a 'private' romance shows a lack of reverence. The lack of metaphysical depth not only in Moore's thinking but also in most romantic narrative literature is suddenly revealed by this one extreme example, and the Wordsworth disciple and conservative Anglican North hastens to point this out and brand Moore's poem, with a characteristic reference to Milton, as tasteless and 'impious'.

Today it seems rather surprising that in this context North allows Byron's *Heaven and Earth* to be an 'epic' on a par with the works of Milton. In spite of the beauty of the language, this lyric, dramatic and epic mixture now bears more resemblance to a libretto for a romantic oratorio, if not for a French opera with chorus, ballet and full use of the stage machinery, than to a true mystery or the first part of a biblical epic in dialogue form; and Byron's humanization of holy beings now appears a lamentable mistake, especially when this poem is compared with that great work *Cain*. It must not be forgotten, however, that Byron did succeed in conveying the cosmic tragedy of the situation, which put his work way above Moore's sentimental and purely worldly treatment of the subject.

In his assessment of Moore, North is to be commended for the healthy instinct that led him to react against the beautifying and romanticizing of religious stories, as this was an instinct that became increasingly rare later in the nineteenth century. One has only to think of the hopeless mixture of Christian iconology with romantic, worldly ideas that characterized the Pre-Raphaelites, or the embarrassing, watered-down version of the Christian 'myth' in Rossetti's *Blessed Damozel*, who has taken her worldly sufferings and longings and her earthly body with her to Paradise, which is peopled with female figures, some of whom are well-known saints of the church, and some fantasy figures with fashionable Victorian names, and which is dotted with mystic trees, in the branches of which the Holy Spirit is 'sometimes' to be seen.

Thus Moore's attempt at an important subject, as represented by *The Love of the Angels*, only serves to confirm Hazlitt's judgement of the author of *Lalla Rookh*: 'There is in all this a play of fancy, a glitter of words, a shallowness of thought, and a want of truth and solidity that is wonderful, and that nothing but the heedless, rapid glide of the verse could render tolerable.'[15] Tastes have changed to such an extent since then that even the last part of this verdict no longer has any validity: even the skilful handling of verse in Moore's narrative poems cannot render them of interest to the modern reader.

Leigh Hunt

> We have said that Lord Byron is a sublime coxcomb: why should we not say that Mr. Hunt is a delightful one?
>
> Hazlitt in *The Spirit of the Age*, p. 343

There are noticeable parallels between the reaction of the *Blackwood's Magazine* critics to Moore's *Love of the Angels* and their reaction to Leigh Hunt's *Story of Rimini*, which suggest important developments in the romantic verse narrative genre. It is on account of these parallels, rather than the superficial similarity of the two poets – which led Hazlitt to deal with Moore and Hunt together in one chapter of his *Spirit of the Age* – that they are placed next to one another in this study. It would not be appropriate here to go into detail about Hunt's services to literature as an importer of Italian literature,[16] as an innovator in the area of verse technique,[17] as the young Keats' teacher and model, as head of the Cockney School and as a critic. These are aspects that are dealt with in every longer history of literature, and are only of secondary importance for this genre study. The only thing that is of interest to us here is the effect of *The Story of Rimini* on the public when it was published, and the implications of this for the internal history of the romantic tale in verse as a genre.

The poem was begun by Hunt in 1811, in his twenty-seventh year. Most of it was written during his imprisonment in Horsemonger Lane Gaol in London from 3 February 1813 to 3 February 1815. It is a romantic, descriptive, free adaptation of the Paolo and Francesca episode in Dante's *Inferno*. From the seventy-two verses of the original Hunt produced five cantos totalling around 1,700 lines. The metre is a heroic couplet with run-on lines, frequent feminine rhymes, neologisms and colloquialisms, the same metre that Keats later used in an even freer fashion in *Endymion*. Hunt's descriptions, as Lockhart noted in the *Blackwood's Magazine* review of November 1817, owe much to Scott, and for his representations of feelings he is equally indebted to Byron. When, in his article of March 1820 *Some Observations upon an Article in B.M. Nr. 29* of August 1819, Byron says that Hunt, 'who had power to have made the "Story of Rimini" as perfect as a fable of Dryden, has thought fit to sacrifice his genius and his taste to some unintelligible notions of Words-worth which I defy him to explain', he is almost certainly not thinking of the content but of the language. In his opinion Hunt, in his endeavour to free the verse language from the shackles of the classicistic school, to which he himself always remained true, is copying the ideas of Wordsworth's famous Preface of 1800.[18] Lockhart too describes Hunt as an imitator of Words-worth, which, given the moral stance of *The Story of Rimini*, he considers almost as an insult to the head of the Lake School; in addition Hunt seems to him to be making futile attempts to equal Byron and Moore.[19]

It was thus evident to everyone that Hunt's *Story of Rimini* belonged to the modern romance genre. It was, however, equally evident that he did not have the same models as Scott or Byron. This is how Jeffrey attempted to place the work in relation to other contemporary works of literature.[20] Hunt, he writes, does not belong to any of the 'schools'. He is neither metaphysical like Wordsworth, nor whimsical like Coleridge, nor 'monkish' like Southey, but he does have one thing in common with these schools: he goes back to the age before the French School of poetry, to which all modern poetry seems to look for inspiration. Hunt has selected other, less exploited areas of early literature, some of which are older than those imitated by the other poets: the Italians of the early Renaissance period and Chaucer. In addition to Dante's *Inferno* (V, 70 – 142), Hunt has also used Petrarch's *Trionfo d'Amore* (III) and Tassoni's *La Secchia Rapita* (V, 43 and VII, 29) as sources for his *Story of Rimini*. There is nothing left of the spirit and style of the most famous of these models – Dante – which is just as well, since anyone who tries to imitate or even enlarge on Dante's style can only fail. Hunt has avoided this pitfall by imparting to the material Boccaccio's sensuousness, Ariosto's smiling grace, Chaucer's homeliness of diction and the freshness and naturalness of his own youth. Certain objections could theoretically be made to Hunt's language and verse treatment (there follows a list of offences similar to that found in all reviews of *The Story of Rimini*), but the overall effect of the poem is nevertheless pleasing, fresh and original.

Before we proceed to the reviews in the other journals, one point should be made clear. Politics played a much more important part in the critics' reactions to Hunt than in their reactions to any other poet of the time: the radical-liberal journalist Hunt, just released from prison where he had been sent for severely insulting the Prince Regent (in an article in the *Examiner* of 22 March 1812) was first and foremost a political figure and only secondarily a poet. It is even questionable whether Jeffrey would have been so forgiving of Hunt's 'deliberate, forced lightness' and his 'very English, but also very careless and sometimes even vulgar style' if the young poet had not been a fellow party member who was considered a martyr in the cause of freedom. We know from his attitude to Scott and Wordsworth that he did not approve of such licence as far as form was concerned.

The reviews of Hunt's political opponents, however, are so obviously motivated by irreconcilable hatred of Hunt as a person that the core of objective truth that they doubtless contain mustbe carefully disentangled from the mass of unpleasant journalistic polemics. The article in the *Quarterly Review*[21] avoids all obvious political references. It concedes that the problematic subject is narrated discreetly and that here and there one finds good passages. However, the critic denounces the poetic principle that governs Hunt's work with a ferocity that betrays the political background: his prose in the Preface is bad and his verses are even worse, his freedom amounts to licence and his idiomatic language is a sign of vulgar taste. The wording of the dedication to Lord Byron – addressing him as 'Dear Byron' without his title – is a piece of impudent familiarity that marks Hunt as an upstart. The reviewer is particularly critical of Hunt on account of two passages – III, 535 ff. and IV, 307 – that are said to be nothing but metrical transcriptions of parts of George Ellis' *Specimens of Early English Romances*; Ellis, it should be noted, wrote for the *Quarterly Review*. The critic sums up by saying that *The Story of Rimini* may be read with enjoyment if one had already read John Galt (whose works were evidently considered the ultimate in bad taste at the time) but it is not serious poetry.

The first two articles (in the October and November issue of 1817) in the series entitled *On the Cockney School of Poetry*, Lockhart's best-known contribution to *Blackwood's Magazine*, are devoted to Leigh Hunt and *The Story of Rimini*. Lockhart makes four very serious criticisms of Hunt, accusing him of Jacobinism, lack of education, arrogance and immorality. The first of these accusations is of no interest to us here, as it has nothing to do with the work, and the second two are a more strongly worded version of opinions already voiced in the *Quarterly Review*.[22] In the fourth accusation, however, if we ignore the polemics, are to be found those parallels to the reviews of Moore's *Love of the Angels* that were mentioned at the beginning of this section, which reveal some important points about the development of the genre.

Like many contemporary poems which attempt to analyse the passions, says Lockhart, *The Story of Rimini* deals with the subject of incest (Paolo knowingly commits adultery with the wife of his brother). This unpleasant subject is only acceptable in poetry if it is described with the utmost seriousness and consciousness of the guilt of the characters and the moral outrageousness of their behaviour. All the great poets who had dealt with the problem of incest had been clear about this: the Greeks, Racine, Schiller, Alfieri and Byron. With his *Story of Rimini*, however, Hunt had written a 'genteel comedy of incest'. Instead of suggesting guilt and tragedy right from the beginning of the poem, as Byron does in his *Parisina*, Hunt opens his story with gaiety and laughter. Instead of describing the event in brief, as Dante does, he expands it with descriptions of medieval costumes and festivals worthy of Scott, although he knows no more about the Middle Ages than what he has gleaned from a few London museum exhibits. Instead of arousing the reader's pity and moral sense as Dante does by intimating that the sinful lovers will suffer in a hell which is made to appear even more horrific than the guilt which has got them there, Hunt leaves hell out of the story and thus separates the tragedy from its cosmic and ethical context, which was Dante's prime reason for recounting the story. All that remains is a 'pleasant romance'. The reader does not realize that the poet is encouraging him to sympathize with characters who are freely committing a great wrong and are not being punished for it with hell but with emotional suffering and death as a consequence of their love for one another, which poetically transfigures their sin (at the close of the story young lovers make night-time pilgrimages to pray at the grave of Francesca and Paolo).

This criticism is more than defamation of a party opponent's morals. It shows that a new attitude to genre, that is at the same time a logical continuation of traditional ideas, is beginning to form. This attitude is not so much centred around the form, but the statements that it is appropriate to make with particular subjects. The *Blackwood's Magazine* reviews of Moore's *Love of the Angels* and Hunt's *Rimini* firmly point out the limits of the 'pleasant romance'. They emphasize that as a genre of a lower, or at best intermediate level of style, it becomes frivolous when it misappropriates subjects that require an elevated style.

The problem had not arisen up until then: in spite of his occasional speculations about the rebirth of the epic from the spirit of the romance,[23] Scott was sufficiently modest and poetically tactful to stick strictly to the intermediate level of style. He did not even deviate from it in the epic vista of *Don Roderick*, and the first section of this work contains, in poetic form, his justification of this approach.

In spite of all his experiments with form, Southey retained the elevated style of the epic to such an extent that what happened in his case was rather the opposite of what the *Blackwood's Magazine* reviewers reproach Moore and Hunt for: there was a discrepancy between the elevated nature of the message and the trivial material, that was often merely an oriental fairy-tale or an exotic horror novel. Where his subjects were more weighty, as in *Joan of Arc* and later *Roderick*, he also avoided all 'romantic trifling' with the form, and raised the level of the overall message such that the formal difference between these works and works belonging to the sublime epic genre became inessential.

Most of the other works that we have examined keep to the intermediate level suitable for the romance in both style and subject matter, and the authors do not misappropriate themes that pose a threat to the 'accepted unconscious metaphysic' of the majority of their readers, namely the Christian tradition and Christian mythology. When we came across romantic tales in verse that had actually advanced to the level where they were offering original metaphysical interpretation – which might have a Christian orientation, but might also be based on quite contrary beliefs – we always found that either the poet had made a mistake in using Scott's romance form (e.g., in the *White Doe*) or that he had abandoned it to produce a new type of elevated style (such as is to be found in the works of Keats and Shelley). Byron kept mainly to the intermediate level of style, and only occasionally – for example in *Prometheus, Heaven and Earth* and *Cain* – does his language have some of the titanic, mythical attributes of Shelley's, however different the two poets are basically from one another.

It is only Moore, in *Love of the Angels*, and Hunt in *The Story of Rimini* who offend poetic sensibility and reduce subjects that are traditionally dealt with at a higher stylistic level and hence must be rooted in some form of metaphysical belief (or revolutionary unbelief) to the level of an agreeable romance, where they are treated in a superficial manner and their deeper implications ignored. This is what the critics were so indignant about, and the point they were thus really making was that the modern romance (in the fashionable form that had established itself in the previous ten years) was incapable by its very nature of metaphysical interpretation – unless it abandoned its characteristic generic style and moved on to a completely different plane.

After *The Love of the Angels*, Moore stayed strictly within his limitations. As a musical lyric poet, mild satirist, skilful prose narrator and loyal but not militant Irish patriot he was assured of a place in literary history: as Tom Little – the agreeable poet who beguiled the hours for his contemporaries with his talent for sounds, colour and emotion, and has given the world at least one song that it still loves and sings. Hunt, the journalist and *littérateur* who was not known for his sensitivity, the man with little conscience and tact but much superficial skill, continued, up until his death in 1859, to write other verse narratives ('little painted crockery pots' as a reviewer in *Blackwood's Magazine*[24] called his poems). Undeterred by the critics and the examples set by his friends Keats, Shelley and Byron during their brief careers when the romance acquired a new superiority and forcefulness, he produced short romantic stories and ballads with a half-serious, half-humorous tone, drawing on the classical world (*Hero and Leander*), the Middle Ages (*The Palfrey, Godiva*, etc.) and the Orient (*Mahmoud, Jaffar* and that undying anthology piece *Abou ben Adhem*). And when he encountered a subject with deeper mythical significance, as was the case with the longer poem *Bacchus and Ariadne* (1819), he playfully ignored its depths, just as he had in the story of Paolo and Francesca. He remained what he was – 'a delightful coxcomb'.

The minor poets

> A good imitation is better than the most original mediocrity.
>   Jeffrey about Barry Cornwall (*ER*, 65, article 8 of January 1820)

Among the lesser poets who allied themselves with a school right from the start, two became so popular that the reviewers were obliged to pay greater attention to them: Bryan Waller Procter – alias Barry Cornwall – the most peace-loving representative of the group of poets known since Lockhart's series of articles in *Blackwood's Magazine* as the Cockney School of poetry, and John Wilson – alias Christopher North – the best-known of the younger generation of the Lake School of poetry and a fervent advocate of the Wordsworthian approach to poetry.

The most noticeable attributes of Barry Cornwall's work[25] are his lack of originality (something he always admitted himself), his mildness, his espousal of poetry that was concerned with natural rather than exalted feelings, and his adoption of the most important characteristics of the Cockney School.[26] Jeffrey loved his works: he wrote[27] that in Cornwall he found once again the mild, healing effect of poetry and that legitimate escape from the cares of life into a realm of soothing beauty that he thought had been lost altogether since most narrative poetry concentrated on 'tremendous agitations' and 'boisterous and agonizing events'. Barry Cornwall was not very original, but he had selected good models and had blended them in well. *Blackwood's Magazine*, however, called him a 'Rider on a Pony-Pegasus in the midst of lancers'.[28] 'Keats could have been a great poet if he had not poured out his wine while it was still must. His poetry was the music of an – imperfectly played – spinet, but by comparison Barry Cornwall's was the music of a mouth organ.'

'This is a new recruit to the company of the Lake Poets.' These were the words with which Jeffrey opened his article on John Wilson's first long poem *The Isle of Palms* that had been published at the beginning of 1812.[29] After this rough classification he then attempts to define the position of this new poet within the 'school'. Although Wilson uses a type of verse derived from Southey's *Kehama* metre, he is evidently a scholar of Wordsworth. Like his master he grafts strong, even exaggerated emotions onto everyday matters. Like Wordsworth he despises material pleasures and purely worldly aims. Like him he sometimes concentrates so hard on simplicity that his works lose their poetic force. However, some aspects of his work differ to his advantage from those of his model: his material is free of the contrived fantasy that characterizes many of Wordsworth's subjects. He also avoids Wordsworth's absurdities and unpoetic objects such as spades, sparrow's eggs, leeches, wash tubs, etc. There has never been a poem that contains so few facts about the plot and so much description and reflection as the *Isle of Palms*, but 'there is matter for delight'. The similarity between Wilson and Wordsworth is not automatically obvious today, aside from the absence of the classicistic style, which was after all still prevalent around 1812, and a few details such as the enthusiasm of both poets for nature and the elevated status of the child in their works.

The story – the Robinson Crusoe saga of the bridal couple shipwrecked on a paradisiacal South Sea island and found after seven years, when they return, with the child born in the meantime, to the mother of the young man, who has been steadfastly waiting for them – is reminiscent of Bernadin de Saint-Pierre's *Paul et Virginie*. It is precisely the attribute that Jeffrey found so praiseworthy, the absence of Wordsworthian realism, that makes it so unpalatable today. In no other romantic tale in verse are there so many 'Ahs' and 'Ohs', so many 'thou' apostrophes, so much moonshine or so many dreams, prayers or angels, and in no other tale does the word 'romantic' occur so frequently. The poet attaches no value whatsoever to the probability of the story; while, for example, everyone else is drowned in the shipwreck, the two lovers are borne – separately! – by the waves onto the reef which saves them, and the only remaining boat is also promptly washed up there, which enables them to row to the palm island. The way in which the child is introduced into the story is typical of the unrealistic and unromantically supernatural style of the narrative: there is nothing about the consummation of the marriage, pregnancy or birth; the little girl is suddenly there, appearing like an angel in the midst of the beauties of radiant nature:

> Was her birth not drawn from heavenly sire, and from the breast
> Of some fair spirit, whose sinless nature glow'd
> With purest flames, enamour'd of a God,
> And gave this child of light in realms of rest.

Wilson bears a certain resemblance to Barry Cornwall, although he naturally did not think very highly of Cornwall, as one of the Cockney Poets. His poetry is full of the same sentimentality as the latter's; for all its rapture, it is just as mild and lacking in substance – and it has just as little to say.

Wilson also failed to overcome these weaknesses in his *City of the Plague* (1816), when he took a passage full of action from Defoe's *Journal of the Plague Year* and turned it into a 'Dramatic Poem' in three acts. Here too the plot is swamped by the mass of reflection and description. The verse narrative *The Convict*, written in the same year, describes the rescue and rehabilitation of a man wrongly condemned to death, at the last minute before he is executed. In this work too Wilson in no way approaches Wordsworth: there is nothing of the latter's Godwinian urgency, the psychology is commonplace and predictable throughout, and the whole tone is unbearably sentimental. It is thus not surprising that the poet John Wilson is today a name known only to literary experts, while the critic Christopher North, author of *Noctes Ambrosianae*, who is one and the same person, is a well-known historical figure in the annals of English romantic literature.

The study of these two minor poets has shown that here there is little more
to be gleaned about the history of the romantic tale in verse. All it has to offer
is diluted mixtures and variations of the same elements that we have already
analysed in the works of the more important poets. Any further names will
thus be omitted, as also the works – most of which were written later on and
have rightly been forgotten – of other, better-known poets such as Joanna
Baillie, Felicia Hemans, John Hamilton Reynolds, Winthrop Mackworth
Praed, Thomas Hood, George Darley, John Cam Hobhouse, Baron
Brougham, Charles Lloyd, Mary Tighe, etc., and we will now turn to
contemporary evidence that the romantic tale in verse lost so much of its
popularity in the 1820s that it can be said to be finished as a genre, in spite
of the occasional revival of the once current form by the Victorians.

The final decline in popularity of the genre, 1818–1830

> ... the world is growing old ... What 'niche' remains unoccupied? What path
> untried? What is the use of doing anything, unless we could do better than
> all those who have gone before us? What hope is there of this?
>
> Hazlitt, *The Spirit of the Age*, p. 194 f.

The history of the genre can be roughly divided into five stages, as follows:

up to 1808	constant increase in popularity;
1808 to 1812	slow decline in popularity;
1812	renewed enthusiasm for the genre after the appearance of Byron;
1812 to approx. 1818	the genre's popularity continues unabated, and at the same time there is a tendency towards a short form, and towards the founding of schools, ramification and dissolution;
from 1818 onwards	increasing signs that the popularity of the genre is fading. This development is clearly reflected in Jeffrey's reviews, and its consequences vividly illustrated in Byron's letters (cf. pp. 159ff.) and the discussion in T. L. Peacock's *Four Ages of Poetry* (1820).

Jeffrey, as we have already mentioned, warmly welcomed the new genre
in his review of *The Lay of the Last Minstrel*;[30] in his review of *Marmion*[31] he
warned of the adverse effects that imitation of the medieval verse romance
would have on public taste and aesthetic standards in poetry, and withdrew
all his basic objections after the appearance of Byron. During this period
Jeffrey was so infected with the general enthusiasm for the genre that he even
warmly recommended the achievements of Scott and Byron – interesting

subjects, excitement, passion, identification, absence of the neo-classical 'distance' of the poet, etc. – to those authors whose works were lacking in these qualities. Even though he continued to reject the Lake Poets, his basic goodwill towards the tales in verse of Byron, Hunt, Keats, Moore, Cornwall, Campbell and even Wilson leads one to suspect that his reservations about the genre had been overcome.[32]

From 1818 on – in other words after the popularity of the romantic tale in verse genre definitely began to decline – Jeffrey reviewed fewer works of this type. Since, in addition, the relevant articles written between 1818 and 1828 mainly concern poets whom he had reviewed before, they add little that is new. Jeffrey appears finally to have reconciled himself to the genre that, prior to 1808, he had issued warnings about. However, in September 1828 he then writes a review of Atherstone's *Fall of Nineveh*[33] in which he makes a strange assessment of the narrative poetry of the previous thirty years. In the *Noctes Ambrosianae* 40 Christopher North bluntly called this article 'Jeffrey's Decline and Fall of Poetry'.[34] Jeffrey starts by describing the situation in 1828. Since Byron's death there had been no other king of poetry. The old masters of narrative poetry are silent: Scott, Southey and Moore only write prose; Crabbe, Coleridge and Wordsworth are burnt out, and Campbell and Rogers are resting on their laurels. The young poets of whom greater things were hoped have all died young, such as Keats, Kirke White and Pollok or Shelley, who was 'perhaps a genius' and has never been dealt with by Jeffrey before. The poets still writing today can be described as no more than talented: Mrs Hemans, Milman, Hunt, Atherstone ...

Jeffrey's further remarks no longer apply solely to the immediate present, but are a résumé of the whole romantic epoch. Of course, he writes, since his youth, when Hoole and Hayley were highly thought of as poets, poetry has made great progress. Never before has so much been written in verse, but it is 'miracles of the heart' that are lacking. Never before have contemporary critics made such good, tolerant assessments of the poetry of their age; but there are no great, creative geniuses. All the poetry of the present generation reflects works from the distant past; this is an age of imitators. The dearth of original works in the eighteenth century is always being pointed out; but the nineteenth century is also overshadowed by great models from the past. The Romeos of the present day are like actors playing heroes, who are not heroes themselves. They describe, but they do not invent. They tell of deeds, things, characters and emotions, but their poetry is not the unconscious expression of nature and true passion. They have great abilities, but their works are lacking in substance, enthralling human subjects and subjects dealing at greater depth with the present age. It is for this reason that these tales are so unoriginal, their fictional characters so puppet-like or academic and so lacking in 'human' qualities, for this reason that the emotion in them is so over-strained and rhetorical, and the reflections so bombastic and mystical. When the nineteenth-century poets do write longer tales, they do not produce action pictures but still lifes full of drapery, and describe places which are either under a spell or unpopulated. Only the shorter forms of tale – formerly the province of women – are still mastered. No one can portray real people any more. The bitter prognosis is thus that the present-day poets will sooner or later be consigned to oblivion with the poetasters of the late eighteenth century, the Hooles and the Hayleys.

This article is of course full of bias, contradictions and erroneous judgements, which history has in the meantime corrected. It reflects Jeffrey's basic inability to understand the change in poetry introduced by Wordsworth, which has led him to assess all the poetry of the period inaccurately. However, it is precisely Jeffrey's bias from which so much can be learned. It results from a reaction against the lyrical and subjective spirit of romanticism and a longing for great epic poetry. Seen in this light Jeffrey's article is not an inaccurate assessment. The romantic verse narrative dethroned the epic, in order that an epic type appropriate to the age might be created. That was the original aim but in practice this was never achieved.[35] However, in the attempt, many important discoveries were made: hybrid genres of great beauty and expressiveness were produced and a higher class of light fiction in verse came into being which delighted thousands because it was more understandable and dealt with subjects with which it was possible to identify, by contrast with the neo-classical epic, in which the emotions were subdued by reason, the will and a controlled style, and with the classic epic from a remote period of history. Another of the many important consequences of this attempt was the development of the symbolic and allegorical continuity on which all great romantic poetry is based. All this Jeffrey overlooked. However, he did see that in the course of this development the romantic epic was not becoming a reality, and that the 'interpretive' narrative poem of the romantic era, the epic based on the 'accepted unconscious metaphysic' of his epoch was nevertheless not being written. Is his out-of-date neo-classical outlook the only reason why this to him was evidence of the 'Decline and Fall of Poetry'? The answer will be left to the final chapter, and we will turn instead to other writers and critics who during the period from 1818 to 1830 established with disillusionment that the form of romanticism initiated by Scott and the Lakers had sacrificed the sublimity and formal unity of great epic poetry to versatility and that the 'Great Poem' of the age had not been written.

We are already familiar with Byron's deprecatory, and self-critical, assessment of the poetry of his epoch. The sentences 'we are all wrong except Rogers, Crabbe, and Campbell' and 'All with the exception of Crabbe, Rogers, and Campbell ... will survive their own reputation, without attaining any very extraordinary period of longevity' from the open letter *Some Observations upon an Article in B.M.* take on a new aspect in the light of the general disillusionment that set in around this time (Byron's article was written in March 1820). It is evident that these words are not just the personal belief of a man who supported the neo-classical school against the romantic schools with their dissolution of form, but that they corresponded to a widespread feeling of dissatisfaction with the poetic achievements of the time. The conclusions Byron drew from this have already been described.[36]

The process of disillusionment is even more apparent in the reviews of *Blackwood's Magazine* than in the comments of Jeffrey and Byron. The periodical was founded in April 1817, and it is greatly to its credit that it constantly pointed out the extent to which Wordsworth's work had influenced the development of poetry, while Jeffrey was assessing him so inaccurately, – although Jeffrey's error does tell us a great deal about the development of the genre. Nevertheless, in the course of time *Blackwood's Magazine*'s assessment of romantic narrative poetry comes more and more to resemble Jeffrey's. At first the general tone is very optimistic, and this optimism does not come to an abrupt stop, but is still being voiced up until 1830, and occasionally even after this, especially when it is a question of opposing the *Edinburgh Review*. 'We are the most poetic age since the Elizabethans, and the great masters of our time are Scott, Byron and Wordsworth', triumphed North in July 1818 in his review of Wordsworth's *White Doe*,[37] and he repeated this view often with slowly waning conviction and an increasing number of qualifications.[38] With slowly waning conviction ...

The 'but' that follows the positive assessments of contemporary poetry becomes increasingly audible in North's reviews, and also in those of his colleagues writing for *Blackwood's Magazine*, from 1818 on. (In the following quotes, the term poetry of course also includes poems that do not belong to the genre that is the subject of this book. In the context from which the quotes are taken, however, most of this 'poetry' – at least two thirds – does in fact consist of romantic tales in verse.) First the reviewers establish that the upswing of English poetry since the beginning of the nineteenth century has resulted in too much being written. In his notorious article on Keats[39] Lockhart speaks of the 'metromania' of the age. Since the successes of Burns and Joanna Baillie, every labourer and every society lady thinks he or she can write poetry (this same complaint had already been made by Jeffrey, in his review of *Kehama*).[40] The consequences of this excess have not been slow to take effect: the public is saturated and no longer reads poems. An article in *Blackwood's Magazine*, 65, June 1822 ('Lights and Shadows of Scottish Life') begins by saying 'the writing of verses is at present an unpopular and unprofitable exercise', and goes on to describe the situation in detail. Scott, Crabbe and Coleridge are no longer writing verse, Wordsworth only has a very small circle of readers, Southey is only admired by the young, no one reads the Cockneys, Campbell's *Gertrude* has become an old lady, Hogg has turned to sheep-breeding, the success of *Lalla Rookh* was only short-lived,

Joanna Baillie's *Metrical Legends* were a failure and even Byron's fame is fading – *Don Juan* is not selling well.

Five years later the situation is even worse. In October 1827 North writes in his review of Montgomery's *Pelican Island*:[41] 'Poetry ... has long been a drug in the market – there has for many years been a glut of that commodity – nor will either wholesale or retail dealers, nor persons not in trade, on any account buy any sorts of it, even at the most reduced prices.' A break is much needed. North already thinks he sees signs of approaching change, but as we shall see, this hope was deceptive. He writes:

Supposing then, that about some half dozen years ago the thing was rather overdone; that the genius of poetry was too creative under the desire which it had awakened for its products; that the muses, forgetting the law of markets, continued too long in a state of inspiration; that Messrs. Longman and Co., Mr. Murray, Mr. Blackwood, and Mr. Constable, would launch out into speculation and adventure in Parnassian produce, even after the reading public had exhibited symptoms of a nausea or overdose – has not the evil cured itself?

A new demand for poetry is already evident, and the demand is even in excess of the supply, because the old poets have grown 'fat and lazy' and the young ones are in Byron's shadow and dare not venture forth. The optimistic conclusion of this critical discussion is rather lacking in conviction. North does not want to believe in a decline of the power of poetry in his day, and he also does not believe that prose will become more popular than poetry. In his opinion every age has the geniuses it needs, and the nineteenth century has neither too many great nor too many minor poets. 'One sun at a time is enough'[42] and 'there is no harm in "small-beer" – it is the best drink for the masses to quench their thirst with'.[43] Much of the decline in popularity of the verse narrative is due to the progressive intrusion of prose into the area of narrative poetry.

Wordsworth's assertion in the Preface to the *Lyrical Ballads* that there is theoretically no basic difference between the language of poetry and the language of prose may have already paved the way for this development. But since in practice he continued to write in verse, his suggestion at first only had the effect of bringing about a change in poetry itself: it freed verse language from the rigid forms of poetic diction. The practical rehabilitation of prose as 'poetry' only began with the success of the Waverley Novels, which were initially published anonymously. (In his review of *Ivanhoe*, of January 1820[44] Jeffrey called it 'a splendid Poem').[45]

As it gradually became known that Scott, one of the first verse narrators of the time, was the author of these novels, his example was followed by other poets, and verse narrators such as Moore, Hunt and Cornwall attempted to change over to romantic tales in prose.[46] There was then also the occasional review which rehabilitated prose from a theoretical point of view as a medium of poetic narration. Although Wordsworth's influence can be seen in these articles, the arguments usually go further than the theories in the famous Preface. While North, in the *White Doe* review of July 1818, is still saying that 'It is easy to see in what feelings, and in what faculties, our living Poets excel their duller prose brethren', a review of Moore's prose tale *The Epicurean* in *Blackwood's Magazine*, 130, September 1827, attempts to prove that a tale can be told just as poetically in prose as in verse, provided it is a real poet who is doing the telling. All prose that deals passionately with a particular subject is potentially poetic, even if the subject concerned is political economy. For this reason the prose form is interchangeable with the verse form, without the character of the contents necessarily being altered. 'Seeing ... that our living poets cannot write long poems and will not write short ones, and seeing also, that they are all excellent prose-writers, each in his degree, what better can any single individual of the whole set do than set himself to work in that department, and ... produce a moral and religious tale, story or fiction?'

North is already remarking on the tendency of writers to use prose for poetic narration in his article 'Lights and Shadows of Scottish Life'.[47] At first he interprets this as a fashionable whim which will pass of its own accord, and advises that where the subject is particularly poetic, the verse form should be retained. 'It would have been a great pity if Wordsworth had written his "Ruth" in prose!' – but he is not basically against poetic narrative prose. In his reviews 'On Montgomery's Pelican Island' and 'Preface to a Review of the Chronicles of the Canongate'[48] he maintained the same reserved, even if not altogether dismissive attitude.

One consequence of the over-abundance of literary works at this time, which also hastened the end of the romantic tale in verse, was the exhaustion of the supply of subjects as all the possibilities – the Bible, classical antiquity, the Middle Ages, the Middle and Far East, the early history of the Celtic and Germanic peoples, the Italian Renaissance, Spain, America, the world of the missionaries, Switzerland and contemporary village life were plundered of their romantic themes. In his book on *Boccaccio in England*, H.G. Wright reveals that some *Decameron* novellas such as IV, 5 (the pot of basil) and V, 9 (the falcon) had been used three and four times as material for romantic tales in verse. We have already seen how stock romantic figures such as the noble criminal or the girl disguised as a page become less interesting as a result of repetition. Even subjects as unromantic as the time before the Flood or the end of the world were used a number of times in the first twenty-five years of the nineteenth century.[49] The review of Moore's *Epicurean* in *Blackwood's Magazine*, 130, September 1827 mentioned above discusses in detail this phenomenon which threatens the continued existence of the romantic tale in verse.[50] Although the reviewer opens his discussion of the subject by saying 'We should be sorry to think human life was exhausted', he then admits that it is in fact almost impossible to find subjects that have not already been used.

'That man is fortunate, who either stumbles by accident, or is led by sagacity, on some nook of virgin soil that will return a sudden harvest of an hundredfold.' The poet who does find such a nook of virgin soil is acclaimed as a genius; the poet who is not so fortunate remains unknown and goes bankrupt, even though he may be equally gifted. Many once famous poets are today in this unhappy position – even though most of them are now pursuing middle-class professions and can outlive the fame of the poems that have proved such a bad capital investment in financially secure circumstances. The reviewer closes by saying: 'So easy is it to write a good Tale, a good subject being given, that we should be happy on such condition, during our leisure hours, to furnish one per week, for the next ten years.'

Around 1827 – after only twenty-five years of popularity – the verse narrative branch of English romantic poetry is thus producing the same reaction as epic poetry of the old school a hundred years before: people believe that for anyone who has mastered the rules of the game, writing verse narrative is a matter of routine and does not require genius, provided of course that a subject has been found. Here the situation in which the romantic poets found themselves differs from that of the neo-classicists: it differs because Scott's type of romantic poetry had resulted in a major shift of the interest of the poetry-reading public from the form to the subject, from the design to the excitement of the plot, and from convention to invention. The price is now being paid for this: the romantic tale in verse is no longer able to satisfy the hunger for novelty that it has aroused. The accusations of plagiarism and unoriginal imitation become more and more frequent, the 'schools' rapidly become unpopular, and all ends in disappointment. Suddenly what Scott, the 'inventor' of the genre, knew right from the beginning is generally acknowledged: namely that the epic revival that for two decades had been regarded as the gateway to vast new areas of poetry was nothing but a passing fashion.[51] This generation was scarcely aware that the most important poets of the epoch – Wordsworth, Coleridge, Keats and Shelley – really had ventured into new areas. Their knowledge of their great poets was sadly deficient, and they did not understand them. They judged according to the subject and narrative aspects. And they were disillusioned because the romantic intoxication had suddenly come to an end.

One of the few literary figures who understood the situation better was North. He recognized the full significance of Wordsworth, and for this reason would not be drawn altogether into the general mood of pessimism. In September 1828, when the critics were at their most pessimistic, he inveighed against Jeffrey's Atherstone article, stressing that Scott was more than an imitator of the chivalric poetry of the feudalistic Middle Ages, and the Wordsworth of *The Excursion* and the *Sonnets* more than a modern ballad imitator. In his harsh criticism of modern poetry, Jeffrey had also overlooked

Keats' *Lamia* and *Isabella*, the two poems 'in which Keats's genius is seen to the best advantage'.[52]

From 1830 on, North is of course also prepared to admit that most popular romantic poetry has proved unsatisfactory, as is shown in his review of Keble's *Christian Year*[53] and in the article 'An Hour's Talk about Poetry'.[54] In the first article North speaks of the intellectual force of poetry in Milton's day, which is absent from the works of modern poets: 'Scott and Byron are remarkable for the confusion of intellectual processes and the violation of intellectual laws, almost throughout their composition. They rest upon conception. Imagination and Passion yield them abundant creation; language, vivid and living, clothes the brood of their minds in visible forms, and that is their composition.' As a description of the romantic creative process this neither shows much understanding, nor is it a very deep analysis, but North nevertheless does see what is new about the romantic poets. He continues: 'When these poetic products are analysed according to the laws of logic, the lack of substance of the ideas becomes obvious. Whole passages of great beauty are seen to be incomprehensible.' North suspects that with their imaginative fictions these poets are not trying to appeal to the reader via the intellect but via 'sympathy' – but he nevertheless reproaches Scott and Byron for being undisciplined thinkers, for all their intellectual ability. When the imagination of the genius fails, it can be seen how thin the philosophy behind it is, as thin and as weak as the intellectuality of the whole age. 'This defect has not impeded their living reputation, but it may possible obstruct their future.' Only when the precise thinking of the old school dies out altogether will the moment come when educated people will also be able to acknowledge such poets without reservation.

This article might theoretically have been intended as a hymn – though not acknowledged as such by the author – to Wordsworth, the 'philosophic mind', but in practice North does not dare to put his 'teacher' as the strong intellectual poet of the age before Scott and Byron, and does not mention him at all in this context. His assessment of contemporary poetry in this review is thus basically very similar to that in Jeffrey's Atherstone article.

North's essay 'An Hour's Talk about Poetry' also provides significant evidence of the doubts that arose during this period about the aesthetic value of contemporary narrative verse. The first sentence of the article sets the tone: 'This is an age that has produced a great deal of poetry, but have we got a great poem?'

In the 'Canongate' article of November 1827, North had written that a 'great poem', is probably the highest form of art. Now, in 1830, he reveals what he means by a 'great poem': which is purely and simply the epic – not of course the classic Heroic Poem, but the poem, the concept of which is not bound to a specific age but offers an interpretation of a particular world, and is what Shelley had in mind when he spoke in *The Defence of Poetry* of the 'title of epic in its highest sense'. What North means is the concept that has also been used throughout this book. According to North, the particular characteristics of the 'great poem' are originality and a consistent plan, an important, 'general', 'all-embracing' interest as the source of inspiration and a greatness that he tries to define by means of expressions such as 'feelings soaring on eagle's wings' and 'cathedrals of the spirit'. He does not talk about the narrative qualities. The central question of the article is: had this ultimate in poetry been achieved in the early nineteenth century? North goes through the poets and the longer poems produced by his generation in turn. A large number of the important works that have been examined in this book are listed and summarized in a few words.[55] And every one of these works is turned down as a 'great poem', even Wordsworth's *Excursion*, which is 'not a great poem but only a series of short pieces without an overall plan', and *Childe Harold*, which is much too uneven in intellectual depth and poetic achievement. (One wonders whether Wordsworth's *Prelude*, then still unpublished, would have been denied the rank of a 'great poem'.) His final conclusion is as follows: What, then, was the last great English poem? What is the 'great poem' of the present age? The answer is: Milton's *Paradise Lost*. This assessment accurately reflects the literary situation at the end of the eighteen-twenties. The romantic tale in verse, which Scott initiated at the beginning of the nineteenth century with the revival of the medieval verse romance, never developed to produce the 'great poem' of its age. This failure – and to some extent also the causes of it – was generally recognized around 1830. It dealt the genre, which had already sunk in the estimation of the public and the critics for the other reasons already mentioned, virtually the final blow: the romantic tale in verse was exposed as light poetry for the masses, and even if, up to the end of the century, it was repeatedly resurrected by poets such as Macaulay, Matthew Arnold, Tennyson and Browning, its heyday was over – the metrical romance died with the romantic movement.

Conclusion

The poetry of the age of Wordsworth ... is great, we say to ourselves but why is it not greater still? It shows a wonderful abundance of genius: why does it not show an equal accomplishment? The disappointment that we feel attends ... mainly our reading of the long poems.

A. C. Bradley, 'The Long Poem in Wordsworth's Age', in *Oxford Lectures on Poetry*, p. 177

The Romantic poets ... found a new language, but clung to old forms; yet their best poetry transcends the limitations of those forms which conflict with the essential purposes of the poet, and the completion of the ostensible structure ceases to matter.

R. A. Foakes, *The Romantic Assertion*, p. 58

To Generalize is to be an Idiot.

William Blake, *Marginalia to Sir Joshua Reynolds' Discourses* (1798)

We have now followed the history of the romantic tale in verse from its beginnings up until the time when it was practically at an end. As in a mosaic we have pieced together the details. Has a recognizable pattern been identified? Has it been possible to understand the 'generic character' of this type of poetry? Have we found the 'key' to this whole field, which W. M. Dixon said did not exist?[1]

If we have to some extent been successful in defining this historical literary phenomenon, we should now be able to apply Hugo Kuhn's three categories of genre problem:[2] we should feel that answers to the problem of the formative idea or type, the sociological context of the literature and the entelechy of the genre have been provided by this study even though it has not been designed methodically around these three points.

The main emphasis has been the 'problem of type', with the greater part of the study concentrating on the adoption, development and mixture of certain constants with respect to content, form and poetic intention. While the presence of these constants varies enormously, and they do not usually appear in a pure form, they are revealed by the analysis of all the works of the genre – and this is what after all makes it possible to speak of a genre in the widest sense. Here no further clarification should be necessary. To list these constants would be merely to repeat what has already been said.

221

The 'class problem', putting the literary phenomena in their sociological context, has been dealt with in so many individual cases throughout the book that the question can be considered settled.

What still requires clarification is the 'entelechy problem', the question of the historical purpose of the genre and the extent to which it achieved this purpose. This is probably the most important question that we have to answer if we are to evaluate the whole phenomenon objectively. Here however we encounter considerable difficulties. All generalizations are dangerous in this context, and all positive claims hypothetical. If what is nevertheless being offered here is an interpretation, it is offered in full consciousness of the one-sidedness of the theories involved.

In the course of this study, many comments have been quoted which suggest that the more important verse narrators of the English romantic period started out with the idea of establishing a contemporary epic free of all rules and conventions, and from the disillusioned reviews of Jeffrey and North of 1828 and 1831 it is clear that the general feeling of disappointment generated by contemporary poetry was because this goal had not been attained. On the other hand of course an equal number of comments have been encountered that seem to prove that the romantic poets wrote romances because they no longer thought that the epic, the great narrative that set out to 'interpret the world', was possible, and also no longer wanted it. Even right at the outset there was a certain amount of confusion on this point: between 1780 and 1800 just as many people thought the epic outdated and dead as thought it the greatest and most desirable form of poetry. This conflict continued throughout the history of the genre and was of course bound up with such contemporary associations as influence the evaluation of pure generic types in all periods: ideology, literary 'taste', different attitudes to the past or to the concept of historic necessity, etc.

Scott knew that an epic of Homeric greatness was not something he or his age could achieve. He did not even want his children to read his verse narratives, since this would spoil their taste (this in any case was what his daughter told a visitor). He also drew Southey's attention to the fact that a mixture of epic and romance themes was impracticable – and he then, in the Introduction to *The Bridal of Triermain*, nevertheless toyed with the idea of such a synthesis and enumerated the aspects of the romantic narrative poem that were superior to the *Iliad*.

The critics of the period on the one hand praised the modern genre for the fact that it had detached itself from the traditional epic type, which was already unsuited to the modern age on account of its length alone – and on the other bemoaned the lack of 'epic dimensions' in the poems of their contemporaries.

The poets of the period were all trying to break away from the neo-classical commitment to established genres. They nevertheless repeatedly assigned the works, as far as the longer narrative poems were concerned, to the epic genre – if they were not obviously shorter forms with ballad or verse novella characteristics – and hence could not help judging them according to epic standards. In spite of this lack of consistency, the entelechy of the romantic tale in verse is still in the opinion of this author the modern epic born of the spirit of the romance. The constant comparisons with the 'great poem', the constant mentions of the great epics of the past, of the epic rules that were infringed because the poets believed they were replacing them with something better, and of the points the works have in common with the epic poets of antiquity and of Italy and with Spenser, Camoens and Milton would seem to be clear indications of this. Those verse narratives that deliberately broke away from the 'Great Poem' as far as length and style were concerned and tended more towards the ballad or novella, with the sole aim of being entertaining or visionary tales, were an offshoot of the actual line of development, a by-product that spread all the more as people increasingly realized that the contemporary epic poem born of the spirit of the romance was Utopian.

What has hypothetically been called here the entelechy of the romantic tale in verse was indeed Utopian. It was doomed to failure right from the start: epic and romantic poetry are mutually exclusive – in whatever way the word romantic is interpreted.[3] It is not necessary to repeat the reasons for this assertion: they were indicated in the section on genre definitions and have been confirmed all through the history of our genre, from Southey and Scott to Keats and Shelley. In addition the reader is referred once again to the important essay by A. C. Bradley entitled 'The Long Poem in Wordsworth's Age'; there Christopher North's assessment (in the article 'An Hour's Talk about Poetry')[4] is examined more closely along the lines pursued in this study, and the question whether the romantically inspired 'great poem' might be possible by the end of the century is explored further. The entelechy of the romantic tale in verse could thus never be achieved. The diagram (Fig. 2) is an attempt to show more clearly the individual consequences of the absolute impossibility of creating a romantic epic. The poets of the romantic generation are envisaged as it were as archers whose narrative poems are arrows aimed at the Utopian target: the idea of the 'Great Poem of the Nineteenth Century'. And the impossibility of creating a long interpretative poem of true epic character in the generation of 1800 to 1830 that was individualistic, bourgeois, prosaic, industrialized, and – as a result of the revolution – politically uncertain, and longed for myths but was remote from them, is envisaged as a wall deflecting all these arrows and causing them to fly in the direction of other either fashionable or subjectively unique generic forms.

The diagram is divided into an upper and a lower part to show the two general directions in which the romantic tales in verse moved away from the ideal unity of interpretation of the world, nearness to historic reality and true narrative treatment of both the spiritual and material concerns of the

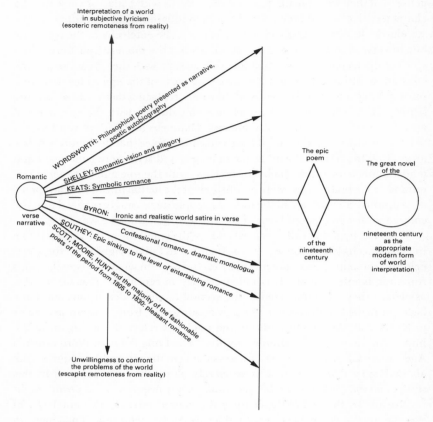

Figure 2

contemporary world which characterize the true epic: the deviation upwards
is the tendency towards 'lyric' visionary poetry, i.e., subjective esoterics with
abstract ideas where the secure relationship to society necessary for the true
epic no longer exists; the deviation downwards indicates the tendency of the
poets to escape from their own world into irony, into a 'private' or pseudo-
reality, a tendency that is usually coupled with a loss of formal intensity. In
the literary productions of this category, narration becomes increasingly the
end in itself or the means of escape, and thus sinks to the level of mass
entertainment. The upward lines could be continued on after Wordsworth,
Shelley and Keats, incorporating an increasing adjunct of the 'Byronic' irony
of *Don Juan*, into French Symbolism. They would, for English poetry,
terminate with Eliot, Pound and Yeats (and nearly all modernistic poetry).
The downward lines could be followed on from Scott's *Lady of the Lake* and

Moore's *Lallah Rookh* via the opera libretti of the nineteenth century, which so often have a lot in common with the romantic tales in verse, to the modern film and cheap novel.

The eloquent defence of the escapism of romantic literature in the article on Crabbe's *The Borough* which appeared in the *Quarterly Review*, 8, article 1, November 1810, has already been mentioned twice. It is significant that the discussion of this topic should have been provoked by the realistic tales of an antiromantic like Crabbe. The whole question is part of the wider topic of pleasure in poetry, which is as old as poetry itself and too wide to be discussed here. The English romantics gave much thought to it, from Wordsworth in his Preface to the *Lyrical Ballads* and Coleridge in the eighteenth chapter of *Biographia Literaria* to the lesser poets, to whom that 'pleasure' simply meant popularity and large sales. The defence of escapism in literature in the *Quarterly Review* is, however, so characteristic of the (Tory) criticism of those days that it should be summarized here when we are talking of the decline of 'romantic poetry' to a popular market product.

The reviewer starts with his personal reactions to Crabbe's poetry: twenty years ago, when Crabbe first became known to the public with the publication of *The Village*, readers were so cloyed with the idyllic insipidity of much late Augustan poetry that Crabbe's virile attempt at a realistic description of country life was welcomed in spite of the rude unpleasantness of many details. Today however the situation had changed: against the background of the abundance of good poets in England the misdirection of Crabbe's poetic endeavours had become apparent. People were not looking in poetry for a reflection of reality but for an escape from it, 'that we may take shelter from the realities of life in the paradise of fancy'. The author goes on to defend escapism in literature as a psychological necessity that man has always yielded to. The gods of antiquity owed their popularity if not their existence to it, 'and when that visionary creation was dissolved, the same powerful instinct supplied the void with the fays and genii and enchantments of modern romance'. With this need for escape, pleasure was even found in sad and terrifying subjects as long as they were invented and imaginary. Just as in life we turned away from reality towards memories of the past, so also in poetry we preferred past and remote things, that which had no actual being. This form of self-deception helped us to endure our existence. If it was a 'moral necessity' in life it must also be allowable as a 'legitimate stratagem' in poetry.

There were in poetry two ways of escape from reality: escape to a world of objects which moved and excited us (this was the case with 'fictions of epic and chivalrous romance') and escape to a world which soothed our feelings (this was the case with the idyllic 'presentation of rural manners and scenes'). The contention that the 'romantic' distortion of reality might in both cases render readers unfit for social interaction is then rejected. Life itself, writes the reviewer, takes care that we do not take the pleasing or edifying fancies of the poets for reality. The reviewer finds it more difficult to refute a further moral objection: 'The Masters of romance contrive to identify the good with the beautiful.' Someone who reads large quantities of such poetry might be in danger of taking the beauty that the poet intended as a mere ornament of virtue for an attribute of it. When he does not find that beauty in life, his faith in the existence of goodness is likely to be shaken, or at least he will be induced to see in virtue nothing but the cold routine of abiding by the law and overlook its intrinsic beauty. While realizing this risk the reviewer believes that time will correct such a defective view: it is not possible to oppose this danger by prohibiting all works of fiction, since an even greater moral danger would be the consequence: if people's urge to escape into the realm of fancy were to be frustrated, that urge would find a different and presumably more dissolute outlet in unrestrained indulgence in shallow sensuality. The best remedy was not to prohibit 'deluding' literature but rather to educate people to distinguish between virtue and beauty and thus elevate the idea of goodness above all association with sentimental aesthetic illusions.

By comparison with Wordsworth's, Shelley's and Keats' struggle for a synthesis of beauty with truth, these ideas may seem rather superficial, and their shallowness becomes even more obvious in a later passage where the reviewer goes as far as to claim that literature should turn away from misery and depravity, just as we do in real life, and focus on more pleasant objects. The article nevertheless contains ideas that are of major importance to a modern evaluation of the romantic verse narratives, and it is significant that so detailed a discussion of the escapism of both poets and readers should have appeared at a time when a sizeable increase in the number of (often uneducated) readers and the production of quantities of 'pleasing' romantic tales made the phenomenon more real than ever before.

It is not possible here to explore further the conclusions that can be drawn from these two cultural developments. All that is being pointed out is that the twentieth-century gulf between solitary, esoteric, unpopular and – in Northrop Frye's terminology – 'ironic' pure art and the devaluation of popular art to a market product – T. W. Adorno's central problem – began to open in the romantic period, and was particularly noticeable in our 'genre'. A final line has been added to the diagram that passes through the 'unattainable' verse epic of the romantic period into the modern period and leads on to the great novel. Are the 'encyclopaedic' novels of Balzac, Zola, Tolstoy, Dostoyevsky, Proust and Joyce the epopees of modern times? They are interpretative, all-embracing – even if not optimistic – narratives in the sense of our definition of the epic. However, this line is drawn as a dotted line: the concept of the epic in these works has undergone a mutation of form and representation that excludes it from our definition; it may be related in its aims, but it is an independent generic form.

In this much broader context most of the romantic tales in verse, to which of necessity greater importance was attached in the pages of this book than is generally the case today, shrink back as if of their own accord to the relatively small degree of importance they have when measured by objective artistic standards. This is of no matter. The romantic tale in verse has had its day and played its part. It provided a starting point for a number of important poems that freed themselves from their period, and for the rest has rightly become unfashionable. It was certainly not the intention of this book to re-evaluate these works which are no longer read. However, if this genre history has brought to life a period which still influences us in many ways today, if the study of the partially forgotten works of this genre has shed new light on those poems from that period that we still value today, and if an intelligible picture has been given of how genres are created, live and die, using this type of poetry as an example, then the purpose of this journey through the history of the romantic tale in verse in England has been achieved.

Notes

Preface

1. Brian Wilkie, *Romantic Poets and Epic Tradition* (Madison and Milwaukee, 1965); M. H. Abrams, *Natural Supernaturalism: Tradition and Revolution in Romantic Literature* (New York, 1971); Thomas McFarland, *Romanticism and the Forms of Ruin: Wordsworth, Coleridge, and Modalities of Fragmentation* (Princeton, 1981); for the chapter on Shelley the following two studies provided me with a broader basis than I had in 1962: Earl R. Wasserman, *Shelley: A Critical Reading* (Baltimore, 1971) and Stuart Curran, *Shelley's Annus Mirabilis: The Maturing of an Epic Vision* San Marino, Calif., 1975).

   I am indebted to the many Byron specialists whom it has been my privilege to meet since 1974 through my contacts with the International Byron Society, and although space does not permit me to list all the names and book titles involved, my indebtedness has increased more than it may appear by comparison of this new edition with the first version of the book: what I wrote then with some uncertainty as a result of my own speculations has been proved to me through these contacts and friendships to be justifiable and correct.

2. Karl Kroeber comes the closest with his book *Romantic Narrative Art* (Madison, Milwaukee and London, 1960), a work with which I had become acquainted just before the first edition was printed. Kroeber however focuses more on 'narrative tendencies' than on the way the poets, their critics and the reading public understood the genre.

3. Since the extracts from the *Edinburgh Review* (abbreviated to *ER*), the *Quarterly Review* (*QuR*) and *Blackwood's Magazine* (*BM*) are only occasionally given word for word in the first edition, and are usually abbreviated summaries of the contents in German, what is not a direct quotation in the new edition may sometimes deviate from the wording of the original texts: these summaries are probably further from the original wording of the articles through having been translated back into English than would have been the case with summaries written in the same language.

Introduction

1. Such readers as have an aversion to Northrop Frye's much disputed theories may be assured that the 'archetypal' criticism that will be found in some later chapters is not being applied as a rigid adherence to the psychoanalytical school of criticism but rather as a tool likely to be of help in cases where other methods fail to yield serviceable results. For a more detailed discussion see pp. 166–69, 191 and 194ff.

2. L. P. Smith's essay 'The Romantic History of Four Words' in his *Words and Idioms* (London, 1925), chapter 3, dates from the first use of the 'Anglo-Franco-German

term' English romanticism as late as the seventies of the nineteenth century. The idea of a 'school' of romantic poets was, however, already in existence in England at the end of the second decade of that century, although it does not, of course, correspond to the present-day meaning but rather denotes all those poets whom Byron in a letter to John Murray of 15 September 1817 accused of being all in the wrong. 'Scott – Southey – Wordsworth – Moore – Campbell – I ... we are upon a wrong revolutionary poetical system – or systems', in other words, all those who figure in the present study as authors of romantic verse narratives. Keeping that meaning of 'romantic' apart from the present-day 'Anglo-Franco-German' signification is not the least of the difficulties this genre study has to grapple with.

3. W. M. Dixon, *English Epic and Heroic Poetry* (London, 1912), p. 279.

4. See for instance Dixon, or E. M. W. Tillyard, *The English Epic and its Background* (London, 1954).

5. Tillyard includes Bunyan and Gibbon in the history of the epopee and considers Cervantes and Fielding as legitimate heirs of the epic tradition; in other words, he is resolved to contemplate prose forms such as the puritan allegory, the great history and above all the novel as logical continuations of the classical epic. His definition of the epic poem (pp. 17ff.) is detached from formal criteria to such an extent that neither verse nor heroism is in his opinion an indispensable component of the genre.

6. In his *The Age of Wordsworth* (London, 1897) and in the Introduction to his edition of *Narrative Poems of P. B. Shelley* (London, 1918) Herford has also made some illuminating remarks on the question of genre in romantic narrative poetry.

7. See in particular p. 56 ff.

8. Wilkie, p. viii.

9. Other terms such as 'metrical romance', 'lay' or 'ballad epic' are too narrow to cover everything appertaining to the genre that is to be investigated here.

10. Many people in England were of course familiar with Mme de Stael's definition of romantic poetry, which is a simplified version of Friedrich Schlegel's original concept: 'Le nom de *romantique* a été introduit nouvellement en Allemagne pour désigner la poésie dont les chants des troubadours ont été l'origine, celle qui est née de la chevalerie et du christianisme' (*De L'Allemagne*, I, part 1, p. 211); see also I, part 2, p. 167 n. 1, where Mme de Stael compares the English literature of her time with German romantic literature: 'Les poètes anglais de notre temps ... ont adopté le même système. La poésie didactique fait place aux fictions du Moyen Age, aux couleurs pourprées de l'Orient.' Apparently Mme de Stael does not distinguish, as we do, between the wild *Sturm-und-Drang* romanticism known in England as 'German', the Weimar classicism of Goethe and Schiller, and the philosophic romanticism of Novalis and her friends the Schlegels (quotations from the Garnier-Flammarion edition, Paris, 1968).

11. Compare pp. 146, 162 and 212ff.

12. The most famous examples are Tennyson's *Enoch Arden* (1864), and *Maud* (1855), Matthew Arnold's *Sohrab and Rustrum* (1853), Macaulay's *Lay of Ancient Rome* (1842) and Longfellow's *Evangeline* (1847).

13. E.g., Oscar Wilde's *Ballad of Reading Gaol* (1898) or W. B. Yeats' and John Masefield's narrative poems.

1. Genre definitions

1. R. Wellek and A. Warren, *Theory of Literature* (New York, 1941), p. 215; quoted from N. H. Pearson, *English Institute Annual*, 1940.
2. See Chapter 17 in Wellek and Warren and W. Kayser, *Das sprachliche Kunstwerk* (Berne, 1948), Chapter 10.
3. The word 'romance' presents a tricky terminological problem. Its use in this book excludes the meaning 'fictitious narrative in prose'. On the one hand the connection with the character of medieval romance and its history and such phrases as 'the age of romance' or 'the decline of romance' should always be kept in mind; on the other hand the word is also made to serve as a denomination for the revived form of romance which was inaugurated by Scott and is the subject of this book. 'Ballad' which in English also has the meaning 'scurrilous, sensational or political poem, broadside' is used, like 'romance', both for the kind of older poetry that was collected by Bishop Percy, Ritson, *et al.* and for the imitations of this by poets of the later eighteenth and nineteenth centuries.
4. Sitzungsbericht der Bayerischen Akademie der Wissenschaften (Philosophisch-Historische Klasse), Jahrgang, 1956, Heft 4.
5. The fact that this idea was strongly advocated by a German romantic, Johann Gottfried Herder, is surely not an argument against its application to this study of a romantic genre. Here is a translation of Herder's opinion: 'A philosophical theory of the beautiful in all art and learning is impossible without the inclusion of the historical aspect ... Why? Nowhere, or at least very rarely, do we find in this field ideas which are axiomatic or posited arbitrarily (as in mathematics or in the more general concepts of metaphysics), what we do normally find here are concepts that have arisen from a multitude of concrete experiences and which occur in many classes and forms of things – in short concepts where their genesis and gradual development are everything' (Herder, *Werke*, ed. by B. Suphan (Berlin, 1877 – 1909), III, p. 380).
6. For the definitions of 'epic' in this section and for its distinction from 'romance' the author owes much to the work of L. Abercrombie, C. M. Bowra, J. Clark, W. M. Dixon, W. Kayser, W. P. Ker, E. Staiger, E. M. W. Tillyard, *et al.* (for titles see the bibliography at the end of this book). The discovery made by this author during the completion of the book that their definition in many ways agreed not only with his own but also with the ideas of the romantic period about the two genres was seen by him as a confirmation of his decision to let this chapter on 'genre definitions' stand as it was first conceived.
7. None of the attempts to extend the genre concept for the 'epic poem' to prose narrative genres has prevailed. These attempts range from Fielding's definition of his own kind of novel as a 'comic epic in prose' (Preface to *Joseph Andrews*) to Francis Jeffrey's calling *Ivanhoe* a 'Poem' (*ER*, 65, article 1, January 1820) and to the inclusion of great novels like *Don Quixote* and *The Pilgrim's Progress*, or great historical works like Gibbon's *Decline and Fall of the Roman Empire* by some modern critics in the genre of the epopee (see e.g. George Lukàcs, *Die Theorie des Romans* (Berlin, 1920), Chapters 2 and 3, or Tillyard (see notes 4 and 5 to the Introduction of this book).
8. Those critics who reduce the definition of 'heroism' to its merely military sense find themselves forced to deny Virgil's 'pius Aeneas' the title of an 'epic hero': they can only concede him the status of a monk or founder of a religious order.

Nevertheless the *Aeneid* will always remain one of the prototypes of epic poetry (see Dixon, p. 4; for romantic critics who were of that opinion see D. M. Foerster, 'The Critical Attack upon the Epic in the English Romantic Movement', *PMLA*, 69 (1954), 444 f.). If Dante and Milton are allowed to be poets who wrote genuine epics, the conception of the hero's heroism has to be shifted even further away from military valour; heroism in their poems rather takes the form of firm adherence to some principle which is accepted by the reader to be of an importance over and above the hero's personal interest.

9. *Das sprachliche Kunstwerk* (Berne, 1948, 4th edn, 1956), p. 356.
10. See Dixon, p. 4 ff. The question whether 'heroic' mythology makes a narrative poem an epic will be of major importance when the genre of the great mythological poems of Keats and Shelley has to be defined.
11. It is not, of course, quite legitimate to restrict the thematic range and weight of the greatest medieval romances – Arthurian or Grail cycles – to a formula such as 'private interest' or 'interest of a class' nor are we justified in applying the present-day concept of 'entertainment' to such literature. For the purposes of this book, however, it seemed justifiable to narrow the definition of 'romance' in this way. There are four reasons for this. (a) The majority of Middle English romances, in particular those which Scott had in mind when he revived the genre, are in fact works in which the high standard of the romances of Chrestien, Wolfram von Eschenbach and the authors of the original *Tristan* has declined to the level of aristocratic or popular entertainment, in which all connections with the mythical roots or 'all-embracing interest' of the original models have been lost sight of (Scott certainly did not see them). (b) The purpose of the definitions given in this section was to provide as rigorous a distinction between epic and romance as possible – and all genre definitions are after all simplifications descriptive of tendencies rather than formulae fitting the complexity of literary works in every detail. (c) The definition had to suit both the medieval and the romantic verse narratives, even if in the hands of the major romantics some of the latter go beyond the limits of our formula and acquire a mythical or symbolical depth comparable to that of the major romances of the twelfth and thirteenth centuries. (d) The 'private interest' and 'entertaining excitement' established in the majority of the medieval as well as the nineteenth-century romances are the main reasons for the popularity of both, and 'private' or individual problems are what the trivial romantic verse narratives have in common with the sublime works of the great romantics with their concentration on individual experience and subjective inspiration.
12. Tillyard, p. 13. See also Abercrombie's essay 'Epic' in the series *The Art and Craft of Letters* (London, n.d.) and Kroeber, p. 84 ff. Tillyard draws attention to Nietzsche's conviction that only in an optimistic age is the creation of epics possible.
13. This distinction is not the same as that between 'authentic' and 'literary' epic. A literary epic, e.g., the *Aeneid* or *Paradise Lost*, can just as easily be dominated by an 'all-embracing interest' or present an 'interpretation of the World' as an authentic one. This is why, for the purpose of this discussion, the distinction between 'authentic' and 'literary' epics has not been taken into consideration.
14. According to Bowra, genuine epic poems were still being produced in some parts of the Soviet Union in the twenties.
15. T. Medwin, *Journal of the Conversations of Lord Byron* (London, 1824), p. 274 ff.; see also *Don Juan* I, CC and passim.
16. This point will be dealt with in the chapter on Byron. See also H. Read, *The True*

Voice of Feeling (London, 1953), p. 308. For affinities of *Don Juan* with the novel see E. F. Boyd, *Byron's Don Juan: A Critical Study* (London, 1945; 2nd edn, 1958), pp. 33 f. and 43, and G. M. Ridenour, *The Style of Don Juan* (New Haven, 1960), chapter 4 and appendix A: 'Epic and Romaunt'. In his *Journal* of 9 January 1821, Byron himself admitted that the 'vanity of human wishes' was the real subject of *Don Juan*.

17. See Kayser, p. 359. Similar views are not infrequently to be encountered in English literary criticism of the romantic age.

18. See *The Prelude* (1850), III, 181: 'This is, in truth, heroic argument' and the Miltonic opening of the Prospectus to *The Recluse*. For a carefully argued view of the genre of *The Prelude* see A. F. Potts, *Wordsworth's Prelude* (Ithaca and New York, 1953) and M. H. Abrams, *Natural Supernaturalism: Tradition and Revolution in Romantic Literature* (New York, 1971), pp. 74–80.

19. Wilkie, p. 4 f. and Kroeber, p. 4.

20. N. Frye, *Anatomy of Criticism* (Princeton, 1957), p. 57; see also T. McFarland, *Romanticism and the Forms of Ruin* (Princeton, 1981) passim, on the 'disparactic' inspiration of the romantics.

21. See Dixon, p. 3. Tasso's view of the epic hero is stated in his *Discorsi dell' Arte Poetica*, Part I. The importance of this text for the theory of the epic is pointed out in Tillyard, p. 230.

22. Goethe's *Hermann und Dorothea*, which comes to mind in this connection, is an idyll rather than an epic, in spite of its weighty content; its Homeric style, though certainly not the expression of a nostalgic escapism, is used as a reminder of an exemplary standard in the past. Goethe does not use this style for the purpose of interpreting the world of his time, but rather with the intention of educating his contemporaries by projecting their problems into the perfect aesthetic form of a great past, a form that he considered to be the reflection of the humanism of that remote period. See A. W. Schlegel's essay on the poem in his *Sämtliche Werke* (Leipzig, 1846–7), p. 183 ff. For Goethe's own reflections on the epic see his essay 'Über epische und dramatische Dichtung' (On epic and dramatic poetry) of 1797, which he wrote in collaboration with Schiller, and the correspondence between the two poets of the same year. When Goethe calls the epic hero 'der ausser sich wirkende Mensch' (Man directing his creative energy outwards) he comes very close to our own view as expressed in this chapter.

23. Lucan, Tasso, Davenant and Lord Kames disagree markedly on the subject of the desirable time interval between the period in which the epic poet lives and the period of his subject matter (see Dixon, p. 2). Their views are of course only applicable to the literary epic.

24. Traces of this are to be found in the *Iliad*, e.g., the sacrifice of twelve Trojan youths beside the funeral pyre of Patroclus.

25. This alludes to a theory, first evolved by U. von Wilamowitz-Moellendorf in 1916 and taken up by W. Schadewaldt in *Von Homers Welt und Werk* (Stuttgart, 1951), p. 97, according to which the *Iliad* was written with the genealogical interests of the princes of Lycia and Troas in mind.

26. See L. L. Schücking, 'Das Königsideal im Beowulf' (The ideal of Kingship in Beowulf), *Englische Studien*, 67 (1932), 1–14.

27. See Dixon, p. 230, where Boileau's indignation at the polite heroes of the seventeenth-century French epics and prose romances is mentioned: Boileau expressed the view that their heroism was confined to mere courtly gallantry.

28. For interesting information on the 'tangible' realism of certain details in the epics of all cultures, see Bowra, *Heroic Poetry from Virgil to Milton* (London, 1952), pp. 178 and 214.
29. Dixon, p. 18.
30. Dixon, p. 98 ff. Here *La Chanson de Roland* is assigned to the romance genre whereas *Beowulf* is called an 'authentic' epic. Dixon's otherwise correct view of the two genres appears to have been blurred by the original meaning of 'romance', i.e., the verse narrative of medieval France.
31. See Herford's short introduction to his *English Tales in Verse* (London, 1924).
32. Sometimes the life of a romance hero is followed up until his death, the most definitive conclusion of a plot which is based mainly on the private life of a hero. Here the difference in breadth of the 'area of life' embraced by these works of literature is particularly evident: the death of an epic hero is both grandiose eclipse and fulfilment, it is a national event upon which are directed the eyes of heaven and earth (see e.g. Canto 22 of the *Iliad* or Laisses 174, 175 and 178 of *La Chanson de Roland*). The death of a romance hero, however great the emotional shock to his entourage and to the reader, is something 'private', it is, as it were, his last adventure:

> Tristan murut pur sun deseir
> Ysolt, qu'a tens n'i pout venir;
> Tristan murut pur sue amur
> E la bele Ysolt pur tendrur.
> (from the *Roman de Tristan*)

(Tristan died of his love-desire, Ysolt because she did not arrive in time; Tristan died of his love and beautiful Ysolt of her tenderness for him).

33. The author's consciousness of a fundamental difference between the fictitious world of romance and the real world he lives in has been very well expressed in the *lamentatio temporis acti* of the opening of Chrestien's *Yvain*. The poet is referring to Amors, i.e., idealized courtly love:

> ... son covant
> ... lors estoit riches et buens,
> Mais or i a mout po de suens;
> Que a bien pres l'ont tuit leissiee,
> S'an est amors mout abeissiee;
> Car cil, qui soloient amer,
> Se feisoient cortois clamer
> Et preu et large et enorable.
> Or est amors tornee a fable ...
> Mes por parler de caus, qui furent,
> Laissons caus, qui an vie durent ...
> (from *Yvain*, I, 1 ff.)

(... his royal household was then rich and good; but today he has few followers, nearly all have left him. For this reason Amors is sorely debased: for those who used to love in the past did everything with the intention of being called courteous and valiant and worthy of respect. Now, however, love has been turned into a falsehood ... So, in order to speak of those that were, let us rather leave those that live today.)

34. See Bowra, pp. 178–214. He points to the importance that is given in all epic poems of all countries to the circumstances of arrival and departure, rising in the morning and going to bed in the evening, dressing and arming, assuming disguise, etc. as well as to details of hospitality, festivities, seafaring and horsemanship.

The medieval romances are of course just as full of all this, but in them a transition from the real to the unreal is much easier and always possible.

35.   '... Seignurs baruns, Carles nus laissat ci;
              Pur nostre rei devum nus ben murir.
              Crestientét aidez a sustenir!
              Bataille avrez, vos en estes tuz fiz,
              Kar a vos oilz veez les Sarrazins.
              Clamez vos culpes, si preiez Deu mercit!
              Asoldrai vos pur voz anmes guarir.
              Se vos murez, esterez seinz martirs,
              Sieges avrez el greignor pareis.'
              Franceis de[s]cendent, a tere se sunt mis,
              E l'arcevesque de Deu les beneist:
              Par penitence les cumande[t] a ferir.
              (Quoted from the text of the Oxford manuscript)

('Noble barons, Charlemagne left us here; we must be prepared to die for our King. Give your assistance to the preservation of Christendom! You will have a battle, you are quite assured of that because before your eyes you see the Saracens. So confess your sins and ask God for his mercy! I shall shrive you to cure your souls. If you die you will be holy martyrs and have a seat in the greater paradise.' The French dismount, they kneel down and God's archbishop blesses them and charges them to strike valiantly in penitence.)

36. In Layman's *Brut* for instance there is a mixture of heroic and romantic features, and in the verse 'romances' of Wace and Benoit de Sainte More we find the typical concern with the descent of the national hero from an illustrious ancestry which often characterizes authentic epics. In the Renaissance epics of Italy classical elements of the heroic poem are constantly interspersed with characteristics of the medieval romance.

37. For most epics an archaic style means the adoption of those formulae of earlier heroic poetry that resulted from the original form of presentation, mostly oral recitation. The epic's concern for national history also seems to reinforce its tendency towards conservatism of form.

38. See E. Auerbach, *Mimesis* (Berne, 1946), chapter 1, where these words are applied to Homer's epics. For the handling of time in the epic see (in addition to the remarks of Goethe, Schiller and A. W. Schlegel already quoted) R. Wellek, *History of Modern Criticism 1750–1950* (New Haven, 1955), I, *passim*.

39. This is not entirely applicable to the versification of Middle High German and Italian narrative poetry, which proves that it is nearly impossible in this field to define hard and fast rules since the various historical influences and the inherent laws of the languages render matters too complicated for subjection to a rigid system.

40. Where the art ballad substantially departs from its popular model (as e.g., in the *Lyrical Ballads*) other interests replace the norms of the original genre; all that remains of them is the metre and an intentional primitivism in the language, and (according to Wordsworth's famous Preface) possibly a 'tempering and restraining' of the often painful feelings aroused by the subject matter in order to safeguard the pleasure which is the objective of all poetry.

41. Buchan, *A History of English Literature* (London, 1933), p. 39.

42. Letter to Goethe of 21 April 1797.

43. See 'Über epische und dramatische Dichtung', in *Goethes Werke*, ed. E. Trunz (Hamburg, 5th edn, 1960), XII, pp. 249–51 and 674.

44. A case in point is the fifteenth-century *Lytell Geste of Robyn Hoode*, which is more a series of ballads about the same hero than an epic.
45. For an elucidation of the metrical freedom of the old ballads from a musical point of view see J. Stevens, *Music and Poetry in the Early Tudor Court* (Oxford, 1960), Part I.
46. In England the romantics were clear about the difference between romance and ballad as a consequence of the intensive study of medieval literature by such antiquarians as Ritson, Leyden, Scott and Ellis, whereas in Germany the poets – for instance Bürger and Goethe – were quite confused in their terminology owning to their equating of the word 'Romanze' (of Spanish origin) with the word 'Ballade' and their use of both indiscriminately for either serious or comic poems. There is, of course, no equivalent for 'romance' in German.

2. The initial situation

1. Henry More, *The Immortality of the Soul* (London, 1659), p. 228. For this and the following quotations from Adam Smith and Adam Ferguson cf. Herbert Mainusch, *Romantische Ästhetik: Untersuchungen zur englischen Kunstlehre des späten 18. und frühen 19. Jahrhunderts* (Berlin/Zurich, 1969), pp. 23 ff., 41 and 40.
2. A. Smith, *Lectures on Rhetoric and Belles Lettres*, ed. John M. Lothian (London, 1963), p. 100. The passage is to be found in the nineteenth lecture, given on 10 January 1763.
3. A. Ferguson, *An Essay on the History of Civil Society* (Edinburgh, 1767), p. 265.
4. Cf. Bishop Percy's Preface to his *Reliques of Ancient English Poetry*, ed. M. M. Schröer, 2 vols. (Heilbronn, 1889–93).
5. Walter Scott, *Minstrelsy of the Scottish Border*, ed. J. Lockhart (Edinburgh, 1833), 'Introductory Remarks on Popular Poetry', pp. 39, 25.
6. The promoters of the Medieval Revival extended the 'rude' Middle Ages well into the sixteenth century. Scott's 'last minstrel' even sings his Lay, which describes events taking place in the middle of the sixteenth century, as late as 1690. As most old ballads dated from the late fifteenth and sixteenth centuries, the literature of that period was lumped together with that of the earlier centuries to form that vague group that was termed 'the works of our old poets' and included even Spenser and Shakespeare and was often called 'simple, wild, rude, ancient, and Gothic'. This view is a hangover from the seventeenth century and the age of Queen Anne; it prevailed throughout the eighteenth century. It was only the appreciation of the 'old' literature and its 'rude' and 'Gothic' charms that changed. It is important to bear in mind this extension of the 'Middle Ages', since it explains such phenomena as the primitivistic associations that even the style and stanza of Spenser carried with them and which rendered them so popular with the romantics, or the curious mixture of Shakespearean elements with the 'modern Gothic' in such plays as Wordsworth's *The Borderers* (which takes place in the thirteenth century) or the 'German dramas', of which more will be said later in this chapter. The historical vagueness of this concept of the 'Middle Ages' is largely responsible for the blatant anachronisms for which Scott, Southey and other 'romantic writers' were constantly blamed by the critics, most of all by Francis Jeffrey.
7. In his Introduction to *The Lay of the Last Minstrel* written for the 1830 edition of his *Poetical Works* Scott states as a further reason that in 1805 'the practice of ballad-writing was out of fashion' and that 'any attempt to revive it ... would certainly

fail of success: The ballad measure, which was once listened to as to an enchanting melody, had become hackneyed and sickening from its being the accompaniment of every grinding hand-organ.'

8. Compare T. Evans, *Old Ballads* (1777 and 1784) with R. H. Evans' new edition of 1810.

9. Cf. Introduction to *The Lay of the Last Minstrel* (1830): 'the translations from Bürger had been unsuccessful'.

10. See Friedrich Brie, 'Pope's Brutus', *Anglia*, 62 (1939), 144–85; Wordsworth's *Prelude* (1850) I, 158–233; J. D. Campbell, *S. T. Coleridge* (London, 1896), pp. 64, 78 f. and 248; T. Moore, *The Life of Byron* (London, 1851) and Byron's letters to Elizabeth Pigot of 2 August 1807 and 11 August 1807; Brian Wilkie, p. 145 (on Keats' *Hyperion* as an epic); Dorothy Hewlitt, *A Life of Keats* (London, 1937), p. 30 (on Keats' translating parts of the *Aeneid* when a boy).

11. *QuR*, 9, article 2, February 1811.

12. Dryden translated the *Iliad* I (in *Fables Ancient and Modern*, 1700) and the *Aeneid* (1697), Pope the *Iliad* (1715–20) and the *Odyssey* (1725–6) and Statius' *Thebais* I (1712); Macpherson supplied a prose translation of the *Iliad* (1773), Cowper an *Iliad* and an *Odyssey* (1791); Nicholas Rowe translated Lucan's *Pharsalia* (1718).

13. Cf. F. Brie, *Englische Rokokoepik 1710–1730* (Munich, 1927); George Kitchin, *A Survey of Burlesque and Parody in English* (2nd edn, New York, 1964); Ulrich Broich, *The Eighteenth-Century Mock Heroic Poem* (Cambridge, 1990); Richmond P. Bond, *English Burlesque Poetry 1700–1750*, Harvard Studies in English (Edinburgh and London, 1931).

14. Cf. W. Davenant's *Discourse upon Gondibert* (1650–1) in J. E. Spingarn, *Seventeenth Century Critical Essays*, III (Oxford, 1908); H. T. Swedenberg, Jr, *The Theory of the Epic in England 1650–1800* (Berkeley, 1944); Donald M. Foerster, 'The Critical Attack upon the Epic in the English Romantic Movement', *PMLA*, 69 (1954), 422 ff. See also W. M. Dixon, p. 242.

15. Dixon, p. 11.

16. Cf. René Wellek, *History of Modern Criticism 1750–1950* (New Haven, 1955), vols. I and II; E. M. W. Tillyard, last chapter. Scott writes in the Introduction to the First Edition of *The Bridal of Triermain* (March, 1813): 'To modern readers, the poems of Homer have many of the features of pure romance.' See also D. M. Foerster, *Homer in English Criticism* (New Haven, 1947) and Rudolf Sühnel, *Homer und die englische Humanität* (Tübingen, 1958).

17. *QuR*, 11, article 13, October 1811.

18. In his article on 'The Critical Attack upon the Epic' (see above) D. M. Foerster admits that just as long an article could be written about faith in and admiration for the epic in the English romantic movement.

19. In his article on Jane Austen's *Emma* in the *QuR*, 27, article 9, October 1815, Scott writes: 'There are some vices in civilized society so common that they are hardly acknowledged as stains upon the moral character, the propensity to which is nevertheless carefully concealed, even by those who frequently give way to them; ... One would almost think that novelreading fell under this class of frailties, since among the crowd who read little else, it is not common to find an individual of hardihood sufficient to avow his taste for these frivolous studies. A novel, therefore, is frequently "bread eaten in secret".' Compare also J. T. Taylor, *Early Opposition to the English Novel: The Popular Reaction from 1760 to 1830* (New York, 1943).

20. Dixon, p. 242 f. quotes these critical comments from John Dennis, *Some Reflexions*

on a Book entitled *Prince Arthur, an Heroic poem* [Blackmore's *Prince Arthur* of 1695] (1696). Dennis as well as Henry Pemberton – in *Observations on Poetry, Especially on the Epic, Occasioned by the Late Poem upon Leonidas* [Richard Glover's *Leonidas* of 1737] (1738) – still seriously thought that the existence of established rules made the composition of an epic a mechanical and comparatively easy task, whereas Pope in his 'Receipt to make an Epic Poem' in the *Guardian*, 78, 10 June 1713 poked fun at such a view. See also L. Sterne, *Tristram Shandy* II, p. 12.

21. 'Throughout the eighteenth century, narrative verse, unless quickened by the zest of satire or burlesque, was something of a *tour de force*, the recounting pen willingly meandered into description, or subsided into sentiment.' C. H. Herford, Preface to *English Tales in Verse* (London, 1924).

22. This is even true of eighteenth-century blank verse. In his first essay on Milton (1936) T. S. Eliot writes: 'On the whole, the blank verse of Dr. Johnson's age might more properly be called unrhymed verse ... each line cries out for a companion to rhyme with', *On Poetry and Poets* (London, 1957), p. 158. That Shenstone's and Beattie's Spenserians are not an ideal medium for story-telling goes without saying.

23. 'The Manner of Proceeding in Certain Eighteenth and Nineteenth Century Poems', Warton Lecture on English Poetry, *Proceedings of the British Academy*, 34 (London, 1948).

24. Tillotson bases this view on a passage in Boswell's *Life of Johnson* (Oxford, 1965), p. 747. He might also have mentioned Johnson's ridiculing of ballads (pp. 510 and 842 f.), his contempt for French novels (p. 442), his deprecatory comparison of Fielding with Richardson (p. 480).

25. Jeffrey applied this epithet to Moore's 'The Veiled Prophet', the first of the four stories in *Lalla Rookh*. Cf. his review of Moore's poem in the *ER*, 57, article 1, November 1817.

26. For contemporary explanations of 'this degrading thirst after outrageous stimulation' see Wordsworth's Preface to the *Lyrical Ballads* of 1800: 'a multitude of causes, unknown to former times, are now acting with a combined force to blunt the discriminating powers of the mind'. He mentions 'the great national events which are daily taking place, and the increasing accumulation of men in cities, where the uniformity of their occupation produces a craving for extraordinary incident, which the rapid communication of intelligence hourly gratifies'. And he deplores the fact that 'The invaluable works of our elder writers ... are driven into neglect by frantic novels, sickly and stupid German Tragedies, and deluges of idle and extravagant stories in verse.' For Jeffrey's view of the matter see p. 51 f.

27. Cf. M. Summers, *The Gothic Quest* (New York, 1963) and *A Gothic Bibliography* (New York, 1964). G. R. Thompson (ed.), *The Gothic Imagination: Essays in Dark Romanticism* (Seattle, 1974); L. Abensour (ed.), *Romantisme noir* (Paris, 1978); D. P. Varma, *The Gothic Flame* (New York, 1960).

28. Scott certainly felt no personal affinity for 'German' horrors and villain heroes. He even ridiculed his own translation of Goethe's *Erl-King* by adding the note: 'To be read by a candle particularly long in the snuff.' Yet he did use the villain hero in *Marmion*. Here as elsewhere his decision may have been influenced by the *lucri bonus odor* which, as Coleridge wrote in the 'Critique on Bertram', 'would conciliate a bill of health to the plague in person'. At any rate he did it to win favour with his readers. Byron, on the other hand, at first followed the German fashion, and imitated its gloomy hero as a means of expressing as well as camouflaging his personal troubles. Only after having witnessed the extraordinary success of this

blend of the subjective with the fashionable did he repeat it as a stereotype. See P. Thorslev, *The Byronic Hero: Types and Prototypes* (Minneapolis, 1962). Jeffrey significantly called Byron's *Giaour* a mixture of Marmion and Bertram with Childe Harold (in the *ER*, 42, article 2, July 1813).

29. James Hervey's *Meditations among the Tombs* and *Contemplations on the Night* (both 1746/7) were highly popular in Germany, as were also the other authors mentioned in this passage. It should however be added that the 'bloated style' of Hervey had become even more bloated in German *Sturm-und-Drang* literature by the addition of mixtures of Gessner with the German translations of 'Ossian'.

30. As early as 1799 Southey, in a letter to W. Wynn of 5th April, had written: 'The German plays ... are thoroughly Jacobinical in tendency.' See also Stockley, *German Literature as Known in England 1750 – 1830* (London, 1929), p. 9: 'With the progress of the anti-revolutionary wars and the strengthening of the Tory party in England, the *Sturm-und-Drang* literature of Germany came to be regarded as synonymous with all that was revolutionary in politics and free-thinking in philosophy.'

31. Cf. Winfield H. Rogers, 'The Reaction against Melodramatic Sentimentality in the English Novel 1796 – 1830', *PMLA*, 49 (1934), 98 – 122, and Stockley, pp. 130 and 138.

32. See Schirmer, *Der Einfluss der deutschen Literatur auf die englische im 19. Jahrhundert* (Halle, 1947), p. 516.

33. Cf. Scott's translation of Goethe's *Goetz von Berlichingen* and his seven *Ballads from the German*; Wordsworth, *The Borderers* (1795); Byron, *Werner* (1822); Shelley, *The Wandering Jew, Zatrozzi, St Irvyne* (all before 1801). H. Kraeger was the first critic to show that the 'Byronic Hero' absorbed many German elements; see his *Der byronische Heldentypus* (Ph.D. thesis, Munich, 1898). Margaret W. Cooke, 'Schiller's *Robbers* in England', *MLR*, 11 (1916), 156 – 75 deals with another important aspect of the German influence.

34. See his review of Scott's *Marmion* in the *ER*, 23, article 1, April 1808: 'reminiscent of a bad German novel'; one passage is said to be taken from Schiller's *Robbers*; and his reviews of Moore's *Lalla Rookh* (see footnote 25 above) and of Byron's *Corsair* and *Bride of Abydos* in the *ER*, 45, article 9, April 1814).

35. Cf. Byron's letters to John Murray (15 September 1817) and to Thomas Moore (2 February 1818).

36. Did Byron resent the long passage about 'the happy balance of the generic with the individual' which Maturin was reproached with having failed to establish? Coleridge compared the Spanish Don Juan (*Atheista Fulminato*) as a 'character representative and symbolical, therefore instructive' with Maturin's 'tragic Macheath' and 'misanthropic hero' Bertram and argued that to reward such 'criminals whom law, reason, and religion have excommunicated from our esteem' with 'all the sympathies which are the dues of virtue' was a Jacobinical 'subversion of the natural order of things in their causes and effects'. This may have seemed to Byron to be a reference to his own heroes. It is significant that the very letter in which he mentions Coleridge's 'attack upon the Committee of Drury Lane Theatre – for acting *Bertram*' contains the first mention of *Beppo*, his first tale without the typical Byronic hero, and that the following summer he began his own *Don Juan*, which indeed strikes a 'happy balance of the generic with the individual'.

37. Cf. Jeffrey's opinion (expressed in his review of Byron's *Corsair* and *Bride*) that only the wish to represent and analyse strong and uncontrolled emotions had caused the poets to go back to the Middle Ages; but the same results could,

of course, be obtained if the poets turned to wild exotic countries as did Byron, or to contemporary 'savages' in our own country (here he is obviously thinking of Crabbe's *Peter Grimes*). To Jeffrey going back to the age of romance seems to be the easier way because of the poetical charm of the old world and the rich supply of models for imitation.

38. In his review of Southey's *The Curse of Kehama* in *ER*, 24, article 11, February 1811, Jeffrey resented the fact that any milkmaid, any shoemaker or drunkard could now be palmed off upon the public as a poet if only they find a patron who 'makes' them. Among the 'poets' promoted in this way were a disproportionate number of women. Owing to the general decline of taste that species of poetic production did not, as it would have done in former times, fall into the oblivion it deserved. See also A.S. Collins, 'The Growth of the Reading Public during the Eighteenth Century', *RES*, 2 (1926), 284–9 and 428–38; and R.H. Havens, 'Changing Taste in the Eighteenth Century', *PMLA*, 44 (1929), 501–36.

39. In a review of Milman's *Samor: A Heroic Poem* in *QuR*, 38, article 3, December 1818, there is a most interesting passage about the 'decline' of literary criticism that ran parallel to the change of taste in the public. It says that in the past literary criticism had been a laborious and highly responsible task, a scholarly activity that had always confined itself to the limits of the object it dealt with. It had been an analysis of literary form and had derived its standards from the observance of certain time-honoured rules which concerned design, moral and choice of subject. Today, however, criticism had become the pursuit of amateurs and was guided by subjective preferences and bias in favour of schools rather than adherence to received systems and principles. As the critics no longer felt obliged to analyse works of literature but dwelt on topics that were attractive in themselves, no special knowledge was now required for the job.

Thus we have highly wrought, and not very short descriptions of poetry in general, ingenious theories respecting poetic power, genius and association, parallels drawn, and contrasts exhibited between the sister arts; rapturous declamations of fancy, the picturesque, natural beauty, and harmony, general comparisons between the fables of different poems, and the characteristic qualities of different poets, with an artful selection either of the best or worst passages of the work under consideration.

In addition a futile dabbling in metaphysics had become fashionable in literary criticism, and all this was perhaps rather pleasant and entertaining, but the taste of both poets and public was no longer educated by such criticism. As a consequence the rules disappeared and the poets, who no longer regarded the critics as their advisers and teachers but as rivals for the favour of the public, set up their own standards, which were based on such entirely subjective and inadequate principles as 'feeling' and 'strong effect'.

40. The virtual lubricity of Richardson's novels and the coarseness of Swift's *Gulliver's Travels* were increasingly exposed and criticized after 1800. The author of the article 'Odoherty on *Don Juan*' in *BM*, 70, September 1823, maintained that Byron's *Don Juan* was neither lewder than *Tom Jones* nor more irreverent than Voltaire's writings but that, on the other hand, Richardson's 'pious' *Pamela* contained more obscenities than Byron, Fielding and Voltaire taken together; Byron had of course said much the same in a letter to Murray of 25 January 1819 (P.S.). A further example of the increasing prudery of the period is Southey's remark, in the Preface to his *Joan of Arc*, that, although

he had read all other poetical treatments of the Jeanne d'Arc legend, he had left out Voltaire's *La Pucelle* because a person could only soil himself by reading it.

41. This, and not his sticking to the style of the Augustans, was the reason why Crabbe was more appreciated by educated than by uneducated readers. The point was discussed in the reviews of Crabbe's *Tales* (1812) of both the *ER* and the *QuR* towards the end of 1812. While Jeffrey of the *ER* advocated the social utility of Crabbe's poetry of humble or middling life and deplored the tendency of the lower classes to prefer in narrative poetry 'the trappings of splendid fortune and high station' the reviewer of the *QuR* was sure that middle-class readers would always despise works in which their own circumstances were depicted; and they were disinclined to sympathize with their own kind. Two years before, the *QuR* had eloquently defended the escapism of 'romantic' literature (see the review of Crabbe's *The Borough* in *QuR*, 8, November 1810). The strategies that the Victorian social novelists adopted in order to break down these mental attitudes are impressively analysed in Norbert Platz, *Die Beeinflussung des Lesers* (Tübingen, 1986).

42. See pp. 143 and 263 f. In his review of Southey's *The Curse of Kehama* in *ER*, 24, article 11, February 1811, Jeffrey stated that today ten times more people read poems than in the age of Dryden and Pope, and that fifty times more people believed they were qualified to have a say in matters of poetry.

43. *ER*, 40, article 2, November 1812.

44. *QuR*, 31, article 9, October 1816.

45. *BM*, 60, January 1822.

46. See Southey's letter to W. Wynn of 5 April 1799: 'The theatrical taste of the public is very bad; but the managers are more to blame than the public.'

47. *BM*, 74, March 1823, 'Remarks on Mr. Barry Cornwall's New Poems'.

48. *ER*, 45, article 9, April 1814. Comparable views are so frequent in contemporary essays and periodical articles that it is impossible to exhaust the topic here. They are all similar in their evolutionistic historical approach but differ greatly in the conclusions for the present age they arrive at. Whereas Jeffrey in the article under consideration ventures something like a historical justification of the modern craving for sensation, Wordsworth in his Preface to *Lyrical Ballads* of 1800 rejects 'this degrading thirst after outrageous stimulation'. It will be shown in the chapter on Byron that even Byron came to consider his earlier oriental tales as 'exaggerated nonsense'.

49. The works at which the lines quoted literally hint are easily discovered: a title or hero of a romantic verse narrative or drama can be substituted for every one of Jeffrey's generalized examples. See also p. 142. As in most criticism of the period no distinction is made between Byron, Crabbe, Wordsworth and Southey. They are considered as a unity, irrespective of the 'school' they belong to, and regarded as representatives of that 'modern' literature whose character, according to Jeffrey, was the necessary expression of a specific phase in the historical development of Europe.

50. See pp. 107 ff.

51. Jeffrey's critical acumen in the review of Byron's *The Corsair* and *Lara* is also admirable where he proceeds from merely stating the reasons for the contemporary hunger for 'strong passion' to a more general analysis. From his cyclical view of history he deduces two significant points: the wish of the contemporary reader to be presented with characters he or she can identify with, and – as a consequence – the striking anachronism of the poets' character-drawing. He is not, however,

really worried about the distortion of reality which accompanies that anachronism: it may offend the thinker but is legitimate in the poet.

52. The connection between the changes in society and the intentions behind the metrical romance genre invented by Scott is very succinctly stated in the review of Scott's *The Lord of the Isles* in *QuR*, 26, article 1, July 1815:

> The works of modern bards ... are obviously calculated for a much larger description of readers; the characters and sentiments which they contain, the species of interest which they inspire are ... level to all capacities; while their faults and deficiencies are such that none but persons of refined and practiced taste are in any sensible degree affected by them. Whether this be a sort of merit which indicates great and uncommon talents, may perhaps admit of doubt; but at all events it is a very useful one to the public at large. The productions of Mr. Scott possibly bear no more proportion to the *Iliad* or the *Paradise Lost*, than the excellent tales of Miss Edgeworth to the *Histories* of Tacitus or Clarendon; but ... such men as Homer or Milton are of rare occurrence; in the mean time we are in the enjoyment of a description of poetry, which is adapted to the genius of a greater number of writers, and is capable of affording amusement to a greater variety of readers than any which antiquity possessed.

In other – sociological – terms, Scott's type of narrative poem is the bourgeois descendant of the 'aristocratic' epic of the three preceding centuries.

3. Early forms

1. With respect to Southey, see Wilkie, chapter 2, and this volume p. 58–71. Shelley's admiration for *Gebir* is confirmed by Mary Shelley in her Note to *Queen Mab*, cf. T. Hutchinson (ed.), *The Complete Poetical Works of Shelley* (Oxford Standard Authors 1905 and 1948), p. 837. Hogg in his *Life of Shelley* (1858 and 1906) records the following amusing anecdote. Some time during Shelley's period at Oxford a visitor found the young poet so engrossed in Landor's poem that, in order to attract his attention, he had to snatch the book away and throw it out of the window. Without uttering a word Shelley went out to fetch it back and continued reading.

2. See the passage about *Gebir* in Southey's Preface to the fourth volume of the *Collected Works* of 1837–8. With respect to the question of genre see also Stanley G. Williams, 'The Story of *Gebir*', *PMLA*, 36 (1921), 624 ff. and Wilkie, chapter 2.

3. For a detailed analysis of the style of *Gebir* see R. D. Havens, *The Influence of Milton on English Poetry* (New York, 1961), p. 293 f. and Douglas Bush, *Mythology and the Romantic Tradition in English Poetry* (New York, 1957), p. 236 ff. E. Nitchie, *Virgil and the English Poets* (New York, 1919), p. 207 ff. discusses Virgilian influences in Landor's work.

4. 'To Wordsworth' in Stephen Wheeler (ed.), *The Complete Works of W. S. Landor*, XV (III), (Oxford, 1937), pp. 55 ff. and 144.

5. Unpublished Postscript to *Gebir*, written 1800, quoted in William Bradley, *The Early Poems of W. S. Landor* (London, 1914), p. 65.

6. W. Bradley, pp. 59–94.

7. Preface to the first edition of *Gebir*, quoted by W. Bradley, p. 97.

8. Wilkie, pp. 53 and 57.

9. In order not to become embroiled in the terminological controversy concerning metaphor and symbol it has proved expedient for the purposes of this book to resort occasionally to R. A. Foakes' very useful distinction between 'images of thought' and 'images of impression': the former term defines the intellectual recognition of 'correspondences' (as e.g., in metaphysical poetry), the latter defines the use

of images which evoke a rich aura of associations and emotional responses. The consequences of the great romantic poets' turning towards an 'imagery of impression' and the way this influenced their narrative poetry will be discussed in a later chapter, see pp. 170–8. Cf. R. A. Foakes, *The Romantic Assertion* (London, 1958).

10. Foakes, p. 58.
11. Cf. note 16 below.
12. Cf. p. 88 ff.
13. Cf. p. 138 f. This influence was already pointed out by Christopher North in his article 'Preface to a Review of the Chronicles of the Canongate' in *BM*, 132, November 1827.
14. Jeffrey's essay on 'John Ford's Dramatic Works' in the *ER*, 36, article 1, August 1811, shows clearly how the poetic language of the romantic poets was felt to be very closely related to the style of the Elizabethans. Jeffrey even reproaches the Lake Poets with imitating their Elizabethan models more closely than the classicists had imitated their Roman ones.
15. W. Hazlitt, *Lectures on the English Poets* (London, 1910), p. 156.
16. Wordsworth saw many of his own intentions reflected in the old ballads: they were unaffected poems about passionate and often painful subjects in which, however, the regularity of the metre made the excessive emotions evoked by the events not only bearable but pleasurable. Yet the addition of 'Lyrical' made it quite clear that the authors were not presenting just another collection of narrative ballads. See F. B. Bateson, *Wordsworth: A Re-Interpretation* (London, 1954), p. 137 and K. Kroeber, *Romantic Narrative Art* (London, 1960), p. 42. Two further reasons for the authors' choice of the ballad genre are obvious: (1) the ballad is the most concentrated narrative form and is thus particularly well suited as a medium for symbolic content which is not just one image but a dynamic structure or, as W. K. Wimsatt called it, an extended metaphor without an expressed tenor, see his *The Verbal Icon* (Louisville, Kentucky, 1954), p. 800; (2) Even some of the old ballads contained such symbolic structures – the journey, the quest, exile, or communication with a supernatural being which might be termed archetypal 'images of impression'. It is obvious that Wordsworth and Coleridge felt attracted by a lyrical genre that offered them these possibilities, and it is also clear that the typically romantic use of short narratives such as the ballad and the 'tale' for symbolic utterance was inspired by such texts as *The Ancient Mariner* and *Lucy Gray, or Solitude*, to name only two. Cf. also Foakes, p. 58.
17. Coleridge's subjectivism of course differed significantly from Wordsworth's 'egotistical sublime'. In the *QuR*, 27, article 10, October 1815 (on *The White Doe of Rylstone*) Wordsworth is reproached – not entirely without justification – with always writing about himself, and particularly about those of his experiences in which he differs most from all other men. Coleridge on the other hand said that 'the choice of subjects very remote from the private interests and circumstances of the writer himself' was a sign of genius, cf. *Biographia Literaria*, chapter 15. Both poets however agreed about the contribution of the subjective mind to the workings of the imagination, and that explains why they were both constantly blamed by the public for their esoteric egotism which made it impossible for the ordinary reader to follow them. Their fancies were said to be 'entirely too poetical to please the common reader', *BM*, 18, September 1818, 'Some Remarks on the Use of the Preternatural in Works of Fiction'. See also Abrams, *Natural Supernaturalism*, pp. 21–31.

18. Preface to the *Lyrical Ballads* of 1800.
19. Hazlitt writes: '[Wordsworth's] poetry is ... internal; it does not depend upon tradition, or story, or old song; he furnishes it from his own mind, and is its own subject. He is the poet of mere sentiment' (*Lectures on the English Poets*, p. 156). An article in *BM*, 21, December 1818, 'On the Habits of Thought inculcated by Wordsworth' calls him the Englishman's Rousseau. Since all English philosophers are empiricists, it falls to the task of the poets to take care of metaphysics, the universe, and the soul. Wordsworth in doing just that had reached a greatness that placed him far above the clamour of the 'Satanic School'.
20. Kroeber, *Romantic Narrative Art*, title of chapter 4: 'Visionary Lyrics'.
21. Jeffrey was right in saying that the subject matter of *The White Doe of Rylstone* was only weighty enough for a ballad, see *ER*, 50, article 4, October 1815; and North was right when, in *BM*, 123, November 1817, he wrote that *The Excursion* was not a great poem, but a series of small poems strung together without a firm plan. Compare also T. McFarland, for another quotation from Hazlitt and a more comprehensive view of this particular question. Would the contemporary critics have judged differently if *The Prelude* had already been accessible to them? See p. 20f.
22. C. H. Herford, Introduction to *English Tales in Verse*.
23. Cf. Jeffrey's review of *Childe Harold* III, *ER*, 54, article 1, December 1816; his review of *Thalaba*, *ER*, 1, article 8, October 1802, and his review of *The Corsair*, *ER*, 45, article 9, April 1814. The contemporary critics blamed the German influence for an emotionalism in poetry which, however, was the consequence of the expressive theory of art – as described by Abrams in his *The Mirror and the Lamp*, (Oxford, 1953), pp. 70 – 99, on the 'lower' literary forms.
24. *BM*'s reviews of Wordsworth, usually written by Christopher North (John Wilson), invariably emphasize the distance between Wordsworth and the 'loud' school of Scott.
25. For the nature and limitations of Wordsworth's gift for narration see A. C. Bradley, *Oxford Lectures on English Poetry* (London, 1909), p. 99 ff.
26. None of Coleridge's other poems could be described as a captivating narrative. *Love* (1798/9), which, next to *The Ancient Mariner*, was the best-known of Coleridge's poems in his time, is nothing but a 'soft and doleful' love poem in ballad form which includes thirty lines of an unfinished 'old and moving story'; its Introduction, *The Dark Lady* (1798) is very similar in form and character. *The Three Graves* (1797 – 1809) is a rather weak imitation of Wordsworth's style and lacks all narrative dynamism; in *Sibylline Leaves* (1817) Coleridge called it 'the fragment, not of a Poem, but of a common ballad tale', and said: 'Its merits, if any, were exclusively psychological.' *Alice du Clos* (published 1834) is a belated piece of balladry, impressive, but hardly an example of exciting story-telling. For Coleridge's attempts at drama, cf. Byron's remark in a letter to John Murray of 17 September 1817: 'there was every disposition on the part of the [Subcommittee of the Drury Lane Theatre] to bring forward any production of his were it feasible – the play he offered [*Zapolya*] though poetical did not appear at all practicable'.
27. See Byron's footnote to *The Siege of Corinth*, l. 522 and his letter to John Murray of 30 September 1816 as well as his letter to T. Moore of 24 September 1816.
28. The article 'Some Remarks on the Use of the Preternatural in Works of Fiction' in *BM*, 18, September 1818, paid Coleridge the dubious compliment of calling him 'the prince of superstitious poets', which was repeated in another article just

about Coleridge in *BM*, 31, October 1819. The first of these articles expresses the view that Coleridge fully belongs to the category of authors of 'romance and fictions' that followed the German fashion. See also Hazlitt, *Lectures on the English Poets*, p. 166 on *The Ancient Mariner*; after having called this poem a work of genius Hazlitt goes on: 'It is high German, however, and in it he seems to "conceive of poetry but as a drunken dream".' Compare also E. K. Chambers, *S. T. Coleridge* (Oxford, 1938), p. 113, where a number of contemporary views are quoted.

29. The *QuR* never dedicated a whole article to Coleridge. Jeffrey of the *ER* managed to avoid commenting on the 1816 publication of *Christabel*, *Kubla Khan* and *The Pains of Sleep* and had the review written by a man who apparently had a personal and political grudge against Coleridge, and whose article was correspondingly aggressive and offensive, see *ER*, 12, article 4, September 1816. 'Timothy Tickler' in the June 1818 issue of *BM* (No. 15) countered the attack, the real identity of whose author has never been discovered, cf. Elizabeth Schneider, 'The Unknown Reviewer of Christabel: Jeffrey, Hazlitt, Tom Moore?', *PMLA*, 70 (1955), 417–42, and, taking the opposite view, H. H. Jordan, 'Thomas Moore and the Review of Christabel', *MP*, 54 (1956), 95–105.

30. *BM*, 65, June 1822, 'Lights and Shadows of Scottish Life'.

31. Herbert Read, *The True Voice of Feeling* (London, 1953), p. 21. The danger inherent in Coleridge's poetology as well as the difficulties arising from its incompatibility with the realities of modern life are pointed out in the article on Coleridge in *BM*, 31, October 1819. The fragmentary character of *Christabel*, the author says, arises from the fact that Coleridge's inspiration is 'too passive'; the poet's will should step in where his inspiration fails. Once his inspiration has furnished him with the basic idea of a poem he should consciously apply his will to the creation of the formal aspects and the final shape. 'Carefulness above all is necessary to a poet in these latter days, where the ordinary medium through which things are viewed is so far from being poetical – and when the natural strain of scarcely any man's associations can be expected to be of that sort which is most akin to high and poetical feeling.'

32. Defending the rhymeless verse of *Thalaba* Southey writes in the Preface to the first edition of this poem (1801): 'Let me not be supposed to prefer the rhythm in which it is written, abstractedly considered, to the regular blank verse ... For the following poem I have preferred it because it suits the varied subject: it is the Arabesque ornament of an Arabian tale ... I do not wish the improvisatore tune, but something that denotes the sense of harmony, something like the accent of feeling.' A similar remark in defence of the 'free' verse of *The Curse of Kehama* occurs in the Preface to Vol. VIII of the *Collected Edition* of 1837/8. See also the motto to *Kehama*, which, in the words of John Withers, advocates liberation from the ties of convention. But all these remarks lack a philosophical basis, they just repeat the pre-romantic tenet that 'the heart' and 'nature' should be the poet's sole teachers.

33. Whereas for the older generation of romantics – particularly Coleridge – it took an extraordinary effort of the intellect to institute the new philosophy of poetry, its basic tenets had become almost a matter of course for the younger poets of romanticism. This comes out very clearly in Shelley's Advertisement to *Rosalind and Helen* (1819): 'I resigned myself, as I wrote, to the impulse of the feelings which moulded the conception of the story, and this impulse determined the pauses of a measure, which only pretends to be irregular in as much

as it corresponds with and expresses the irregularity of the imagination which inspired it.'

34. Though Scott had only once heard *Christabel*, when it was read to him by John Stoddard, he imitated the metre and incorporated four lines from it into his *Lay of the Last Minstrel* (I, 1, 12 and II, 26 and 27).

35. For earlier uses of the so-called *Christabel* metre cf. G. Saintsbury, *A History of English Prosody* (London, 1910), III, p. 77 f. Scott ascribes to Coleridge only the invention of the use of this metre for serious poetry, since it had already been made use of by several recent poets for comic works (see Scott's Introduction to the *Lay* in the *Collected Poetry* of 1830). One should not forget to mention in this connection the endeavours of Matthew G. Lewis to make the narrative tetrameter as well as the ballad metre less rigid by interspersing it with dactyls and anapaests. Lewis, who was Scott's mentor in questions of versification, had been given the idea of this mixed metre by the German ballads written in the *Sturm-und-Drang* period, whose authors had in turn been influenced by Percy. All this contributed to the formation of the metre of Scott's *Lay* which, undoubtedly, surpasses the *Christabel* metre in freedom and irregularity.

36. See Jeffrey's article on Byron's *The Corsair* in *ER*, 45, article 9, April 1814 and *ER*, 25, article 13; 24, article 11; 27, article 1; 32, article 1. After 1815 it was no longer Southey but Byron whose name was coupled with Scott's by the reviewers when they wrote about the 'new poetry'.

37. See Southey, *A Vision of Judgement*, IX.

38. The history of the composition and publication of *Joan of Arc* and details about Coleridge's additions to it, which were later published under the title *The Destiny of Nations*, are given in the introductory remarks on this poem in E. H. Coleridge's edition of *The Complete Poetical Works of S. T. Coleridge* (Oxford, 1912). In the second edition of *Joan of Arc* (1798) Southey eliminated all allegorical machinery from the poem.

39. Compare p. 41.

40. With his 'epic' ambition, Southey was profoundly irritated when Scott in his review of *The Curse of Kehama* (*QuR*, 9, article 2, February 1811) ignored the difference between a 'story of mere amusement' and a work of 'high imagination'. See Southey's letter to Captain T. Southey of 5 December 1811. See also his letter to Hill of 5 February 1811. Both letters are to be found in *Selections from the Letters of Robert Southey*, 4 vols., ed. J. W. Warter (London, 1856).

41. Although there are faint traces of the fashionable admiration of the noble savage in *Madoc* as well as in the *Tale of Paraguay* and *Oliver Newman*, these are outweighed by a self-righteous condemnation of the heathen religions as 'systems of atrocious witchcraft' (Preface to vol. V of the *Collected Edition of Robert Southey's Poetical Works*, 10 vols., London, 1837/8, henceforth quoted as *CE*). Southey's simplistic way of allotting good or bad moral marks even to primitives is based on a rationalist belief in the equality of the moral character in people of all nations and races. Equally uncomprehending is his view of medieval catholicism as it is reflected in his *Ballads and Metrical Tales*.

42. See Southey's letter to Grosvenor C. Bedford of June 1801. His plan 'of exhibiting the most remarkable forms of mythology which have at any time obtained among mankind, by making each the groundwork of a narrative poem' goes back to his school-days at Westminster (see the Preface to vol. VIII of the *CE*).

43. See Wordsworth's *Excursion* IV, 1062 – 77.

44. See Preface to vol. V of the *CE* for Southey's account of his reasons for choosing shorter subdivisions and altering his 'original conduct of the piece'.

45. In a letter to Landor of 30 September 1809 Southey contemplated calling the subdivisions in *The Curse of Kehama* 'canticles' but rejected the idea because of associations with the *Song of Songs*.

46. Four of these are taken from Spenser, three from medieval Latin sources, one from a ballad by Ben Jonson, one from an early Jewish author and one from an Arabic poem. This mixture is quite characteristic of Southey, the polymath turned romancer.

47. In the Original Preface, *Thalaba* is called a romance and an Arabian Tale. Brian Wilkie, chapter 2, adopts Southey's own 'careful distinction between his three genuine epics and his romances, *Thalaba* and *Kehama*' (p. 36). He neglects, however, most of the evidence adduced by this author that points to a more complicated view of the case.

48. Southey was convinced that his irregular metre was the best verse form to suit his 'varied' subject; he called it the 'Arabesque ornament to an Arabian Tale' (see the Original Preface to *Thalaba*, the Preface to vol. VIII of the *CE*, and Southey's letter to Captain T. Southey of 5 December 1812.

49. See letters to W. Taylor of 24 February 1799 and to William Wynn of 5 April 1799. In the latter he places *Thalaba* between Wieland's *Oberon* and Ariosto's *Orlando Furioso*. See also C. H. Herford, *The Age of Wordsworth* (London, 1897), p. 208.

50. In a letter of John May written in 1803 Southey claims that *Thalaba* is second in originality only to *The Faerie Queene*.

51. See G. Saintsbury, *Essays in English Literature 1780–1860* (London, 1895), p. 25 f. Saintsbury speaks of 'rhymeless pindarics' and 'that antirhyming heresy which nobody but Milton has ever rendered orthodox'. Byron, in a letter to Thomas Moore dated 27 September 1815, wrote jokingly: 'To have Southey's head and shoulders, I would almost have written his Sapphics.' Southey himself mentioned Collins as his model, whereas Scott in his article on *Kehama* (*QuR*, 9, article 2, February 1811) was reminded of Donne's and Cowley's 'pindarics'.

52. The following elements of the conventional heroic style are to be found in *Thalaba*: absolute participle constructions, ellipsis, Miltonic inversion, anthimeria (use of adjective with an adverbial function), compounds (sometimes periphrastic as in 'the all-perceiving Eye', a 'Methodist' way of speaking of God (which was criticized by Jeffrey in his review of *Madoc* in *ER*, 13, article 1, October 1805); many examples of Miltonic syntax (which were criticized by Scott in his review of *Kehama* in *QuR*, 9, article 2, February 1811) and even one classical allusion to Orpheus and to a 'Thracian shepherd' (*Thalaba* VI, 21); biblical language such as the tautological repetition and anaphora frequent in the Prophets and Psalms.

53. Archaic verb forms such as *spake, sate, bare*; epanalepsis, internal rhyme, repeated exclamations and rhetorical questions. Most of these stylistic devices are also to be found in neo-classical heroic diction, but in combination with Southey's metre they often acquire an unmistakable ballad tone. This is particularly the case where an iambic or anapaestic tetrameter is followed by a trimeter:

> On ... on ... with swift and steady pace
> Adown that dreadful way,
> The dogs are fleet, the way is steep,
> The sledge goes rapidly ...
> (*Thalaba* XI, 19)

The avoidance of rhymes in such metrical 'ballad stanzas' has a particularly frustrating effect when such passages are followed by a longer unrhyming line: here – and indeed all through the poem – the ear recognizes conventional rhythmic and stylistic nuclei but is baffled when its expectations are thwarted by a heterogeneous continuation.

54. Dialogues with speech-headings are to be found in both *Thalaba* and *Kehama*. In one case – *Thalaba* III – a dialogue is written wholly in iambic pentameters. In a letter to Wynn of 5 April 1799 Southey speaks of a 'dramatic turn which my thoughts have for some time taken' and says he is contemplating a plan to narrate 'in dialogue, or poems not much longer' historical or other events such 'as would make noble scenes only'. In 1793 – 1802 he wrote five monodramas, and his nine *English Eclogues* of 1799 are written in dialogue form.

55. In the two oriental poems lyrical passages are often highlighted by rhyme, cf. Maimuna's incantatory song in *Thalaba* VIII, 24 – 32, or by metre, cf. the curse in *Kehama* II, 4. Further examples are *Thalaba* II, 28 (anapaests) and *Kehama* XI, 7 – 10 (tetrameter couplets).

56. Cf. the Preface to vol. VIII of the *CE*.

57. Jeffrey called *Thalaba* a 'versified notebook of excerpts' and ascribed its tediousness to the fact that so large an amount of 'poetical material taken from d'Herbetot, Sale, Volney et al.' was bound to destroy the proportions of the story (*ER*, 1, article 8, October 1802).

58. Southey's unwillingness to consider the civilizations he wrote about without prejudice is evinced by the following sentences: 'The plan upon which I proceeded in Madoc was [to represent] the most remarkable religion of the New World such as it was, a system of atrocious priest-craft' (Preface to vol. VIII of the *CE*). 'The religion of the Hindoos is of all false religions the most monstrous in its fables, and the most fatal in its effect' (Original Preface to *The Curse of Kehama*). Of the ornamental illustrations in Persian manuscripts he said that they were 'as absurd to the eye as nonsense-verses to the ear' (footnote to *Thalaba* I, 13, v. 1). He disparaged Firdausi's *Shahnameh* as a bad poem not worthy to be compared with the *Iliad* and blamed the *Arabian Nights' Entertainment* for its 'metaphorical rubbish'. That he showed no understanding for the 'monkish' Middle Ages becomes evident in several of his ballads and metrical tales written between 1798 and 1829.

59. See the *Age of Wordsworth*, p. 208 f.

60. Ibid.

61. In his Preface to vol. IV of the *CE* Southey protested against being called a Lake Poet and denied that he had any affinity with Wordsworth. In the eyes of the public however he was a Laker.

62. There had been only a few earlier attempts to write 'oriental poetry', such as Collins' *Persian Eclogues* of 1742 – 57 and three similar poems by Chatterton. For further information see McFarland, p. 8, note 3.

63. In spite of Southey's alleged indifference to the success of his works some passages in his letters tell quite a different tale: cf. his letters to Wynn of 30 December 1804 and of 11 June and (?) July 1808; to Hill of 2 February 1811; to T. Southey of 5 December 1812 and of 5 January 1815; and to Landor of 3 January 1819. In a letter to T. Southey of 15 January 1798 he expressed a hope that the proceeds from his next publication would enable him to furnish a house – 'for I greatly dislike lodgings' – and adds that 'This desire has already led me to write sometimes in poetry what perhaps otherwise would have been in prose.' Further

financial speculations of Southey's in connection with his work are to be found in letters to Wynn (of 24 January 1800 and 11 June 1808) and to C. Danvers (of 28 March 1801).

64. In the *ER*, 24, article 11, February 1811, Jeffrey approved of the rough outlines of the story in *Thalaba*: it suited the fairy-tale character of the poem quite well, whereas in *Kehama*, which posed as a real epic, the childish tawdriness, which reminded Jeffrey of rococo grottoes, gave the lie to the author's high ambition.

65. In both the Preface and the last lines of the Proem of *A Tale of Paraguay* Southey defends his choice of a shorter narrative form in this tale, 'where Truth and Nature lead my way', 'in quest of no ambitious height' or 'desultory flight'.

66. In many of his letters Southey discussed questions of metre, e.g. his letters to Bedford of 21 December 1820; to the Reverend Herbert Hill of 5 February 1811, where he discusses the suitability of the hexameter for heroic poetry; and to Landor of 14 August 1820. To T. Southey he writes on 5 December 1812: 'My irresolution as to the choice of a suitable metre [for his story of *Oliver Newman*] is very silly, for at last chance rather than choice decides it, and the poem is in that form into which the commencement happens to run when it is poured out.'

67. As late as 1805 Southey contemplated writing a poem about the Flood, 'pitched in a higher key than *Madoc*' (letter to Miss Barker of 6 June 1805). The plan was superseded by the composition of *Roderick*, originally called *Pelayo*.

68. Jeffrey included neither this nor his other two disparaging reviews of Southey's works in his *Contributions to the Edinburgh Review* (London, 1844). Whether he had changed his opinion or Southey's poems were already completely forgotten at that time is difficult to decide. Tactful respect for the recently deceased Poet Laureate is the most likely explanation.

69. The article 'Lights and Shadows of Scottish Life' in *BM*, 65, June 1822, confirms that Southey's narrative poems were still 'a favourite with young men with a classical taste'. Oxford and Cambridge undergraduates would read him eagerly; but they would sell the heavy volumes after their exams and forget those youthful amusements.

70. This is not very likely. Southey had already mentioned the subject in 1805 in a letter to Landor (27 September) and his monodrama *La Cava*, which deals with the same subject matter, was written as early as 1802. *Roderick* was begun in 1809 (see Preface to vol. IX of the *CE*). Its more sober character proceeds from the high seriousness of the historic subject. The exclusion of all miracles is a consequence of the author's Protestant convictions.

71. Both Landor's drama *Count Julian* (1812) and Scott's *The Vision of Don Roderick* (1811) deal with Southey's hero, but neither of these works arouses as much sympathy in the reader. Enthusiasm for Spanish subjects was widespread at the time owing to English admiration for the heroic struggle of the Spaniards and the Portuguese against Napoleon. In Southey's case there was an additional incentive: he had visited the Iberian peninsula twice in 1795–8 and in 1801, and had translated several works of Spanish literature.

72. Cf. his Introduction (of 1830) to *The Lay of the Last Minstrel*.

73. The metre and the initial stanza of *Queen Mab* clearly show the influence of *Thalaba*; it also makes itself felt here and there in *Alastor*. See also p. 186.

74. Cf. Dixon, p. 289.

75. Ibid.

76. Ibid.

77. Cf. *English Bards and Scotch Reviewers*, vv. 127 and 195 – 230 and the footnotes to the latter passage in Murray's edition of *The Poetical Works of Lord Byron* (London and Leipzig, 1860), also *Hints from Horace*, vv. 155 ff. and 197 ff. and 'Some Observations upon an Article in Blackwood's Magazine no. XXIX of 15th March' by Byron. For an approving remark about Southey's work, see Byron's letter to T. Moore of 10 January 1815 as well as his reaction to Southey's *Roderick* as reported by Murray in a hand-written memorandum: 'he thought it one of the finest poems he had ever read' (see E. H. Coleridge's edition of the *Works of Lord Byron*, London, 1900). That Byron constantly associated Southey with the epic is also proved by the first stanza of the Dedication of *Don Juan*, v. 5, where he addresses Southey as 'My Epic Renegade!'.

4. The establishment of the genre

1. A great deal of material documenting Scott's enthusiasm for anything medieval is to be found in Lockhart's *Life of Scott*. Lockhart also indicates some of the motives behind it: the family history of the Scotts, the enthusiasm the boy Walter showed for ballads and old border stories, his gift for narration even as a schoolboy and his keen study of all available sources of Scottish history. For a summary see H. A. Beers, *A History of English Romanticism in the Nineteenth Century* (New York, 1898, 1901), chapter 1.
2. Cf. pp. 61f., 69 and note 34 on p. 245. Apart from his medieval models, modern ballads, and *Christabel*, Scott already knew Southey's *Thalaba*. The extensive metrical freedom of this poem may have confirmed him in his own metrical experiment. He was however too firmly rooted in the neo-classical tradition and too keen on creating a 'medieval' impression to adopt Southey's rhymelessness. He preferred Dr Johnson's poems to any other English poetry and Miss Cranston, at whose suggestion he had written his translation of Bürger's *Lenore* in 1796, detected in it nuances of Burns and Gray. The extent to which Scott's style – under the romantic varnish – was indebted to neo-classical models has been shown by T. Larsen in his article 'The Classical Element in Scott's Poetry', *Transactions of the Royal Society of Canada* (1938).
3. Scott apparently saw no difference between the ballad and the romance as genres. It is not easy to decide what meaning he attributed to the word romance. Oliver Elton in his *Survey of English Literature 1730 – 1830*, (London, 1924) I, p. 297 traces the transformations of Scott's conception of romance: originally a synonym for ballad it gradually came to include the medieval lay and tale in verse, Scott's own verse romances and finally the novel. The lack of a precise distinction is discernible, even in his own poetry. The homeliness of the ballad, which after all is completely absent from the longer medieval romances (at least the courtly ones), pervades all Scott's verse narratives and the majority of his motifs come from ballad rather than from romance tradition. According to Elton this is even true of his historical novels, for instance *The Bride of Lammermoor*. It was through the ballad that Scott approached the metrical romance and this derivation is constantly revealed. Scott's later view of the history and meaning of the term romance is to be found in his *Essay on Romance* of 1823.
4. For the many influences on Scott's romances see T. Larsen, *passim*, and F. W. Stokoe, *German Influence in the English Romantic Period* (Cambridge, 1926), who devoted a whole chapter to Scott, pp. 61 ff. Goethe's *Goetz von Berlichingen*, a play

that Scott had translated in 1799, might have led Scott away from the fantastic unreality of the Gothic novels and tales of wonder towards a more realistic 'romance of history' (see R. P. Gillies, 'Recollections of Sir Walter Scott', *Fraser's Magazine*, September 1835, in book form, London, 1837).

5. This seems to be the case with both English and German versification. Twenty years before Scott's *Lay*, in the Preface to his 'medieval' verse romance *Geron der Adelige*, the German poet Wieland rejected the tetrameter couplet 'in which nearly all the poetry of our old masters and minnesingers is written', because he considered its use in modern poetry better suited to comic narrative and hence incompatible with the dignity of his serious subject matter. In 1813 Byron, when he wrote his *Corsair*, also rejected the tetrameter couplet in favour of the heroic couplet. His reason was, as he wrote in the dedication letter to Thomas Moore, 'the fatal facility of the octosyllabic verse', over which 'Scott alone, of the present generation, has hitherto completely triumphed'. Meanwhile Scott had of course overcome his earlier doubts and written *The Lady of the Lake* and *Rokeby* almost entirely in tetrameter couplets.

6. In the Introduction to the *Lay* of 1830 Scott oddly enough speaks of 'heroic hexameters with all the buckram and binding which belong to them of later days'. He probably did not mean the comparatively rare use of the classical hexameter for heroic poetry in English (in a letter to Hill of 5 February 1811 Southey described his own use of it as absolutely new). Did Scott use the term 'heroic hexameter' for the heroic couplet of the neo-classical epics?

7. A number of older English and American critics extol Scott's 'Homeric spirit', among others Palgrave, Osmond, Hutton, Herford, Beers, Shairp and Dixon. Scott himself, however, made a clear distinction between epic and romance, see his Introduction to *The Bridal of Triermain*.

8. Dixon, p. 282.

9. The most characteristic features of 'the Scott verse music' are described by Larsen and by W. Franke in his Berlin thesis of 1909, *Der Stil in den epischen Dichtungen Walter Scotts*.

10. Cf. Dixon, p. 287. A previous chapter in this book (on Southey) tried to prove how detrimental a discrepancy between the high-flying intentions of a poet and his limited talent can be to his reputation. The reactions of the critics and the public to *Thalaba* may have confirmed Scott in his 'modesty'. On the other hand the example of Coleridge, who abandoned his attempt to complete *Christabel*, proves that an excess of scruples and a strong dependence on sublime inspiration are not very conducive to the creation of lively romances.

11. In Scott's tales fighting is presented as a mixture of political necessity, sport, adventure, affairs of honour and rowdiness. The questionable side of the thoughtless displays of aggression and readiness to kill is never considered. Had his feelings been more delicate, he could not have revived the romance genre (as he saw it). With an attitude to war such as that reflected in Wordsworth's *White Doe*, a narrative poet was unlikely to flourish in those Napoleonic days. By comparison Scott's 'military music' has an undeniable verve which makes the thrill of fighting understandable even to readers who are entirely out of sympathy with single combat and war. The battle scenes in *Marmion* (Canto VI) stirred the hearts of many Regency and Victorian bourgeois readers, people who had never wielded a weapon and would have run away terrified from the sight of a real medieval battle.

12. *ER*, 11, article 1, April 1805.
13. *ER*, 23, article 1, April 1808.
14. See p. 105.
15. E. M. Forster, speaking of *The Antiquary* in his *Aspects of the Novel* (London 1927, 8th edn, 1947), p. 46 ff., somewhat maliciously described the surefire success of Scott's manner of telling stories; and yet Scott's own opinion of his gift for narration is quite similar, as appears from an entry in his *Journal* for 18 October 1826: 'There is one way to give novelty: to depend for success on the interest of a well-contrived story. But woe's me! That requires thought, consideration – the writing out a regular plan or plot – above all the adhering to one – which I never can do, for the ideas rise as I write, and bear such a disproportionate extent to that which each occupied at the first concoction, that (cocksnows!) I shall never be able to take the trouble.' This, of course, refers, as does Forster's ironic remark, to Scott's novels, yet it also applies to his metrical romances. See also Scott's self-criticism in the anonymously published review of his own earlier novels in *QuR*, 33, January 1817. Both passages are quoted in Elton, I, p. 450.
16. 'Preface to A Review of the Chronicles of the Canongate' in *BM*, 132, November 1827.
17. E. M. Forster, p. 35.
18. Lockhart reports that Scott made a thorough study of the landscape and vegetation of the places where his stories are set; once he even timed a ride on horseback from one particular place to another so as to be sure of being factual.
19. In a letter to Captain T. Southey of 5 January 1815, Southey comments on Scott's newly acquired conciseness as well as his greater skill in interpolating lyrical passages in *Rokeby* and *The Lord of the Isles*: 'Scott no longer provokes you in the midst of his story with a string of ballads and songs: what little there is of this is properly and necessarily introduced.'
20. Cf. p. 107 ff.
21. *ER*, 11, article 1, April 1805.
22. Scott's assertion that he had neither the intention nor the ability to make his romances compete with the classical epics is not yet as clearly expressed in the introductory epistles prefixed to the cantos of *Marmion* as it is later in *The Vision of Don Roderick* (I, 3) or in the Introduction to *The Bridal of Triermain*, but it is implied in several passages. Like all Scott's long poems, *Marmion* is interspersed with phrases such as 'my rugged rhyme', 'the desultory song', 'the unpremeditated lay' (compare however *Paradise Lost* IX, 24: 'my unpremeditated verse'). These stereotyped expressions of modesty are of course *topoi* of the *exordium* in classical rhetoric. But phrases such as 'this simple tale', 'my artless lines', 'the careless rhyme' in a pre-romantic work (Beattie's 'The Minstrel') already contain a hint of apology, as though the poet wanted an excuse for his unclassical themes and their 'primitive' handling. This *topos* was passed on through Scott to Byron, whose *Childe Harold* also contains protestations such as 'this lowly lay', 'so plain a tale', 'this too protracted song' and 'inglorious lays'. Both Scott and Byron even surpass this rhetorical modesty by proceeding to personal confessions or justifications; thus in the third introductory epistle in *Marmion* and in the verse Introduction to *Harold the Dauntless* Scott confesses that he is giving way to his love of romance because only this gives him poetic inspiration, even though reason and taste rebel against such frivolities. Byron, in the last but one stanza of *Childe Harold*, apologizes in a very personal way for the inadequacies of his poem:

> Would it were worthier! but I am not now
> That which I have been – and my visions flit
> Less palpably before me

In the introductory epistle to the first canto of *Marmion* Scott, after praising Spenser, Milton and Dryden for their endeavours to re-establish the romance genre, humbly places his own efforts far below theirs:

> Warm'd by such names, well may we then,
> Though dwindled sons of little men,
> Essay to break a feeble lance
> In the fair fields of old romance.

23. Cf. the 1830 Introduction to *Marmion*.
24. In the 1830 Introduction Scott says that he began *Marmion* with the intention of devoting more time than hitherto to the elaboration of this poem, and even though he later on had to hasten its publication, some passages were executed more carefully than had been his wont till then. As far as the versification is concerned, however, that carefulness is hardly discernible: the style of *Marmion* is very similar to that of the *Lay*.
25. Jeffrey's example of Wordsworthian echoes in *Marmion* is taken from Canto IV, line 12:

> And Bishop Gawein, as he rose,
> Said – 'Wilton! grieve not for thy woes,
>   Disgrace and trouble.
> For He, who honour best bestows,
>   May give thee double.

Jeffrey was surely thinking of Wordsworth's *The Tables Turned*. (The *trouble/double* rhyme was also ridiculed by Byron in the passage on Wordsworth in *English Bards and Scotch Reviewers*, see V, 239 f.). For Jeffrey's critique of *Marmion* see *ER*, 23, article 1, April 1808.
26. Cf. Herford, *The Age of Wordsworth*, p. 192.
27. *Lectures on the English Poets*, p. 155.
28. See note 2, p. 264.
29. In *English Bards*, line 931 ff., Byron asked whether no nobler theme was to be found in Caledonia's annals than 'the wild forays of a plundering clan' and 'Marmion's acts of darkness'. The Muses and Scotland demanded 'a hallow'd harp' and not an outlawed hero who, like a second Robin Hood, 'disgraced the name of man'.
30. See Byron's *Journal* of Wednesday, 24 November 1813: 'Scott is undoubtedly the Monarch of Parnassus, and the most *English* bard.'
31. The story of the publication of *The Bridal of Triermain*, besides being amusing, is very characteristic of the trade of literature when Scott was at the height of his popularity. Scott had this little tale published anonymously in order to find out whether his poems after the *Lay* owed their success merely to his name. The opening of the *Bridal* had already appeared – also anonymously – in the *Edinburgh Annual Register*, of which he was one of the founders. This fragment was said to have been intended originally as a pastiche of Coleridge (there is an obvious similarity between its framework and Coleridge's poem *Love*), but because of the even more obvious translucence of Scott's own style it was taken for an imitation of his poetry. Scott seems to have fallen in with this misapprehension when completing the poem: he executed it as an 'imitation of Scott' and had it published

in 1813. In order to add to the mystification he even spread a rumour – not without apprising the person concerned – that William Erskine (the later Lord Kinedder) was the author, and he encouraged this rumour by writing the Introduction in the manner of Erskine, who was reputed to be a good classical scholar, and by including two quotations in Greek, when everybody knew that he himself had hardly any knowledge of that language. The deception was successful, and only when the third edition was about to be issued (the second had appeared in 1817, together with Scott's *Harold the Dauntless*) did Erskine reveal the name of the real author. On reading the reviews in the *QuR*, 18, July 1813, and in *BM*, 1, April 1817 we can imagine what fun Scott must have got out of this successful mystification. *QuR* calls the *Bridal* unoriginal, and good only in those passages in which it follows Scott closely; it finds the comic parts affected but the tone more elegant than in Scott's work. *BM* shows surprise that an exact imitation of Scott, which one would have though impossible, should be successful; the *Bridal* was undoubtedly weaker than Scott's own poems, but its author had come closer to the original than all other imitators (the names mentioned here are Byron and Wordsworth). These details are related here for two reasons: first because Scott seems from then onwards to have acquired a taste for publishing anonymously, which he continued to do when he abandoned the verse romance for the novel; and second because our assessment of his Introduction to the *Bridal* – a text that of all Scott's theoretical pronouncements contains the most interesting reflections on the genre of his metrical tales – will have to take into account the fact that Scott here spoke through the mouth of a different person.

32. The *QuR* praised the characterization of Wilfrid in *Rokeby* as particularly original and lifelife: Scott had here succeeded, without the usual idealization, in arousing sympathy for a character that until now had always been treated as ridiculous in literature: the melancholy lover who is ousted by a more dashing rival (see *QuR*, 16, article 12, December 1812).

33. See *Narrative of the Life of Sir Walter Scott* (Everyman Edition, London, 1906), p. 235.

34. Jeffrey considered *The Lord of the Isles* too polite to the British, too void of the buoyant national enthusiasm that should support such a poem (see *ER*, 48, article 1, February 1815).

35. *QuR*, 26, article 1, July 1815.

36. Like Ellis, Jeffrey interpreted the more serious and historically orientated *Lord of the Isles* as an abortive invasion of the territory of the epic. He even called it a 'modern epic' and found it 'monotonous like all heroic-tragic and sublime things'. In his opinion Scott was more at home in the lighter genres. And like Ellis, Jeffrey disapproved of the imbalance of the historical and fictional parts of the poem (see *ER*, 48, article 1, February 1815).

37.   Be cheer'd, 'tis ended – and I will not borrow,
    To try thy patience more, one anecdote
    From Bartholine, or Perinskiold, or Snorro.
    Then pardon thou thy minstrel, who has wrote
    A Tale six cantos long, yet scorn'd to add a note.

James Hogg of *The Poetic Mirror* and the authors of the *Rejected Addresses* could not have done better.

38. *BM*, 1, April 1817.

39. Scott clearly realized the damage that might accrue to English poetry and taste from his careless versification and style if both were to be imitated by others.

In his (anonymous) review of Campbell's *Gertrude of Wyoming (QuR*, 2, article 1, May 1809) he even warned young poets against himself: a further example of his love of mystification. Having first criticized Campbell's style as 'overlaboured' and patronizingly told the author of *Gertrude* that the majority of his readers did not appreciate a refined poetic technique because they always favoured the 'forward and bold', he checked himself and continued: 'Let no reader suppose that we recommend to imitation that indiscreet and undaunted precipitation with which another popular poet is said to throw his effusions before the public.' That man's slovenliness, he writes, is dangerous because it attracts young novices and encourages them to flood the world with rhapsodic romances full of faulty grammar and vulgar inversions which will ruin the taste of the reading public.

40. See Introduction to *Rokeby*, 1830.

41. See p. 186 f. With the condescension of the expert, Southey writes to Landor on 5 June 1811: 'Scott, you see, is writing up Rodrigo. I am curious to see his poem: there will be a good deal of splendour in it, no doubt, but Visions are difficult things to handle.'

42. Two years before Scott's *Roderick* an anonymous 'Poem' in the Scott manner, *The Battle of Talavera*, had had Wellington for its hero. The reviewer of the *QuR*, 4, November 1809, felt reminded of the sixth canto of *Marmion* because of metrical similarities.

43. The critics were unanimous in their opinion of Scott's *Roderick*. Jeffrey called it 'a pantomime in three acts' and 'a romantic vestibule without a palace'; the reason for Scott's failure was that in this topical poem he had had to give up all those things which up to now had made his poetry captivating: suspense, novelty, singularity. The romance elements were nothing but irksome machinery (*ER*, 36, article 6, August 1811). In the *QuR*, 11, article 13, October 1811, W. Erskine was of a similar opinion, although he palliated his harsh verdict by adding a lengthy attack on the principles of Jeffrey's criticism. He conceded the *Vision* the title of an epic, since it contains a plot, suspense, action and pathos.

44. See p. 94 f.

45. See p. 97 f.

46. See notes 34 and 36.

47. *ER*, 21, article 1, August 1810.

48. The following passage from a review of *Harold* and the *Bridal (BM*, 1, April 1817) proves that his contemporaries saw in Scott the principal promoter of the shift from manner to matter in literature:

> The character of Mr. Scott's romances has effected a material change in our mode of estimating poetical composition. In all estimable works of our former poets, from Spenser down to Thomson and Cowper, the plot seems to have been regarded only as good or bad, in proportion to the advantage which it furnished for poetical description: but of late years, one half, at least, of the merit of a poem is supposed to rest on the interest and the management of the tale.

This is then said to be true not only of those people who, spoilt by novel-reading, had always read and judged merely according to the subject matter, but even of the best reviewers: as a result, they now concentrated almost exclusively on logical coherence and probability not only with respect to the plot but also with respect to the descriptive details, at the cost of the aesthetic merits of both form and fancy.

49. The *QuR* commented on the change of taste initiated by Scott (see its review of *The Lord of the Isles* in No. 25, article 1, July 1815): 'Since all that the purchasers of

poetry seem now to insist upon is an interesting story, spirited narrative, and good and picturesque descriptions of visible objects, it cannot be expected that poets should feel very anxious to furnish them with any thing besides.'

50. *Lectures on the English Poets*, p. 155.
51. *The Spirit of the Age*, p. 225.
52. *QuR*, 6, article 16, May 1810.
53. See Schiller's letters *Über die ästhetische Erziehung des Menschen* (1795).
54. See pp. 82 f. and 99 as well as notes 19, 31, 32, 35, 41, 49; see also note 2, p. 264.
55. *QuR*, 27, article 9, October 1815.
56. See note 19, p. 236 and cf. J. T. Taylor, *Early Opposition to the English Novel: The Popular Reaction from 1760 to 1830* (New York, 1943).
57. In the *QuR* article on *The Bridal of Triermain* (18, January 1813), the reviewer comments on the moral view behind Scott's stories: the heroes and heroines of his tales are invariably victorious and are rewarded accordingly; they are thus made worthy of the reader's respect, even if their sentiments are only seldom dwelt upon; the heroes deserve admiration because of their patriotism, the heroines because of their chastity.
58. See p. 103.
59. Scott's readers by no means considered his metrical romances as mere entertainment, even though some contemporary intellectuals were of this opinion (cf. Hazlitt's remarks quoted on p. 105). There were many who extolled Scott as the greatest poet of the period and found in his tales depths that a present-day reader is not likely to see. Christopher North (in his 'Preface to a Review of the Chronicles of the Canongate' in *BM*, 132, November 1827) maintained that Scott had actually tackled the same problems as Wordsworth, he had only approached them by a different route, that of the historical romance. His real subject however was not so much the past as human life in general, and especially the life of the lower classes. In devoting an equal share of warmth and deep feeling to the palace and to the peasant's cottage, he had shown more social sympathy and a fuller understanding of human existence than Crabbe, the Whig poet, with his gloomy pictures of poverty which lacked the most important colour of the poor man's life: the glory of the virtue that shines the brighter for the misery that surrounds it. These remarks were obviously dictated by political sympathies: they read like a belated retort to Jeffrey's opposite view in his review of *The Lady of the Lake*.
60. See p. 42 ff.
61. See, for example, *The Vision of Don Roderick* I, 1:

> Lives there a strain, whose sounds of mounting fire
> > May rise distinguish'd o'er the din of war;
> Or dried it with yon master of the lyre,
> > Who sung beleager'd Ilion's evil star?

In the same poem, I, 3, Scott says that the deeds of Wellington are a subject worthy of a Homer or Milton,

> But we, weak minstrels of a laggard day,
> > Skill'd but to imitate an elder page,
> Timid and raptureless, can we repay
> > The debt thou claim'st in this exhausted age? ...
> > ... a theme ...
> How much unmeet for us, a faint, degenerate band.

62. The fact that Scott never went so far as to make peasants the heroes of his tales – the only hero without a title is Arthur, the protagonist of the framework story of *The Bridal of Triermain* – suggests that in this retrospective remark he may have included Wordsworth and maybe even Crabbe in his concept of 'romantic poetry'.

63. The review of *The Battle of Talavera* (*QuR*, 4, article 4, November 1809) blames the modern poets for their 'apparent apathy ... to the events which pass over them'; this suggests that criticism of the escapism of the modern romancers began soon after their first works had appeared. See also Byron's harsh words about the escapism or quietism of the other poets including Scott (p. 162).

64. See p. 7.

65. See pp. 98 f.

66. *QuR*, 5, article 5, February 1810.

67. Besides pointing out her indebtedness to Scott, Joanna Baillie emphasizes her independence: she did not choose the easy way of the merely entertaining and intoxicating romance, either national or oriental, but decided for the unpopular and dry task of writing a chronicle of real things in which the chronicler raised the historical truth to a higher poetic level by feeling her way into the historical characters, but never falsified it with romantic veils. Her characters are in fact always taken from history: William Wallace, Christopher Columbus, etc.

68. Cf. *ER*, 47, articles 8 and 9, November 1814.

69. The connecting framework is the story of Tommy Puck and his fairy wife. They were separated and locked into mustard pots by Michael Scott, the very magician whose tomb is opened in Scott's *Lay of the Last Minstrel*. They could only be freed if the prettiest maid of Scotland married the cleverest young Scotsman. The story is of course a very free, and a comic, variant of Shakespeare's Oberon and Titania motif, and the interference of Puck, who helps the aspirant to the hand of the pretty Maggie Lauder, favoured by both the heroine and the reader, is also reminiscent of *A Midsummer Night's Dream*. The description of the contest by means of which the cleverest Scot is to be found is more along the lines of Burns: the combatants have to distinguish themselves in tests such as a donkey race, a sack race, a bagpipe and a storytelling competition. These passages – as indeed many other details – prolong the mock heroic tradition, which is also discernible in the description of the approach of the clans to the Fair, which fills the whole of the second canto. There are of course such catalogues of names and lists of Scottish customs in Scott too – Hogg parodies them amusingly in *The Poetic Mirror* – but Tennant's list of the clans is obviously an imitation of the eighteenth-century mock heroic tradition and thus derives from the classical epic catalogue, even if the style and the national colour are reminiscent of Scott. Pulci's *Morgante Maggiore* furnished the motley joyfulness and the verse form: the ottava rima. Tennant preceded John Hookham Frere (alias Whistlecraft) in his use of that Italian model for English narrative; Byron however does not appear to have read Tennant.

70. Wordsworth's Preface to his *Poems* (1815) is a singularly instructive text and a landmark in the history of poetic genres. Having first discussed the classical genres – the 'various moulds' or 'divers forms' – and conceded first place to 'The Narrative', he then gives up this traditional and objective classification for a different one which he considers more important. It is subjective, and it distinguishes types of poems according to the 'powers of mind *predominant* in the production of [the poems]'. It is also an 'organic' classification, based as it is on the 'order of time, commencing with Childhood, and terminating with Old Age,

Death, and Immortality'. Only when a poem does not fit into this double systematization does Wordsworth fall back on names that point to a traditional 'mould' or 'form' (he does so in the case of his Sonnets and Epitaphs and Elegiac Pieces). A no less significant indication of the gradual disappearance of the fixed genres is Wordsworth's habit of presenting some of his narratives sometimes as self-contained tales in verse, and sometimes as elements incorporated into his long philosophical poems (cf. the history of the publication of *The Ruined Cottage, Vaudracour and Julia, The Matron's Tale* and *The Female Vagrant*).

71. See p. 64 f.

72. In a letter to Southey, the 'master of the supernatural', written on 7 April 1819, Wordsworth comments on this *Prologue*, explaining his personal rejection of the spirit world and the fantastic in greater detail. *Peter Bell* was intended to prove that an everyday, and even a low subject was just as capable of arresting the imagination and providing aesthetic enjoyment as exciting stories of ghosts, fairies and genii.

73. See A. C. Bradley, p. 116: 'The martial parts of *The White Doe of Rylstone* are ... uninteresting, if not painfully tame. The former at least they were meant to be'. Bradley as well as H. A. Beers (in his *History of English Romanticism in the Nineteenth Century*, New York, 1901, p. 17) thinks that the same is true of Wordsworth's other martial poems. The description of the crime which is at the centre of *Guilt and Sorrow* only occupies one line (70): of the earlier misdeeds of Peter Bell so little is said that his beating the donkey is felt to be his worst crime, which is no doubt intended by the poet. Wordsworth's treatment of erotic themes is equally tame, as has been remarked by Bradley, p. 112, and H. W. Garrod, *Wordsworth* (Oxford, 1923).

74. C. H. Herford, *The Age of Wordsworth* (London, 1897), p. 163, traces the influence of Scott, not only in *The White Doe*, but also in the framework of Wordsworth's *Song at the Feast of Brougham Castle* (1807) and in the general tone of *The Force of Prayer* (1807) and *The Horn of Egremont Castle* (1806). Scott himself wrote in his *Journal*: 'Wordsworth could be popular if he would – witness the *Feast at Brougham Castle*' (see Beers, p. 19). See also C. B. Bradford, 'Wordsworth's *White Doe* and Related Poems', *MP*, 36 (1938), 59 ff. Wordsworth's capability as an epic poet is discussed in L. Abercrombie, *The Art of Wordsworth* (London, 1952), p. 60 ff., in H. Lindenberger, *On Wordsworth's Prelude* (Princeton, 1963), passim, in H. Kroeber, (pp. 87 ff. and 208 n. 27) and in Brian Wilkie, Chapter 3. Wordsworth expressed his own opinion of the epic in a letter to Southey of 1815, see E. de Selincourt (ed.), *The Letters of William and Dorothy Wordsworth*, III: *The Middle Years* (Oxford, 1937), p. 633). The reception of *The White Doe* seems to have shown Wordsworth his limitations as a narrative poet. Although he considered his poem as 'in conception his best work' he realized that he was not a born storyteller. On 19 April 1808 he wrote to Coleridge: 'I also told Lamb that I did not think the Poem could ever be popular, first because there was nothing in it to excite curiosity, and next because the main catastrophe was not a material but an intellectual one.' In the Prefatory Note to *The White Doe* – in the *Fenwick Notes* of 1834, see A. B. Grosart's Edition of the *Prose Works of William Wordsworth*, (London, 1876), III, p. 122 ff. – the poet discusses at some length the affinities of his poem with Scott's romances, and as late as 1836 he told Justice Coleridge 'he should devote much labour to perfecting the execution of it in the mere business part of [*The White Doe*]'. The most interesting explanation of his intention in this poem is to be found in a letter of 1816 to Archdeacon Wrangham (Grosart, III, p. 123). For a modern opinion of the genre of *The White Doe*, see Kroeber, p. 83 f.

75. A further source is Dr Whitaker's *History and Antiquities of the Deanery of Craven*, which presents the story of the white doe as a real event.
76. The stories suggested by the scholar and the student are the same as those that Wordsworth had told in *The Force of Prayer* and *Brougham Castle*. The source for both was the *History of Westmoreland and Cumberland* by Nicholson and Burn.
77. Wordsworth's message is adumbrated by the verse motto at the beginning of Canto I, 'Action is transitory ...', the first six lines of which were taken from *The Borderers* (l. 1,539 ff.) while the rest was added as late as 1837. Equally relevant to the poem's meaning is the motto to Canto VII, 'Powers there are ...' which the poet took from his *Address to Kilchurn Castle*, written in 1803, and inserted in *The White Doe* in 1837.
78. *ER*, 50, article 4, and *QuR*, 27, article 10, both October 1815.
79. *BM*, 16, 'On the Lake School of Poetry I', July 1818.
80. This objection was often made to longer romantic verse narratives. Jeffrey had made it in his discussion of Scott's *Marmion* in 1808 and Southey, usually Jeffrey's opponent, had adopted Jeffrey's view in a letter to Wynn of July 1808. Did a narrative poem of over 1,000 lines in length inevitably lead the critics to associate it with the classical epic and did they resent the fact that neither Scott nor Wordsworth was willing to fulfil the requirement of the traditional genre that it be a 'combined and regular narrative' in the traditional sense?
81. Jeffrey's attacks against Wordsworth in the *ER* are to be found in the following articles: No. 1 of October 1802 (on Southey's *Thalaba*); No. 23 of April 1808 (on Wordsworth and Crabbe); No. 38 of November 1814 (on *The Excursion*) and No. 50 of October 1815 (on *The White Doe*).
82. Vol. III, *The Romantic Age*, p. 110–20.
83. McFarland, p. 383.
84. *QuR*, 23, article 5, October 1814.
85. *BM*, 185, September 1831.

5. 'The postscript of the Augustans'

1. See Byron's letter to Moore of 2 February 1818.
2. This remark of Goethe's was recorded in a letter written by J. Guillemard, an Englishman who visited Goethe on 29 July 1829; see W. Beattie, *The Life and Letters of Thomas Campbell* (London 1850), III, p. 441.
3. Scott thought that Campbell's *The Pleasures of Hope* combined 'the sweetness of Goldsmith with the strength of Johnson' and was as far removed from a servile imitation of neo-classicism as from the 'babbling and jingling simplicity of ruder minstrels'. By the latter he obviously meant himself and his 'school'. See his review of *Gertrude of Wyoming* in *QuR*, 2, article 1, May 1809.
4. This is mentioned in Scott's review (see note 3 above).
5. See H. M. Fitzgibbon's Introduction to his edition of *Gertrude of Wyoming* (Oxford, 1891) p. 1, note 1, where a list of parallels with *Atala* is given. An exhaustive study of this particular question was published by Albert M. Bierstad in *JEGP*, 20 (1921), 491–501. Beattie, whose biography of Campbell contains various details concerning the composition of *Gertrude*, does not mention Chateaubriand.
6. *Barneck und Saldorf* is Vol. II of Lafontaine's *Familiengeschichten* (Frankfurt, Leipzig, Berlin, 1804). Beattie was the first to draw attention to this borrowing and quoted the pages of the novel in question in his biography. The passage corresponds to *Gertrude*, I, 15–20.

7. *Lectures on the English Poets*, p. 149.
8. Leigh Hunt, *Sketches of the Living Poets*, No. 3; *The Examiner* of 21 August 1821, pp. 506 – 8; also in L. H. Houtchens, *Leigh Hunt's Literary Criticism* (New York, 1956), p. 159 ff.
9. *QuR*, 2, article 1, May 1809, see note 39, p. 253.
10. Quoted in Fitzgibbon's Introduction (see note 5 above).
11. *ER*, 27, article 1, April 1809.
12. *Lectures on the English Poets*, p. 325.
13. *Spirit of the Age*, p. 325 ff.
14. See E. H. Coleridge's edition of *The Works of Byron* (London, 1898), I, p. 429.
15. Pope, *Imitations of Horace*, 'The First Epistle of the Second Book of Horace', l. 280 f.
16. Quoted from John Murray's edition of *The Poetical Works of Lord Byron* (London and Leipzig, 1860).
17. Here and elsewhere the quotations from Byron's *Letters and Journals* are taken from Leslie Marchand's edition (New York and London, 1973 – 82).
18. See Campbell's footnote to this stanza, where he quotes two-and-a-half pages from Isaac Weld's *Travels through the States of North America* (London, 1799), II.
19. It is probably Campbell's lack of skill at rounding off a Spenser stanza with a convincing Alexandrine which made George Saintsbury write (in his *History of English Prosody*, III, p. 90: 'The Spenserians of *Gertrude* ... are among the least successful effects in that great metre made by any poet who has done elsewhere really good things.'
20. *Spirit of the Age*, p. 328.
21. Ibid., p. 327.
22. *Lectures on the English Poets*, p. 149.
23. *BM*, 96, January 1825, criticized the unpoetic sentimentality of the subject, which had more in common with material for a women's magazine than with Byron's passionate and Wordsworth's tranquil humanity; the review also identified certain 'Cockneyisms' in the poem – obviously out of political spite directed at the Whig poet Campbell. In its first number of 1825 the *QuR* was no less harsh in its judgement. Even Jeffrey, while praising the profound tranquillity of *Theodric* – something he had not appreciated at all in Wordsworth's *White Doe* – and trying to defend the poem, could not help noting its rather unpoetical character and the improbability of its content. Thus all three periodicals, though differing in the degree of censure according to their political bias, agreed that *Theodric* was much weaker than *Gertrude* and that such sentimental transformations of neo-classical 'domestic poetry' into romantic verse narrative stood no chance of success with the public in the age of Scott, Byron and Wordsworth.
24. There is an interesting passage in a letter Southey wrote to Landor on 3 January 1819 about the aridity of neo-classical poetry as it went into decline at the end of the eighteenth century, and the sudden abundance of minor poets in England who all cultivated the kind of verse narrative inaugurated by Scott. Southey begins his letter by praising Wordsworth as a poet and thinker of rare quality. Before him England had only had one genius to match him: Milton (since Shakespeare belonged to a different class). He continues: 'Of all inferior degrees of poets no age and no country was ever so prolific as our own: every season produces some half dozen poems, not one of which obtains the slightest attention, and any of which

would have made the author celebrated above all contemporaries five-and-twenty years ago.'

25. Jeffrey's review of *Thalaba* (*ER*, 1, article 8, October 1802) is a source of information about the relationship thought to exist between romanticism and revolution. Here the moral character of the Lake Poets is considered to be thoroughly revolutionary: these poets are said to be against the existing political order, against civilization, against everything that had up to now protected and guaranteed the existence of society – prisons, the gallows and the workhouse. To them these institutions only meant oppression. People who had offended (but only the poor amongst them) were exonerated and the blame was laid entirely on the institutions; the whole movement was in addition pacifist. If culprits had to be found they were invariably members of the wealthy and ruling class. This attack against the Godwinism of the young Lakists is all the more significant for coming from the pen of a confirmed Whig.

26. The tetrameter stanzas at the beginning of Rogers' *Columbus* are said to be the inscription on the old Spanish manuscript from which the author pretends to have translated the poem. Appended to the fragments is a fictitious translation and synopsis of a poem 'written in the romance or ballad measure of the Spaniards' with which the manuscript is said to conclude. It tells of a visit by Cortés and Pizarro to a memorial for the deceased Columbus, where both pay homage to their forerunner. As an equivalent for the Spanish ballad measure Rogers chose Scott's free narrative metre.

27. The Original Preface to *Columbus* places more emphasis on the universal significance of the subject matter – the hero's virtue and divine mission, the 'most memorable voyage in the annals of mankind', etc. – than the Preface to the second edition. Here Rogers even deemed it necessary to defend the 'romantic' elements, which he had after all introduced deliberately, as the extravagant consequences of the early sixteenth-century belief in miracles.

28. This sentence from the second edition of *Columbus* is further clarified by a remarkable footnote. In it Rogers declares that romantic subjects taken from modern times – 'however wild and extravagant' – are perfectly suitable provided the action takes place in exotic countries. In defence of this 'daring' opinion he quotes from Racine. It is just possible that Byron – who adopted the fragmentary form for his first oriental tale, *The Giaour*, and dedicated that poem to Rogers, whom he admired – was first inspired to write his 'modern' and exotic romances by that footnote.

29. In a note on the last couplet of *Columbus*, Rogers defends the fragment form with a mixture of romantic and neo-classical arguments. He points out the charm of the fragments of old tapestries and of reflections in water that are broken and jumbled up as in a kaleidoscope by the stroke of an oar, and expresses a hope that the reader's imagination will fill the gaps better than the poet would have been able to do. Towards the end of the note, however, Pliny the Elder is quoted to prove that with the ancient Greeks fragmentary works often became more popular than complete ones.

30. Campbell's borrowings are sometimes literal quotes: the most famous line about earthly pleasures in *The Pleasures of Hope*, 'like angel visits short and far between', was in fact taken from Blair's *The Grave*, and in *Gertrude* Scott found borrowings from Burns and Leyden (see *QuR*, 2, article 11, May 1809). In Rogers' *Columbus* there are literal borrowings from Dante, Tasso and Milton, acknowledged in

footnotes. The verse has a Miltonic ring: the heroic couplet is given a certain freedom by frequent run-on lines, and syntax and diction are also often Miltonic (inversions, the use of relative pronouns to link sentences, litotes, etc.). An unclassical idiosyncrasy which occurs in Rogers' two verse narratives and is also frequent in Southey is the extensive use of punctuation – dashes, dots and exclamation marks – for the purpose of dramatic emphasis.

31. *ER*, 23, October 1813.
32. *QuR*, 17, March 1813.
33. Cf. the conclusion to this book, *passim*.
34. *Jacqueline* is in three parts and is no longer than 350 lines. It is written in the irregular metre which Byron, following Scott's example, had developed for his *Giaour* and *Bride of Abydos*; Rogers did not however adopt the stanzaic division of Byron's verse.
35. The *QuR* (21, article 11, July 1814) found it incomprehensible that this 'highly refined but somewhat insipid pastoral tale' should be linked with Byron's *Lara*, but nobody else seems to have noticed the difference in quality; most readers thought Southey was the author of *Jacqueline*, which shows how interchangeable the style and manner of these minor poets were. Murray made a considerable sum of money with this volume.
36. See Byron's letter to John Murray of 15 September 1817.
37. *BM*, 31, October 1819.
38. In addition to *The Missionary* there were other verse romances that dealt with foreign missions, such as Southey's *Tale of Paraguay*; Montgomery's *Greenland*, however, does not belong to this category as it is almost entirely devoid of narrative elements.
39. See Elton, II, p. 263: 'little more than prize poems'.
40. See the General Preface to his *Poetical Works* (London, 1841).
41. See Southey's review of Montgomery's *Poems* (*QuR*, 12, article 4, December 1811). Here Southey calls this mixing of genres a fundamental error in the planning of the poem, for which all its other merits could not compensate.
42. Percy's *Reliques*, Series I, Book 2, No. 18.
43. *ER*, 18, article 6, January 1807.
44. By playing off the Lake Poets, for whom he had so far shown little liking, against Montgomery, Jeffrey incurred the displeasures of Southey, who in his *QuR* article on Montgomery's poems accused Jeffrey of lack of principle.
45. Montgomery had been a journalist in Sheffield writing under the pseudonym Alcaeus. The 'northern blast' and 'Caledonian gales' are of course Jeffrey's harsh words in his *ER* article. 'Classic Sheffield' refers to Montgomery's lyrical output, which was entirely conventional. Byron was sorry for Montgomery because of the rough treatment meted out to him by Jeffrey. In his note to ll. 418 ff. of *English Bards* (added in 1816) he called him 'a man of considerable genius' and said of *The Wanderer of Switzerland* that it was 'worth a thousand Lyrical Ballads' and at least fifty 'degraded epics'.
46. *ER*, 19, article 14, April 1807.
47. Cf. Bertha Reed, *The Influence of Solomon Gessner upon English Literature* (Philadelphia, 1905). Stockley, p. 306, also mentions several imitations of *The Death of Abel*, one of them being Coleridge's *Wanderings of Cain*. Both Scott and Byron complained of the boredom they had experienced with Gessner's prose poem when it was forced on them at school as instructional reading in their German lessons.
48 *QuR*, 21, article 6, April 1814.

49. North praised *The Pelican Island* warmly in a long article (*BM*, 131, October 1827) although he had had little to say in favour of Montgomery's earlier works, in particular the popular *Wanderer*. His commendation of *The Pelican Island* seems to be genuine even if slightly patronizing. His only criticism concerns the ending: the poet's vigour seemed to slacken the moment Man appeared on the scene and from then on the poem, which had begun as a poetic vision, declined into disagreeable reality.

50. To the modern reader the similarity of the beginning of *The Pelican Island* with comparable allegories in Shelley is rather conspicuous, although after reading a dozen lines the evident discrepancy between the grand visionary stance and the quite innocent content betrays the enormous distance in poetic quality between the work of Montgomery and Shelley.

51. In a letter to J. N. White of 30 September 1808, Southey called Crabbe an 'antithesizer of Goldsmith'. The numerous references to *The Deserted Village* in Crabbe's *The Village* and *The Parish Register*, both 'anti-idylls', prove that Southey had understood Crabbe's intention quite well. Crabbe's 'primitive' villagers are an impassioned rejection of the 'innocent' country life described in eighteenth-century pastoral poetry.

52. Crabbe's attitude to what his contemporaries understood by 'romantic' poetry is a complex subject. In *Ellen Orford* (letter XX of *The Borough*) and in *The Library* (in the last but one paragraph) he repudiates all romantic themes. His ghost story *The Cathedral Walk* (in *Tales of the Hall* of 1819) terminates in a very unromantic anticlimax, while the spiritism in *Lady Barbara; or the Ghost* is demystified by a psychoanalytical explanation (this last story is also one of the *Tales of the Hall*). Whenever the word 'romantic' occurs in Crabbe's works it has the derogatory meaning characteristic of its use in the earlier eighteenth century. The rise of the word to a nobler meaning in the early romantic period appears to be unknown to him: in *The Widow's Tale* (*Tales* of 1812, seventh tale) the phrase 'romantic views' denotes the eccentric snobbery of a sentimental country girl who has been rendered temporarily unfitted for a country existence through a sojourn in town, and in *The Maid's Story* (*Tales of the Hall* XI) the sentimental attachments of young girls are criticized by a realistic mother as 'The bane of our romantic triflers'. In *Belinda Waters* (*Posthumous Tales* 1834, ninth tale) and *The Preceptor Husband* (*Tales of the Hall* IX) he takes the same view of the enthusiasm of silly females for 'romantic' literature as Jane Austen in *Northanger Abbey*. Crabbe's criticism of 'romantic fancies' does not however represent a total rejection, but only a warning to uncritical young people who are not aware of the danger resulting from a blurring of the limit between fancy and reality (for examples of a more objective attitude to the world of romance in both Crabbe's work and life, see Elton, I, p. 48). In a little tale about Harun Alrashid, which forms the conclusion of *The Confident* (*Tales* XVI), Crabbe even pays tribute to the fashion of the 'oriental romance', and from many passages in his work we may infer that in his youth he liked reading Gothic novels and that he was less averse to pure romance than to the pseudo-realism of such sentimental literature as Richardson's novels. See also Kroeber, p. 115 ff. and Lilian Haddakin, *The Poetry of Crabbe* (London, 1955).

53. 'Lights and Shadows of Scottish Life', *BM*, 65, June 1822.

54. See note 66 below.

55. The external structure of *Sir Eustace Grey* is rather similar to that of Shelley's *Julian and Maddalo*: an inmate of a lunatic asylum tells his story to two visitors. Crabbe

may have drawn – as he often did – on personal experience. He does not however treat the story as a social and psychological problem, as Shelley would have done, but as a religious and moral one. Sir Eustace's madness is a consequence of his sin, misdemeanour and self-righteousness, and can only be cured by the consolations of the Christian religion. The same is true of the gypsy's story in *The Hall of Justice*: despite its similarity with some of Wordsworth's poems it is a conventional preacher's example illustrating the contrition of a penitent sinner rather than a 'lyrical ballad' inspired by faith in the indestructible goodness of even the basest human beings. A. Pollard expresses a similar opinion in the Introduction to his edition of *New Poems by George Crabbe* (Liverpool, 1960) and adduces *Hester*, the best piece in his volume as an example. For a more recent detailed discussion of Crabbe's work see New, *George Crabbe's Poetry* (London, 1976).

56. Elton, I, p. 49.
57. Compare p. 140 f.
58. Cf. Edmund Blunden's Preface to his *Life of George Crabbe* (London, 1948), p. xii: 'his cassock haunts his later work in the tendency towards moralizing his tales'; Francis Berry expresses a similar view in *Poet's Grammar: Person, Time and Mood in Poetry* (London, 1958).
59. For the growth of Crabbe's skill as a storyteller see A. Sale, 'The Development of Crabbe's Narrative Art', *The Cambridge Journal* (May 1952), 480 ff.; for his increasing metrical skill see W. C. Brown, *The Triumph of Form: A Study of the Later Masters of the Heroic Couplet* (Chapel Hill, 1948). Crabbe's type of verse narrative differs essentially from Scott's in that it is from the start designed as a 'short story' in verse, as F. R. Leavis pointed out in *Revaluation* (London, 1936), p. 105. He composed it with the compelling logic of a scientific experiment, whereas Scott, although he tried to construct a sound plot with a climactic peripeteia – recognition, solution of the mystery, convergence of the various threads, decisive battle – is prone to improbable coincidences and to stifling the plot by a surplus of details. Scott's tales always, as he knew himself, betray their descent from the old romances with their fairly casual concatenation of adventures. Elton, who called Crabbe's tales 'petty epics' and 'novelettes in heroic couplets' and spoke of the poet himself as a 'novelist in verse', has expressed what other critics have tried to imply by speaking of Boccaccio or Chaucer as Crabbe's poetic ancestors.
60. See *ER*, 40, article 9, April 1812.
61. Ibid.
62. Cf. p. 83.
63. *ER*, 45, article 9, April 1814.
64. See p. 51.
65. *ER*, 31, article 2, April 1810.
66. The romantic poets were constantly reflecting on the strange fact that in poetry pleasure can be derived from sad or painful subjects. Wordsworth pondered over it in works ranging from *The Old Cumberland Beggar* (see ll. 87–105) and the *Ode to Immortality*'s 'soothing thoughts that spring / Out of human suffering' to the quiet submission to God's will in the face of the sad destinies of the buried villagers in the sixth and seventh books of *The Excursion*.
67. *QuR*, 8 article 1, November 1810.
68. The author of the article may have been Gifford, but he cannot be identified with certainty. In his opinion the idyllic insipidity of much neo-classical poetry of the 1890s justified Crabbe's early attempt to counteract it with his crude and

unpleasant description of rural life in *The Village*. This roughness is, however, inexcusable in an age so rich in exciting poetry as the present. Crabbe misapplies his talents and has an erroneous conception of the pleasure that the readers expect to derive from poetry: they do not want poetry to be a mirror of reality but an escape from it: 'that we may take shelter from the realities of life in the paradise of fancy'. This kind of 'legitimate stratagem' is then presented as a psychological necessity; the gods of antiquity owed to it their popularity, maybe even their existence, 'and when that visionary creation was dissolved the same powerful instinct supplied the void with the fays and genii and enchantments of modern romance'. Even painful and sad elements can contribute to the satisfaction of that genuine desire for escape as long as they are imaginary. There are two ways of escape in literature: that of 'fictions of epic and chivalrous romance', which carries us into past or remote worlds, and that of the idyllic presentation of 'rural manners and scenes'. The author grants that certain distortions of our view of the world may result from the romantic beautification of reality or from the romancers' tendency 'to identify the good with the beautiful', but he believes that the experience of the real world and a suitable education will sooner or later correct such errors. They are in any case much less dangerous than a general ban on works of fiction; for a frustration of the legitimate hunger for escape into fantasy must necessarily result in an exploding of that desire in a morally dangerous direction, i.e. in the excesses of a crude sensuality.

69. *BM*, 132, November 1827.
70. See chapter 3, p. 62.
71. Many contemporaries felt that Crabbe's gift for description had more of the painter's than of the narrative poet's art. Hazlitt (in *The Spirit of the Age*, p. 332) and the critics of the periodicals sometimes compared Crabbe with Dutch painters such as Teniers or Hobbema. The reviewer of the *QuR* (8, article 1, November 1810) challenges this view: whereas painting is able to dissolve the objects so that the viewer's interest is directed exclusively to the execution, poetry, which deals with words and their semantic content, cannot do that.
72. Elton, I, p. 55.
73. *Lectures on the English Poets*, p. 98.
74. *The Spirit of the Age*, p. 333.
75. 'In a word, if Mr. Crabbe's writings do not add greatly to the store of entertaining and delightful fiction, yet they will remain ''as a thorn in the side of poetry'', perhaps for a century to come.' (*The Spirit of the Age*, p. 335).

6. Ramification and dissolution

1. Cf. p. 103.
2. As early as 1808, immediately after the publication of *Marmion*, Southey wrote to Wynn: 'There is a buzz of envy beginning against Scott ... unless I am mistaken Scott has killed the goose that laid the golden eggs ... the world are looking for blemishes in *Marmion* as eagerly as they hunted for beauties in the *Lay*.' Sales were however still very high. They dropped noticeably with *Rokeby*: '*Rokeby* certainly was not popular', Southey wrote to Captain Thomas Southey on 5 January 1815, and Byron, looking back in 1821, wrote in his *Journal* of 12 January: 'Scott's poetry ... only ceased to be so popular, because the vulgar learned were tired with hearing ''Aristides called the Just'' and Scott the Best, and ostracised him.' See also pp. 212 ff.

3. Scott's review of *Childe Harold* III in the *QuR*, 31, article 9, October 1816, shows that the earlier 'romantic' poetry he had inaugurated had objectivity as its aim and prided itself on having achieved this. The poets of those earlier years had imitated their classicistic forerunners in following the principle: 'Sine me, liber, ibis in urbem.' The special position of the poet as a man destined 'to make sport by his solitary exertions for escape' and excluded 'from the usual business of life' was in Scott's opinion far from being a modern phenomenon; it had in fact gone out of fashion a long time ago. The irritability of the 'genius irritabile' had decreased considerably since the poets had learnt to curb their excessive enthusiasm. Scott mentions Burns as the only exception; but he ascribes Burns' extravagance to his fate rather than to his genius. He does not mention the more complicated subjectivism of the Lake Poets since he is only concerned with 'private' egotism, i.e., the proneness to self-analysis and confession, which he considers Byron to embody, as the great exception to the general tendency towards reticence of modern poets.

4. See Thilo von Bremen, *Lord Byron als Erfolgsautor: Leser und Literaturmarkt im frühen 19. Jahrhundert* (Wiesbaden, 1977).

5. In his Introduction to the 1830 Edition of *Rokeby* Scott, after talking about the phenomenon of the gradual exhaustion of any genre or manner and explaining some of the reasons why the popularity of his 'school' had been fast decaying since 1812, mentions as an additional reason the appearance of Lord Byron's *Childe Harold* and 'the great chance of his taking the wind out of my sails'. See also the passage from Byron's Ravenna *Journal* of 12 January 1821, note 2 above.

6. In 1820, when Byron had turned to writing classical tragedies his financial success as a writer declined considerably. The article 'Odoherty on Werner' in *BM*, 71, December 1822 states that Byron's cabinet dramas hardly sold any better than any new publications by Southey or Wordsworth; they did not even achieve second-rate success, and Murray was now compelled to advance all the money he had once gained by those 'charming little tales'. See also the first paragraph of Scott's review of *Childe Harold* IV in *QuR*, 27, article 9, April 1818.

7. In a letter to Murray of 20 February 1816 Byron both defended his careless versification and drew attention to the metrical variability of his romances: 'The versification of *The Corsair* is not that of *Lara*; nor the *Giaour* that of the *Bride*; *Childe Harold* is again varied from them; and I strove to vary the last [*The Siege of Corinth*] somewhat from all the others ...'

8. At the beginning of his review of Scott's *The Lord of the Isles* – *QuR*, 26, article 1, July 1815 – George Ellis wrote: 'The works of our modern bards ... are obviously calculated for a much larger description of readers: the characters and sentiments which they contain, the species of interest which they inspire, are, for the most part, level to all capacities.' Byron had doubts about publishing *The Giaour* because the obscurity of the fragmentary narrative and the unfamiliar Turkish names might discourage the readers and prevent their enjoying the tale. See Byron's letters to Lord Holland of 3 April 1813, to Murray of 13 June 1813, to Hodgson of 6 June 1813 and 8 June 1813, to E. D. Clarke of 17 June 1813 and to Moore of 1 September 1813.

9. See Byron's *Journal* of 17 November 1813 and of 15 March 1814 with its modest reactions to all comparisons of Scott's achievement with his own, and also his letter to Coleridge of 27 October 1815.

10. See Byron's letters to Murray of 12 October 1813 and 26 April 1814 (b).

11. See Byron's letter to Murray of 3 February 1816. In the case of Gulnare/Kaled, who follows Lara in the disguise of a pageboy or squire, it is difficult to decide whether Byron adopted the motive from Renaissance literature, where it is frequent, or from Scott, who had first used it in *Marmion* and later repeated it in *The Lord of the Isles* and *Harold the Dauntless*, much to the displeasure of the reviewer of the latter poem, who, in *BM*, 1, April 1817, complained of this 'very affected and unnatural' device, 'now rendered trite by repetition'. The same reviewer states openly that Byron, like many other poets of the day, is an imitator of Scott.

12. See Byron's letters to Murray of 15 September 1817 and to Moore of 2 February 1818.

13. See for instance Byron's letter to Murray of 12 October 1818.

14. *Childe Harold* IV, stanza 40. See also the letter to Murray of 12 October 1813: 'Scott I no further meant to follow than in his *Lyric* measure – which is Gray's – Milton's & any one's who likes it.'

15. See Byron's letter to Murray of 17 September 1817.

16. See Byron's *Journal* of 17 November 1813 and that of 12 January 1821.

17. E.g., George Ellis in his review of *The Corsair* and *Lara* in *QuR*, 21, article 11, July 1814.

18. *ER*, 54, article 2, December 1816.

19. In a letter to W. Miller of 30 July 1811 Byron said of his *Childe Harold* IV that it was written 'on *Ariosto's plan*, that is to say on *no plan* at all'. Scott, when reviewing *Childe Harold* IV in *QuR*, 27, article 9, April 1818, wrote: 'the plan hovers between a descriptive and a philosophical poem'. Jeffrey, in his review of *Childe Harold* III in *ER*, 54, article 1 of December 1816, stated that 'In Lord Byron, the interest of the story, where there happens to be one, which is not always the case, is uniformly postponed to that of the character itself.' G. Ellis objected to the subtitle 'A Romaunt': 'an appellation, perhaps, rather too quaint, but which, in as much as it has always been used with considerable latitude of meaning, and may be considered applicable to all the anomalous and non-descriptive classes of poetical composition, is not less suited than any other title to designate the metrical itinerary we are about to examine here'. It was impossible to know whether Lord Byron had planned *Childe Harold* as an epic. The subject might be suited to such a treatment, had not Homer himself made the travels of Ulysses the subject of a regular and grand composition. But Byron had mismanaged the execution: the hero did not give the work the cohesion promised by the author, nor did the anachronistic medievalism support the epic character of the poem (*QuR*, 13, March 1812). Christopher North, too, felt reminded of Homer: the last scene of *Childe Harold* IV made him think of Achilles who, in the eighteenth canto of the *Iliad*, is, like Harold, found by the side of the ocean – mourning the death of Patroclus. North, however, is not prepared to honour *Childe Harold* with the title of 'a Great Poem', because Byron 'has celebrated no mighty exploit, or event, or revolution in the destinies of mankind, nor brought before us one majestic portion of the history of our species' (*BM*, 14, May 1818).

20. See e.g. Byron's letters to Dallas of 7 September 1811 and to W. Miller of 30 July 1811.

21. See *Childe Harold* I, st. 92 and II, st. 95–6.

22. Byron's letter to Dallas of 11 October 1811.

23. Letter to Dallas of 7 September 1811. In the manuscript version of *Childe Harold*

I, st. 3, line 1 the hero was called 'Childe Buron'; but in the letter of 11 October 1811 Byron disclaimed the title 'Childe of Harrow' for his poem.

24. See also the letter to Dallas of 7 September 1811: 'Before Childe Harold left England, it was his full intention to traverse Persia, and return by India.' Byron did not even omit his 'little page' (Robert Rushton) in the *Adieu*-poem of the first canto.

25. Letter to Dallas of 31 October 1811; see also Preface to *Childe Harold* I and II and the letter to Cawthorne of 30 August 1811: 'I wished to be anonymous but Mr D[allas] teazed me out of it.'

26. In the same letter to Cawthorne, of 30 August 1811, Byron writes: 'the subject being descriptive'.

27. Preface to *Childe Harold* I and II.

28. G. Ellis called Byron's 'moral anatomy of passion' unpoetical while admitting that it helped the simple reader to identify with the events of the narrative (see his review of *The Corsair* and *Lara* in *QuR*, 21, article 11,, 11 July 1814).

29. In an article in *BM*, 60, June 1822 Byron is said to belong to the tradition of confessional literature alongside Montaigne and Rousseau; the reviewer's somewhat drastic words for that tendency in Byron are: 'he was said to have gutted himself body and soul, for all the world to walk in and see the show'.

30. See Byron's letter to Mrs Catherine Gordeon Byron of 7 October 1808.

31. Jeffrey mentioned Chateaubriand's René as a prefiguration of the Byronic hero (in his review of Moore's *The Love of the Angels* and Byron's *Heaven and Earth* in *ER*, 75, article 2, February 1823). Scott points to Cowper (in his review of *Childe Harold* IV in *QuR*, 27, article 2 of April 1818). Before 1818 the surprise at the 'novelty', 'singularity', or 'originality' of Byron's poetry impeded such insights into the web of possible historical affiliations.

32. Scott's perspicacity made him discover the reasons for Byron's success (see his review of *Childe Harold* III in *QuR*, 31, article 9, October 1816).

33. In Jeffrey's opinion the modern poet's discarding of rules and models represented a return to the aesthetics of the Elizabethans: Jeremy Taylor's prose was more poetical than all the epics of his own time or of later epochs. The French School of poetry had interfered with that independence and naturalness, but the moderns were trying to regain it by imitating the Elizabethans (see his review of Henry W. Weber's edition of *The Dramatic Works of John Ford*, *ER*, 36, article 1, August 1811).

34. Owing to both his traditionalist and emotionalist convictions Jeffrey resented the inclusion of topical or political material in narrative poems: that kind of poetry wanted new and extraordinary subjects, but they had to be remote and fabulous (see his review of Scott's *The Vision of Don Roderick* in *ER*, 36, article 6 of August 1811 and his review of *Childe Harold* III in *ER*, 54, article 1, December 1816); in the latter review however he allows Byron to be the only contemporary who has succeeded admirably in writing poetry about topical events such as the battle of Waterloo.

35. *QuR*, 27, article 2, April 1818.

36. See Byron's letter to Murray of 24 November 1818.

37. *QuR*, 22, article 11, July 1814.

38. Review of *Childe Harold* I and II, *ER*, 38, article 10, February 1812.

39. *ER*, 42, article 2, July 1813.

40. *ER*, 45, article 9, April 1814; see also pp. 51 ff.

41. *ER*, 54, article 1, December 1816.

42. As has been shown earlier in this book, Scott did eventually realize that it would be better if modern 'epic' poets abandoned 'the great occurrences of history' and confined their poetry to 'Two or three figures, well grouped' so as to excite 'those sentiments which it is the very purpose of poetry to inspire' (Scott's anonymous Introduction to *The Bridal of Triermain*, 1813). This insight, though in some ways describing his own manner of proceeding, was however overshadowed in his historical verse narratives by his antiquarian interest in battles, pageantry and national history, while on the other hand his ability to compete with Byron in the description of 'those passions which agitate the human heart with most violence' (Introduction to *Rokeby* of 1830) was comparatively limited.

43. An article in *BM*, 66, July 1822 contains a most discerning analysis of the generic characteristics of the contemporary 'dramatic poems' as well as of the motives which made the poets write such works.

44. Byron soon came to realize that he was not a born dramatist. In a letter to Murray of 4 January 1821, i.e., at a time when he had written only one of his classicistic dramas, he wrote: 'many people think my talent *"essentially undramatic"*, and I am not at all clear that they are not right'.

45. Letter to Murray of 9 April 1817: 'You must call *Manfred* "a poem" for it is *no drama.*'

46. See pp. 194 ff. As it is almost unnecessary to point out, with their subjective inspiration the romantics – including Byron – were hardly ever able to create actable stage drama. The novel, however, was also a genre that it was impossible for Byron to adopt, as he says in his Journal of 17 November 1813: 'I began a comedy, and burnt it because the scene ran into *reality* – a novel, for the same reason. In rhyme, I can keep more away from the facts.' Though he wrote this with his affair with Augusta in mind, it is obvious that even later he would have had to give up more of his masks and poses in order to write a novel than would have been compatible with his need for gentlemanly discretion. In addition, Byron lacked the gift of dispassionate analysis which allowed writers like Stendhal or Balzac to compose novels that were both romantic and analytical.

47. Byron refers to his freedom from the bonds of genre in his letter to Hobhouse of 11 November 1818, in which he describes the first book of *Don Juan* as 'as free as La Fontaine and bitter in politics – too – ... when I say *free* I mean that freedom – which Ariosto Boiardo and Voltaire Pulci – Berni – and all the best Italian and French – as well as Pope and Prior among the English permitted themselves'.

48. For significant changes in Byron's narrative technique in the course of his development see Robert Escarpit, *Lord Byron, un tempérament littéraire*, 2 vols. (Paris 1955–7).

49. See Byron's letters to Lord Holland of 3 April 1813, to Lady Melbourne of 31 August 1813, to Moore of 1 September 1813, to Lord Holland of 25 October 1813, to E. D. Clarke of 15 December 1813 as well as the Advertisement and the last footnote to *The Giaour*. For a full account see J. J. McGann (ed.), *The Complete Poetical Works of Byron* (Oxford, 1981), III, p. 414.

50. For a deeper analysis of the frequency of fragments, deliberate or otherwise, in romantic literature see Thomas McFarland, *Romanticism and the Forms of Ruin*, a book dealing with the general 'fragmentation' of experience in the romantic period.

51. Letter to Lord Holland of 3 April 1813; see also the letter to Murray of 13 June 1813. Byron dedicated *The Giaour* to Rogers.

52. The first 167 lines are an elegiac description of Greek landscapes in the author's own voice. The first narrator, a Turkish fisherman, who then takes over, changes from an objective spectator to a passionate partisan of Hassan, and curses the Giaour. After line 787 we hear the fisherman's voice six years after the events of the first half of the tale and in a different country. His inquiry of a monk about the Giaour, who now lives in a convent, leads to the monk's objective tale about the Giaour's solitary gloom in the convent, and this tale is in turn followed by the Giaour's passionate and unrelenting 'confession' (from line 971 onward). See also Kroeber, *Romantic Narrative Art*, p. 140 and McGann (ed.), III, p. 412 f.

53. Letter to Lady Melbourne of 28 September 1813.

54. When in his 1830 Introduction to *Rokeby* Scott pondered the secret of Byron's success and found it in the presentation of 'those passions which agitate the human heart' he made no distinction between the passions of Byron's heroes and those of the poet himself. In his review of *Childe Harold* IV he had still made this distinction. Even though there too he felt that the success of the work was derived from the fact that the protagonist was a 'real' character who clearly stood for the author, he added that Lord Byron had obviously tried to put a check on his self-portraiture and that perhaps Harold was not exactly Byron himself but his masked image, resembling him only as far as the external attributes were concerned – which, of course, Byron had admitted in his Preface, i.e., the dedication letter to Hobhouse of 2 January 1818.

55. See Byron's *Journal* of 14 November and 5 December 1813 and his letter to W. Gifford of 12 November 1813.

56. See in particular stanza 20 of Canto II. These lines are the 'reflection' which Murray had requested Byron to add to Selim's speech: 'eighteen lines in decent couplets, of a pensive, if not ethical tendency' (Byron to Murray on 23 November 1813). The necessitarianism of these lines which interprets Selim's readiness to commit carnage in order to preserve his freedom as a kind of natural law,

> Yet there we follow but the bent assign'd
> By fatal Nature to man's wavering mind …

seems to anticipate the philosophy of *Cain*.

57. See Byron's *Journal* of 10 March (Thor's Day) 1814.

58. Dedicatory letter to Moore of 2 January 1814.

59. *QuR*, 31, article 9, October 1816.

60. See p. 154.

61. See Byron's letter to Moore of 4 March 1822: 'My ideas of a character may run away with me: like all imaginative men I, of course, embody myself with the character while I *draw* it, but not a moment after the pen is off the paper.' See also Byron's *Observations upon an Article in B.M. No. 29, August, 1819* addressed to J. D'Israeli on 15 March 1820: 'I must here observe … that my case, as an author is peculiarly hard, in being everlastingly taken, or mistaken for my own protagonist …'

62. For a detailed discussion of the Byronic hero see P. L. Thorslev, *The Byronic Hero: Types and Prototypes* (Minneapolis, 1962).

63. In an as yet unpublished paper on 'Byron's "Wrong Revolutionary System" and Romanticism' read to the International Byron Seminar held at Trinity College, Cambridge in July 1988. The essay will be included in a volume edited by Andrew Rutherford, which is to be published by Macmillan in 1990.

64. Letter to Murray of 15 September 1817.
65. Letter to Moore of 2 February 1818.
66. See Byron's letter to Murray of 20 September 1821.
67. Letter to Moore of 5 July 1821.
68. See Byron's letter to James Hogg of 24 March 1814.
69. Letter to Moore of 5 July 1821.
70. Letters to Murray of 12 September 1821 and 25 December 1822.
71. Letter to Shelley of 20 May 1822.
72. *Some Observations upon an Article in Blackwood's Magazine* (written 1820).
73. Most clearly by A. Rutherford in *Byron: A Critical Study*, (1961) Sections II, III and VI.
74. This author cannot subscribe to certain modern attempts to reevaluate Byron's *The Island* by interpreting it as an 'allegory' or 'prophecy' of 'man's farthest hopes' and thus to place it in a similar category to Shelley's *Prometheus Unbound*, as does J.J. McGann in *Fiery Dust* (Chicago, 1968), p. 201 f. However it is certainly a semi-ironical settling of affairs with the old Byronic hero (Christian), who is here hurled over a cliff and washed away by the ocean; and it doubtless contains a vision of an earthly paradise, as do many of Byron's narrative works, see R. F. Gleckner, *Byron and the Ruins of Paradise* (Baltimore, 1967), pp. 347 – 50. But is it legitimate, considering Byron's deliberate turning away from the 'wrong revolutionary system' of romanticism after 1817, to see in *The Island* more than a belated indulgence in nostalgic dreams of his happy days in Athens in August 1810, when it was once granted to him to enjoy freedom, love, and aquatics together; and indulgence, too, in his wish to cater to the taste of that section of his public which he had shocked by works such as *Cain* and *Don Juan*? While it most certainly represents wishes on the part of the poet, it looks back to the past – 'the yet infant world' (as the last line of the poem has it) – and not ahead to a Utopian future.
75. Letter to Moore of 25 March 1817. 'Story' or 'romance' seem more acceptable to Byron than 'tale'.
76. The fact that he leaves *Childe Harold* and *Manfred* out of that general condemnation proves that it was mainly the verse romance that he had come to detest; cf. his letters to Murray of 26 April 1814 (!), 6 April 1819 (b) and 24 September 1821 (Postscript). His letters however reflect a growing aversion to almost everything romantic, including the 'mystery' and 'mystification' of the poetry of the Lakists, the 'vulgarity' of the Cockney Poets and also the 'madness', 'sin' or 'Babel' which Scott and he had initiated. Poetry is not a profession but a mere habit or – still worse – the 'effluvia of uneasy minds'. Byron now hates 'things all fiction', denies that poetry ever changes anything, and asserts first that poetry must be based on experience and not on mere imagination, and finally that a commitment to the causes of humanity and freedom should be rated much higher than 'scribbling' or 'sweating poetry' (for references see my paper mentioned in note 63 above).
77. To these longer dramatic monologues should be added the shorter *Prometheus*, written only a few weeks after *The Prisoner of Chillon*.
78. This is the 'count of far and high descent' with whose wife, Theresa, Mazeppa had had an affair, in consequence of which the count had him bound on a wild horse's back.
79. *Byron*, p. 202.
80. P. D. Fleck, 'Romance in Byron's *The Island*', in *The Byron Journal*, 3 (1975), 4 – 23.

81. Letter to Murray of 11 September 1820.
82. Letter to Moore of 2 February 1818; see also the letter to Lord Holland of 17 November 1813.
83. Letters to Murray of 15 September 1817 and 25 January 1819.
84. Letters to Moore of 2 April 1823: 'I am as low in popularity and bookselling as any writer can be'; and to Shelley of 20 May 1822: 'now that I have really composed some things which sh^d "not willingly be let die"', the whole herd snort and grumble and return to wallow in the mire'. See also Byron's letter to J. Hunt of 17 March 1823.
85. Letter to Shelley of 26 April 1821.
86. Letter to J. Hunt of 17 March 1823.
87. Letter to Murray of 25 March 1817. Other letters contain words such as 'corps', 'Grub Street' and 'suburb of Babylon'.
88. Cf. Byron's *Journal* of 23 November 1813 (Tuesday morning).
89. Letter to Moore of 1 June 1818.
90. Letter to J. Hogg of 24 March 1814. See also *Journal* of 23 November 1813 (Tuesday morning).
91. Byron referred to Southey's self-love in the aforementioned letter to J. Hogg (24 March 1814); he accused Leigh Hunt of self-love in a letter to Moore of 1 June 1818 and made a similar accusation of Keats in the letter to Shelley of 26 April 1820.
92. See Byron's letter to Murray of 3 November 1821.
93. Letter to Murray of 2 April 1817.
94. See the entry in Byron's *Journal* mentioned above (23 November 1813, Tuesday morning): 'No one should be a rhymer who could be any thing better – Scott, Moore, Campbell, Rogers – mere spectators', or Byron's letter to Moore of 28 April 1821, which expresses his disappointment at the failure of the insurrection of the Carbonari at Ravenna: 'And now let us be literary; – a sad falling off, but it is always a consolation', etc. As early as 1813 Byron had written in his *Journal* (24 November): '"Action – action", said Demosthenes; "Actions – actions", I say, and not writing, – least of all rhyme. Who would write who had any thing better to do.' In 1820 Byron even suggested that he and Moore found a newspaper, to 'give the age some new light upon policy, poesy, biography, criticism' (see his letter to Moore of 25 December 1820).
95. Letter to R. Belgrave Hoppner of 25 November 1818.
96. Letter to Moore of 14 May 1821 about Keats' '*yielding* sensitiveness' and to Murray of 9 November 1820 on Keats' 'viciously solliciting his own ideas into a state, which is neither poetry nor any thing else but a Bedlam vision'.
97. Letter to Leigh Hunt of 4–6 November 1815 (?).
98. See letters to Murray of 6 April 1819, to Moore of 14 May 1821, to Shelley of 20 May 1822, and to Moore of 2 April 1823. For the decrease in the volume of sales see von Bremen, pp. 18–24.
99. Byron's *Journal* of 23 November 1813.
100. See Gerhart Hoffmeister, *Byron und der europäische Byronismus*, Erträge der Forschung, 188 (Darmstadt, 1983), p. 157 ff. In spite of the unreliability and inaccuracy of these pages on Byron and music, they give an idea of the strength of Byron's influence on the composers of opera. It is incontestable that there were dozens of works based on Byron's metrical tales, in particular works by Italian composers, from Rossini's *The Siege of Corinth* (1826; first performed under the

title *Maometto Secondo* in 1820) to Mascagni's *Parisina* (1913); Donizetti and Verdi were also prominently represented with a *Parisina* by the former (1833) and *Il Corsaro* by the latter (1848). Hoffmeister is surely right in pointing out the influence of the Byronic Hero on such operatic characters as Verdi's desperately bewildered Manrico (in *Il Trovatore*) and – of course – the two protagonists in his *I Due Foscari*.

101. All Keats' letters are quoted from H. Buxton Forman (ed.), *The Letters of John Keats* (Oxford, 3rd edn, 1947/8). Had Keats read the following sentence in Coleridge's *Biographia Literaria*, XIV, published in the same year? 'The reader should be carried forward, not merely or chiefly by the mechanical impulse of curiosity, or by a restless desire to arrive at the final solution; but by the pleasureable activity of mind excited by the journey itself ... at every step he pauses and recedes, and from the retrogressive movement collects the force which again carries him onward.'

102. *ER*, 42, article 2, 2 July 1813.

103. Compare Coleridge, *Biographia Literaria*, XIV: 'a poem of any length neither can be, nor ought to be, all poetry'. Keats and Coleridge arrived at a conclusion which thirty-two years later received its most famous formulation in Edgar Allan Poe's *The Poetic Principle*: ' "a long poem" is simply a flat contradiction in terms'.

104. In a letter to his publishers Taylor and Hessey of 21 March 1818 Keats insists on having *Endymion* designated as a 'Romance' in the title – 'for a romance is a fine thing notwithstanding the circulating Libraries'. He is obviously thinking of the popular prose fiction which had brought the word 'romance' into discredit, but possibly also of the many superficial tales in verse being consumed by the reading public. That he had something much more exalted in mind when he called *Endymion* a romance is borne out by his dedicating the poem to the memory of Chatterton. It was Chatterton rather than Scott whom he considered the true modern continuer of the romance tradition.

105. Keats' attitude to Scott and Byron and their poetry was rather cool. There are, it is true, a few echoes of *The Lay of the Last Minstrel* in *The Eve of St Agnes*, and the tone of both *La Belle Dame Sans Merci* and *The Eve of St Mark* may have been influenced a little by Scott's style, though Coleridge's influence is more likely (see J. C. Jordan, 'The Eve of St Agnes and The Lay of the Last Minstrel', *MLN*, 46 (1928), 38 ff.). Keats' medievalism, to use H. A. Beers' distinction (p. 119) is 'Southern' rather than 'Northern Gothic', being derived from Chaucer, Spenser, Chatterton and Hunt rather than from Scott and his medieval models. As to Keats' attitude to Byron, it changed from an early admiration – expressed in his Sonnet to Byron of 1814 – to an increasing reserve and even disapprobation. Their different opinions on the subject of Pope and the Augustans was one of the reasons. (See Keats' letters to Bailey of 8 October 1817, and to George and Georgiana Keats of 14 February to 3 May and of 16 December to 4 January 1819. In the latter he confesses his total indifference to the 'fashionable slang literature of the day': the works of the 'literary Kings' of his time, Scott and Byron, now seem dead to him.)

   Keats' suspicion that Scott was the author of the hostile *BM* articles 'On the Cockney School of Poetry' (see his letter to George and Georgiana Keats of 23 January 1818) and his indignation at Byron's cynicism in *Don Juan* (reported by Richard Monckton Milnes, Baron Houghten, in *The Life, Letters, and Literary Remains of John Keats*, London, 1848, vol. II and quoted in Sir Sidney Colvin's

John Keats: his Life and Poetry, his Friends, Critics and Afterfame (London, 1917),
p. 496) increased his alienation towards the end of his life.

106. While Keats was planning *Hyperion* he once referred to it as a romance (see his
letter to B. R. Haydon of 28 September 1817), but thereafter always called it
a poem. Another letter to Haydon of 23 January 1818 states what he meant by
poem, by comparison with the romance of *Endymion*: 'in *Endymion* ... you ... have
many bits of the deep and sentimental cast – the nature of *Hyperion* will lead
me to treat it in a more naked and grecian Manner – and the march of passions
and endeavour will be undeviating – and one great contrast between them will
be – that the Hero of [*Endymion*] being mortal is led on ... by circumstance;
whereas the Apollo of *Hyperion* being a fore-seeing god will shape his actions like
one.' Compare also Keats' letter to George and Georgiana Keats of 16 October
1818, written while he was at work on *Hyperion*: 'shapes of epic greatness are
stationed around me'.

NB: In this chapter the genre names are no longer used as normative designations. In order to be able to deal with the dissolution of the traditional genres
which took place in the second generation of the romantics, we use them with
a more extended meaning. Hence we abstain from labelling Keats' two long verse
narratives, preferring to discuss the mixture of features characteristic of the
'archetypal romance' as Northrop Frye has defined it and features characteristic
of the epic, in the sense of an 'interpretation of the world'.

107. The introductory passage of the second book of *Endymion* (ll. 1 – 34) is a poetical
rejection of the heroic world of the epic in favour of the world of romance. In
its defence of private themes (in this case love) and in its repudiation of all heroic
subject matter it resembles Scott's apology of romance in his Introduction to *The
Bridal of Triermain* as well as some passages in Southey's Preface to his *Joan of Arc*.

108. Frye, p. 60.

109. Ibid., p. 52 ff.

110. If Keats' use of myth is called philosophical here, this does not of course mean
that he was consciously illustrating a philosophical system. The romantic myths
he created were free of all abstraction, they were part of his experience as a poet.
Douglas Bush's *Mythology and the Romantic Tradition* was perhaps the first
systematic analysis of the structure and functions of romantic uses of myth. Frye's
more anthropological contribution to this topic (in his chapter 'The Theory of
Modes', pp. 33 – 67), has proved useful in this author's discussion of 'genre' in
romantic poetry at the point where traditional concepts of genre were obviously
no longer adequate. One need not share Frye's dependence on a C. J. Jung type
of psychoanalytical belief in the 'collective unconscious' to acknowledge the
plausibility of his 'system', at least in so far as it helps to define a concept of
romance which covers both the great medieval romances and the verse narratives
of the English romantics. The passage about the origin of myths in Wordsworth's
Excursion (IV, 717 – 62 and 846 – 87), as Leigh Hunt and, in our century, de
Selincourt and Bush realized, stimulated Keats to revive old myths in his poetry
as well as create new ones. In *I stood tiptoe ...* he proposed this to himself as a
task, in *Endymion*, *Hyperion*, the Hermes passage of *Lamia* and the Odes he
provides highly personal examples of romantic mythology or myth-making.

111. Frye, p. 57.

112. The reference to Scott's *Lay of the Last Minstrel* has been inserted here to indicate

the shallowness of Scott's relation to the romance. The 'memory' of a fulfilled life guided by genuine myths has in his poem declined to the sentimental dallying of a cultural historian and antiquarian with his material.

113. Frye, p. 59. Much is to be said for Frye's way of bridging the gap between medieval and romantic romance by equating the quest hero of yore with the romantic poet of the nineteenth century, even though he tends to over-schematize, and skips over all more detailed historical evidence. For a much better documented discussion of the common biblical, neo-Platonic or esoteric roots of certain medieval and romantic 'myths' see M. H. Abrams, *Natural Supernaturalism*, Chapter 3 and *passim*.

114. Frye, p. 59.

115. Frye, p. 60.

116. By 'encyclopaedic tendency' Frye means the poetic endeavours of all ages to arrive at a comprehensive and imaginative interpretation of their 'world' on the basis of the 'central episodic themes' of their time. This concept thus corresponds roughly to the idea of the epic as defined at the beginning of this book, even though Frye's 'encyclopaedic tendency', like his concept of romance, has to be conceived as a general principle divested of both external literary form and particular historical realization. The genre concepts of this study are on the contrary always defined with an eye to the historical models of narrative poetry.

117. In his malevolent fourth article of the series 'On the Cockney School of Poetry' (*BM*, 17, August 1818), all Lockhart had to say about the ending of *Endymion* was 'and so, like many other Romances, terminates the "Poetic Romance" of Johnny Keats, in a patched up wedding'. This unappreciative remark proves that Keats, by giving his poem the subtitle 'A Poetic Romance', exposed himself to comparison with the romances of the Scott type, or even with the popular novels of the period. Since his poem lacked their narrative appeal, it was attacked as a failure.

118. Frye, p. 57.

119. Drayton's influence was affirmed by Claude Finney – in an article in *PMLA*, 39 (1924), 805 ff. and in *The Evolution of Keats' Poetry* (Cambridge, Mass.), 1936 – and by Amy Lowell in her *John Keats* (Boston, 1925). Douglas Bush attacked this opinion and pointed to a series of other possible influences. Jeffrey had been the first critic to look for possible literary echoes in *Endymion* (*ER* 67, article 10, August 1820). He mentioned pastoral models such as Theocritus, Jonson's *Sad Shepherd* and Fletcher's *Faithful Shepherdess*. The likelihood of Christoph Martin Wieland's *Oberon* (1780) having influenced *Endymion* was discussed (and exaggerated) by W. W. Beyer in *Keats and the Daemon King* (Oxford, 1947).

120. See *BM*, 74, March 1823, 'On B. Cornwall's New Poems' and 17, August 1818, 'On the Cockney School of Poetry IV: Keats'. Byron had a higher opinion of Keats' reanimation of Greek myth. In spite of his antipathy to Keats' poetry he acknowledged Keats' genius, after the latter's death, in *Don Juan* XI, LX and in a manuscript note to *Some Observations upon an Article in Blackwood's Magazine*. In both cases he referred to the authenticity of the dead poet's treatment of Greek subjects.

121. *QuR*, 37, article 7, April 1818.

122. *ER*, 67, article 10, August 1820.

123. According to Jeffrey there are only three instances in classical literature when the passions of a divine being are described: the love song of the Cyclops in

Theocritus' eleventh idyll, Venus' lament for Adonis in Moschus and the legend of Amor and Psyche in Apuleius.

124. Abrams, *Natural Supernaturalism*, p. 11.

125. See note 122.

126. Since George Saintsbury in his *History of Nineteenth Century Literature* (London, 1896), p. 89 wrote that 'Keats begat Tennyson and Tennyson begat all the rest', many critics have traced the lines of development from such romantic poets as Keats and Shelley, Novalis and Hölderlin, Gérard de Nerval and Edgar Allan Poe to the French Symbolists and the great poets of the first decades of the twentieth century. Two more recent studies of some of these lines are Abrams, *Natural Supernaturalism* (cf. p. 121 f. and p. 445) and Paul de Man, *The Rhetoric of Romanticism* (New York, 1984).

127. The critic who in our century opened the attack against too high an estimation of Keats as a poetic thinker and symbolist was H. W. Garrod, in *Keats* (Oxford, 1926). He was followed by R. H. Snow, in 'Heresy Concerning Keats', *PMLA*, 43 (1928), 1,142 ff., and H. N. Fairchild, in *The Romantic Quest* (New York, 1931). After the Second World War, E. C. Pettet (in *On the Poetry of Keats*, Cambridge, 1957) took a similar line. It should by now be clear that this author cannot share their point of view.

128. Cf. p. 17 ff.

129. Cf. p. 24 and 30 ff.

130. See p. 167.

131. The artist's *mimesis* of reality has taken on an even more problematic character in the course of the critical discussions of the last twenty years. We have had such a crop of theories that it is not possible to work the present-day state of the theoretical discussion (if the word 'state' is admissible in a case where one would rather use the word 'crisis') into this study, the first draft of which dates back to the late fifties.

132. Frye, p. 84.

133. In other words, the unquestioned acceptance of this distance broke down with the coming on of what Frye calls the 'low mimetic mode'.

134. Wordsworth's main reasons for writing in verse are stated in the paragraph of the Preface to the *Lyrical Ballads* beginning with 'It will now be proper to answer an obvious question ...'

135. See note 39 and p. 155.

136. *ER*, 40, article 2, November 1812.

137. The further increase in and poetic rehabilitation of narrative prose, which marked subsequent developments and was commented on by Scott's contemporaries and which eventually won the day over the verse narrative fashion, will be discussed in a later section (see pp. 216 ff.).

138. See note 63 and cf. Haddakin, who has a chapter called 'Why in Verse?'; see also Kroeber, p. 211, note 5.

139. The relationship between art and nature was a topic which was passionately debated all over Europe in the days of the romantics. Since the Aristotelian balance of the two spheres had been lost and the literary conventions that had been based on that balance destroyed, it proved necessary to establish a new relationship which took into account both the 'natural' themes of Rousseauism (including its subjective, associationist and emotionalist interests) and the romantic striving for transcendent truth and universal validity. Instances of this struggle are to

be found everywhere, from Goethe (*Dichtung und Wahrheit*) and Beethoven (*Pastoral Symphony*) to Goya, Géricault and the English romantic poets. The following two quotations illustrate how this theme was reflected in the English periodicals of the period: 'A generation of poets has appeared in our day who have gone back to Nature, and have sought the element of Poetry immediately in the world of Nature and of human life.' (*BM*, 167, June 1830, on John Keble's anonymously published *The Christian Year* of 1827. The article analyses the special relationship to 'Nature' of almost all the poets discussed in this genre study with the exception of the 'Cockneys'.) The second quotation is taken from an article on Moore's *Irish Melodies* (*BM*, 60, January 1822), which discusses a then widespread critical opinion, viz. that Moore's poetry was nothing but artificial frippery: 'Moore is not, like Wordsworth and Coleridge, the poet's poet, nor is it necessary, in order to enjoy his writings, that we should create a taste for them other than what we received from Nature and our horn-books.' The reviewer thought it paradoxical that one should be compelled to reflect and develop a progressive taste merely to be able to understand the meaning of the alleged 'naturalness' of the Lake Poets, while it sufficed to rely on one's 'common feeling' to enjoy Moore's 'artificial' poetry. In the end the reviewer urges the reader to leave the hackneyed topic of 'nature vs. art' alone – since it had been platitudinized too much. He advises waiting for the churned-up mud to settle, and then it will be possible to see clearly to the bottom of the question.

140. W. K. Wimsatt, *The Verbal Icon: Studies in the Meaning of Poetry* (Louisville Kentucky, 1954), p. 80 f.

141. Cleanth Brooks, *The Well-Wrought Urn* (London, 1947), p. 139.

142. If traditional genre names were to be applied at any cost, *Endymion* would have to be called a pastoral epic, *Hyperion* a heroic one. Keats, as has been said already, called both works romance or poem indiscriminately.

143. Cf. McFarland, pp. 31 – 4.

144. Keats composed *Lamia* in the period of his most intense infatuation with Fanny Brawne. Some sentences in a letter which he sent her on 27 July 1819 express ideas which are related to the experience communicated symbolically in *Lamia*: 'I have been all day employ'd in a very abstract Poem and I am deep in love with you ... all I can bring you is a swooning admiration of your beauty ... You absorb me in spite of myself ... I tremble at domestic cares ... I have two luxuries to brood over in my walks, your Loveliness and the hour of my death. O that I could have possession of them both in the same minute. I hate the world: it batters too much the wings of my self-will, and I would I could take a sweet poison from your lips to send me out of it.'

145. See Keats' letter to Woodhouse of 27 October 1818.

146. For a characterization of Scott's narrative method see pp. 90 ff.; for Byron's narrative gift see T. S. Eliot's essay on Byron in *On Poetry and Poets*, pp. 193 – 206. Eliot overlooks Scott's and overrates Coleridge's influences on Byron's tales.

147. *QuR*, 37, article 7, April 1818.

148. Letter to Woodhouse of 21 September 1819.

149. See Keats' letter to George and Georgiana Keats of 17 to 27 September 1819: 'I am certain there is that sort of fire in it which must take hold of

people some way – give them either pleasant or unpleasant sensation. What they want is sensation of some sort.'

150. W.J. Bates, *John Keats* (Cambridge, Mass., 1963), pp. 546 f., 553.
151. Cf. letter to Reynolds of 21 September 1819.
152. H.W. Garrod, *Keats, passim.*
153. Cf. letter to Haydon of 22 December 1818: 'I admire Human Nature but I do not like Men' and his letter to Shelley of 16 August 1820; 'My imagination is a Monastery and I am its Monk.'
154. Cf. Keats' letter to George and Georgiana Keats of 21 September 1817.
155. See J.M. Abrams, *Natural Supernaturalism, passim.*
156. See A.C. Bradley, p. 199.
157. Ibid.
158. *BM*, 185, September 1831, 'An Hour's Talk about Poetry'; see also p. 00.
159. Keats seems to have been conscious of the generic kinship of the dream vision (in *The Fall of Hyperion*) with the romance and that of the *Hyperion* fragment with the epic (even though he once called the fragment a romance): he divided the former into cantos, the latter into books.
160. Foakes, p. 56 f.
161. See Abrams, *Natural Supernaturalism*, p. 67.
162. London, 1918, 2 vols.
163. Herford classifies *Queen Mab* as 'visionary mythology' and points to the strong influence of Southey's *Thalaba*; *The Revolt of Islam* is 'less an epic, than a romance, of revolution', owing to Shelley's enthusiastic reading of Spenser at the time of its composition; for *Rosalind and Helen* Herford feels compelled to use a mixed generic description, calling it 'a modern novelistic eclogue' without however paying attention to the features Shelley borrowed from contemporary verse narrative: Coleridge's *Christabel* metre and the tone of certain Wordsworthian poems. For the rest of Shelley's narrative poems Herford dispenses with traditional genre names: *Alastor* is a 'dreamy voyage', *The Sensitive Plant* 'delicate symbolism', *Julian and Maddalo* combines 'Attic ease' with 'high-bred familiarity' or, in terms of influence, Byron's lightness of touch (without his vulgarity) with Hunt's less strict handling of the couplet (without his lack of discipline). *The Witch of Atlas* is 'a poet's play at myth-making' and a 'Shelleyan fantasia', *Arethusa* 'a lovely echo of Greek legend', *Marianne's Dream* 'a dreamlike tale of marvel', etc. When Herford finally comes to *The Triumph of Life* he returns to traditional terminology, calling the work 'a sublime allegory' and pointing out that the symbol of the chariot is modelled on Petrarch's *Trionfi* and the imagery of ancient Rome (p. 1 ff.).
164. D. King-Hele, *Shelley: His Thought and Work* (London, 1960), p. 31.
165. Letter to Leigh Hunt, Pisa, 22 June 1821.
166. 'Note on *Queen Mab* by Mrs. Shelley', in R. Ingpen and W.E. Peck (eds.), *The Complete Works of Percy Bysshe Shelley*, in 10 vols. (London, 1926–30), vol. I, p. 165.
167. Ibid.
168. See also p. 192 and note 197. For a more detailed discussion of the genre of *Queen Mab* and, indeed, most of Shelley's major poems see Stuart Curran, *Shelley's Annus Mirabilis: The Maturing of an Epic Vision* (San Marino, Calif., 1975). Making use of the conclusions arrived at by Wilkie, Kroeber and Foerster, Curran presents well-founded theories about the 'epic' character

character of Shelley's 'Epic Ventures'. Particularly relevant to our study are pp. 6–12; here Curran quoted material proving his thesis that 'Epic was a fever of the time' and points out that William Hayley's *Essay on Epic Poetry* (1782) was 'The major impetus' behind the revival of the epic in the romantic period and had a strong effect on Southey. Hayley had also suggested the 'rich sources of Eastern mythologies as a mean to renew the moribund epic genre'.

169. Ingpen and Peck, I, p. 173. Earl R. Wasserman, *Shelley: A Critical Reading* (Baltimore, 1971), p. 203.
170. Northrop Frye, p. 57 (cf. a more detailed account of Frye's theories of mode and genre in our section on Keats, p. 167).
171. *Defence of Poetry*, Ingpen and Peck, VII, p. 116.
172. Wilkie, chapter 4: 'holy and Heroic Verse'.
173. Curran, pp. 24–32.
174. Ingpen and Peck, I, p. 239 ff.
175. F. L. Jones, *Letters of Percy Bysshe Shelley*, (Oxford, 1964), II, p. 271.
176. *The Halliford Edition of the Works of Thomas Love Peacock*, ed. by H. F. B. Brett-Smith and C. E. Jones (repr. New York, 1967), pp. 1–25. Quote on p. 20.
177. Jones, II, p. 271. Shelley's letter should not be considered as a wholesale rejection of all romantic verse narrative. It has already been stated that he admired *Gebir* and *Thalaba*. In his adolescence he chose lines from Scott's *Lay* and *Marmion* for mottoes to some of the chapters of his Gothic novel fragments, and his poem *The Wandering Jew* clearly shows the influence of Scott and Southey. His admiration for Byron's poetry and his early recognition of Keats' greatness were based on qualities other than narrative, but he considered Thomas Moore as superior to himself and admired 'the character no less than ... the genius' of Moore, as he wrote in a letter to Horace Smith of 11 April 1822 (see Jones II, p. 412) and in a further letter to Smith of 29 June 1822 (Jones, II, p. 442).
178. 'Epic Ventures' is the title of chapter 1 of Stuart Curran's *Shelley's Annus Mirabilis*.
179. In his Introduction to *Shelley's Narrative Poems*.
180. Carlos Baker, *Shelley's Major Poetry: The Fabric of a Vision* (Princeton, 1948), pp. 4, 6 and 217.
181. M. Kelsall, *Byron's Politics* (Brighton and Totowa, New Jersey, 1987).
182. See *Shelley: The Critical Heritage*, ed. James E. Barcus (London, 1975), pp. 106–43.
183. Jones, I, p. 576 f.
184. Ingpen and Peck, III, p. 146.
185. Ingpen and Peck, III, p. 137.
186. Ingpen and Peck, IV, p. 15 f.
187. Ingpen and Peck, II, p. 156 f.
188. Ingpen and Peck, II, p. 5.
189. Ingpen and Peck, II, p. 67 f.
190. See Wasserman, *Shelley* part I, section 3 and *passim*.
191. *The Letters of John Keats*, ed. Hyder E. Rollins, (Cambridge, 1958), II, p. 234 f.
192. Northrop Frye, p. 57.
193. *BM*, 27, June 1819. The author of this review was either John Wilson (alias Christopher North) or John Lockhart, see G. M. Matthew (ed.), *Keats: The Critical Heritage* (London, 1971), p. 152.

194. Elton, II, p. 193.
195. See note 188.
196. Like *Rosalind and Helen*, *Ginevra* (1821) and the unfinished *Fiordispina* (1820) could be described as attempts to write purely narrative romantic fiction, whereas *The Cenci* (1819) is – at least at the outset – an attempt to compose an objective romantic drama.
197. The choice of words in Mary Shelley's note on *Rosalind and Helen* and the *Poems of 1820* (Ingpen and Peck, II, p. 45 and IV, p. 78 ff.) indicates clearly that she would have liked to change the direction of Shelley's poetry: 'Shelley had no care for any of his poems that did not emanate from the depth of his mind, and develop some high or abstruse truth. When he does touch on human life and the human heart [as in *Rosalind and Helen*], no picture can be more faithful, more delicate, more subtle, more pathetic – [*The Witch of Atlas*] is peculiarly characteristic of his tastes – wildly fanciful, full of brilliant imagery, and discarding human interest and passion, to revel in the fantastic ideas that his imagination suggested.'
198. *The Sensitive Plant* is perhaps best described as an allegorical illustration of Shelley's conviction that 'Poetry is the record of the best and happiest moments of the happiest and best minds. We are aware of the evanescent visitations of thought and feeling, sometimes associated with place and person ... and always arising unforeseen and departing unbidden, but elevating and delightful beyond all expression, etc' (*Defence*, Ingpen and Peck, VII, p. 136 f.). *Epipsychidion* on the other hand, which Shelley compared with the *Vita Nuova* of Dante, is the poetical record of a love experience, from which the story, i.e., 'The matter-of-fact history of the circumstances, to which it relates' (Advertisement to *Epipsychidion*) had been taken out. The three early drafts of the Preface to the poem could be read as an endeavour to cope with both the difficulty of assigning to it a traditional genre ('seem to have been written as a sort of dedication of some work to have been presented to the person whom they address'; 'apparently ... intended as a dedication to a longer poem or series of poems') and the difficulty of eliminating by a process of distillation as much of the dross of the material story as was possible without making the poem unintelligible.
199. See *BM*, 32, November 1819. According to James E. Barcus, *Shelley: The Critical Heritage*, p. 101, this review was written by Lockhart rather than John Wilson.
200. In his Preface to *The Revolt of Islam* Shelley wrote: 'The Poem ... is narrative, not didactic' and asserted that he refused to 'recommend the motives which I would substitute for those at present governing mankind by methodical argument'. In the Preface to *Prometheus Unbound* he was more outspoken: 'Didactic poetry is my abhorrence; nothing can be equally well expressed in prose that is not tedious and supererogatory in verse.' The *Defence of Poetry* is, of course, full of philosophical arguments supporting this view. Particularly relevant to Shelley's attitude to narrative poetry is the paragraph beginning with: 'A poem is the very image of life expressed in its eternal truth' with its distinction between 'story' and 'poem' (Ingpen and Peck, VII, p. 115).
201. See *Defence* (Ingpen and Peck, VII, p. 112): 'The grammatical forms which express the moods of time, and the differences of persons, and the distinction

of place, are convertible with respect to the highest poetry without injuring it as poetry.' The effect of this view on Shelley's poetry is discussed in William Keach, *Shelley's Style* (New York and London, 1984). See also Earl R. Wasserman's discussion of Shelley's *Defence of Poetry* in his *Shelley: A Critical Reading*, pp. 204–20.

202. Ingpen and Peck, VII, p. 110.
203. Jones, I, p. 576 ff.
204. Ingpen and Peck, VII, p. 112.

7. The subsequent fate of the genre

1. See pp. 103 and 212.
2. See Scott's Introduction to *Rokeby* of 1830.
3. There is a slight possibility that Moore may be the author of thirty-two versified versions of *Decameron* novellas which appeared in 1812 under the title *The Spirit of Boccaccio's Decamerone*. H. G. Wright has adduced convincing evidence pointing to Moore as the author (see his article in *RES*, 23 (1947), p. 337 ff. and his *Boccaccio in England from Chaucer to Tennyson* (London, 1957)), but the question has still not been settled.
4. See Byron's letter to Moore of 10 July 1817.
5. *On Poetry and Poets*, p. 43.
6. This was also Byron's opinion, see his letter to Murray of 15 September 1817.
7. 'Byron', p. 199.
8. Elton, I, p. 392, maintains that Moore's Fadladeen is a satire on Jeffrey and tries to prove it with quotations.
9. *ER*, 57, article 1, November 1817.
10. *BM*, 3, June, and 4, August 1817.
11. Moore had also begun a metrical romance called *Alciphron* which, however, he left unfinished because he wanted to use the subject for a prose novella, *The Epicurean*. This was published in 1827 and, judged by modern standards, appears as his best narrative work.
12. See Byron's letters to Moore of 28 August and 1 September 1813. A similar rivalry had arisen in 1812 when Byron decided to give up a plan of writing a story about a Peri because Moore had already conceived the idea of his *Paradise and the Peri*.
13. *ER*, 75, article 2, February 1823.
14. *BM*, 72, January 1823, and *BM*, 74, March 1823 (two articles).
15. *Spirit of the Age*, p. 339.
16. Italian influence on the English romantics is of course to be found everywhere, but credit is due to Hunt for pointing out the store of narrative material and the wealth of formal variation in Italian Renaissance literature to his contemporaries at a moment when the world of indigenous medieval romance had been exploited almost to exhaustion. Credit is also due to Hazlitt who had been praising Boccaccio's genius in lectures and essays since 1814 (see Wright, *Boccaccio in England*, p. 342 ff.).
17. Hunt's remarks about English versification in the Preface to his *Stories in Verse*, published in 1855 and the appended *Study in Versification* (first published as Preface to his *Poetical Works* of 1832) are well worth reading not only as

first-hand information about his intentions with regard to metre but also as proof of his veneration for Chaucer, the 'father of English poetry' who, Hunt believes, is still misunderstood and underrated by the English.

18. See also Byron's letter to Moore of 1 June 1818. Hunt revised *The Story of Rimini* several times in later years. The different versions as well as a number of annotations which Byron had written in pencil in a copy of the first edition and on some manuscript sheets of Hunt's poem with the intention of giving him advice are given in the Appendix to H. S. Milford's edition of *The Poetical Works of Leigh Hunt* (London, 1923). A comparison of the different versions with the detailed criticism of Hunt's 'reformation' of English verse language that Jeffrey, Lockhart and the critic of the *QuR* had advanced in their reviews shows that Hunt gave in to many of their arguments; maybe he did so because Byron had tried to bring him back to classical standards. In some cases, however, he abode by his first decision and many of these cases concerned lines that Byron had especially commended.
19. *BM*, October 1817.
20. *ER*, 53, article 11, June 1816.
21. *QuR*, 28, January 1816.
22. The full extent of Lockhart's ideological opposition to Hunt becomes apparent when he exposes Hunt's partiality to Voltaire's philosophical tales and to the *encyclopédistes* and traces Hunt's lack of genuine feeling for nature back to his lack of religion: here Lockhart obviously plays off Wordsworth's message against Hunt's sensual and metropolitan materialism.
23. Cf. Scott's Introduction to *The Bridal of Triermain*.
24. *BM*, 61, March 1822.
25. Two feeble imitations of Byron's *Beppo* – *Gyges* and *Diego di Montilla* (1820); some serious romances such as *A Sicilian Story* (1820), which can hardly be called a rival to Keats' *Isabella*, though it is making use of the same *Decameron* story, and the rather more Byronic *Marcian Colonna* (1820), which is a semi-dramatic tale of a luckless Italian Renaissance hero.
26. In a letter to John Murray of 4 January 1821, Byron said of Barry Cornwall's *Tales in Rhyme* that they were 'quite spoilt by I know not what affectation of Wordsworth – and Hunt – and Moore – and Myself – all mixed up into a kind of Chaos'.
27. *ER*, 65, article 8, January 1820.
28. *BM*, 74, March 1823.
29. *ER*, 38, article 6, February 1812.
30. *ER*, 11, article 1, April 1805.
31. *ER*, 23, article 1, April 1808.
32. Jeffrey never quite relinquished his doubts about the lasting value of most of the poetry of the period. His article on Campbell's *Specimens of the British Poets* in the *ER*, 62, article 2, March 1819, foreshadows the negative verdict on the poetry of the whole period that he expressed more fully nine years later in his review of Atherstone's *The Fall of Niniveh* (*ER*, 95, article 3, September 1828). The latter article is discussed in the text of this chapter. In the former he tried to predict the future reputation of the leading contemporary poets. The article culminates in a forecast for the year 1919: Campbell would by then have retained about half of his present popularity, Byron a quarter, Scott a sixth, Crabbe a tenth, and Southey 3 per cent. Apart from the error concerning Campbell this was not a bad prognosis.

33. See note 31.
34. *BM*, 146, December 1828.
35. This author's reasons for not counting *The Prelude* and *Don Juan* among the great epics of world literature were stated in chapter 1.
36. See p. 159 ff.
37. *BM*, 16, 'Essays on the Lake School of Poetry I'.
38. *BM*, 38, May 1820, 'On Wordsworth's River Duddon'; 74, March 1823, 'Remarks on Mr. B. Cornwall's New Poems'; and 167, June 1830 on Keble's *Christian Year.*
39. *BM*, 17, August 1818, 'On the Cockney School of Poetry IV'.
40. *ER*, 24, article 11, February 1811.
41. *BM*, 131, October 1827.
42. Did North have a particular poet in mind? A few lines above this he had mentioned Byron, but he was known to be an ardent admirer of Wordsworth. We may be assured that he did not mean Scott. He did, it is true, appreciate Scott's poetry and even once called him the Scottish counterpart of Wordsworth (*BM*, 132, November 1827, 'Preface to a Review of the Chronicles of the Canongate'). Behind this praise we may however suppose political and personal sympathies. North's most sincere verdict on Scott is probably what he wrote in his review of Wordsworth's *White Doe* (*BM*, 16, July 1818); there he said Scott was an original as Wordsworth but greatly inferior to him in all other respects.
43. North expressed similar thoughts in his 'Preface to a Review of the Chronicles of the Canongate' (see note 42) and 'Noctes Ambrosianae 40' in *BM*, 146, December 1828.
44. *ER*, 65, article 1.
45. See Jeffrey's review of *Ivanhoe*, *ER*, 65, article 1, January 1820.
46. Moore, it will be remembered, had given *Lalla Rookh* a prose framework in 1817 and embarked on a verse romance before 1827, which however he recast in prose. Cornwall published *Tales in Prose* in 1853, some of which had however already appeared in 1823, 1828 and 1833.
47. *BM*, 65, June 1822.
48. See notes 40 and 41.
49. Romantic verse narratives about the time before the Flood are: Montgomery's *World Before the Flood*, Coleridge's *Wanderings of Cain*, Dale's *Irad and Adah: A Tale of the Flood*, Moore's *Love of the Angels* and Cornwall/Procter's *Flood of Thessaly*. The end of the world figures at the end of Pollock's *The Course of Time*, a blank verse poem in ten books, and in two short poems, Campbell's *The Last Man* and Byron's strange poetic vision *Darkness.*
50. As early as 1813, in a letter to Moore of 28 August, Byron had spoken of the complete exhaustion of all subjects suitable for romantic narratives with the exception of the East and quotes Mme de Stael as being of the same opinion.
51. Byron had always known this, see p. 159 ff.
52. *BM*, 146, 'Noctes Ambrosianae 40', of December 1828.
53. *BM*, 167, June 1830.
54. *BM*, 185, September 1831.
55. The poets North discusses in 'An Hour's Talk about Poetry' are: Rogers, Crabbe, Bowles, Campbell, Montgomery, Moore, Wordsworth, Coleridge, Southey, Scott, Byron, some peasant poets such as Burns, Hogg, etc., the most important

early romantic poets and the 'female geniuses' such as J. Baillie, F. Hemans etc. Keats, Shelley and Hunt are not mentioned.

Conclusion

1. See p. 2.
2. See p. 12.
3. In his novel *Small World* (London, 1984, 2nd edn, 1985), p. 322, David Lodge half jokingly illustrates the basic difference between the 'male' epic and the 'female' or 'vaginal' romance with sexual imagery which underlines the mutual exclusiveness of the two. While this imagery would seem to point to the possibility of a fruitful union, the plot of the novel shows this to be Utopian.
4. See p. 219 f.

Bibliography

I. Primary sources of authors discussed

Bowles, William Lisle: *Poetical Works*, ed. G. Gilfillan (Edinburgh, 1855)

Byron, George Gordon: *Works*, ed. E. H. Coleridge and R. E. Prothero, 13 vols. (London, 1894, 1900, 1904)

    Poetical Works, collected and arranged with notes ..., ed. J. Murray (London and Leipzig, 1860)

    Byron's Letters and Journals, ed. L. Marchand (New York and London, 1973–82)

    Complete Poetical Works, ed. J. J. McGann (Oxford, 1981)

Campbell, Thomas: *Complete Poetical Works*, ed. J. L. Robertson (Oxford, 1907)

    Gertrude of Wyoming, ed. Fitzgibbon (Oxford, 1891)

Coleridge, Samuel Taylor: *Complete Poetical Works*, ed. E. H. Coleridge, 2 vols. (Oxford, 1912)

    Biographia Literaria, ed. J. Shawcross, 2 vols. (Oxford, 1907)

Crabbe, George: *Poetical Works*, ed. A. J. and R. M. Carlyle (Oxford, 1908)

    New Poems, ed. A. Pollard (Liverpool, 1960)

Hogg, James: *The Poetical Works of the Ettrick Shepherd*, 5 vols. (Glasgow, 1838–40)

Hunt, Leigh: *Poetical Works*, ed. H. S. Milford (London, 1923)

    Stories in Verse (London, 1855)

    Literary Criticism, ed. L. H. Houtchens (New York, 1956)

Keats, John: *Poetical Works*, ed. H. B. Forman (Oxford, 1908)

    Poems, ed. E. de Selincourt (London, 1905)

    The Letters, ed. H. B. Forman (Oxford, 3rd edn, 1947–8)

    The Letters, ed. H. E. Rollins, 2 vols. (Cambridge, 1958)

Landor, Walter Savage: *Poems*, ed. C. G. Crump, 2 vols. (London, 1891–3)

    Complete Works: Poems ed. S. Wheeler, 7 vols. (Oxford, 1937)

Montgomery, James: *Poetical Works* (London, 1841)

Moore, Thomas: *Poetical Works, with a Life of the Author*, centenary edition (Berlin, 1879)

    Memoirs, Journals and Correspondence, ed. J. Russell, 8 vols. (London, 1853–6)

Procter, Bryan Waller, alias Barry Cornwall: *Poetical Works of Barry Cornwall*, 3 vols. (London, 1822)

    The Flood of Thessaly, The Girl of Provence, and Other Poems (London, 1823)

    Essays and Tales in Prose, 2 vols. (Boston, 1853)

Rogers, Samuel: *Poetical Works, with a Memoir*, ed. E. Bell (London, 1892)

Scott, Walter: *Poetical Works*, ed. J. L. Robertson (Oxford, 1908)

    Minstrelsy of the Scottish Border, ed. J. G. Lockhart (Edinburgh, 1833)

Shelley, Percy Bysshe: *Complete Poetical Works*, ed. T. Hutchinson (Oxford, 1905, 1948)

    The Narrative Poems of Percy Bysshe Shelley, ed. C. H. Herford (London, 1918)

    Complete Works, ed. R. Ingpen and W. E. Peck, 10 vols. (London, 1926–30)

    Letters of Percy Bysshe Shelley, ed. F. L. Jones, 2 vols. (Oxford, 1964)

Southey, Robert: *Poetical Works*, complete in one vol. (London, 1847). The text
corresponds to the *Collected Edition* 1837–8 (quoted as *CE*)
Selection from the Letters, ed. J.W. Warter, 4 vols. (London, 1856)
Tennant, William: *Anster Fair*, with a Memoir and Notes (Edinburgh, 1871)
Wilson, John, alias Christopher North: *Poems: A New Edition in Two Volumes* (Edinburgh
and London, 1825)
Wordsworth, William: *Poetical Works*, ed. E. de Selincourt and H. Darbishire, 5 vols.
(Oxford, 1937, 1940, 1949)
Prose Works, ed. A. Grosart, 3 vols. (London, 1876)
Letters, ed. E. de Selincourt, 6 vols. (Oxford, 1935–9)

II. Other primary sources

Barcus, James E. (ed.): *Shelley, the Critical Heritage* (London, 1975)
Boswell, James: *Life of Johnson*, (Oxford, 1965)
Evans, R.H. (ed.): *Old Ballads*, new edition (1810)
Evans, T. (ed.): *Old Ballads* (1777 and 1784)
Goethe, Johann Wolfgang von: *Werke*, ed. E. Trunz, 14 vols. (Hamburg, 5th edn,
1960)
Hazlitt, William: *Lectures on the English Poets* and *The Spirit of the Age*, Everyman edition
(London, 1910)
Herder, Johann Gottfried von: *Werke*, ed. B. Suphan, 33 vols. (Berlin, 1877–1913)
Jeffrey, Francis: *Contributions to the Edinburgh Review*, 4 vols. (London, 1844)
Lafontaine, August: *Familiengeschichten* (Frankfurt/Leipzig/Berlin, 1804)
Lockhart, John G.: *Memoirs of the Life of Scott*, 2 vols. (Edinburgh, 1837–8)
Narrative of the Life of Sir Walter Scott, begun by himself and continued by J.G.
Lockhart, Everyman edition (London, 1906)
Matthew, G.M. (ed.): *Keats, the Critical Heritage* (London, 1971)
Peacock, Thomas Love: *The Halliford Edition of the Works of Thomas Love Peacock*,
ed. H.F.B. Brett-Smith and C.E. Jones (repr. New York, 1967)
Pope, Alexander: *Prose Works*, ed. N. Ault, Vol. I (Oxford, 1935)
Schlegel, August Wilhelm: *Sämtliche Werke* (Leipzig, 1846–7)
Spingarn, J.E. (ed.): *Seventeenth Century Critical Essays* (Oxford, 1908)
de Stael, Germaine, *De L'Allemagne* (Paris, 1968)

III. Secondary sources

Abensour, L. (ed.): *Romantisme noir* (Paris, 1978)
Abercrombie, L.: *The Art and Craft of Letters* (London, n.d.)
The Art of Wordsworth (London, 1952)
Abrams, M.H.: *The Mirror and the Lamp* (Oxford, 1953)
Natural Supernaturalism: Tradition and Revolution in Romantic Literature (New York, 1971)
Auerbach, E.: *Mimesis* (Berne, 1946)
Baker, C.: *Shelley's Major Poetry: The Fabric of a Vision* (Princeton, 1948)
Bateson, F.W.: *Wordsworth: A Re-Interpretation* (London, 1954)
Beattie, W.: *The Life and Letters of Thomas Campbell*, 3 vols. (London, 1849–50)
Beers, H.A.: *A History of English Romanticism in the Nineteenth Century* (New York, 1901)
Berry, F.: *Poet's Grammar: Person, Time and Mood in Poetry* (London, 1958)
Beyer, W.W.: *Keats and the Daemon King* (Oxford, 1947)

Bierstadt, A. M.: 'Gertrude of Wyoming', *JEGP*, 20 (1921), 491–501
Blunden, E. (ed.): *The Life of George Crabbe by His Son* (London, 1948)
Bond, Richmond P.: *English Burlesque Poetry 1700–1750*, Harvard Studies in English (Edinburgh and London, 1931)
Bowra, C. M.: *Heroic Poetry from Virgil to Milton* (London, 1952)
Boyd, E. F.: *Byron's Don Juan, a Critical Study* (London, 1945, 2nd edn, 1958)
Bradford, C. B.: 'Wordsworth's *White Doe* and Related Poems', *MP*, 36 (1938), 59–70
Bradley, A. C.: *Oxford Lectures on Poetry* (London, 1909)
Bradley, W.: *The Early Poems of W. S. Landor* (London, 1914)
Bremen, Thilo von: *Lord Byron als Erfolgsautor: Leser und Literaturmarkt im frühen 19. Jahrhundert* (Wiesbaden, 1977)
Brie, F.: *Englishe Rokokoepik 1710–1730* (Munich, 1927)
    'Pope's Brutus', *Anglia*, 62 (1939), 144–85
Broich, Ulrich: *The Eighteenth-Century Mock Heroic Poem* (Cambridge, 1990)
Brooks, C.: *The Well-Wrought Urn* (London, 1947)
Brown, W. C.: *The Triumph of Form: A Study of the Later Masters of the Heroic Couplet* (Chapel Hill, 1948)
Buchan, J.: *A History of English Literature* (London, 1933)
Bush, D.: *Mythology and the Romantic Tradition in English Poetry* (Cambridge, Mass., 1937 and New York, 1957)
Campbell, J. D.: *Samuel Taylor Coleridge* (London, 1896)
Chambers, E. K.: *Samuel Taylor Coleridge* (Oxford, 1938)
Clark, J.: *A History of Epic Tradition* (London, 1900)
Collins, A. S.: 'The Growth of the Reading Public During the Eighteenth Century', *RES*, 2 (1926), 284–94, 428–38
Colvin, Sydney: *John Keats: His Life and Poetry, his Friends, Critics and Afterfame* (London, 1917)
Cooke, M. W.: 'Schiller's *Robbers* in England', *MLR*, 11 (1916), 156–75
Curran, Stuart: *Shelley's Annus Mirabilis: The Maturing of an Epic Vision* (San Marino, Calif., 1975)
Dixon, W. M.: *English Epic and Heroic Poetry* (London, 1912)
Eliot, T. S.: *On Poetry and Poets* (London, 1957)
Elton, O.: *A Survey of English Literature 1780–1830*, 2 vols. (London, 1924)
Escarpit, R.: *Lord Byron, un tempérament littéraire*, 2 vols. (Paris, 1955–7)
Fairchild, H. N.: *The Romantic Quest* (New York, 1931)
Ferguson, A.: *An Essay on the History of Civil Society* (Edinburgh, 1767)
Finney, C.: 'Drayton's Endymion and Phoebe and Keats' Endymion', *PMLA*, 39 (1924), 805–13
    The Evolution of Keats's Poetry (Cambridge, Mass., 1936)
Fischer, Hermann: 'Byron's "Wrong Revolutionary System" and Romanticism', in Andrew Rutherford (ed.), *Byron: Augustan and Romantic* (in preparation)
Fleck, P. D.: 'Romance in Byron's *The Island*', *The Byron Journal*, 3 (1975) 4–23
Foakes, R. A.: *The Romantic Assertion* (London, 1958)
Foerster, D. M.: 'The Critical Attack upon the Epic in the English Romantic Movement', *PMLA*, 69 (1954), 432–47
    Homer in English Criticism (New Haven, 1947)
Forster, E. M.: *Aspects of the Novel* (London, 1927, 8th edn, 1947)
Franke, W.: 'Der Stil in den epischen Dichtungen Walter Scott's' (Thesis, Berlin, 1909)

Frye, N.: *Anatomy of Criticism* (Princeton, 1957)
Garrod, H.W.: *Wordsworth* (Oxford, 1923, revised 1927)
  Keats (Oxford, 1926, 1939)
Gillies, R.P.: *Recollections of Sir Walter Scott* (London, 1837)
Gleckner, R.F.: *Byron and the Ruins of Paradise* (Baltimore, 1967)
Haddakin, L.: *The Poetry of Crabbe* (London, 1955)
Havens, R.D.: 'Changing Taste in the Eighteenth Century', *PMLA*, 44 (1929),
  501–36
  The Influence of Milton on English Poetry (New York, 1961)
Herford, C.H.: *The Age of Wordsworth* (London, 1897)
  (ed.), *English Tales in Verse* (London, 1924)
  see also Shelley
Hewlitt, D.: *A Life of John Keats* (London, 1937)
Hoffmeister, Gerhart: *Byron und der europäische Byronismus*, Erträge der Forschung, 188
  (Darmstadt, 1983)
Hogg, T.J.: *Life of Shelley* (London, 1858, 1906)
Jordan, H.H.: 'Thomas Moore and the Review of Christabel', *MP*, 54 (1956),
  95–105
Jordan, J.C.: 'The Eve of St Agnes and the Lay of the Last Minstrel', *MLN*, 43
  (1928), 38 ff.
Kayser, W.: *Das sprachliche Kunstwerk* (Berne, 1948, 4th edn, 1956)
Keach, William: *Shelley's Style* (New York and London, 1984)
Kelsall, M.: *Byron's Politics* (Brighton and Totowa, 1987).
Ker, W.P.: *Epic and Romance* (London, 1896)
King-Hele, Desmond: *Shelley: His Thought and Work* (London, 1960)
Kitchin, George: *A Survey of Burlesque and Parody in English* (New York, 2nd edn,
  1964)
Kraeger, H.: *'Der byronische Heldentypus'* (Ph.D. thesis, Munich, 1898)
Kroeber, K.: *Romantic Narrative Art* (Madison, Milwaukee, London, 1960)
Kuhn, H.: *Gattungsprobleme der mittelhochdeutschen Literatur*, Proceedings of the Bayer-
  ischen Akademie der Wissenschaften, Philos.-Hist. Klasse (1956), 4
Larsen, T.: 'The Classical Element in Scott's Poetry', *Transactions of the Royal Society
  of Canada* (1938)
Leavis, F.R.: *Revaluation* (London, 1936)
Lindenberger, H.: *On Wordsworth's Prelude* (Princeton, 1963)
Lodge, David: *Small World* (London, 2nd edn, 1985)
Lowell, A.: *John Keats* (Boston, 1925)
Lukàcs, Georg von: *Die Theorie des Romans* (Berlin, 1920)
Mainusch, Herbert: *Romantische Ästhetik: Untersuchungen zur englischen Kunstlehre des
  späten 18. und frühen 19. Jahrhunderts* (Berlin and Zurich, 1969)
Man, Paul de: *The Rhetoric of Romanticism* (New York), 1984)
Mason, E.C.: *Deutsche und englische Romantik* (Göttingen, 1959)
McFarland, T.: *Romanticism and the Forms of Ruin: Wordsworth, Coleridge, and the
  Modalities of Fragmentation* (Princeton, 1981)
McGann, J.J.: *Fiery Dust* (Chicago, 1968)
Medwin, T.: *Journal of the Conversations of Lord Byron* (London, 1824)
Moore, T.: *Life of Lord Byron* (London, 1951)
More, Henry: *The Immortality of the Soul* (London, 1659)
New, P.: *George Crabbe's Poetry* (London, 1976)

288   *Bibliography*

Nitchie, E.: *Virgil and the English Poets*, Columbia University Studies in English and Comparative Literature (New York, 1919)
Pearson, N. H.: *English Institute Annual*, 1940
Peckham, M.: 'Toward a Theory of Romanticism', *PLMA*, 66 (1951), 5–23
Percy, Thomas: *Reliques of Ancient English Poetry*, ed. M. M. Schröer, 2 vols. (Heilbronn, 1889–93)
Pettet, E. C.: *On the Poetry of Keats* (Cambridge, 1957)
Platz, Norbert: *Die Beeinflussung des Lesers* (Tübingen, 1986)
Potts, A. F.: *Wordsworth's Prelude* (Ithaca and New York, 1953)
Read, H.: *The True Voice of Feeling* (London, 1953)
Reed, B.: *The Influence of Solomon Gessner upon English Literature* (Philadelphia, 1905)
Richter, H.: *Geschichte der englischen Romantik*, 3 vols. (Halle, 1916)
Ridenour, G. M.: *The Style of Don Juan* (New Haven, 1960)
Rogers, W. H.: 'The Reaction against Melodramatic Sentimentality in the English Novel 1796–1830', *PMLA*, 49 (1934), 98–122
Rutherford, Andrew: *Byron: A Critical Study* (1961)
Saintsbury, G.: *Essays in English Literature 1780–1860* (London, 1895)
  History of Nineteenth Century Literature (London, 1896)
  History of English Prosody, 3 vols. (London, 1910)
Sale, A.: 'The Development of Crabbe's Narrative Art', *The Cambridge Journal* (May 1952)
Schadewaldt, W.: *Von Homers Welt und Werk* (Stuttgart, 1951)
Schirmer, W. F.: *Der Einfluss der deutschen Literatur auf die englische im 19. Jarhundert* (Halle, 1947)
Schneider, E.: 'The Unknown Reviewer of Christabel: Jeffrey, Hazlitt, Tom Moore?', *PMLA*, 70 (1955), 417–32
Schücking, L. L.: 'Das Königsideal im Beowulf', *E Studien*, 67 (1932), 1–14
Smith, A.: *Lectures on Rhetoric and Belles Lettres*, ed. John M. Lothian (London, 1963)
Smith, L. P.: *Words and Idioms* (London, 1925)
Snow, R. H.: 'Heresy Concerning Keats', *PMLA*, 43 (1928), 1,142–9
Staiger, E.: *Grundbegriffe der Poetik* (Zurich, 1946)
Stevens, J.: *Music and Poetry in the Early Tudor Court* (Oxford, 1960)
Stockley, V.: *German Literature as Known in England 1750–1830* (London, 1929)
Stokoe, F. W.: *German Influence in the English Romantic Period* (Cambridge, 1926)
Sühnel, R.: *Homer und die englische Humanität* (Tübingen, 1958)
Summers, M.: *The Gothic Quest* (New York, 1963)
  A Gothic Bibliography (New York, 1964)
Swedenberg, H. T. Jr: *The Theory of the Epic in England 1650–1800* (Berkeley, 1944)
Taylor, J. T.: *Early Opposition to the English Novel: The Popular Reaction from 1760 to 1830* (New York, 1943)
Thompson, G. R. (ed.): *The Gothic Imagination: Essays in Dark Romanticism* (Seattle, 1974)
Thorslev, P. L.: *The Byronic Hero: Types and Prototypes* (Minneapolis, 1962)
Tillotson, G.: 'The Manner of Proceeding in Certain Eighteenth and Nineteenth Century Poems', Warton Lecture on English Poetry, from the Proceedings of the British Academy, 34 (London, 1948)
Tillyard, E. M. W.: *The English Epic and its Background* (London, 1954)
Varma, D. P.: *The Gothic Flame* (New York, 1960)
Wasserman, Earl R.: *Shelley: A Critical Reading* (Baltimore, 1971)
Wellek, R.: *History of Modern Criticism 1750–1950*, Vols I and II (New Haven, 1955)

Wellek, R. and Warren, A.: *Theory of Literature* (New York, 1941)

Wilkie, Brian: *Romantic Poets and Epic Tradition* (Madison and Milwaukee, 1965)

Williams, Stanley G.: 'The Story of Gebir', *PMLA*, 36 (1921), 624 ff.

Wimsatt, W. K.: *The Verbal Icon: Studies in the Meaning of Poetry* (Louisville, Kentucky, 1954)

Wright, H. G.: 'Thomas Moore as the Author of "Spirit of Boccaccio's Decameron"', *RES*, 23 (1947), 337–48

    Boccaccio in England from Chaucer to Tennyson (London, 1957)

IV. Literary criticism from the following periodicals of the English romantic period

Edinburgh Review
Quarterly Review
Blackwood's Magazine